THE
PUSHCART PRIZE, XVI:
BEST OF THE
SMALL PRESSES

THE PUSHCART PRIZE XVI

BEST OF THE SMALL PRESSES

*Edited by
Bill Henderson
with the
Pushcart Prize
editors.
Introduction by
Edward Hoagland
Poetry Editors:
Marvin Bell,
Carolyn Kizer
Essays Editor:
Anthony Brandt*

A Touchstone Book
Published by Simon & Schuster
New York   London   Toronto   Sydney   Tokyo   Singapore

TOUCHSTONE
Simon & Schuster Building
Rockefeller Center
1230 Avenue of the Americas
New York, New York 10020

10 9 8 7 6 5 4 3 2 1

ISBN 0-671-73435-0

Note: Nominations for this series are invited from any
small, independent, literary book press or magazine in
the world. Up to six nominations—tear sheets or copies
selected from work published, or about to be published,
in the calendar year—are accepted by our December one
deadline each year. Write to Pushcart Press, P.O. Box
380, Wainscott, N.Y. 11975 for more information.

Acknowledgements

Introduction © 1991 Edward Hoagland
Glossolalia © 1990 Shenandoah
Anonymity © 1990 North American Review
The Cleaving © 1990 TriQuarterly
Bill Weisler © 1990 Kenyon Review
Three Propositions: Hooey, Dewey and Looney © 1990 American Poetry Review
Little Owl Who Lives In The Orchard © 1990 Ploughshares
Night Sweats © 1990 American Poetry Review
The Gift © 1990 Confluence Press
Bocci © 1990 Iowa Review
Visitors © 1990 Grand Street
Sweet Ruin © 1990 Moon Pony Press
Against the Text 'Art is Immortal' © 1990 Agni
The Box © 1990 Milkweed Editions
One Thousand Words On Why You Should Not Talk During A Fire Drill © 1990 North
American Review
Mighty Forms © 1990 ZYZZYVA
Long, Disconsolate Lines © 1990 The Iowa Review
The Dream © 1990 Antaeus
The Hair © 1990 Partisan Review
Writers and Their Songs © 1990 Michigan Quarterly Review
Strong Pomegranate Flowers and Seeds of the Mind © 1990 Black Warrior Review
When They Leave © 1990 Amicus Journal
Woman Who Weeps © 1990 Antioch Review
Nosotros © 1990 Shenandoah
Books Oft Have Such A Charm: A Memory © 1990 North Dakota Quarterly
Chinese Fireworks Banned In Hawaii © 1990 Bamboo Ridge
1989, Gillette, Our Navy © 1990 The Sun
Jane Addams © 1990 Beloit Poetry Journal
The Stuff Men Are Made Of © 1990 Dalkey Archive Press
Maintenance © 1990 The Georgia Review
Gift Shop In Pecs © 1990 Partisan Review
Sesame © 1990 ZYZZYVA
Seeing You © 1990 American Poetry Review
Raisin Faces © 1990 Virginia Quarterly Review
River Girls © 1990 Northern Lights
Third Dungeness Spit Apocalypse © 1990 Bellowing Ark
Stories © 1990 Threepenny Review
Text © 1990 The Quarterly
Portable People © 1990 Paris Review
The Dead Body Itself © 1990 Agni
What They Wanted © 1990 American Poetry Review
The Limbo Dancer © 1990 Grand Street
Past, Future, Elsewhere © 1990 Ploughshares
Two Stories © 1990 Tikkun, Conjunctions

In memory of Nona Balakian (1918–1991) and Paul Engle (1908–1991), Founding Editors of The Pushcart Prize series

"HOLY FOOLS"

by EDWARD HOAGLAND

MY ENGLISH FRIEND Aaron Judah, raised in a mercantile family in Bombay, didn't mind me occasionally teasing him with the name "Jude the Obscure," because we were all pretty obscure. His first novel, "Clown of Bombay," was about to come out. My second, "The Circle Home," had just been published and had crashed in flames, as I liked to say, though total invisibility would have been a better word for it. With a few other struggling artists—a Maori painter named Ralph Hoteri, an Oregon novelist named Don Berry—we were comfortably couched under the protection of the beautiful Countess Catherine Karolyi in her little art colony in the village of Vence in the Alpes Maritimes in the south of France. When not at work, we would visit the Matisse Chapel or hike up an augerlike river canyon, past deep caves which underground springs gushed out of, and past otter pools, dizzy cliffs, swimming holes, waterfalls—my wife Amy and Ralph's wife Betty enlivening the crew. I was living on the Lower East Side of New York otherwise, on $2,500 a year, as was commonly the case among writers thirty years ago, before big book contracts and university writing programs had been invented to boost their incomes. Not just the Beat spirit Seymour Krim, but Philip Roth lived on East 10th Street too.

The countess was the widow of the Hungarian patriot Mihaly Karolyi, whose brief presidency in 1919 had been a beacon of democratic enlightenment between authoritarian regimes. She was vibrant, passionate, the friend or lover of Bertrand Russell, Gordon Craig and other flamboyant intellectual figures of prewar days, and now in her sixties was beloved by her large German shepherd. She lived with a middle-aged Englishwoman in this declining epoch, but had such zest that, hearing of the giddy canyons we had discovered, she galvanized herself to accompany us. And as a colony founded by a generous patroness to nurture the arts, hers was the very type of several I stayed at later, on Ossabaw Island, off Georgia, in Sweet Briar, Virginia, and at Saratoga Springs, up the Hudson River. Paying six dollars a week for a room in 1955, fifty dollars a month for a room in 1958, a hundred dollars a month for an apartment in the early '60s, I was a "low-rent" writer, in Tom Wolfe's phrase—"downwardly mobile," as Gay Talese used to kid me at publication parties (there were no *Pushcart Prizes* then)—and needed a break.

But my friend "Jude the Obscure" startled us all at that point by fainting from hunger. He was cut from that rare category of person whom I think of as "holy fools," and whom I like to draw very close friends from. But he was a gloomier personality than my own quite standard brand of New Englander's transcendentalism, or Don Berry's Oregon frontier go-do-it energy, for that matter. He had been gloomy in India, in England, and Israel, and had skipped too many meals for the sake of completing his work, and now he was starving. Ralph and Betty found him lying on his bed unconscious.

Countess Karolyi of course soon put a stop to the hunger, and her companion, his countrywoman, I think may have succored him just as directly. She had offered to succor me also, but, being married, I had refused. Later, unmarried, I visited her in Paris and was startled all over again to discover her studio apartment decorated with paper skulls and cut-out skeletons to remind her of "how bizarrely little time I have left." Her doctor had told her that she was terminally ill.

Succor your starving artists while ye may, might be a good motto. I never saw my hunger artist again, and I'm writing of an ancient era when artists were mostly male. People knew the sculptor Mary Frank, not as *Mary Frank*, but as the photographer Robert Frank's wife, Mary—and the theatrical innovator Jo Anne Akalaitis, not as *Jo Anne Akalaitis*, but as the composer Philip Glass's wife, Jo Anne. Yet I've known women who comforted an array of men, ranging from Donald Barthelme to Marlon Brando, Edward Abbey to John Berryman, and never regretted it. Abbey and Berryman, red-eyed and coughing, used

13

to look in on me on their trips to the city, and speak gratefully of bosoms opened to them, though, as always, such flings could be complicated. An old pal might throw a shoe at them too. I knew a kind-natured Playboy Playmate who owned a whole shelf of presentation copies, and bore no writer a grudge (at least in that heyday). On the other hand, a wealthy woman who made a practice of taking in lorn famous writers like Berryman told me she fed them according to their income level. Rich ones got steak; poor ones spaghetti. It was her pleasure, as well, when she bought a painting, to make love with the artist on the floor under it after the gallery had closed. Sadism was surely part of her thrill, and as with housing a doomed gladiator, the sense in his ardor that *We who are about to die salute you.*

This must still go on, but the milieu has changed. A youngish writer recently asked me to recommend him for a stay at the MacDowell Colony on the strength of a $300,000 advance-against-royalties he had received. He'd not previously published a book, but wanting to do a travel volume, had announced to various publishing houses that he would only set forth if he received a $200,000 advance. Now having done quite a bit better, he was seeking quarters for the winter while he wrote up his notes.

I didn't know how to reply. Great travelers, from Wilfrid Thesiger to Colin Thubron, tend to operate on a shoestring, but there is a feeling of entitlement among many new writers: budding novelists who want lifetime job tenure at a college somewhere and a Volvo in the garage. The particular angst, anguish, poverty or precarious circumstances they describe in their minimalist fiction should never be visited upon them. People quote Samuel Johnson's celebrated line that "No man but a blockhead ever wrote except for money" (though Johnson's own career refuted the idea, like his affection for the ragged genius, Christopher Smart). The low-rent life of William Blake or Dostoyevsky seems absurd.

It wasn't like that as we struggled in those years—Richard Yates, Ivan Gold, Joe Flaherty, Joel Oppenheimer, Marge Piercy, Hayden Carruth, Frederick Exley, Galway Kinnell. During my apprenticeship in shoeleather, as I called it, which I served for the first twenty years after I got out of the army in 1957, I reached my largest audience with an essay called "The Courage of Turtles," for which I received $35. (That was in 1968; for *this* essay I will pocket $100.) And I was glad to, because it was a newsprint audience, in the *Village Voice*, bigger than I'd had. My third novel had also crashed in invisible flames—"A Typical Example of Fictional Blight" was the *Times'* headline—sales of nine hundred copies after five years' work. For my next novel I shifted from ballpoint pens to using a typewriter, but that one took twenty years to do.

Meanwhile, however, I'd hit the ground running with a travel journal from British Columbia and a fluent exuberance that greased my wheels: in effect, my first essay, a form I discovered I had been made for. Like my previous books, I could recite the entire thing by heart when I was through, and like the first, I slept with it under my pillow the night the first copy arrived in the mail. But I let my hopes scud too high. When "Notes From the Century Before" scarcely received any notice at all in the *Times*, sold two thousand copies, and got good but scanty reviews elsewhere, what I did was go to the country to lick my wounds. They were bloody, and after licking them for a week or two, I vomited, vomited blood.

For me it ranked as an equivalent crisis to when my poor avatar, Jude the Obscure, had fainted from hunger. He'd looked for changes to institute in his life, and so did I. I'd begun teaching, for $300 per semester, at the New School for Social Research; and for $50, did book reviews for the *Herald Tribune*. My rent by 1970 had risen to $200. I had grown up in an expensive suburb of New York, going on to prep school and Harvard—but a writer's life is leveling. My father had tried to discourage me from embarking on my career; then had asked that if I must, I use a pen name; then had written to Houghton Mifflin's attorney to ask that the publication of my first novel be stopped, arguing that it was "obscene"; and finally had pretty much cut me out of his will. So when I published stories in the *Paris Review*, the *Transatlantic Review*, the *New American Review*, it was important to me just as it's crucial to many writers who appear in the journals represented here. My policy was that once it was finished, no story should be allowed to spend a night at home. If they bounced back from one magazine in the morning, out they went to another that same afternoon. Even so, the boost of seeing them in print might take twelve submissions. The very first, called "Cowboys," wound up at Saul Bellow's magazine, *The Noble Savage* (five issues, 1960–62—with Bellovian generosity, he wired me when he accepted it), which I suspect he had started in the aftermath of his anger at *The New Yorker*'s rejection of his short masterpiece, "Seize the Day," which had then appeared in *Partisan Review*.

Antaeus, Witness, Pequod, New England Review, like alternative publishers such as North Point Press and *The Hungry Mind Review*, have counted for me, just as their counterparts did for so many writers I knew—Kenneth Rexroth, Gary Snyder, Craig Nova, Hilma Wolitzer, Tobias Schneebaum, John Haines, Gilbert Sorrentino, Jonathan Raban, Hortense Calisher, Wendell Berry, George Dennison. Raymond Carver was homeless, broke, "belly-up," as he said, when I met him, adrift, shortly before his first success, on his way to El Paso from Iowa City. Those of my friends who felt that inspiration lay partly in gin and cigarette ends (and they may have been right) didn't live quite as long, but their hardships were all of a piece with the rest of us. Buildings where the furnace broke or caught fire or the boiler blew up, where leaks developed in the ceiling that were not fixed for endless weeks, where tenants suffering a nervous breakdown ran through the hallway wielding a knife.

Does one still meet "starving" artists? Yes: a poet off an ore boat who has driven to the East Village and is being "eaten alive" by New York, he says. And regularly there are brand-name writers who need help in getting a cancer operation; regularly, young strugglers coming up—Fae Myenne Ng, Elizabeth Tallent, Sara Vogan, Clarence Major, Charlie Smith, Howard Mosher. But whether they think of their work as being improvised like a jazz riff, or plotted like a piano sonata, whether they ramble through wilderness country or case the Big Apple, choose their subject matter from what they love like John McPhee, or what they hate like Joe McGinniss, "go Hollywood," lobby for a position on a magazine's masthead, or chair an English department, writers do tend to turn bitter. In fact I can't recall ever meeting a middle-aged writer who wasn't somewhat bitter. Greeting-card and comic-book writers, thriller writers, sci-fi or sitcom writers, American Academy of Arts and Letters writers, front-page of the *New York Times Book Review* writers, sports-page or mule-train writers—in forty years in the trade I've known hundreds. The big divide seems to be between the free spirits who sit down

16

every morning to speak their minds without first calculating the market for it and staff writers in what I call mule trains—well-fed, nicely harnessed, with bits in their mouths and bottoms upraised for the whip of an editor—who write cover stories for *Time* or dance attendance upon the mindset of *Vanity Fair,* perhaps, on retainer.

There are talented people of my generation who devoted the meat of their careers to anticipating the tastes of *The New Yorker's* "legendary" William Shawn, with his three-year inventory of profiles and stories, all bought and paid for (oh, *would* he use yours!). The crotchets of Mr. Shawn, like those of his predecessor, Harold Ross, recounted with an anxious edge to the voice, were fodder for thousands of cocktail parties. I went to the Sudan and to Maine for Mr. Shawn ("You won't be political, will you?" he asked), and to Alaska for *Vanity Fair's* Tina Brown (whose interest was limited to its millionaires), but in each case my attention strayed to politics and to the mountains.

The price of independence is occasional despair, however. You see it in Melville, Dreiser, Hemingway, Faulkner—whoever. Bernard Malamud, among recent writers, has elaborated best upon the uses to which despair can be put, like a kind of elixir at last. I remember lunches with Donald Barthelme in Greenwich Village and suppers with Hayden Carruth in Johnson, Vermont fifteen or twenty years ago, in which each writer—separately, and at the height of his powers—expressed the belief that he was played out and about to die: like Raymond Carver "belly up," at about the same time, and Philip Roth virtually paralyzed with despondency, as he has described.

Stubborn, foolhardy, profitless writing—the small press ideal—may free one to say something new. John Updike, E. L. Doctorow, William Gaddis, Grace Paley, Paul Theroux, and Bellow have also marked me with lessons I've tried to learn—about modesty, fecundity, self-preservation, stamina, gaiety, and ingenuity. The core of writing well is to tell your tale at your own pace, just as you wish, taking your chances. From the Bible to *Peter Rabbit*, that's how it's been done. We all want to strike the perfect pitch that will win us an hour's ease and aplomb, heart to heart with a million readers, fathoming their fears and their funnybones, with our own loneliness only a fortifying toxin, or sort of like how heavy hitters swing two or three bats before going to

17

work. If the middle-aged writers I speak of had been simply bitter they would have got nothing done. An ebullient open-heartedness and mischief-making has enlivened even the most choleric ones, like John O'Hara and Edward Dahlberg.

O'Hara relished money and Dahlberg pined for it, but surely money has never meant more to authors than it does now. The smiley buzz and slippery hustle of agents, auctions, talk tours, mall blitzes, "pencil" editors versus "belly" editors (who "just do lunch"), and young writers standing around at soirées like brat-pack bond salesmen comparing "scores," are a far cry from my fond hunger artist, Jude the Obscure, following his inner compass and maybe winning a Pushcart Prize. But greed and integrity do their dance down through the ages, and in each of us. For every Kafka-pure anorexic you could cite a couple of geniuses of the fat strutting stripe of Dickens or Twain, in whom the two drives intertwined fruitfully also.

I don't see any Kafkas, Dickenses or Twains around, but who knows? Among the bohemians camped in voluntary or involuntary squalor (and they inhabited crevices of even the Eighties too), there may be a boomingly, lusciously talented soul, neurotic, fretful, and bereft of hope, but churning out radiant prose. Too many writing courses are being offered, too many aspiring novelists stoop over word screens, for the number of earnest readers at large. It seems as if writing has become a therapy for loneliness, or part of the new search for solitude, like "meditation" or jogging, like Walkmans, Jacuzzis, a societal symptom, instead of an individual aptitude too pressing to ignore. Writers are prickly, blithe, callous, and manipulative, the top-of-the-food-chain when it comes to processing other people's experiences, eavesdropping upon them, milking them of their bewilderment, happiness or grief. Tell me your story and I'll make it mine, they say. It's a higher gossip, a mixmaster process, but once in a blue moon—in Becky Sharp, Ebenezer Scrooge—the tale becomes *ours*. All the posturing, the ego-swagger, the pinched nerves that go with having writers around appear to be worth it.

Evidence of that worth is in the pages that follow.

THE PEOPLE
WHO HELPED

FOUNDING EDITORS—*Anaïs Nin (1903–1977), Buckminster Fuller (1895–1983), Charles Newman, Daniel Halpern, Gordon Lish, Harry Smith, Hugh Fox, Ishmael Reed, Joyce Carol Oates, Len Fulton, Leonard Randolph, Leslie Fiedler, Nona Balakian, (1918–1991), Paul Bowles, Paul Engle (1908–1991), Ralph Ellison, Reynolds Price, Rhoda Schwartz, Richard Morris, Ted Wilentz, Tom Montag, William Phillips, Poetry editor: H. L. Van Brunt.*

EDITORS—*Walter Abish, Ai, Elliott Anderson, John Ashbery, Russell Banks, Joe David Bellamy, Robert Bly, Philip Booth, Robert Boyers, Harold Brodkey, Joseph Brodsky, Wesley Brown, Hayden Carruth, Frank Conroy, Paula Deitz, Steve Dixon, Rita Dove, Andre Dubus, M. D. Elevitch, Louise Erdrich, Loris Essary, Ellen Ferber, Carolyn Forché, Stuart Freibert, Jon Galassi, Tess Gallagher, Louis Gallo, George Garrett, Reginald Gibbons, Jack Gilbert, Louise Glück, David Godine, Jorie Graham, Linda Gregg, Barbara Grossman, Donald Hall, Helen Handley, Michael Harper, Robert Hass, DeWitt Henry, J. R. Humphreys, David Ignatow, John Irving, June Jordan, Edmund Keeley, Karen Kennerly, Galway Kinnell, Carolyn Kizer, Jerzy Kosinski, Richard Kostelanetz, Seymour Krim, Maxine Kumin, James Laughlin, Seymour Lawrence, Naomi Lazard, Herb Leibowitz, Denise Levertov, Philip Levine, Stanley Lindberg, Thomas Lux, Mary MacArthur, Thomas McGrath, Jay Meek, Daniel Menaker, Frederick Morgan, Cynthia Ozick, Jayne Anne Phillips, Robert Phillips, George Plimpton, Stanley Plumly, Eugene Redmond, Ed*

19

Sanders, Teo Savory, Grace Schulman, Harvey Shapiro, Leslie Silko, Charles Simic, Dave Smith, Elizabeth Spencer, William Stafford, Gerald Stern, David St. John, Bill and Pat Strachan, Ron Sukenick, Anne Tyler, John Updike, Sam Vaughan, David Wagoner, Derek Walcott, Ellen Wilbur, David Wilk, David Wojahn, Bill Zavatsky.

CONTRIBUTING EDITORS—Sandra Alcosser, John Allman, Philip Appleman, Jennifer Atkinson, Rick Bass, Charles Baxter, Linda Bierds, Marianne Boruch, Michael Bowden, Michael Dennis Browne, Christopher Buckley, Richard Burgin, Michael Burkard, Barry Callaghan, Henry Carlile, Kelly Cherry, Naomi Clark, Judith Oritz Cofer, Henri Cole, Michael Collier, Peter Cooley, Stephen Corey, Richard Currey, Philip Dacey, John Daniel, Lydia Davis, Susan S. Deal, Carl Dennis, Toi Derricotte, Rita Dove, John Drury, Stuart Dybek, Karen Fish, Jane Flanders, H. E. Francis, Kenneth Gangemi, Reginald Gibbons, Patrick Worth Grey, Marilyn Hacker, Sam Hamill, Ehud Havazelet, Daniel Hayes, Robin Hemley, DeWitt Henry, Kim Herzinger, Brenda Hillman, Edward Hirsch, Jane Hirshfield, Edward Hoagland, Andrew Hudgins, Lynda Hull, T. R. Hummer, Sandy Huss, Colette Inez, Richard Jackson, Mark Jarman, David Jauss, Laura Jenson, Diane Johnson, Rodney H. Jones, Mary Karr, Dave Kelly, Thomas Kennedy, Richard Kostelanetz, Maxine Kumin, Wally Lamb, Dorianne Laux, Li-Young Lee, David Lehman, Melissa Lentricchia, Philip Levine, Stanley Lindberg, Gerry Locklin, David Madden, Clarence Major, Kathy Mangan, Michael Martone, Dan Masterson, Lou Mathews, Cleopatra Mathis, Robert McBrearty, Lynne McFall, Kristina McGrath, Lynne McMahon, Wesley McNair, Sandra McPherson, Susan Mitchell, Jim Moore, Lisel Mueller, David Mura, Joan Murray, Kent Nelson, Fae Myenne Ng, Josip Novakovich, Sigrid Nunez, Joyce Carol Oates, Sharon Olds, Cynthia Ozick, Frankie Paino, Greg Pape, Walter Pavlich, Johathan Penner, Mary Peterson, Robert Phillips, Robert Pinsky, Joe Ashby Porter, C. E. Poverman, Francine Prose, Tony Quagliano, Bin Ramke, Eugene Redmond, Donald Revell, Alberto Alvaro Rios, Kenneth Rosen, Gibbons Ruark, Sharman Russell, Vern Rutsala, Sherod Santos, Lloyd Schwartz, Laurie Sheck, Jim Simmerman, Arthur Smith, Lee Smith, James Solheim, Chris Spain, Elizabeth Spencer, David St. John, Maura

20

CONTENTS

GLOSSOLALIA

fiction by DAVID JAUSS

from SHENANDOAH

THAT WINTER, LIKE every winter before it, my father woke early each day and turned up the thermostat so the house would be warm by the time my mother and I got out of bed. Sometimes I'd hear the furnace kick in and the shower come on down the hall and I'd wake just long enough to be angry that he'd wakened me. But usually I slept until my mother had finished making our breakfast. By then, my father was already at Goodyear, opening the service bay for the customers who had to drop their cars off before going to work themselves. Sitting in the sunny kitchen, warmed by the heat from the register and the smell of my mother's coffee, I never thought about him dressing in the cold dark or shoveling out the driveway by porchlight. If I thought of him at all, it was only to feel glad he was not there. In those days my father and I fought a lot, though probably not much more than most fathers and sons. I was sixteen then, a tough age. And he was forty, an age I've since learned is even tougher.

But that winter I was too concerned with my own problems to think about my father's. I was a skinny, unathletic, sorrowful boy who had few friends, and I was in love with Molly Rasmussen, one of the prettiest girls in Glencoe and the daughter of a man who had stopped my father on Main Street that fall, called him a "goddamned debt-dodger," and threatened to break his face. My father had bought a used Ford Galaxie from Mr. Rasmussen's lot, but he hadn't been able to make the payments and eventually Mr. Rasmussen repossessed it. Without a second car my mother

27

couldn't get to work—she had taken a job at the school lunchroom, scooping out servings of mashed potatoes and green beans—so we drove our aging Chevy to Minneapolis, where no one knew my father, and bought a rust-pitted yellow Studebaker. A few days later Molly Rasmussen passed me in the hall at school and said, "I see you've got a new car," then laughed. I was so mortified I hurried into a restroom, locked myself in a stall, and stood there for several minutes, breathing hard. Even after the bell rang for the next class, I didn't move. I was furious at my father. I blamed him for the fact that Molly despised me, just as I had for some time blamed him for everything else that was wrong with my life—my gawky looks, my discount-store clothes, my lack of friends.

That night, and others like it, I lay in bed and imagined who I'd be if my mother had married someone handsome and popular like Dick Moore, the PE teacher, or Smiley Swenson, who drove stock cars at the county fair, or even Mr. Rasmussen. Years before, my mother had told me how she met my father. A girl who worked with her at Woolworth's had asked her if she wanted to go out with a friend of her boyfriend's, an Army man just back from the war. My mother had never agreed to a blind date before, or dated an older man, but for some reason this time she said yes. Lying there, I thought about that fateful moment. It seemed so fragile—she could as easily have said no and changed everything—and I wished, then, that she had said no, I wished she'd said she didn't date strangers or she already had a date or she was going out of town—anything to alter the chance conjunction that would eventually produce me.

I know now that there was something suicidal about my desire to undo my parentage, but then I knew only that I wanted to be someone else. And I blamed my father for that wish. If I'd had a different father, I reasoned, I would be better-looking, happier, more popular. When I looked in the mirror and saw my father's thin face, his rust-red hair, downturned mouth, and bulging Adam's apple, I didn't know who I hated more, him or me. That winter I began parting my hair on the right instead of the left, as my father did, and whenever the house was empty I worked on changing my voice, practicing the inflections and accents of my classmates' fathers as if they were clues to a new life. I even prac-

28

ticed one's walk, another's crooked smile, a third's wink. I did not think, then, that my father knew how I felt about him, but now that I have a son of my own, a son almost as old as I was then, I know different.

If I had known what my father was going through that winter, maybe I wouldn't have treated him so badly. But I didn't know anything until the January morning of his breakdown. I woke that morning to the sound of voices downstairs in the kitchen. At first I thought the sound was the wind rasping in the bare branches of the cottonwood outside my window, then I thought it was the radio. But after I lay there a moment I recognized my parents' voices. I couldn't tell what they were saying, but I knew they were arguing. They'd been arguing more than usual lately, and I hated it—not so much because I wanted them to be happy, though I did, but because I knew they'd take their anger out on me, snapping at me, telling me to chew with my mouth closed, asking me who gave me permission to put my feet up on the coffee table, ordering me to clean my room. I buried one ear in my pillow and covered the other with my blankets, but I could still hear them. They sounded distant, yet somehow close, like the sea crashing in a shell held to the ear. But after a while I couldn't hear even the muffled sound of their voices, and I sat up in the bars of gray light slanting through the blinds and listened to the quiet. I didn't know what was worse: their arguments or their silences. I sat there, barely breathing, waiting for some noise.

Finally I heard the back door bang shut and, a moment later, the Chevy cough to life. Only then did I dare get out of bed. Crossing to the window, I lowered one of the slats in the blinds with a finger and saw, in the dim light, the driveway drifted shut with snow. Then my father came out of the garage and began shoveling, scooping the snow furiously and flinging it over his shoulder, as if each shovelful were a continuation of the argument. I couldn't see his face, but I knew that it was red and that he was probably cursing under his breath. As he shoveled, the wind scuffed the drifts around him, swirling the snow into his eyes, but he didn't stop or set his back to the wind. He just kept shoveling fiercely, and suddenly it occurred to me that he might have a heart attack, just as my friend Rob's father had the winter before. For an instant I saw him slump over his shovel, then

29

collapse face-first into the snow. As soon as this thought came to me, I did my best to make myself think it arose from love and terror, but even then I knew part of me wished his death, and that knowledge went through me like a chill.

I lowered the slat on the blinds and got back into bed. The house was quiet but not peaceful. I knew that somewhere in the silence my mother was crying and I thought about going to comfort her, but I didn't. After a while I heard my father rev the engine and back the Chevy down the driveway. Still I didn't get up. And when my mother finally came to tell me it was time to get ready, her eyes and nose red and puffy, I told her I wasn't feeling well and wanted to stay home. Normally, she would have felt my forehead and cross-examined me about my symptoms, but that day I knew she'd be too upset to bother. "Okay, Danny," she said. "Call me if you think you need to see a doctor." And that was it. She shut my door and a few minutes later I heard the whine of the Studebaker's cold engine, and then she was gone.

It wasn't long after my mother left that my father came home. I was lying on the couch in the living room, trying to figure out the hidden puzzle on "Concentration," when I heard a car pull into the driveway. At first I thought my mother had changed her mind and come back to take me to school. But then the back door sprang open and I heard him. It was a sound I had never heard before and since have heard only in my dreams, a sound that will make me sit up in the thick dark, my eyes open to nothing, and my breath panting. I don't know how to explain it, other than to say it was a kind of crazy language, like speaking in tongues. It sounded as if he was crying and talking at the same time, and in some strange way his words had become half-sobs and his sobs something more than words—or words turned inside out, so that only their emotion and not their meaning came through. It scared me. I knew something terrible had happened, and I didn't know what to do. I wanted to go to him and ask him what was wrong, but I didn't dare. I switched off the sound on the TV so he wouldn't know I was home and sat there staring at Hugh Downs' smiling face. But then I couldn't stand it anymore and I got up and ran down the hall to the kitchen. There, in the middle of the room, wearing his Goodyear jacket and work-clothes, was my father. He was on his hands and knees, his head hanging as though it were too heavy to support, and he was rocking back and forth and babbling in a rhythmical stutter. It's funny, but the first thing I thought when I saw him like that was the way he used to let me ride on his back, when I was little, bucking and neighing like a horse. And as soon as I thought it, I felt my heart lurch in my chest. "Dad?" I said. "What's wrong?" But he didn't hear me. I went over to him then. "Dad?" I said again and touched him on the shoulder. He jerked at the touch and looked up at me, his lips moving but no sounds coming out of them now. His forehead was knotted and his eyes were red, almost raw-looking. He swallowed hard and for the first time spoke words I could recognize, though I did not understand them until years later, when I was myself a father.

"Danny," he said. "Save me."

Before I could finish dialing the school lunchroom's number, my mother pulled into the driveway. Looking out the window, I saw her jump out of the car and run up the slick sidewalk, her camel-colored overcoat open and flapping in the wind. For a moment I was confused. Had I already called and told her what had happened? How much time had passed since I found my father on the kitchen floor? A minute? An hour? Then I realized someone else must have told her something was wrong.

She burst in the back door then and called out, "Bill? Bill? Are you here?"

"Mom," I said, "Dad's—" and then I didn't know how to finish the sentence.

She came in the kitchen without stopping to remove her galoshes. "Oh, Bill," she said when she saw us, "are you all right?"

My father was sitting at the kitchen table now, his hands fluttering in his lap. A few moments before, I had helped him to his feet and, draping his arm over my shoulders, led him to the table like a wounded man.

"Helen," he said. "It's you." He said it like he hadn't seen her for years.

My mother went over and knelt beside him. "I'm so sorry," she said, but whether that statement was born of sorrow over something she had said or done or whether she just simply and guiltlessly wished he weren't suffering, I never knew. Taking his hands in hers, she added, "There's nothing to worry about. Everything's going to be fine." Then she turned to me. Her brown

31

hair was wind-blown, and her face was so pale the smudges of rouge on her cheeks looked like bruises. "Danny, I want you to leave us alone for a few minutes."

I looked at her red-rimmed eyes and tight lips. "Okay," I said, and went back to the living room. There, I sat on the sagging couch and stared at the television, the contestants' mouths moving wordlessly, their laughs eerily silent. I could hear my parents talking, their steady murmur broken from time to time by my father sobbing and my mother saying "Bill" over and over, in the tone mothers use to calm their babies, but I couldn't hear enough of what they said to know what had happened. And I didn't want to know either. I wanted them to be as silent as the people on the TV, I wanted all the words to stop, all the crying.

I lay down and closed my eyes, trying to drive the picture of my father on the kitchen floor out of my head. My heart was beating so hard I could feel my pulse tick in my throat. I was worried about my father but I was also angry that he was acting so strange. It didn't seem fair that I had to have a father like that. I'd never seen anybody else's father act that way, not even in a movie.

Outside, the wind shook the evergreens and every now and then a gust would rattle the windowpane. I lay there a long time, listening to the wind, until my heart stopped beating so hard.

Some time later, my mother came into the room and sat on the edge of the chair under the sunburst mirror. Her forehead was creased, and there were black mascara streaks on her cheeks. Leaning toward me, her hands clasped, she asked me how I was feeling.

"What do you mean?" I wasn't sure if she was asking if I was still feeling sick or if she meant something else.

She bit her lip. "I just wanted to tell you not to worry," she said. "Everything's going to be all right." Her breath snagged on the last word, and I could hear her swallowing.

"What's wrong?" I asked.

She opened her mouth, as if she were about to answer, but suddenly her eyes began to tear. "We'll talk about it later," she said. "After the doctor's come. Just don't worry, okay? I'll explain everything."

"The doctor?" I said.

"I'll explain later," she answered.

Then she left and I didn't hear anything more until ten or fifteen minutes had passed and the doorbell rang. My mother ran to the door and opened it, and I heard her say, "Thank you for coming so quickly" and "He's in the kitchen." As they hurried down the hall past the living room, I caught a glimpse of Dr. Lewis and his black leather bag. It had been years since the doctors in our town, small as it was, made house calls, so I knew now that my father's problem was something truly serious. The word *emergency* came into my mind, and though I tried to push it out, it kept coming back.

For the next half-hour or so, I stayed in the living room, listening to the droning sound of Dr. Lewis and my parents talking. I still didn't know what had happened or why. All I knew was that my father was somebody else now, somebody I didn't know. I tried to reconcile the father who used to read to me at night when my mother was too tired, the man who patiently taught me how to measure and cut plywood for a birdhouse, even the man whose cheeks twitched when he was angry at me and whose silences were suffocating, with the man I had just seen crouched like an animal on the kitchen floor babbling some incomprehensible language. But I couldn't. And though I felt sorry for him and his suffering, I felt as much shame as sympathy. *This is your father,* I told myself. *This is you when you're older.*

It wasn't until after Dr. Lewis had left and my father had taken the tranquilizers and gone upstairs to bed that my mother came back into the living room, sat down on the couch beside me, and told me what had happened. "Your father," she began, and her voice cracked. Then she controlled herself and said, "Your father has been fired from his job."

I looked at her. "Is that it?" I said. "That's what all this fuss is about?" I couldn't believe he'd put us through all this for something so unimportant. All he had to do was get a new job. What was the big deal?

"Let me explain," my mother said. "He was fired some time ago. Eight days ago, to be exact. But he hadn't said anything to me about it, and he just kept on getting up and going down to work every morning, like nothing had happened. And every day Mr. Siverhus told him to leave, and after arguing a while, he'd go. Then he'd spend the rest of the day driving around until quitting time, when he'd finally come home. But Mr. Siverhus got fed up and changed the locks, and when your father came to work today he couldn't get in. He tried all three entrances, and when he found his key didn't work in any of them well, he threw a trash barrel through the showroom window and went inside."

She paused for a moment, I think to see how I was taking this. I was trying to picture my father throwing a barrel through that huge, expensive window. It wasn't easy to imagine. Even at his most angry, he had never been violent. He had never even threatened to hit me or my mother. But now he'd broken a window, and the law.

My mother went on. "Then when he was inside, he found that Mr. Siverhus had changed the lock on his office too, so he kicked the door in. When Mr. Siverhus came to work, he found your dad sitting at his desk, going over service accounts." Her lips started to tremble. "He could have called the police," she said, "but he called me instead. We owe him for that."

That's the story my mother told me. Though I was to find out later that she hadn't told me the entire truth, she had told me enough of it to make me realize that my father had gone crazy. Something in him—whatever slender idea or feeling it is that connects us to the world and makes us feel a part of it—had broken, and he was not in the world anymore, he was outside it, horribly outside it, and could not get back in no matter how he tried. Somehow I knew this, even then. And I wondered if some day the same thing would happen to me.

The rest of that day, I stayed downstairs, watching TV or reading *Sports Illustrated* or *Life*, while my father slept or rested. My mother sat beside his bed, reading her ladies magazines while he slept and talking to him whenever he woke, and every now and then she came downstairs to tell me he was doing fine. She spoke as if he had some temporary fever, some twenty-four hour virus, that would be gone by morning.

But the next morning, a Saturday, my father was still not himself. He didn't feel like coming down for breakfast, so she made him scrambled eggs, sausage, and toast and took it up to him on a tray. He hadn't eaten since the previous morning, but when she came back down a while later all the food was still on the tray. She didn't say anything about the untouched meal; she just said my father wanted to talk to me.

34

"I can't," I said. "I'm eating." I had one sausage patty and a few bites of scrambled egg left on my plate.

"Not this minute," she said. "When you're done."

I looked out the window. It had been snowing all morning, and the evergreens in the back yard looked like flocked Christmas trees waiting for strings of colored lights. Some sparrows were flying in and out of the branches, chirping, and others were lined up on the crossbars of the clothesline poles, their feathers fluffed out and blowing in the wind.

"I'm supposed to meet Rob at his house," I lied. "I'll be late."

"Danny," she said, in a way that warned me not to make her say any more.

"All right," I said, and I shoved my plate aside and got up. "But I don't have much time."

Upstairs, I stopped at my father's closed door. Normally I would have walked right in, but that day I felt I should knock. I felt as if I were visiting a stranger. Even his room—I didn't think of it as belonging to my mother anymore—seemed strange, somehow separate from the rest of the house.

When I knocked, my father said, "Is that you, Danny?" and I stepped inside. All the blinds were shut, and the dim air smelled like a thick, musty mixture of hair tonic and Aqua Velva. My father was sitting on the edge of his unmade bed, wearing his old brown robe, nubbled from years of washings, and maroon corduroy slippers. His face was blotchy, and his eyes were dark and pouched.

"Mom said you wanted to talk to me," I said.

He touched a spot next to him on the unmade bed. "Here. Sit down."

I didn't move. "I've got to go to Rob's," I said.

He cleared his throat and looked away. For a moment we were silent, and I could hear the heat register ticking.

"I just wanted to tell you to take good care of your mother," he said then.

I shifted my weight from one foot to the other. "What do you mean?"

He looked back at me, his gaze steady and empty, and I wondered how much of the way he was that moment was his medication and how much himself. "She needs someone to take care of her. That's all."

"What about you? Aren't you going to take care of her any-more?"

He cleared his throat again. "If I can."

"I don't get it," I said. "Why are you doing this to us? What's going on?"

"Nothing's going on," he answered. "That the problem. Not a thing is going on."

"I don't know what you mean. I don't like it when you say things I can't understand."

"I don't like it either," he said. Then: "That wasn't me yester-day. I want you to know that."

"It sure looked like you. If it wasn't you, who was it then?"

He stood up and walked across the carpet to the window. But he didn't open the blinds; he just stood there, his back to me. "It's all right for you to be mad," he said.

"I'm not mad."

"Don't lie."

"I'm not lying. I just like my father to use the English language when he talks to me, that's all."

For a long moment he was quiet. It seemed almost as if he'd forgotten I was in the room. Then he said, "My grandmother used to tell me there were exactly as many stars in the sky as there were people. If someone was born, there'd be a new star in the sky that night, and you could find it if you looked hard enough. And if someone died, you'd see that person's star fall."

"What are you talking about?" I asked.

"People," he answered. "Stars."

Then he just stood there, staring at the blinds. I wondered if he was seeing stars there, or his grandmother, or what. And all of a sudden I felt my eyes start to sting. I was surprised—a moment before I'd been so angry, but now I was almost crying.

I tried to swallow, but I couldn't. I wanted to know what was wrong, so I could know how to feel about it; I wanted to be sad or angry, either one, but not both at the same time. "What *hap-pened?*" I finally said. "*Tell* me."

He turned, but I wasn't sure he'd heard me, because he didn't answer for a long time. And when he did, he seemed to be an-swering some other question, one I hadn't asked.

"I was so arrogant," he said. "I thought my life would work out."

I stood there looking at him. "I don't understand."

"I hope you never do," he said. "I hope to God you never do."

"Quit talking like that."

"Like what?"

"Like you're so *smart* and everything. Like you're above all of this when it's you that's causing it all."

He looked down at the floor and shook his head slowly.

"Well?" I said. "Aren't you going to say something?"

He looked up. "You're a good boy, Danny. I'm proud of you. I wish I could be a better father for you."

I hesitate now to say what I said next. But then I didn't hesitate. "So do I," I said bitterly. "So the hell do I." And I turned to leave.

"Danny, wait," my father said.

But I didn't wait. And when I shut the door, I shut it hard.

Two days later, after he took to fits of weeping and laughing, we drove my father to the VA hospital in Minneapolis. Dr. Lewis had already called the hospital and made arrangements for his admission, so we were quickly escorted to his room on the seventh floor, where the psychiatric patients were kept. I had expected the psych ward to be a dreary, prison-like place with barred doors and gray, windowless walls, but if anything, it was cheerier than the rest of the hospital. There were sky-blue walls in the hallway, hung here and there with watercolor landscapes the patients had painted, and sunny yellow walls in the rooms, and there was a brightly lit lounge with a TV, card tables, and a shelf full of board games, and even a crafts center where the patients could do decoupage, leatherwork, mosaics and macramé. And the patients we saw looked so normal that I almost wondered whether we were in the right place. Most of them were older, probably veterans of the First World War, but a few were my father's age or younger. The old ones were the friendliest, nodding their bald heads or waving their liver-spotted hands as we passed, but even those who only looked at us seemed pleasant or, at the least, not hostile.

I was relieved by what I saw but evidently my father was not, for his eyes still had the quicksilver shimmer of fear they'd had all during the drive from Glencoe. He sat stiffly in the wheelchair and looked at the floor passing between his feet as the big-boned nurse pushed him down the hall toward his room.

We were lucky, the nurse told us, chatting away in a strange accent, which I later learned was Czech. There had been only one private room left, and my father had gotten it. And it had a *lovely* view of the hospital grounds. Sometimes she herself would stand in front of that window and watch the snow fall on the birches and park benches. It was such a beautiful sight. She asked my father if that didn't sound nice, but he didn't answer.

Then she wheeled him into the room and parked the chair beside the white, starched-looking bed. My father hadn't wanted to sit in the chair when we checked him in at the admissions desk, but now he didn't show any desire to get out of it.

"Well, what do you think of your room, Mr. Conroy?" the nurse asked. My mother stood beside her, a handkerchief squeezed in her hand.

My father looked at the chrome railing on the bed, the stainless steel tray beside it, and the plastic-sealed water glasses on the tray. Then he looked at my mother and me.

"I suppose it's where I should be," he said.

During the five weeks my father was in the hospital, my mother drove to Minneapolis twice a week to visit him. Despite her urgings, I refused to go with her. I wanted to forget about my father, to erase him from my life. But I didn't tell her that. I told her I couldn't stand to see him in that awful place, and she felt sorry for me and let me stay home. But almost every time she came back, she'd have a gift for me from him: a postcard of Minnehaha Falls decoupaged onto a walnut plaque, a leather billfold with my initials burned into the cover, a belt decorated with turquoise and white beads. And a request: would I come see him that weekend? But I never went.

Glencoe was a small town, and like all small towns it was devoted to gossip. I knew my classmates had heard about my father—many of them had probably even driven past Goodyear to see the broken window the way they'd drive past a body shop to see a car that had been totaled—but only Rob and a couple of other friends said anything. When they asked what had happened, I told them what Dr. Lewis had told me, that my father was just overworked and exhausted. They didn't believe me any more than I believed Dr. Lewis, but they pretended to accept that explanation. I wasn't sure if I liked them more for that pretense, or less.

It took a couple of weeks for the gossip to reach me. One day during lunch Rob told me that Todd Knutson, whose father was a mechanic at Goodyear, was telling everybody my father had been fired for embezzling. "I know it's a dirty lie," Rob kept saying, "but some kids think he's telling the truth, so you'd better do something."

"Like what?" I said.

"Tell them the truth. Set the record straight."

I looked at my friend's earnest, acne-scarred face. As soon as he'd told me the rumor, I'd known it was true, and in my heart I had already convicted my father. But I didn't want my best friend to know that. Perhaps I was worried that he would turn against me too and I'd be even more alone.

"You bet I will," I said. "I'll make him eat those words."

But I had no intention of defending my father. I was already planning to go see Mr. Siverhus right after school and ask him, straight out, for the truth, so I could confront my father with the evidence and shame him the way he had shamed me. I was furious with him for making me even more of an outcast than I had been—I was the son of a *criminal* now—and I wanted to make him pay for it. All during my afternoon classes, I imagined going to see him at the hospital and telling him I knew his secret. He'd deny it at first, I was sure, but as soon as he saw I knew everything, he'd confess. He'd beg my forgiveness, swearing he'd never do anything to embarrass me or my mother again, but nothing he would say would make any difference—I'd just turn and walk away. And if I were called into court to testify against him, I'd take the stand and swear to tell the whole truth and nothing but the truth, my eyes steady on him all the while, watching him sit there beside his lawyer, his head hung, speechless.

I was angry at my mother too, because she hadn't told me the whole truth. But I didn't realize until that afternoon, when I drove down to Goodyear to see Mr. Siverhus, just how much she hadn't told me.

39

Mr. Siverhus was a tall, silver-haired man who looked more like a banker than the manager of a tire store. He was wearing a starched white shirt, a blue and gray striped tie with a silver tie tack, and iridescent sharkskin trousers, and when he shook my hand he smiled so hard his crow's feet almost hid his pale watery eyes. He led me into his small but meticulous office, closing the door on the smell of grease and the noise of impact wrenches removing lugs from wheels, and I blurted out my question before either of us even sat down.

"Who told you that?" he asked.

"My mother," I answered. I figured he wouldn't try to lie to me if he thought my mother had already told me the truth. Then I asked him again: "Is it true?" But Mr. Siverhus didn't answer right away. Instead, he gestured toward a chair opposite his gray metal desk and waited until I sat in it. Then he pushed some carefully stacked papers aside, sat on the edge of the desk, and asked me how my father was doing. I didn't really know—my mother kept saying he was getting better all the time, but I wasn't sure I could believe her. Still, I said, "Fine."

He nodded. "I'm glad to hear that," he said. "I'm really terribly sorry about everything that's happened. I hope you and your mother know that."

He wanted me to say something, but I didn't. Standing up, he wandered over to the gray file cabinet and looked out the window at the showroom, where the new tires and batteries were on display. He sighed, and I knew he didn't want to be having this conversation.

"What your mother told you is true," he said then. "Bill was taking money. Not much, you understand, but enough that it soon became obvious we had a problem. After some investigating, we found out he was the one. I couldn't have been more surprised. Your father had been a loyal and hardworking employee for years—we never would have put him in charge of the service department otherwise—and he was the last person I would have expected to be stealing from us. But when we confronted him with it, he admitted it. He'd been having trouble meeting his mortgage payments, he said, and in a weak moment he'd taken some money and, later on, a little more. He seemed genuinely sorry about it and he swore he'd pay back every cent, so we gave him another chance."

"But he did it again, didn't he?" I said.

I don't know if Mr. Siverhus noticed the anger shaking my voice or not. He just looked at me and let out a slow breath. "Yes," he said sadly. "He did. And so I had to fire him. I told him we wouldn't prosecute if he returned the money, and he promised he would."

Then he went behind his desk and sat down heavily in his chair. "I hope you understand."

"I'm not blaming you," I said. "You didn't do anything wrong."

He leaned over the desk toward me. "I appreciate that," he said. "You don't know how badly I've felt about all of this. I keep thinking that maybe I should have handled it differently. I don't know, when I think that he might have taken his life because of this, well, I—"

"Taken his life?" I interrupted.

Mr. Siverhus sat back in his chair. "Your mother didn't tell you?"

I shook my head and closed my eyes for a second. I felt as if something had broken loose in my chest and risen into my throat, making it hard to breathe, to think.

"I assumed you knew," he said. "I'm sorry, I shouldn't have said anything."

"Tell me," I said.

"I think you'd better talk to your mother about this, Danny. I don't think I should be the one to tell you."

"I need to know," I said.

Mr. Siverhus looked at me for a long moment. Then he said, "Very well. But you have to realize that your father was under a lot of stress. I'm sure that by the time he gets out of the hospital, he'll be back to normal, and you won't ever have to worry about him getting like that again."

I nodded. I didn't believe him, but I wanted him to go on.

Mr. Siverhus took a deep breath and let it out slowly. "When I came to work that morning and found your father in his office, he had a gun in his hand. A revolver. At first, I thought he was going to shoot me. But then he put it up to his own head. I tell you, I was scared. 'Bill,' I said, 'that's not the answer.' And then I just kept talking. It took me ten or fifteen minutes to get him to put the gun down. Then he left, and that's when I called your mother."

41

I must have had a strange look on my face because the next thing he said was, "Are you all right?"

I nodded, but I wasn't all right. I felt woozy, as if I'd just discovered another world inside this one, a world that made this one false. I wanted to leave, but I wasn't sure I could stand up. Then I did.

"Thank you, Mr. Siverhus," I said, and reached out to shake his hand. I wanted to say more but there was nothing to say. I turned and left.

Outside in the parking lot, I stood beside the Chevy, looking at the new showroom window and breathing in the cold. I was thinking how, only a few months before, I had been looking through my father's dresser for his old Army uniform, which I wanted to wear to Rob's Halloween party, and I'd found the revolver tucked under his dress khakis in the bottom drawer. My father had always been full of warnings—don't mow the lawn barefoot, never go swimming in a river, always drive defensively—but he had never even mentioned he owned this gun, much less warned me not to touch it. I wondered why, and I held the gun up to the light, as if I could somehow see through it to an understanding of its meaning. But I couldn't—or at least I refused to believe that I could—and I put it back exactly where I found it and never mentioned it to anyone.

Now, standing there in the bitter cold, I saw my father sitting at a desk that was no longer his and holding that same gun to his head. And I realized that if he had killed himself with it, the police would have found my fingerprints on its black handle.

I didn't tell my mother what I had learned from Mr. Siverhus, and I didn't tell anyone else either. After dinner that night I went straight to my room and stayed there. I wanted to be alone, to figure things out, but the more I thought, the more I didn't know what to think. I wondered if it was starting already, if I was already going crazy like my father, because I wasn't sure who I was or what I felt. It had been a long time since I'd prayed, but that night I prayed that when I woke the next day everything would make sense again.

But the next morning I was still in a daze. Everything seemed so false, so disconnected from the real world I had glimpsed the day before, that I felt disoriented, almost dizzy. At school, the chatter of my classmates sounded as meaningless as my father's babble, and everything I saw seemed out of focus, distorted, the way things do just before you faint. Walking down the hall, I saw Todd Knutson standing by his locker, talking with Bonnie Kahlstrom, a friend of Molly Rasmussen's, and suddenly I found myself walking up to them. I didn't know what I was going to say or do, I hadn't planned anything, and when I shoved Todd against his locker, it surprised me as much as it did him.

"I hope you're happy now," I said to him. "My father *died* last night." I'm not sure I can explain it now, but in a way I believed what I was saying, and my voice shook with a genuine grief.

Todd slowly lowered his fists. "What?" he said, and looked quickly at Bonnie's startled, open face.

"He had *cancer*," I said, biting down on the word to keep my mind from whirling. "A tumor on his brain. That's why he did the things he did, taking that money and breaking that window and everything. He couldn't help it."

And then my grief was too much for me, and I turned and strode down the hall, tears coming into my eyes. As soon as I was around the corner and out of their sight, I broke into a run. Only then did I come back into the world and wonder what I had done.

That afternoon, my mother appeared at the door of my algebra class in her blue uniform and black hair net. At first I thought she was going to embarrass me by waving at me, as she often did when she happened to pass one of my classrooms, but then I saw the look on her face. "Excuse me, Mr. Laughlin," she said grimly, "I'm sorry to interrupt your class but I need to speak with my son for a moment."

Mr. Laughlin turned his dour face from the blackboard, his stick of chalk suspended in mid-calculation, and said, "Certainly, Mrs. Conroy. I hope there's nothing the matter."

"No," she said. "It's nothing to worry about."

But out in the hall, she slapped my face hard.

"How *dare* you say your father is dead," she said through clenched teeth. Her gray eyes were flinty and narrow.

"I didn't," I answered.

She raised her hand and slapped me again, even harder this time.

"Don't you lie to me, Daniel."

I started to cry. "Well, I wish he *was*," I said. "I wish he was dead, so all of this could be over."

My mother raised her hand again, but then she let it fall. She didn't have enough left in her to hit me again. "Go," she said. "Get away from me. I can't bear to look at you another minute."

I went back into the classroom and sat down. I felt awful about hurting my mother, but not so awful that I wasn't worried whether my classmates had heard her slap me or noticed my burning cheek. I saw them looking at me and shaking their heads, heard them whispering and laughing under their breath, and I felt humiliation rise in me like nausea. I stood up, my head roiling, and asked if I could be excused.

Mr. Laughlin looked at me, then without even asking what was wrong, wrote out a pass to the nurse's office and handed it to me. As I left the room, I heard him say to the class, "That's enough. If I hear one more remark . . . "

Later, lying on a cot in the nurse's office, my hands folded over my chest, I closed my eyes and imagined I was dead, and my parents and classmates were kneeling before my open coffin, their heads bowed in mourning.

After that day, my mother scheduled meetings for me with Father Ondahl, our priest, and Mr. Jenseth, the school counselor. She said she hoped they could help me through this difficult time, then added, "Obviously, I can't." I saw Father Ondahl two or three times, and as soon as I assured him that I still had my faith, though I did not, he said I'd be better off just seeing Mr. Jenseth from then on. I saw Mr. Jenseth three times a week for the next month, then once a week for the rest of the school year. I'm not sure how these meetings helped, or even if they did. All I know is that, in time, my feelings about my father, and about myself, changed.

My mother continued her visits to my father, but she no longer asked me to go along with her, and when she came home from seeing him, she waited until I asked before she'd tell me how he was. I wondered whether she'd told him I was seeing a counselor, and why, but I didn't dare ask. And I wondered if she'd ever forgive me for my terrible lie.

44

Then one day, without telling me beforehand, she returned from Minneapolis with my father. "Danny," she called, and I came out of the living room and saw them in the entryway. My father was stamping the snow off his black wingtips, and he had his suitcase in one hand and a watercolor of our house in the other, the windows yellow with light and a thin swirl of gray smoke rising from the red brick chimney. He looked pale and even thinner than I remembered. I was so surprised to see him, all I could say was, "You're home."

"That's right," he said, and put down the suitcase and painting. "The old man's back." Then he tried to smile, but it came out more like a wince. I knew he wanted me to hug him and say how happy I was to see him, and part of me wanted to do that, too. But I didn't. I just shook his hand as I would have an uncle's or a stranger's, then picked up the painting and looked at it.

"This is nice," I said. "Real nice."

"I'm glad you like it," he answered.

And then we just stood there until my mother said, "Well, let's get you unpacked, dear, and then we can all sit down and talk."

Despite everything that had happened, our life together after that winter was relatively peaceful. My father got a job at Firestone, and though for years he barely made enough to meet expenses, eventually he worked his way up to assistant manager and earned a good living. He occasionally lost his temper and succumbed to self-pity as he always had, but for the rest of his life he was as normal and sane as anybody. Perhaps Dr. Lewis had been right after all, and all my father had needed was a good rest. In any case, by the time I was grown and married myself, his breakdown seemed a strange and impossible dream and I wondered, as I watched him play with my infant son, if I hadn't imagined some of it. It amazed me that a life could break so utterly, then mend itself.

But of course it had not mended entirely, as my life had also not mended entirely. There was a barrier between us, the thin but impenetrable memory of what we had been to each other that winter. I was never sure just how much he knew about the way I'd felt about him then, or even whether my mother had told him my lie about his death, but I knew he was aware that I hadn't been a good son. Perhaps the barrier between us could

45

have been broken with a single word—the word "love" or its synonym "forgive"—but as if by mutual pact we never spoke of that difficult winter or its consequences.

Only once did we come close to discussing it. He and my mother had come to visit me and my family in Minneapolis, and we had just finished our Sunday dinner. Caroline and my mother were clearing the table, Sam was playing on the kitchen floor with the dump truck my parents had bought him for his birthday, and my father and I were sitting in the living room watching "60 Minutes." The black pastor of a Pentecostal church in Texas was talking to Morley Safer about "the Spirit that descends on us and inhabits us." Then the camera cut to a black woman standing in the midst of a clapping congregation, her eyes tightly closed and her face glowing with sweat as she rocked back and forth, speaking the incoherent language of angels or demons. Her syllables rose and fell, then mounted in a syntax of spiraling rapture until finally, overcome by the voice that had spoken through her, she sank to her knees, trembling, her eyes open and glistening. The congregation clapped harder then, some of them leaping and dancing as if their bodies were lifted by the collapse of hers, and they yelled, "Praise God!" and "Praise the Lord God Almighty!"

I glanced at my father, who sat watching this with a blank face, and wondered what he was thinking. Then, when the camera moved to another Pentecostal minister discussing a transcript of the woman's speech, a transcript which he claimed contained variations on ancient Hebrew and Aramaic words she couldn't possibly have known, I turned to him and asked, in a hesitant way, whether he wanted to keep watching or switch channels.

My father's milky blue eyes looked blurred, as if he were looking at something a long way off, and he cleared his throat before he spoke. "It's up to you," he said. "Do you want to watch it?"

I paused. Then I said, "No" and got up to change the channel.

Perhaps if I had said yes, we might have talked about that terrible day he put a gun to his head and I could have told him what I had since grown to realize—that I loved him. That I had always loved him, though behind his back, without letting him know it. And, in a way, behind my back too. But I didn't say yes, and in the seven years that remained of his life, we never came as close to ending the winter that was always, for us, an unspoken but living part of our present.

46

That night, though, unable to sleep, I got up and went into my son's room. Standing there in the wan glow of his night light, I listened to him breathe for a while, then quietly took down the railing we'd put on his bed to keep him from rolling off and hurting himself. I sat on the edge of his bed and began to stroke his soft, reddish blond hair. At first he didn't wake, but his forehead wrinkled and he mumbled a little dream-sound.

I am not a religious man. I believe, as my father must have, the day he asked me to save him, that our children are our only salvation, their love our only redemption. And that night, when my son woke, frightened by the dark figure leaning over him, and started to cry, I picked him up and rocked him in my arms, comforting him as I would after a nightmare. "Don't worry," I told him over and over, until the words sounded as incomprehensible to me as they must have to him, "it's only a dream. Everything's going to be all right. Don't worry."

Nominated by Henry Carlile, Joyce Carol Oates, Dennis Vannatta, David Wojahn and Shenandoah.

ANONYMITY

by SUSAN BERGMAN

from THE NORTH AMERICAN REVIEW

> Turandot—*Gli enigmi sono tre, la morte una!*
> Caleph—*No, no! Gli inigmi sono tre, una la vita!*
> —Puccini

1. WITHOUT THE REAL NAME OF THE AUTHOR

THE SUMMER OF 1977, after my sophomore year in college, I took a job lifeguarding at a rooftop hotel swimming pool eight stories above the Boardwalk in Atlantic City. It was the summer gambling muscled in, and the sleepy ghetto town was intoxicated with the crisp new bills casino lords waved under every soon to be displaced nose. July, the Marlborough-Blenheim Hotel still lent the ramshackle grandeur of its lobby to deals deals deals, regardless of the wrecker ball that within weeks would polish off what explosives hadn't collapsed. Crime's entourage the white haired ladies stood in town meetings to decry had assembled. What I hadn't seen before that summer in the way of off-center sex and other permutations of greed, I learned breathing salt air in the company of transients and gamblers, and those who serviced them. Joe tended poolside bar on weekends when the mostly foreign tourists drank blender mixups that made them sink when I tried to teach them to swim. "Mickey Finns," Joe scraped his voice into my ear with a laugh. "It'll put 'em on the bottom every time." On steamy afternoons before the blackjack tables' first cards had been dealt, to the carnival rantings of the penny arcade below, I stayed sober on the virgin mint nostalgia coolers Joe concocted in honor of the ferris wheel, or the green and white striped trolley, or the faded beach umbrellas. "Here's to you, Sappho (he kept an eye on me), to saving lives. Do it while there's still time!"

Joe first started calling me Sappho on one of the few rainy Saturdays that summer. *He pulled it like a paisley handkerchief from his hat,* or out of the overcast air, I guessed. At the time the name stood for the whole secret world to which he alluded and belonged—Mafia dandies, union men, the multicolored women who came and went for free drinks and a couple of laughs. I held my image of his image of me like a pose hardly apropos for an out-of-her-element Ohio girl taking in, for the first time, an Atlantic seaboard town. Sappho was a woman in a black bathing suit that buttoned down the front.

By the time Joe finished his crossword puzzle, the laundry crew sent up the day's hot from the dryer towels which were my living: a dollar tip per towel draped over the gentleman's arm, a two-dollar tip to show the lady to her chaise. There were the man and woman who pulled up a chair for me between them and spoke in slurred voices about many-partner sex. How it worked, how it would feel. My experiments toward physical intimacy had been modeled on Western Literary Romance as commonly available in the *Poetry of Love Anthology,* historical novels, or the comic books in my grandparents' Backwater Grocery store, which as a child I snuck under my skirt to read in the garage. One male and one female, a gradual crescendo in the same covered wagon train, glances, "Shall I compare thee to a summer's day?" a mountain pass, soda shop, the top down, taken by storm, "There be none of Beauty's daughters / With a magic like thee"; marriage. With nothing in my life up to that point to help translate what the couple were asking me to do, I can't remember much of what they described except that as I got up to go the gray-skinned man rolled his head on his shoulder and said, "Think about it, Pussy Pussy?" Arm's length and refusal, yet I had participated, listening, my awkwardness a hitch of conscience even as she began to coax, my fear the green trapeze I swung on over their heads. They seemed lonely to me, so I went with them for a lobster dinner after work and rode my bicycle down the Boardwalk home.

There was the flawless, smooth-skinned girl exactly my age, who Joe said Mr. Koroner kept, and whose red toenails he would rub as he walked by her chair. She simply sat, without a book, in the sun, and never went near the water. If the general questions I posed could be met with one-word answers, she would say yes or no; if not she looked at the door, or petted the subtle incline under her ribs with her long spread fingers until I went away. Some days it was just the two of us for hours. I wanted to know where she'd found her scanty armor, and the way it worked.

The queens who snuck in in pods of three despised me for my breasts. They giggled in vigorous falsettos and spat directly at my feet, rubbing themselves against the pool lights, or the wooden slats of the chairs, or the deck rails. Masquerading as girls, they played out their episodes of how girls must behave, naming a hair out of place deshabille, trading an orange bracelet for a purple fringed scarf. My thighs were not right, the way they didn't rub together at the top like theirs. I could see why they preferred men. They leaned way out over the Boardwalk, all calling at once. They primped and rehearsed, the artifice of gendered accoutrement cubed. At first they came to swim, and chide, but as summer wore on and the crowds thinned, so did their act. My part in their carnival was cut to stage-hand, towel bearer. They had gotten to me and found the target wanting, or too easy.

For the photographer, who milled around the sun deck in plaid trunks with cameras hanging off his back, I was a sunny prop. In the back of my disorderly cupboards I still find the inch-by-inch blue plastic key-chain peek portraits of the French/Canadian duo with their arms around Sappho, smiling; the Hollywood mogul with his black bikini and me; Ed, the other lifeguard, who loved the racetrack, and me. It was part of the resort appeal of souvenirs and sideshows that went with the job. And there were two identical twin would-be gynecologist pool managers, whom we could not tell apart and who liked it that way. They were my boss and would jump in the water after me when I was swimming and try to pull me under. I slicked on suntan lotion before diving in, and one or the other of them would wrestle the great oily half-fish Sappho till she nearly drowned.

The hotel manager who gave me the job was what I called then a bachelor friend of my father's. Fortyish, masterfully handsome, the rumor was that he had fathered the child the owner's wife was about to have. But the owner wasn't worried. "It's his own rumor," Joe confided to me. "The fellow likes it behind closed doors." *Queen* was the "bachelor's" term for men who frolicked in

50

the open. He owed my father a favor was how I heard it, so my friend got a job in the office answering phones for the summer and I got to work at the pool. I heard my father arguing with him past midnight some nights on the telephone. He would wrap and unwrap himself in the rubber cord. That summer I knew nothing of being kept, or of my father and his friends, or of the other Sappho, but I liked that name better than my old one. Joe made it sound learned and notorious, and when he introduced me, no one mixed me up with anyone else.

2. OF UNKNOWN NAME

August in Ohio emptied out horses and baseball, marigold gardens and salamander streams. We toted books and coins to the tree house and traded stories for silver dollars. I'd turned twelve in May. If a boy loved me he could hold me out over the edge of the wood plank platform in the air for an hour without letting go. If a boy loved you he would tie your wrists to a high branch with a thousand knots.

My first poems I didn't sign. They fit on 3-by-5 cards the exact size of what I thought and felt, which was the perfect size to report on Hopi Indians, or The Declaration of Independence, or nightingales and their nests. No name—that way Jackie, the neighbor's German cousin visiting for the summer, would be overcome with a pure, undesignated passion when he discovered them rolled up and tied with ribbons, tucked under his pillow, or in his shoes.

The beloved turns the handwritten page over to look for a name, any name. Who could have sent me this? It means what I mean. I will never have to speak again. It is what my life has meant all along to discover. Finding no name, he turns back to the words which burn behind his eyes, it is the words of the one whom he has loved forever—THE WORDS. I will go to her she is here with me. We will take us in our arms.

I pictured that if I left off my name, the words would loosen from me and the page so they could float out toward a cosmic, amorphous love-at-large that would somehow settle on Jackie as he slept. Isn't that what potions do? I would happen along, the poem's remedies cast over him. He would declare his mutual

51

absorption in the nameless vocabulary of hearts and moons. We would wander in the fields and woods, or sit on the roof of the house being built down the road. He would hold out his hand in a fist in front of me and ask me to pull up on his thumb, which he liked me to do so that he could fart. Then he would kiss me. He was bodily and courageous enough to do such things even in front of parents. He was seventeen. He had an accent.

What happened was, my great grandmother had died and left me all her books. My family had driven to her house in Indiana and told me that I could take as many as would fit into one cardboard box, which I filled and emptied and rearranged until I could fit all of James Whitcomb Riley Hoosier Poet, Byron, Keats and Shelley, some sheet music with Art Nouveau ladies in flowing dresses, a few bound copies of an early women's magazine, and her notebooks and genealogies. What her dying did was to start me thinking about death and poems. So I promptly requested baptism into my parents' separatist Baptist church of 16 or so parishioners—to give up my life and replace it with the Word, to die as the pastor laid me back in the water, and to resurrect. And I began to transform lines from Byron's poems into facsimiles of my own, layering grace over ardor.

As though no one would notice—who had ever read George Gordon, Lord Byron but my great grandmother?—I borrowed liberally. Revision meant a shift of focus from description of the beloved, to being the beloved. I was the *thee* of the lines, I the beauty, the one waiting, the betrayer, no credit to the original. There were places I could go in the poems that I could not trespass in the everyday. Things to be. I was in the air of the poems, I the articulating will that compelled the circle of desire to turn around me, and to return. There were ladders and hallways, chandeliers, forbidden keys, long golden hair, a wand, a mountain I moved or moved through. I would read Byron's poems, then open to the front of the volume and carefully lift the yellow tissue back from the poet's portrait etched on the flyleaf, for inspiration. He was my first and last muse (a concept I have since understood to be a corruption of female-as-inspiration). But he worked for me. Every other line rhymed without fail or slant.

In Ohio, no one did notice they were Byron writ adolescent. But the pastor who had baptized me, the uncle of my love, either found one of the poems in its hiding place and demanded to have the complete work, or, as I suspect happened, was presented with the series, ribbons and all, as a great, hilarious betrayal of me by the villain Jackie. He knew. The poems would be burned ceremonially in the incinerator the two families shared. How did he know? Our lives leave clues. Passion and words are neither pure nor undesignated. Their spells wear off. You wake up to find you have adored an ass.

A sort of tribunal of spiritual discipline took place that evening, structured like the trial of Hester Prynne. I remember the "logical conclusions," prostitution and fornication, as they rhymed. My mother left the room. My father spoke to me in a rushed voice about how inappropriate such lustful poems were coming from a member of the Bride of Christ. I was part of them, he said, an ambassador, the old man of me put away, the new man wearing a white wedding dress. I don't say this to mock him now, and less to mock my own sincere participation in the outward acts of faith. He was both terrified and compelled by my imagination, and his own, which could only have its roots, he feared, in the wicked practices of the World from which he had withdrawn.

I'm not sure which was worse in his mind, the poems or the illustrations. My father handled them like snakes. You cannot fix snakes with poke root or goat's milk, though a shovel will do. There are so many of them. They multiply before your eyes. They look like your worst image of you, crawling on your lascivious belly. They get into the garden; every row of dirt you turn, you find them. They say those things. Plagued House of Pharaoh, the locust, blood, scabie, first-born Uh, uhhoww, even in the water. Is there no one to deliver us of this . . . ? That which I would not, that I do. If you stand in the center of the room cringing to have granted birth, if you shame the snake and revoke its entire permission, then.

What more graphic way for a child to learn the attachment of words to their source, than for her own—borrowed as they were from a passionate poet—to be read aloud in front of a roomful of people, to convict her, and to horrify them. You write the words: you will carry their praise or blame. These things didn't really happen, I told them. This isn't me, it's someone else. But to my interrogators, words equaled acts; concepts (in the hands of the unsympathetic) crime. I am still torn, actual Reader, between

53

wanting to address you sincerely (as if it were possible), without the interference of art, and wanting the art to show between the two of us. As I listened to my harm it sounded rhythmic and eloquent, and though they stumbled over the loopy cursive, someone in the poems spoke exactly what I meant.

It had failed to work in a mighty way, the anonymity: the words claimed me whether or not I called them by my name. Not only the words but their content. I stopped crying when I slept. They taught me well, whatever else they meant for me to learn, that to write something down is to admit the secret, which will always give you away.

My books were forbidden, as was my writing of poems. For a rare, indecisive moment, my parents and the pastor (who to this day harrows a band of the adamant) discussed whether I should submit to the discipline of excommunication or receive a spank. How old is a twelve year old girl? The pastor sat me on his lap and recited parts of verses I wish I could remember: *the pure of heart, the good the better the best, think on these things*, no doubt. He said I would be watched—vigilance, penitence, abstinence. Didn't I like to play with girls my age? Couldn't I learn to sew? I was not allowed to say goodbye to Jackie, whose eighteenth birthday I also missed. I had wanted it to go: "When we two parted / In silence and tears, / Half broken hearted / To sever for years, / Pale grew thy cheek and cold, / Colder thy kiss; / Truly that hour foretold / Sorrow to this."

3. LACKING A NAME: *as one not assigned to any species*

On the thrust stage of the Guthrie Theater, in slow motion as the house lights dim, a mass of figures in the heat of an Algerian midday advances and recedes to the accompaniment of the Electric Arab Orchestra's whiny short-winded repetitions. Philip Glass has written the music for Jean Genet's "The Screens." The drum beat and the human commotion reduce to the twitch of a shoulder here, the face's tic against flies, a slow hand rising to sweep the forehead there. A shudder, a spasm, the bodies' feel perpetual and chronic.

The whole momentum of the six-hour event—90 characters, the golden skirts of the whore (dinner break of beef with currant and pine nuts, tabouli, eggplant salad), red flames in the orange grove, red umbrellas of the mourners—flushes toward oblivion. "I worked so hard to erase myself," Said, the central character says to his wife, Leila, who is so ugly he keeps her in a full-body veil. And in the end, as Genet tells the story, this is what his character achieves—not a better life, or an afterlife, but nothing.

The play's last three scenes take place overhead in the land of the dead. Heavy netting strung between the ceiling and the audience groans with the weight of its ever-replenished cache. The newly deceased crash one after the other through the paper portals and exclaim, "Oh, this is not what I'd expected!" After the third or fourth time the audience mouths the words with the actors. Said is not well after years in prison, years as society's kicking boy. They expect him any moment now, the dead, who roll, clumped in the net in their white robes like wetted cotton wads, humming. But Said makes it, somehow, outside the realm of people in the net. He escapes both life and afterlife: that one alleviation Genet could conceive for the self from the vantage of his life as orphan, thief, inmate, prostitute, writer. "Said is like me." Leila says, "he wants everything to fuck up as fast as it can."

So did my father, who was not nearly so clever as Genet at aesthetic consolations. Refusing to distinguish between the stage and himself, what oblivion he enacted played in the cramped theater of his body to stiff consequence. He died one stranger at a time until he finally caught it, and could pass it along.

"O you must have a Bluebeard closet!" says Richard Howard, who is not afraid of his. "Everybody does." His seductive poems flaunt in passage after passage what I imagine my father would have liked not to hide. The dead's secrets are tough to urge. A private room in an indigent ward, the name of an Episcopal minister to gay men, phone calls charged to my account that I can trace. I go back over the veiled signals: "Family man," he kept insisting, "Family man—I adore my perfect, model, church-going wife and—what a Family man resists makes him a square in the round world. You know this new scene of mine, Andy Warhol, von Furstenberg, people whisk me around town in their limousines. Clients of mine. I was supposed to meet them at this bar where the Most Gorgeous tall blackhaired woman can't take her eyes off me. She led me toward the back stairs and I tell her Family Man Happily Married, four beautiful children. Upstairs she's a man. Freak of Nature! The entire floor is pulsing with small colonies of partners in the dark. Men more beautiful than the next, with muscle and fiery loins. The pattern breaks—no, more fluid—it absorbs color and momentum, stalk in, stalk out, breath of a single beast, heave, stroke, as if it would dissolve me inside its scales. I didn't belong there, Sweetheart, and knew it as soon as . . . Clients take me there. You would like them. They wouldn't believe I have a daughter your age. Their barbers come to their apartments to shave them."

This is the part of the story he told me, his confidante, better not mention this to your mother. What he told my sister when she walked in on him in the bathroom fumbling with her mascara was that from so far away—a poorly lit room, the raised piano top casting a steep shadow—it would be hard for people to see who he was.

It started as a mystery of masks, whereof
You were the master, charagus, maze: amazing
Trollops, old men, lovers, you transformed them all,
Green-and-white Brighella, Polidoro, motley
Harlequin, the passionate Spaniard, and Elles . . .
("The Comedy of Art")

What kept my father's existence privy was less the lack of evidence, I suppose, than his meticulous track covering and refutation. And, no doubt, there was some confusion on his part *being* the most well-wrought mask he wore. Bluebeard, your family is right here with you. We are the part of the persona most put on and taken off. It is getting stuffy, all these dicks and our mother. The more I write about him, the more I feel like Noah's son, who finding his father drunk and without clothes held back the flaps of his tent and laughed. I am not uncovering my father's nakedness, I am getting some air.

Until the *NY Times Sunday Magazine* put it on the cover, hardly anyone said AIDS. The small-print names of my father's miscellany of diseases I'd been hearing from the Bellevue doctors were euphemisms. Cancer, we told our friends, a mild case of skin cancer and pneumonia. The early cases caught in the most promiscuous. Estimates of 1100 partners average, per life. Within a year, 8 of the 11 cases studied died. To New York and back on

56

business, to San Francisco, the ship coming in, could I lend him air fare he would stay with friends. Could I just read him the numbers on my credit card over the phone, please sorry, he got there but he couldn't get back.

I walked up to the roof of our building and watched a tug-boat on the Hudson haul a rusty barge under the George Washington Bridge. Back downstairs I read the article again. He wasn't Haitian. He didn't use drugs. Maybe he used drugs, I'd look for needle marks. I read it again. Sanctimony is the child of imposture: I was the daughter of a cocksucker.

Just nod, I would say to them at the hospital. I'm not asking for a sentence, just a confirmation.

"You'll have to talk with your father."

In his delirium my father thinks I'm the Union Guard. He hardly breathes, Doctor Dansus, you would think he would want someone he loves to know something about him.

"The prognostic groups he falls into are not good. Anything we know is so inconclusive at this point that . . . "

Anything we ever know, fine, of course it's AIDS or you would tell me. What are you protecting, who . . . ? The cold March sun threaded the eye of the bridge over the East River. Tubes and incisions. The bridge laced all the way over, its neatness tiresome. If not for the random colors of cars outside his window, each with its passengers trying to talk, if not for the low boats, fly at the window. "You nurses are so lazy," my father said from his bed, mistaking me. "I will not let you destroy my life." Along the hospital parking lot they'd planted Acanthus trees that stank like wanton boys. The smell wiped out the disinfectant and his blue gown tied once in the back.

They called me one day that week sorry, wondering if I would release the body to science. There were three dimes, some small tins of hard imported candy, and a jar of bronzing cream in his bedside table drawer. I said no, we would ship the body whole to his mother and sister. They could dress him up.

Your father dies: you wish you didn't think good riddance. Every curse falls flat. What are we celebrating celebrities? What serial killers do we approve? How many patches for the quilt now, O ye who stitch in sympathy? How black is the day of pictures to the gallery wall? I have been waiting to say this. My sisters and I are calmer now. My mother holds a job and calls us.

We are calm. We watch it on television, the parade of VICTIMS. We are calm. We are not men. The men have written poems and empathetic screen jigs for each other, having undergone society's inflictions. Their versions master the neat shift from rage to tenderness, loose ends to closure: they make lousy art out of their losses, hurrying, before the subject is passé. I'm waving my arms now. Courage, dignity, a forced bloom of humor, elevation of *his* suffering, *his* point of view. National Public Radio chronicles the lover's last days. I hurry out to buy the last dress Perry Ellis designed. The men are dead.

After seven years the dreams have stopped. I would dig my fingers into his eye sockets and pull with my thumbs under his chin to try and tear the mask away. He would come into my house and rearrange the furniture, pasting layers of grass cloth on the walls. No one else in the dream recognized him. When I screamed he flinched and blinked, sometimes cowering behind the couch. My father played keyboard instruments, mostly church organs and dinner club grands. He did what he chose to do—I am my father's daughter: so do I.

The homosexual father prays before dinner and compares his calamity to Job's. The homosexual father sits in group therapy with his confused children and unsuspecting wife and discusses phantom trouble. The homosexual father is so frightened of his daughter's ordinary development that he finds a way to torment her for menstruating. The homosexual father contracts hepatitis and insists it was the seafood he ate that the rest of the family swallowed and survived. He is sick and yellow when his children meet the bill collectors at the door. The homosexual father disapproves as his daughters seek substitutes for him. The homosexual father lives as though the only life were his, or for him. "Were they not, devil-fish, angel fish and all the rest, the contents of one infinite, eternal body—his?" ("With the Remover to Remove"). "They will assume another life—their make-up will, by transforming them into 'others,' enable them to try any and every audacity: as they will be unencumbered by any social responsibility," wrote Genet in his rehearsal notes to Roger Blin.

That life, a lack, gaping, insatiable, cast out onto the waters, will come back to your children whom I intend to tell. I will say, you do not belong to the family you believe you do and it is not your fault for thinking the collar and tie before your eyes, the toupee, the poppers he does before he has sex with your mother, just to survive what his father did to him, are safe.

The year before he died—the days he felt back to normal—I would run into him on the street and we would have lunch I would pay for, all right. He would taste his food, lick his fingers and then tear off a piece of meat or cheese he would put in my baby's mouth. Go to HELL, DADDY. Go to Hell, every single fucking jack he ever fucked or was fucked by, the zillion Grand Central Station Royalty men's room flight attendant Times Square fucks. I don't mean it. I mean it but I could never say it to your face. I was holding the baby. You said "I don't think I want him to call me Granddad, please. Teach him to call me, oh, I don't know, SKIPPER."

We would walk back to Peter Stuyvesant's former gracious quarters now owned by Norman Vincent Peale's Church, and chat with the man who kept my father the months after the family was locked out of the beach house for not paying the rent. The man talked about his ministry to the gay community. He was trying to let me in on my father's condition without saying it. He felt around conversationally to see if he could pass the burden of my father's care along. My father was proud of the enormous room and pointed to the oil portraits, stumbling over the names. He looked to Mr. Tweed for correction. His skin was "rowdy," pea, onion peel yellow—it was my father's skin, I cannot get it right. His tongue as he tried to moisten his lips was white with fungus. Take some grapes with you, he offered, for the ride home.

Nominated by North American Review *and DeWitt Henry*

THE CLEAVING

by LI-YOUNG LEE

from TRIQUARTERLY

He gossips like my grandmother, this man
with my face, and I could stand
amused all afternoon
in the Hon Kee Grocery,
amid hanging meats he
chops: roast pork cut
from a hog hung
by nose and shoulders,
his entire skin burnt
crisp, his
flesh I know
to be sweet,
his shining
face grinning
up at ducks
dangling single file,
each pierced by black
hooks through breast, bill,
and steaming from a hole
stitched shut at the ass.
I step to the counter, recite,
and he, without even slightly
varying the rhythm of his current confession or harangue,
scribbles my order on a greasy receipt,
and chops it up quick.

Such a sorrowful Chinese face,
nomad, Gobi, Northern
in its boniness
clear from the high
warlike forehead
to the sheer edge of the jaw.
He could be my brother, but slighter,
and except for his left forearm—engorged,
sinewy from his daily grip and
wield of a two-pound tool—
he's delicate, narrow-
waisted, his frame
so slight a lover, some
rough other,
might break it down
its smooth, oily length.
In his light-handed calligraphy
on receipts, and in his
moodiness, he is
a Southerner from a river province;
suited for scholarship, his face poised
above an open book, he'd mumble
his favorite passages.
He could be my grandfather;
come to America to get a Western education
in 1917, but too homesick to study,
he sits in the park all day, reading poems
and writing letters to his mother.

He lops the head off, chops
the neck of the duck
into six, slits
the body
open, groin
to breast, and drains
the scalding juices,
then quarters the carcass
with two fast hacks of the cleaver,
which blade has worn

into the surface of the round
foot-thick clop-block
a scoop that cradles precisely the curved steel.

The head, flung from the body, opens
down the middle where the butcher
cleanly halved it between
the eyes, and I
see, foetal-crouched
inside the skull, the homunculus,
gray brain grainy
to eat.
Did this animal, after all, at the moment
its neck broke,
image the way his executioner
shrinks from his own death?
Is this how
I, too, recoil from my day?
See how this shape
hordes itself, see how
little it is.
See its grease on the blade.
Is this how I'll be found
when judgment is passed, when names
are called, when crimes are tallied?
This is also how I looked before I tore my mother open.
Is this how I presided over my century, is this how
I regarded the murders?
This is also how I prayed.
Was it me in the Other
I prayed to when I prayed?
This too was how I slept, clutching my wife.
Was it me in the other I loved
when I loved another?
The butcher sees me eye this delicacy.
With a finger, he picks it
out of the skull-cradle
and offers it to me.
I take it gingerly between my fingers
and suck it down.
I eat my man.

The noise the body makes
when the body meets
the soul over the soul's ocean and penumbra
is the old sound of up-and-down, in-and-out,
a lump of muscle chug-chugging blood
into the ear; a lover's
heart-shaped tongue;
flesh rocking flesh until flesh comes;
the butcher working
at his block and blade to marry their shapes
by violence and time;
an engine crossing,
recrossing salt water, hauling

immigrants and the junk
of the poor. These
are the faces I love, the bodies
and scents of bodies
for which I long
in various ways, at various times,
thirteen gathered around the redwood,
happy, talkative, voracious
at day's end,
eager to eat
four kinds of meat
prepared four different ways,
numerous plates and bowls of rice and vegetables,
each made by distinct affections
and brought to table by many hands.
Brothers and sisters by blood and design,
who sit in separate bodies of varied shapes,
we constitute a many-membered
body of love.
In a world of shapes
of my desires, each one here
is a shape of one of my desires, and each
is known to me and dear by virtue
of each one's
unique corruption
of those texts, face, body:

that jut jaw
to gnash tendon;
that wide nose to meet the blows
a face like that invites;
those long eyes closing on the seen;
those thick lips
to suck the meat of animals
or recite 300 poems of the T'ang;
these teeth to bite my monosyllables;
these cheekbones to make
those syllables sing the soul.
Puffed or sunken
according to the life,
dark or light according
to the birth, straight
or humped, whole, manque, quasi, each pleases, verging
to utter grotesquery.
All are beautiful by variety.
The soul too
is a debasement
of a text, but, thus, it
acquires salience, although a
human salience, but
inimitable, and, hence, memorable.
God is the text.
The soul is a corruption
and a mnemonic.

A bright moment
I hold up an old head
from the sea, and admire the haughty
down-curved mouth
that seems to disdain
all the eyes are blind to,
including me, the eater.
Whole unto itself, complete
without me, yet its
shape complements the shape of my mind.
I take it as text and evidence
of the world's love for me,

and I feel urged to utterance,
urged to read the body of the world,
urged to say it
in human terms,
my reading a kind of eating, my eating
a kind of reading,
my saying a diminishment, my noise
a love-in-answer.

What is it in me would
devour the world to utter it?
What is it in me will not let
the world be, would eat
not just this fish
but the one who killed it,
that butcher who cleaned it.
I would eat the way he
squats, the way he
reaches into the plastic tubs
and pulls out a fish, clubs it, takes it
to the sink, guts it, drops it on the weighing pan.
I would eat that thrash
and plunge of the watery body
in the water, that liquid violence
between the man's hands,
I would eat
the gutless twitching on the scales,
three pounds of dumb
nerve and pulse, I would eat it all
to utter it.
The deaths at the sinks, those bodies prepared
for eating, I would eat,
and the standing deaths
at the counters, in the aisles,
the walking deaths in the streets,
the death-far-from-home, the death-
in-a-strange-land, these Chinatown
deaths, these American deaths.
I would devour this race to sing it,
this race that according to Emerson

managed to preserve to a hair
for three or four thousand years
the ugliest features in the world.
I would eat these features, eat
the last three or four thousand years, every hair.
And I would eat Emerson, his transparent soul, his
boring transcendence.
I would eat this head,
glazed in pepper-speckled sauce,
the cooked eyes opaque in their sockets.
I bring it to my mouth and—
the way I was taught, the way I've watched
others before me do—
with a stiff tongue lick out
the cheek-meat and the meat
over the armored jaw, my eating—
its sensual, salient nowness—
punctuating the void
from which such hunger springs and to which it proceeds.

And what
is this
I excavate
with my mouth?
What is this
plated, ribbed, hinged
architecture, this *carp head,*
but one more
articulation of a single nothing
severally manifested?
What is my eating,
rapt as it is,
but another
shape of going,
my immaculate expiration?
O, nothing is so
steadfast it won't go
the way the body goes.
The body goes.
The body's grave,

so serious
in its dying,
arduous as martyrs
in that task and as
glorious. It goes
empty always
and announces its going
by spasms and groans, farts and sweats.

What I thought were the arms
aching *cleave*, were the knees trembling *leave*.
What I thought were the muscles
insisting *resist, persist, exist*,
were the pores
hissing *mist* and *waste*.
What I thought was the body humming *reside, reside*,
was the body sighing *revise, revise*.
O, the murderous deletions,
the keening down
to nothing, the cleaving.
All of the body's revisions end
in death.
All of the body's revisions end.

Bodies eating bodies, heads eating heads,
we are nothing eating nothing,
and though we feast,
are filled, overfilled,
we go famished.
We gang the doors of death.
That is, our deaths are fed
that we may continue our daily dying,
our bodies going
down, while the plates-soon-empty
are passed around, that true
direction of our true prayers,
while the butcher spells
his message, manifold,
in the mortal air.
He coaxes, cleaves, brings change

67

before our very eyes, and at every
moment of our being.
As we eat we're eaten.
Else what is this
violence, this salt, this
passion, this heaven?

I thought the soul an airy thing.
I did not know the soul
is cleaved so that the soul might be restored.
Live wood hewn,
its sap springs from a sticky wound.
No seed, no egg has he
whose business calls for an axe.
In the trade of my soul's shaping,
he traffics in hews and hacks.

No easy thing, violence.
One of its names? Change. Change
resides in the embrace
of the effaced and the effacer,
in the covenant of the opened and the opener;
the axe accomplishes it on the soul's axis.
What then may I do
but cleave to what cleaves me.
I kiss the blade and eat my meat,
I thank the wielder and receive,

while terror spirits
my change, sorrow also.
The terror the butcher
scripts in the unhealed
air, the sorrow of his Shang
dynasty face,
African face with slit eyes. He is
my sister, this
beautiful Bedouin, this Shulamite,
keeper of sabbaths, diviner
of holy texts, this dark
dancer, this Jew, this Asian, this one

with the Cambodian face, Vietnamese face, this Chinese
I daily face,
this immigrant,
this man with my own face.

Nominated by Joyce Carol Oates, Robert Phillips, and Alberto Alvaro Rios

BILL WEISLER

fiction by URSULA K. LE GUIN

from THE KENYON REVIEW

HE DID NOT often go down on the beach. It was too big, too wide and flat, and the water worried him. Why did the breakers always come in, even against the wind? It seemed like they might go out when the tide went out and come in when it came in, but even with an east wind and the tide on the ebb the waves came straight against the land and bashed and broke themselves against it. The sound of them underlying all other sounds in his life was peaceful to him, but not the sight of them senselessly breaking. And sometimes the great breadth of the beach and the sea discomforted him. It was not the terror, the feeling he dreaded so much that his mind would touch it only with the two fingers of the two words he had for it, "falling black," but only an uneasy sense of dwindling, weighing nothing, in the great desolation of the wind. As a kid down on the beach he had enjoyed that feeling of being nothing, free, but that was a long time ago. Back then, too, sometimes there had been nobody else on the beach all day. These days there was always somebody else. Town was full of them, even on weekdays. The only way to keep away from them was to stay in and work.

He had put too much sand in the bucket. It didn't look like a lot, but as soon as he started to lift it he knew the metal handle would pull right out of the plastic. He tipped the faded orange bucket and let sand well out onto sand. When it was half empty he lifted it cautiously and lugged it over the dune onto Searoad. He put the bucket on the floor of his pickup and climbed in, reaching into his right front jeans pocket for the key. The pocket was empty.

He looked around the cab of the pickup for a while and then went back up the dune, following his tracks, which were the only ones in the sand, stooping and peering around among the dune grass. On the ocean side was the little dip where he had filled the bucket with clean sand and then tipped half of it back. There he knelt and scrabbled and sifted sand through his fingers vaguely for a while. It had to be here, or else in the pickup. Didn't it?

He went back to the pickup and looked all over the seat and floor and around under the front wheels and frame. He had to tell himself that he *had* had the key. Because he'd driven the pickup here. To get sand. He always put the key in his right front jeans pocket. He felt in the empty pocket again. There was no hole in it. He felt in all his other pockets again. He did not have the key. It did not make sense. He went back up the dune again, almost on hands and knees, pushing the tough, sharp-edged grass aside. The wind gusted, blowing sand in his face.

"Are you looking for something?"

He jumped. His head jerked sideways, disorienting him for a moment. He stood up and glanced up once. Where had she come from? There had been nobody except some people way off north on the beach. She was an older woman. It was all right. He had to speak to her, though. He said, "Lost my key."

Her voice had been amused on the surface but cold underneath, as if she thought he was suspicious, a trespasser. She came from the solid white house there, the last house on Searoad, summer people, the professor, they had had the house a long time, he didn't remember their name.

She said, "Oh, Mr. Weisler," as if she recognized him all of a sudden. "Your car keys? Oh, let me help you look. What an awful bother. Do you have another set?"

"Home," he said, with a jerk of his head, and pretended to look for the key, pushing the dune grass aside. He couldn't look if she was there. She kept stooping and peering on the ground between the dune and his pickup. She said something else, but his dismay was more than he could bear. He made a break for the pickup and swung up into it while her back was turned. "Going

71

home for the other one," he said to her startled raised face five yards away, and then realized he couldn't drive home. He got out of the pickup and walked away on Searoad, his head drumming and his legs loose at the knees. She called something but he pretended not to hear. After a while he thought she had called, "I'll drive you." But he had got away. He went the shortcut, through town, walking quickly.

He stayed around home a while to be sure she would be gone when he went back. When he did set out, going along the creek and then taking the path across Macdowell Slough, he walked quickly again. He met nobody, though he heard some kids calling in the woods. He was nervous when he came out onto Searoad, but she wasn't in sight, nobody was. The pickup sat waiting with a sad, patient look. He slipped in and started it up with the spare key and drove off without looking again for the lost one. It was gone.

Once he was home and in his workshop he thought gratefully of the old woman trying to help him find the key and offering to drive him home. He had been startled by her appearing like that when he thought he was alone. The trouble with women was he did not know how to talk to them. Men frightened him much more than women did, but there were things he could say to men, ten or twelve things: the weather, how's business, done any fishing lately, the Blazers. They would answer back, or they would say one of the ten or twelve things to him and he would answer back, and it was done. But if there were things to say to women he did not know them; the ten or twelve things didn't work; they wanted to talk. The woman from the square solid house had wanted to talk. But she had tried to help him, and though he hadn't wanted her to, he was able to feel her kindness, now, and to think about her kindly. He had always liked that house, and she was solid and firm-looking like it, with her greyish white hair. She had said his name in a neighborly way, "Oh, Mr. Weisler," when she recognized him. Probably she didn't see well at a distance, and he had been bent over almost on all fours. It was nice of her to call him "Mr." Most people called him Bill, but she hadn't said "Mr. Weisler" in a stand-offish way. People of her generation called people "Mr." until they knew them better than just recognizing their face. When he had to give his own name he always said it all. If he had known her name, he would have called her "Mrs." She had known he was dismayed about losing his key and had tried to do something about it right away. She was a nice woman. His gratitude towards her made him feel pleasant and solid. The loss of the key no longer troubled him, and he forgot the sense of the desolation of the wind and the sand and the bowing, sharp-edged grasses, that huge place where the key had been lost.

He had a box of rawhide thongs for hanging the little wall planters that sold well at Saturday market in Portland, at the stall Conrad ran there. He put the spare ignition key onto a thong and tied it in a loop, then untied it, added his workshop key to it, and retied it. It would be easier to find now, two keys on the strip of rawhide, and he might as well carry the workshop key as hide it behind the loose board, since he never locked the workshop.

The sand in the orange bucket was for coating the outside of cylindrical pierced garden lanterns for candles, another item Conrad had been selling well. Sandman's Lanterns. People would pay forty-five dollars for them. The price seemed too high for the little skill and work it took to make them, but Conrad set the prices and knew what he was doing. "They're too easy, you get bored, so you get paid for getting bored, man!" Conrad said. There was justice in that, though Bill Weisler still thought the boredom wasn't worth more than about twenty-five dollars.

He got to work, because if the surface dried much more it wouldn't hold the sand, and there were twenty lanterns to be coated with the dark grey and creamy, mica-flecked basalt and quartz milled down fine and even by the Pacific Ocean. If making sand was the purpose of the breakers always coming in and never going out, at least they were good at it. They did a good job. Even a river could make sand if it was big enough; the Columbia had sand shores, and he had seen dunes way inland along the Snake River, from the train. But mostly rivers turned out his kind of dirt, the really fine-milled stuff, silt, mud, clay. Even little Klatsand Creek had some pockets of light-textured brown clay that he had dug and cleaned and used, now and then, for small pots and bowls, handling it like terra-cotta. The cool pierced cylinders rolled under his hands and the words in his mind rolled and stilled and vanished into the work the way streaks of color vanish into kneaded clay.

He had always lived in Klatsand, before and after four years in the army in California, Georgia, Italy, and Illinois. His mother had been fifteen years old when he was born and he had been fifteen years old when she died. He thought about those numbers sometimes. It seemed as if they should make some sense, should add up to another number that made sense, at least, but he could not make them do it. It seemed like each subtracted from the other and left nothing. His father, William Weisler, had left town a couple of years after marrying Bill's mother and never came back. She had died of peritonitis or of a ruptured spleen, due to a fall, Ray Zerder said. Ray Zerder told the hospital people about the fall, and they did not ask what kind of fall had knocked out her lower front teeth and broken her cheekbone and turned both her arms black from elbow to wrist as well as rupturing her spleen. Since Ray Zerder had moved in, Bill Weisler had been sleeping in the old woodshed. When Ray Zerder and his mother drank and started yelling and screaming in the house, he would go hang around on the school playground, sometimes with the other town boys his age. When his mother died, his father's mother, Mrs. Robert Weisler, made him move into her house. He never knew what her first name was. She got the little house out back of the lumberyard above the creek cleaned up some and rented it to summer people. Bill Weisler was drafted when he was eighteen, and she died while he was in the army. She left him the house above the creek in her will. He got the letter from the lawyer when he was in Illinois waiting for his discharge. He came across the country on the train to Portland, came on the Greyhound bus to Klatsand, and walked out past the lumberyard and through the spruce woods to his house. The lawyer had written that it was still leased to some Portland people, but with gas rationing they never came over or paid the rent. He broke in by giving the back door a hard yank—it was always stuck, not locked—and so came home. The afghan in red, white, and blue squares that his mother had made when he was ten was still on the couch in the living room. Everything smelled musty. It was perfectly still in the woods at night; only the frogs sang down along the creek, and if you listened you could hear the steady pouring of the sea.

None of the places he had been in the army ever came into his mind, except that for a few years he used to dream sometimes about being in a windowless room with dried blood on the stucco walls. That was in Italy, though he had never actually been in the room in the dream. He thought sometimes about some of the men he had met in the army; some of them had been good men, and he had learned the things to say to them, but they were always being moved, so that he never stayed long in a group. He had been afraid of the colored soldiers at first, but the ones he stayed afraid of were the kind of white men who were looking for trouble. That was what his mother had said: "Oh, that Ray, he's just always looking for trouble!" Bill Weisler kept out of trouble as well as he could. One big, dark brown Negro named Sef had stood up for him in the city in Italy, he didn't know its name, where they had tried to make him go to the whores with them. "You want fuckin crabs and fuckin clap you go right on," Sef had said. "Billy and I ain't interested." None of them wanted to tangle with Sef, so they let them alone. He and Sef had talked a little that night. Sef said he had a wife and a daughter in Alabama. "I never been with a woman," Bill Weisler said to him, the only time in his life he spoke to another person about sex. He had never learned the things to say to men about women. He got by because he listened and nodded at the right times when other men talked about the parts of women. He knew all the words, but they went out of his mind as soon as he stopped hearing them. He remembered the one thing Sef said about his wife in Alabama. "She got this big laugh," he said, and laughed saying it.

The things he remembered from the four years in the army stayed very clear, because there was nothing else ever like them in his life, but there were only a few of them, a few faces and words, like Sef saying "She got this big laugh." The rest had not made sense to him. When he tried to make sense of some things he had seen and done in Italy, he got the feeling of darkness and falling, until he quit.

In the same way he did not think about the times when he had fallen all the way into the black, because thinking about it made it happen. He knew it had happened twice. There was also the time when he had drunk too much beer at the VFW oyster feed, but that time he'd pulled out of it in just a day or two. The two times when he had fallen black had been long. If some people in town thought he was crazy, and he knew they did, they had some reason to. He knew that the second time they had sent Tom James, the sheriff, to take him to the hospital, because he was in his house and hadn't come out or eaten anything for nobody knew how long, days or weeks. It was the hospital up in Summersea, where his mother had died. He remembered leaving it, but later did not know whether that was after his mother died or after they released him, coming down the steps into sunlight.

The sheriff used to check on him every week or two for a long time after that. "Hullo, Bill. Eatin'?" He had been a good man. You didn't have to make conversation with him at all. Once after a firemen's benefit dinner old Hulse Chock, who had been sitting between Bill Weisler and Sheriff James for two hours, said, "Tom, the only trouble with you and Bill is a man can't get a word in for the flow of wit and repartee," and it still struck Bill Weisler funny when he thought of it. Old Hulse had sounded so like he meant it that it made it funny, and anyhow it was a relief to get laughed at for not talking, instead of pitied or resented.

That was what made him feel easy with Tom James, and old Hulse, and a few other people—Conrad in Portland, and Mrs. Hambleton at the grocery, and the woman who had come out to his house that day asking about clay. They didn't take him too seriously. They weren't looking for trouble. They laughed; they cleared things up. Conrad, hippie entrepreneur, had got hold of Bill Weisler's ceramics way back in 1970 and parlayed him right out of the local garden shops where he had made a bare living for twenty years into the city street markets and fairs and boutiques and malls of the seventies and eighties, till he was working seven ten-hour days a week in his workshop to meet the demand and had an incredible eighteen thousand dollars in the bank in savings. "Man, you kill me, you crack me up," Conrad said. "You are unreal!" He laughed whenever Bill Weisler said anything, and sometimes he patted his arm or stroked his shoulder and said, "Oh, man, I love you!" Conrad had made sense to Bill Weisler from the start. Only lately there had been times when he seemed to get serious, to be asking for trouble. One time last month when they were stocking the Saturday Market stall Conrad had started a kind of speech, like somebody talking on TV, talking at you but not seeing you, and kept going on and on about

76

how the insurance racket was ripping people off, and the IRS, and who the people were that were really running the town. "OK, Bill, look at the money that's going into this new convention center, see what I mean? Talk about a pipeline!" He talked so angrily and with so many details and names and amounts of money that Bill Weisler felt that he understood, or should understand, but kept feeling uneasy and almost dizzy, as he stacked the pots and platters and planters on the raw pine shelves.

Conrad was his link to all the people, the competent, confident customers, the shop owners, the families with children, the young men and women who threw Frisbees and made campfires on the beach, the real people who were good at living in the world, and if he lost that link he would be on his own again, without any way to find out if what he thought made sense. When Conrad used to tell him, "Man, you are insane!" it set Bill Weisler's mind at ease, because Conrad couldn't say that if he was.

He couldn't test things on Mrs. Hambleton the way he could on Conrad, because he couldn't actually talk to her, as he could sometimes to Conrad; but she was reassuring, because he could tell that he made sense to her. Pretty much everything did. Nothing fazed her, nobody troubled her; she'd had a hard life, lost two sons, brought up a retarded grandson, kept the grocery going; she looked at Bill Weisler across the counter and said, "How's life treating you, Bill?" or "Selling lots of flowerpots, Bill?" and laughed, because she was easy with him. She had known him sixty years.

The woman who had come to his workshop was different. Her people had come a few years back, but she didn't live in Klatsand until she came to stay with her mother who had cancer. Her father was already dead. Bill Weisler knew that from people talking in the grocery store. He didn't know who she was, exactly, when she came out to his place. She had parked on the road and started to the house and then saw him in his workshop, which was the old woodshed expanded out a good bit. She said her name, "Hi, I'm . . . " whatever it was—he had been too surprised and confused to understand what she said. She was the color of certain roses and azaleas. After her visit he had worked on a glaze for the next set of tall flower vases and had got pretty close to that color, a pink gold with an underlay of deeper reddish peach; on some of them he laid a streak of cobalt, a light dash down one side. She had round arms and was round and full, solid. All this he was aware of while she stood there, as he was aware of what a piece he was throwing on the wheel looked like, without any words, only clear impressions of its wholeness, its completeness, whether it was right. He thought she was right. But of course she was talking and he was not following what she said. It seemed like it had been something about making animals out of clay.

"They have some, at the junior college," he said, waving his clay-encrusted hand to the south, "classes, you know." She understood him and said she couldn't go to a ceramics class because she needed to stay at home, and anyhow she just wanted to fiddle around. "Make an ashtray, like in second grade," she said, smiling. She had what he would call a big smile.

"Well, then, you need," Bill Weisler said, and ran out of words as he turned to lay his hands on the things she would need. A few pounds of dry clay, and she'd have to have a couple of knives, and if she was doing figurines a turntable—the one he hadn't dropped worked better; he dusted it off some and gave it to her, trying to explain how to use these things, how to knead, how to make slip, there was so much she needed to know. She kept smiling and laughing and saying "I see!" and "Got it!" and nodding, and when she repeated what he said she said it better than he did.

"I can put the, what you make, in my kiln, just bring it over," he said. "I fire on Tuesday. Usually. I could any day." She looked blank. She was thanking him and smiling and drawing away, going to her car backwards like she was being pulled to it on a string. "You want to try the wheel," he said, and she looked at the little lazy Susan he had given her. "You know," he said, waving his hand behind him at the workshop. "If you want to bring up stuff on the wheel, any evening, I'm here," thinking that he would come back early when he took the next lot in to Portland, so that he would be there in the evening if she came.

She did not come, but she had to stay with her sick mother. He thought of her often while he worked. He thought of her as a kind person, giving up her freedom to care for her mother, and friendly in the way she talked and laughed. It gave him pleasure to think of her. She was on the right side, like Sef and the old woman who had looked for his key and Mrs. Hambleton and Conrad. If you could keep on their side you would not fall black. They were colored tan, brown, rose, gold and cobalt. They were solid.

When Conrad let him down it was very bad. It made everything threaten to fall. It was only something he said, which Bill Weisler scarcely noticed at first, but it was like the hairline under the glaze that you don't see because you don't want to see it but you do see it. All Conrad said was, "Don't bother sorting out the seconds."

It wasn't till he was driving back home, passing the highway sign that said Ocean Beaches, that he started thinking about Conrad saying that, and thought that it meant he had been selling imperfect pieces, seconds, at the same price as firsts. The idea kept coming back to him, though he could not take it beyond itself and make sense of it. Nor could he get up the courage to telephone Conrad and ask him what he had meant.

Two weeks later when he took in a pickup load of the four-foot vase-planters that were selling so well at the fancy place in the mall, Exterior Decorating, Conrad helped him unpack the pieces in the back room of the shop. They were fragile because they were so big. Bill Weisler couldn't stand handling the plastic foam bits people used now, and packed in straw he got from the feed shop. He had stuck a tab of bright orange marking tape on the six flawed pieces. Conrad was brushing off one of them, and flicked the tab off with his thumbnail.

"Second," Bill Weisler said.

"What's wrong with it?" Conrad said, and then, "Yeah," spotting the flaw in the glaze down one side. "That don't matter," he said.

"It's a second," Bill Weisler said.

"It's nothing. It's sound, isn't it? It'll sell as a first. They don't notice, Bill." Conrad looked over at him. "They don't care."

Bill Weisler picked up the bit of tape from the dirty floor of the back room. He did not dare stick it back onto the big, handsome planter, with its flawed blue and white glaze.

"I'll tell the showroom people to point it out to 'em," Conrad said, "OK?" He waited a minute for an answer, glancing sideways at Bill Weisler and at the planter out of his deepset Indian-looking eyes, obsidian eyes. Conrad was looking a lot older. "It

79

don't make any difference to the use, Bill. It's a desirable imperfection. Shows it's handmade, for Chrissake! We could *raise* the price for it. Listen, you seen those catalogs come all the time in the mail, talking about slubs or stubs or some kind of crap like that in these goddam hundred-and-fifty-dollar silk shirts, little defects so you know they're really genu-wine? So call it a slub, there. Genu-wine Weisler vase with authentic slubs in the absolutely sincere glaze made with true human spit. Orange stickers, two C's; no stickers, one-fifty. Look, Bill. Nothing is perfect. Only what we say is."

"I don't know," Bill Weisler said.

Conrad reached across the planter and patted his arm. "Oh, man," he said, "you are so unreal. I love you when you look so sad! Come on, baby, let's cry all the way to the bank."

It did not make sense, so he could not talk about it. He got afraid to say anything to Conrad. It had all worked so well for so long, now was it going to fall apart? Would Conrad be angry with him?

As he drove west past the Ocean Beaches sign he realized that it was worse than that. He was angry at Conrad.

At the thought, the pickup swerved. A Ford merging lanes honked at him. His heart leaped and thumped for miles. In the Coast Range there were falling places, areas of black. When he drove into Klatsand it looked unfamiliar in a strange orange sunset light full of black pits and streaks. As he got out of the pickup in front of his house his shoe caught on the rubber mat on the floor, pulling a corner of it up. The ignition key was shining there on the floorboard. He picked it up and then looked at his hands because he had a key in each, one on a thong with the workshop key, the other by itself. It took him a minute to understand why he had two keys.

It was the old woman who had looked for the lost key in the dunes that he thought of then, and all night as he worked, for he could not sleep; he was afraid to go to bed, to lie down and fall black. The frogs sang down along the creek, ceasing and beginning again. He worked at the wheel, bringing up a shape he had not made for a long time: bowls about a foot across, rounded in at the top. *Chalices*, a word from a ceramics exhibition once in Astoria. He worked till daylight. He slept on the workshop floor, flat out, his head under the bench, in the dust of clay.

The day was bad. He knew he must not go into the house. If he did he might not be able to come out. He needed a shower, and washed as well as he could at the workroom tap. After a while he could not work.

He could not go to the old woman because he did not know her name, but the one who had come to his place was named Jilly. Mrs. Hambleton had said, "How's it going, Jilly?" to her one day in the grocery store. He knew her house. He knew every house in Klatsand and who lived in it, maybe not by name but by its looks, by its color and shape, its form of being.

He thought about Tom James, but Tom James was dead.

He went to the grey shingle house with the added-on porch in the back and knocked on the door. He knocked very softly because the mother was sick and dying. He fell black and caught himself from falling not once but over and over, brief, deep, dizzying falls. He took a step away from the door. It opened.

The rose and azalea color was paler, puffier; the cobalt was dulled. The smile was not big. She said his name in a soft, flat voice. He held out the bag of dry clay and said his speech: "Thought you might need some more."

She reached out to take what he offered, but she said, "Oh, gee, I still have lots—thanks—see, I just made these little tiny things—" She looked down at the paper sack. "I don't have any time now to, you know, do anything much else," she said, with a different smile; then she looked up into his face. He looked down. She took the sack. "Thank you, Bill," she said. Her voice shook up and down like music. He realized she was crying.

"I wanted to ask you," he said.

She caught her breath and nodded.

"If you make something doesn't come out right . . . " he said.

"Nothing I make comes out right," she said, and laughed on those doubled, shaking notes.

"It's wrong to sell it the same as if it was right," he said.

After a while he glanced up at her.

"I guess so," she said. "Isn't it?"

"It doesn't make sense," he said.

She nodded, then shook her head. "I've got to go back in, Bill," she said. "You know. She's." She said it that way, "She's." He nodded. "Thank you," she said again.

"OK," he said. He turned away. She closed the door. He walked through the front yard to his pickup with its patient look, parked on the unpaved street. He had left the key in the ignition. The light of day was pure, flawless, a clear glaze on the solidness of things. Inside the great bowl he could hear the sound the waves made down on the beach.

Nominated by Pat Strachan

THREE PROPOSITIONS: HOOEY, DEWEY, AND LOONY

by MARVIN BELL

from THE AMERICAN POETRY REVIEW

I HAVE BROUGHT something along to serve as prologue. It's an article by Bob Thomas of Associated Press in which Thomas is interviewing William Shatner about the movie, "Star Trek V: The Final Frontier." This is not the first occasion on which William Shatner, better known as Captain Kirk of the Starship Enterprise, has spoken for me. You may remember that, in "Star Trek IV: The Voyage Home," Captain Kirk and his crew return to Earth in our time. Kirk is eating pizza in a joint in San Francisco with a woman whose help he will need, when he decides to fess up about who he is and where he has come from. The camera circles the room, then homes in on Kirk and his companion as she bursts out with, "YOU MEAN YOU'RE FROM OUTER SPACE?" "No," says Kirk, "I'm from Iowa. I only *work* in outer space."

That was the first time that the Captain spoke for me. The second time occurs in this article. Trying to explain the popularity of "Star Trek," Kirk—I mean, Shatner—says: "Is it possible that we're creating a mythology? . . . The more I read and the more I think about it, I wonder if the key to 'Star Trek' is not all the wonderful stuff we talk about: the character interplay, the sci-fi, action and adventure and all those good things that seem to be on the surface. Somewhere underneath, the chemistry and the concept touch upon a mythological need in modern culture. That's my real thought." And then he backs up just like an artist and says, "I don't quite know what I mean. It would take a far more intelligent and perceptive person to divine what I mean."

* * *

Since we are free in the imagination to begin anywhere, let me begin with three propositions about poets. The first is an analysis in the form of a prediction, the second is an explanation, and the third is a testimonial. Here are the three propositions: 1) The future belongs to the helpless; 2) We all think we are frauds but none of us is rich enough to say so in public; and 3) The rain is too heavy a whistle for the certainty of charity.

First, "the future belongs to the helpless." I phrased it thus to echo the confidence with which the Russian poet, Yevgeny Yevtushenko, some years ago proclaimed that in poetry the future belonged to those poets who could jump the farthest, those who could freely associate most wildly. Although at the time Russian and East European writers often spoke about politics in unpolitical metaphors—hence, a Polish pencil might stand for a Polish bureaucrat—the "free association" to which Yevtushenko was referring was not the coming liberalism of *perestroika*, but that of juxtaposition, which, it can be argued, may be poetry's most constant and visible technique.

But what does one mean by a "constant, visible technique?" First, we have to make some gesture toward defining a playing field where any technique might matter. So here is today's definition of poetry. It has occurred to me, during the ongoing game—and it is only a game: artificial in conception, justified by assumptions, dependent on tacit cooperation, and well-forgotten afterwards—the game of defining poetry, *vis-à-vis* prose, that we might say that prose is prose because of what it includes while poetry is poetry because of what it leaves out.

Juxtaposition is a form of leaving out. Pound wanted more of it, demonstrating its strength in his broad editing of "The Wasteland." In its simplest manifestation, it means leaving out the transitions. The practice overlaps the classroom advice to "Show, don't tell," it reiterates by example Archibald MacLeish's well-known line, "A poem should not mean, but be," and it reaffirms Billie Holliday's "Don't explain."

84

Why should a poem be effective, even "poetic," because it leaves things out? Shouldn't a reader—intelligent, practical, demanding, sensible, reasonable—want to secure a path through the poem at first glance? Whoa! I have imagined a reader who isn't necessarily a reader of poetry. A reader of poetry is not, at the moment of reading, practical, but indulgent; not demanding, but attentive; not sensible, but audacious; not reasonable, but imaginative; not even so much intelligent as simply aware. For poetry, like beauty, is in the eye of the beholder. One cannot make an unwilling reader see the unflowering life of a poem when he or she has something else to do, such as proving a point.

The action of poetry requires a reader. The writer, having found his or her way from the first word of the poem to the last, leaves it to the reader to find the route for himself or herself. Each rereading is a fresh start. As for the Emily Dickinsons of this world, publishing little or not at all during their lifetimes, they must be their own and perhaps only readers, but so are we all as we write and then first see what it is we have written.

Poetry is unparaphraseable. We repeat this maxim, we shove it in the faces of critics, we use it to escape the responsibility of the classroom, and we are allowed to because, yes, it is true. The Imagist Credo: A new cadence is a new idea. Robert Creeley, as quoted by Charles Olson: "Form is never more than an extension of content." Frank Lloyd Wright: "Form follows function." How a poem says what it says *is* what it says. We all know this. Of course no word expresses what another word expresses, we all know this too (there are no absolute synonyms), and this truth is promoted by the phrase and further by the sentence and so is true of all language. In poetry, however, it is true with a vengeance. To apprehend the full expression that is a poem, we have to read between the lines, go outside the borders, engage in metaphor, hear the silences, change direction in the interludes, and, often most importantly, be ready to think many things at once.

In the classroom, despite the best of intentions, this has proven almost impossible. Graduates of what we call our "education *system*," and the academics thereof whose professional standing depends on research into what can only be called, with gross naiveté, "the facts" of literature, often make a poor audience for the poetry in poems. They want to find out what a poem means and how to use it, rather than how to follow and experience it. They have been schooled in getting to the gist of things and moving on, and so they approach poetry as if it were content covered up by words.

I take a back seat to no one in my appreciation of poetry as an occasion for conversation. But there is something overlooked in most of the conversation that surrounds poems, and that something, I have come to believe, is the poetry.

American poetry sometimes seems to be a playground of contesting ideologues, promoting themselves as narrative poets, neo-formalists, language poets, class poets, and so forth. Insofar as the techniques and manners of poetry may serve many motives, some contradictory to one another, and insofar as poetic license is not obtained from any authority other than the expressive self, I suppose that they must be, all of them, in some sense correct, no matter what they say. I think to add only this little epistemological alert: where all things are correct, it is equally true that none are.

So. Helplessness. We are, all of us, trained not to be helpless. We are schooled in what to do, as well as how, when, where, and why to do it. We become purposeful, reasonable, civic, deliberate and . . . predictable and programmable. After all that, art becomes, more and more, the refuge of our helplessness: our purposeless, unreasonable, personal or private, accidental, unpredictable selves. It is where we have a chance to experience the helpless "Yes!" of life, to experience nature and artifice, inner and outer, as if life itself were what there is to life.

As if life is what it is, nothing more. I want to be careful to respect that feeling some have, out of faith or partial research, that there is a life hereafter. Nonetheless, it seems to me that poetry springs from the need and the wish to express what this life feels like. Even when it sings of another life or another world, it sings it in the frequencies of this one.

It is good to recall, in first classes, these four lines by the Spanish poet, Antonio Machado: "People possess four things / that are no good at sea: / anchor, rudder, oars, and / the fear of going down." Poetry is an abandonment of position (or anchor), an abandonment of the deliberate course (or rudder), an utter nonchalance about propulsion (or oars), and, perhaps scarily, a relinquishing of the fear of going down. Goodbye, known ports of call;

goodbye, mapped interstates; goodbye, teacher with one finger held aloft; goodbye, sophisticated schooner of privilege, farewell, burden of right, the lists in the pocket.

The poet comes to his or her helplessness, and to its value, by way of the helplessness of others—and much of that masquerading as help*ful*ness. See if any of you recognize the usual poetry workshop in this description: the poet reads aloud his or her poem, hurrying through it fearfully as if it were prose garbage, and as if the greatest vulnerability is to be seen with one's mouth open. Then the discussion begins. One person says we just can't use a certain word in a poem—it's archaic, or it's crude, or it's fancy, or—God forbid—its meaning has to be looked up in the dictionary. Another thinks the poem should be shorter, or longer, or should start later, or end sooner. The group gradually cuts out all the "bad" lines, leaving, if anything remains, a smaller poem ostensibly of "good" lines. In the end, the group, if it is a smart one, has produced another publishable poem in imitation of a great many other already published poems.

Little artistic growth can come from such talk. First off, one learns nothing from others' bad work, only from one's own. Let me repeat that because I think it may imply a way of life: one learns nothing from others' bad work, only from one's own. Would we attempt to learn to sing by listening to the tone deaf? Do we imagine we could learn to fly by imitating the labors of a kangaroo? To fly, study the eagle or the sparrow—as you prefer. To know the richness of language, read—well, it's obvious, isn't it.

Second, the growth of a poet does not rest in what he or she can do already. It rests in what he or she cannot do yet. In other words, the worst part of a poem may contain the seeds of what will become the next poem and, beyond that, bigger and better poems by that writer.

Behind each poem brought to group discussion may lie a ghost poem, a poem that is bigger (not necessarily longer), more complex (not necessarily more complicated), deeper, richer, more enveloping. To disdain the raw, unrealized portion of such a poem is to relegate the writer to the role of good scout, on the trail of the acceptable. I realize that one comes to a writers' conference not simply to listen, even to writers who are willing teachers, and that there is a nurturing, supportive element to any purposeful group. The truth is, nonetheless, that most of those who one sees on the platforms of writers' conferences are those of us who were too ornery to listen to the crowd, too helpless to take good advice. We were the lucky examples of Blake's dictum, "If the fool persist in his (or her) folly, he (or she) shall become wise."

Ask yourself, not if you are smart enough and clever enough and diligent enough to write the poetry to which you aspire, but if you are dumb enough, bullish enough, helpless enough to get through.

Poems are written not from intelligence but from ignorance. The stores are endless, the paths not yet taken innumerable. For every real poet finds a new way with each poem by which to lose him- or herself. One loses oneself to find oneself, if you will. One walks away from the path—the road marked by reasonable men and women who are expecting one at the other end—and creates a new path as one goes, eventually unto finding its direction, which may or may not rejoin the others where they have built what they call a civilization.

The future belongs to the helpless. I am often presented that irresistible question asked by the beginning poet: "Do you think I am any good?" I have learned to reply with a question: "If I say no, are you going to quit?" Because life offers any of us many excuses to quit. If you are going to quit now, you are almost certainly going to quit later. But I have concluded that writers are people who you cannot stop from writing. They are helpless to stop it.

One final note about helplessness. We see now what pride and planning have brought the so-called civilized world. The seeds of our destruction were always present in the language of our successes. The same language that enabled us to pass along the uses of fire also allows that doubletalk by which mankind creates, permits, and endorses nuclear dump sites, trickle-down economics, and the knee-jerk justifications and falsehoods of every lobby from the gun nuts to the cancer farmers. No other creature tortures; none destroys its homeland with such recklessness. Mankind is God's curse on Nature. In a world that inevitably uses language, not primarily to make art or note fact, but for lies, evasions, and distortions—all of these fed by convention and prejudice—it seems to me not only more interesting, but more useful and, yes, even virtuous—one might say, moral—for serious writing to leave at every turn the path of the willful, to fly from the calcified spine of urbanity, and to get its boots muddy.

Besides, do you really want to succeed by doing it the way you were taught? Ten years, twenty years from now, after you have published that book or books of poetry or prose, will the writing have made a difference to you? I would think it a great pleasure to be able to look in the mirror and know that you followed your instincts and that you did it your way.

*   *   *

Now to the issue of "fraud." I put it as I did because I was quoting a friend: Frank DiGangi, a potter. Recently, while two potters, two painters, and your humble servant were sitting around in the midst of art talk, amused by the distance between what artists know about the making of art and what the world of culture says about it, he said, "We all think we are frauds, but none of us is rich enough to say so in public." Of course, it was a joke, dependent on a sophisticated point of view and a large dose of irony. *We* are not the frauds. The frauds are those who teach poetry as if it were more schooling, another viewing area on the way to some invisible heaven of total understanding where we won't have to be bothered any longer by all this confusion, this ambiguity, this ambivalence, this disorder, this, this, this . . . *life!*

Thus, in the classroom poems are presented as if they were etched in stone by writers who had, above all, A Plan. "Why does the poet say this and why does she say that?," we are asked. The better question is, "What is the *effect* of this or that?" And an even better question may be, "How do you imagine the poet happened on this or that?"

William Stafford has noted that, "Writing poems is easy, like swimming into a fish net," but that explaining how poems are written is difficult, "like swimming out of a fish net." This is not to deny that many writers have made the act of writing sheer hell for themselves. We have all heard how one writes by sitting in a room with a piece of paper until droplets of blood appear on one's forehead, and the one about writing being one-tenth inspiration and nine-tenths perspiration.

But it is equally true that, while ordinary trumpet players trying to play high C above the staff may turn red and threaten to go all the way to blue from the pressure, the virtuoso trumpeter,

89

Rafael Mendez, could do it on a horn suspended by a string, with his hands behind his back.

I believe that for each of us there is a way of writing we can do with one hand behind our back, in a world where the telephone rings, children cry, and sometimes the doctor has bad news. If we are writers, eventually we may have the good luck to find that way. Then, we will understand the true ease of the writer, that ease which seems to give him or her the powers of a medicine man or priest or psychic, and which threatens those self-proclaimed arbiters of their own temporal preferences, which of course they call "standards," but which time clearly shows to be nothing more than opinions.

The difficulty of writing lies in turning from our reasonable, pragmatic selves long enough to idle our way into the imagination. Once there, however, the creative engine runs smoothly and time flies past. Poets know the experience of starting a piece just before bedtime, because one has a line or two, and then finding that it is three hours later. On the other hand, one has also labored over poems of substance which would not breathe or dance or fly, no matter how hard one worked to give them life, only to have a poem emerge suddenly all of a piece, needing little revision afterwards, only a bit of correction, yet putting the other poems to shame by its richness and vitality.

About creative writing, there are some things to admit to oneself. Curmudgeons cannot admit these things, and they will not want you to admit them either. They do not understand Kierkegaard's remark that laughter is a kind of prayer. They have no sense of humor. They do not want you to be freer than they are. They worry about what the critics of *The New Amsterdam Times* or *The New Amsterdammer* will think.

Like the members of a closed guild, they do not want the truth to be known. For the truth is that writing poetry is first a matter of getting into motion in the presence of words; that the accidental, the random, and the spontaneous are of more value to the imagination than any plan; and that it is more valuable to be able to write badly than to write well, for writing well always involves some imitation of the routine while writing badly always involves something original and raw. This is as true for formalists as for informalists and anti-formalists.

So we are all frauds, if it is fraudulent not to know what you are doing until you have done it. The truth about writing is so simple that no one can win a teaching job by admitting it. It is more and more necessary to surround such simple truths as relativity and overlap in the use of language with theories such as "structuralism" and "deconstruction." Theories are pretzel-benders. They tie us in knots.

Perhaps you have heard the saying, "He's so dumb he couldn't empty piss out of a boot if the instructions were written on the heel."

* * *

My third proposal is, "The rain is too heavy a whistle for the certainty of charity." "In actuality," like they say, that sentence is two lines of poetry I wrote more than twenty-two years ago. I knew then that they might not make a lot of sense to many readers, but to me they contained the essence of naturalism, metaphysics, and morality—and, thus, poetry. While I went on writing what I could, these lines stayed with me, suggesting a kind of poem I was not yet prepared to write.

In the beginning, I had tried to go forward from those two lines, in this way:

The rain
is too heavy a whistle for the certainty of charity.
The moon
throws us off the sense.
The wind
happens at night before you drop off.
The mountains
on them sufferance blisters its skin of paint.
The oceans
in which this happens.
The ash
of which we are made.

Later, I used some of the lines in a poem about a home-sewn pillow. The pillow, which supported me for years, is finally shedding its cover and spilling its guts, while these twelve lines of poetry remain pristine and withholding.

91

But not unapproachable. For while I have not yet written the rest of the poem, I feel that I am now closer to it. I understand now—no, I *feel* now—its mix of external and internal, of reaching and reticence. If I have had anything on my mind over the years of writing, beyond each single poem as it came into being, if I have hoped for more than a momentary illumination, it has been for this. So much comes to mind in relation to that ideal that I cannot tell you all of it. On the low side of specificity, there are the many other examples I have found and cared for: this one, for example, by Theodore Roethke, the start of an elegy: "Is that dance slowing in the mind of man / That made him think the universe could hum?" And on the high side of the general, there is Pound's quotation from, he says, De Quincey or Coleridge (he is not himself sure which) to the effect that, "The character of a great poet is everywhere present yet nowhere visible as a distinct excitement."

And where did I find, other than in living day to day, the sense of the complex that made such sense to me? I found it in poems other people did not care about, in the raw language of journals and letters, and in poetry in translation.

More and more I want my poetry raw or abstract. In the words of an old song, I "don't want to mess with Mr. In Between."

Listen to this report by a therapist, written after a session with someone called "Robin":

"I used to call him The Hound of Hell, that's how bad he was. Now he talks. He says, 'When I walk into the house it's like the air has fists.' A mean place he's from. I may be the first who ever held his tears. 'I've been reading Gertrude Stein in the way that you instructed me, just listening to the sounds,' he said, and once he said the word *henceforth*. Nearly fell off my rocker that day. He wrote me a letter, he wrote, 'Amazing how quickly snow disappears.' He wrote he would like to be an athlete or Thomas Mann, he loves that guy. He wrote he thinks I would like his dog better than him. He brought in a book about a boy who thought spiders had ears in their legs which he wanted to discuss instead of his father who shouted Shut Up before he even opened his mouth. 'How does poetry enter the mind,' he asks. 'Gee, and then sometimes it just packs up and leaves.' People grow to love what is repeated, who said that? Today before he goes he makes a

92

kiss and bats it to me, then says, 'Dead writers are best. They stay the same so long.' "

Or how about this helpless, shockingly innocent journal entry from a junior at a high school in Georgia:

"Yesterday I messed around with everything and goofed off all day. I gave away five of my bulldog pups yesterday. Eddie Burgess got three and Lynn Beck and Romeo got two. I went over to Ma's about dark and ate supper. Then I went home.

"I have been writing about my life and I have realized that you don't understand some things. I will explain. I live by myself. I live about a mile and a half from my ma. I used to be married. I was married to Terri Metts. She was five months pregnant. I had a 1966 Chevy Chevelle it had a nice white paint job and rally wheels. It had a 350 4-bolt mane with a four-speed transmission and a 4:11 rear end. Terri never drove it. I let her drive it one day to the Handy Corner in Dawson County. On the way back she wrecked. She lost the baby. She was in the Hospital three months and I never went to see her. I loved my car. She died. I now have a 69 roadrunner it is black and gold with a 440 plus 6 and a 4-speed and high-speed rear end, a 77 Ford ranger, 351 Cleveland and 3 speed on column with a spicer rear end. It is painted black. I also have two motorcycles a Yamaha maxim and Yamaha 360. I dig graves for a living that is how I afford my vehicles."

By the way, I was deliberately exaggerating when I said a moment ago that I wanted my poetry, if not raw, to be abstract. Truly, what attracts me in poetry other than the raw is not abstraction itself, but the quality of abstraction that comes out of the generalized. And what connects the generalized to the abstract is metaphor, with its peculiar ability to contain a thing without it being the thing itself.

Remember, if you will, that, while modern poetry may begin somewhere back in, say, Baudelaire, where the image became the repository for a mixture of the objective and the subjective all at once (that mix came to be the essence of modernism, even a formula for it), something else we might as well call "contemporary poetry" begins in the previously unknown contemporary knowledge of the general condition of man and the universe. Some people might say it begins with "The Bomb," but The

Bomb of the fifties was only a localized blot on the Malthusian landscape. After that, we came to know much more.

Some artists brag about not watching television, not reading newspapers, and the like. One understands their brand of escapism. Some people can sense a totality in private. I will say, however, that I think generalized knowledge, rather than the particularity of book learning—what used to be called wisdom as distinct from intelligence—is one of the signs of contemporary art.

So. I come back to the water and the singing string of charity. I feel with a strength I have not felt earlier the rightness of any line two. When the Exxon-Valdez layered Prince William Sound with oil, the story floated all the way down to the Lower Forty-eight. And there on a day when we fed the marmot, and then the deer, breaking the rules, with a study of pulp mills just about to be released in a new report on cancer, and Chinese armor poised to roll over the student rebellion, and everywhere in the world something else, the DiGangis were celebrating their thirtieth wedding anniversary all year long, so that, feeling the impulse to dance as much as to run, we all knew that, when we talk about poetry, we are talking about a perfect vacancy, resonant and responsive to whomever takes up residence and stays.

Stay up half the night for a week and write one hundred poems. Write badly, rawly, smoothly, accidentally, irrationally . . . Join the disparate. Make the "like" unlike and the "unlike" like. When you can't write, read. Use the word "window" in every line. Write about colors. Set out to write a poem "like a sweater." It makes no difference. The coherence is already within you. Afterwards, you will have learned more about writing than an entire semester of classes can teach you.

In writing, as in the imagination, as in dreams, there is no right way, and there is no one way. Thus, one does not require a compass, just a good supply of nourishment and a push.

* * *

At this point, I am going to interrupt the main thrust of my talk, which has four paragraphs to go, to strengthen or weaken my case with a bit more testimony. Those four paragraphs yet to come, when I reach them, will explain my title and otherwise conclude my presentation.

First, I will use the poem you were handed this morning to illustrate some implications of believing that there is no one way and no right way. The poem before us is not here for praise but for attention. The illustration and testimony I offer is that of a common reader.

LAWN SPRAWLED OUT LIKE A DOG

When the peacock screams out at night, do you think it knows
its cry makes a man look at himself to see if he is suffering?
Perhaps the peacock and all birds realize
the effect of their voices. They carry a musical score in
*   their bones,*

which are so thin—toothpicks, really—their only defenses
are the gluttony that puffs them up, the edges of their songs
*   and cries,*
and the flimsy handkerchiefs on struts
they wave as they fly or run from grass to grass.

Even the tiny mosquito, most blood-thirsty of God's creations,
considering the brevity of its life, must sense the communion
*   to come*
when, shivering and wild,
with nothing to eat, she sings us to the wood like Circe.

Forgive me, I mixed up the horrible little mosquito, an insect,
with the eagle, the loon and the brave, little sparrow.
Forgive me, I only recently learned
to slap down the gnats that hover near the shores of
*   human swans!*

In the reading of poetry, it sometimes seems that one encounters example after example of willful misunderstanding. I would like to propose an opposing attitude: that of willful *un*derstanding. From such small acts of sympathy, great rewards may follow.

Hence, lacking any attribution to the contrary, one could perhaps imagine this poem to have been written in a language other than English and then translated. I rather like that quality myself. Perhaps Spanish, given the surreal quality of the title and last line. Or Russian—Russian writers, we believe, are free with

95

sentiment and such words as "suffering." Or perhaps the poem was translated from one of the languages of Eastern Europe, given the satiric bent of the last two lines, a turn on social expectation and civilized blindness. It could even be British, if I hear the tone of voice correctly in the phrase "toothpicks, really" and sense the exacting attitude that turns bird wings into flimsy handkerchiefs.

All of this interests me. As does the bizarre sympathy of the speaker (or poet?) in stanza three for the mosquito. Who among us has considered a blood bank for mosquitos?

Who is being addressed? We don't know. *I* don't know. Could be it's the reader who is asked to imagine the knowledge, or awareness, possessed by other animals. Easy to do, or at least to think about, perhaps (there's that "perhaps" again), when it's the peacock crying out in the dark with its all-too-human voice. Easy to move from there to bird song at large. There is much less to a bird than we are led to believe by our wishes, our fancy, and its own skillful song. But even if we are made to concentrate, still the eagle is noble; the loon, elegant and mysterious; and the common sparrow, brave beyond number. But the mosquito?

I lean forward as a reader when I come upon, first, a title so imbued—for me, that is—imbued with a suddenness of imagination encircling ordinary things, and second, quickly thereafter an initial sentence that mixes location and involvement and raises the stakes in a hurry. In leaning into the poem, I get caught up by what might be called a "narrative of mind." In this case, the poem plays off the self-serving distinctions we make between ourselves and other sentient beings. This is the sort of theme that engages me when it is left to simmer underneath everything else, because I don't believe in crystal power, I don't think aliens are coming to save us, channelers are frauds, a sucker is born every minute, and the truth will set you free.

In the end, I have to go back to the title, the strangest phrase in the poem. I can make more sense of it than I could before I read the lines that follow it. I see that it combines distance (I hear the echo of the phrase "a sprawling lawn") and locus (I see a sprawled out dog). I see, when I linger on it, that the image is an amalgamation of nature and animal, and that it now parallels the last image in the poem in which animal and human are likewise combined in "the necks of human swans." Of course, swans are swans and humans are humans. Aren't they?

I do not think this poem shies from its human role, nor refuses its guilty survival. I do see that it questions conventional distinctions within a somewhat bizarre frame, and that it handles notions of suffering and survival.

I like this poem because of its "Russian" sentimentality, its "Spanish" imagery, its "East European" irony, its "British" nuances, its strangeness, the elasticity of its line, and other things as well. I like it because I have paid enough attention to it as a reader to have been rewarded. And of course I like it because— and I recommend this reason to all of you—I like it because, yes, because I wrote it. However, I am not employing it here today because of who wrote it, but because of how it was written.

"In actual fact," like they say, I wrote it during a gathering in Fairbanks, Alaska as part of a week's testimonial. I wanted to show my students that I meant it when I recommended that they write more, starting with whatever was at hand and daring to be odd. And so I wrote a poem a day. And at the end included them in a public reading. This is the one I kept. The title is a line reported as having come up in another class which was looking for a starting point for an assignment. It had been mentioned during a panel discussion at the start of the week. Later I realized that, because the line is unconventional, unsocialized, it required of me a human definition. And the human definition, in turn, led me into a brief meditation on the human condition. And so it goes.

* * *

As I approach the end of my talk, I want to refer back to the moment when I realized that it had to have a title. It is sometimes bad to write with a title in mind. With a title in mind, that practical fellow or gal each of us can be sticks to the subject. If I had one minute to tell you a single piece of advice for writing poetry, and if I wanted to be certain your poetry would surprise you and others, and if above all I hoped your poetry would not be simply that kind of writing which goes gently to its end in the interest of soporific culture—if I had but one minute to say one thing, I would say, Don't stick to the subject. (The second thing I would say is, Listen!)

Afterwards—the title comes afterwards. Well, I had three items in mind at the beginning, so "Three Propositions" seemed seductively syllogistic. But those kinds of propositions are not so much fun, so I added three names: Hooey, Dewey, and Loony. If this seems silly, may I remind you that T. S. Eliot and Groucho Marx entered into a correspondence, including an exchange of photographs of themselves, and that, when Marx at last went to dinner at the Eliots, brushing up on "Macbeth" so that he might have the intellectual nourishment he craved, Eliot wanted only to talk about "Duck Soup."

"Hooey," because most of what is said about writing poetry, after the event—often by critics, reviewers, and theorists, but sometimes by the poets themselves—is just that: hooooeeee! "Dewey," because as a schoolboy I had a fond spot for the so-called practical philosopher, John Dewey, who among other things suggested that classroom chairs should not be bolted down. And "Loony," because after all, by any reasonable standard of society at large, anyone who writes what some of us have written, or—heaven forfend—suggests that there might be utter clarity in the lines, "The rain/is too heavy a whistle for the certainty of charity," must certainly be loony.

So let us go then, you and I, when the evening is spread out against the sky like a pigeon poised upon a nickel. Let us not get into a pickle. Or, finding ourselves already deep in the briny pickley flesh, let us find there the seeds of our poetry. What rough beast, its hour come round at last, slouches toward Bethlehem to be born? No one knows. Is this a dish for fat lips? Roethke wasn't sure. Is that dance slowing in the mind of man that made him think the universe could hum? Yes, it is.

Nominated by Richard Jackson, Laura Jensen and David St. John

LITTLE OWL WHO LIVES IN THE ORCHARD

by MARY OLIVER

from PLOUGHSHARES

His beak could open a bottle,
and his eyes—when he lifts their soft lids—
go on reading something
just beyond your shoulder—
Blake, maybe,
or the Book of Revelation.

Never mind that he eats only
the black-smocked crickets,
and dragonflies if they happen
to be out late over the ponds, and of course
the occasional festal mouse.
Never mind that he is only a memo
from the offices of fear—

it's not size but surge that tells us
when we're in touch with something real,
and when I hear him in the orchard
fluttering
down the little aluminum
ladder of his scream—
when I see his wings open, like two black ferns,

a flurry of palpitations
as cold as sleet
rackets across the marshlands
of my heart,
like a wild spring day.

Somewhere in the universe,
in the gallery of important things,
the babyish owl, ruffled and rakish,
sits on its pedestal.
Dear, dark dapple of plush!
A message, reads the label,
from that mysterious conglomerate:
Oblivion and Co.
The hooked head stares
from its blouse of dark, feathery lace.
It could be a valentine.

Nominated by John Daniel

NIGHT SWEATS

by GWEN HEAD

from THE AMERICAN POETRY REVIEW

for Richard Ronan (September 19, 1946—November 3, 1989)

"Bit by bit, grain by grain, the self is taken away.
The other men in my room were covered with KS:
gray skin, tubes everywhere. But they're in a conspiracy
with the doctors, and keep on hoping.

"The night sweats are terrible.
Liters of water—I feel myself dissolving.
But in dreams my body is real, intractable.
In one, I had huge stone hands, red thread, a needle—
the eye impossible to find. I woke up crying.

"In all my dreams, there is—call it a *feeling tone*.
During one of these stomach things I was convinced
I was pregnant, the baby was ramming and kicking me.
All that night two things were physically evident:
One was that there were two of me, the one on the left
bigger, the one on the right, smaller.

"And the other—every time I woke up
and realized I was lying in a pool of sweat,
I knew that this sweat was a woman,
a female that had come out of my body.
And I kept saying to myself, 'It's not you

101

that's sick, Richard. It's this poor
woman, this palpable female entity.'

"At one point, a couple of nurses came in.
I was drugged, convinced I was delivering
a child, and that it was *their* child.
Over and over I dreamed this, a hundred times . . .
the birth of my child, whose face I never saw."

Nominated by Henry Carlile, Sandra McPherson, Joan Swift

THE GIFT

by WILLIAM STAFFORD

from HOW TO HOLD YOUR ARMS WHEN IT RAINS
(Confluence Press)

Time wants to show you a different country. It's the one
that your life conceals, the one waiting outside
when curtains are drawn, the one Grandmother hinted at
in her crochet design, the one almost found
over at the edge of music, after the sermon.

It's the way life is, and you have it, a few years given.
You get killed now and then, violated
in various ways. (And sometimes it's turn about.)
You get tired of that. Long-suffering, you wait
and pray, and maybe good things come—maybe
the hurt slackens and you hardly feel it anymore.
You have a breath without pain. It is called happiness.

It's a balance, the taking and passing along,
the composting of where you've been and how people
and weather treated you. It's a country where
you already are, bringing where you have been.
Time offers this gift in its millions of ways,
turning the world, moving the air, calling,
every morning, "Here, take it, it's yours."

Nominated by Lloyd Van Brunt

103

BOCCI

fiction by RENÉE MANFREDI

from THE IOWA REVIEW

"JESUS CHRIST is a blood clot in my leg," Ellen says. "Right here in my calf, the size of a quarter." She puts her foot up on the bench where her mother, Nina, is sitting in front of the mirror applying makeup. "Do you want to see it?"

"Not now," Nina says, shadowing her eyelids with purple.

Ellen sighs loudly. She is ten, an ordinary little girl whose imagination sometimes intersects inconveniently with truth; all of her imaginary friends die tragic deaths and she grieves for them as though they were real.

Ellen sits on the floor beside Nina. Her mother is pretty today. She is wearing earrings and perfume, which she almost never does.

"Mama—"

"How many times do I have to ask you not to call me 'Mama'? It's infantile."

Ellen pauses. "Mother, my carnation didn't come today."

"It didn't? Maybe your father has finally had enough of spoiling you rotten."

Teresa of Avila, "The Little Flower," is Ellen's favorite saint. Teresa levitated off the bed in her love of God and had visions like those Ellen herself has had: Michael the archangel has appeared to Ellen in dreams, called to her from the top of a white staircase. Until recently, Ellen would shake her head no when Michael held his arms open to her. But one night he sang so sweetly that she walked halfway up and he halfway down. Ellen

104

sat in his white lap and he rocked her and looked at her with his great violet eyes that never blinked and told her that heaven was perfect, but lonely. When he touched her, Ellen felt as though all the light in the world was inside of her and when she awoke the next morning the sunlight seemed dim and she felt a heavy ache in her leg that beat like a heart.

Ellen's father, Sam, indulges her: every Saturday he has a white carnation delivered to the house for Ellen to wear as a corsage. All the nonsense about saints and angels is perfectly harmless, he said to Nina, and if a flower every week keeps her out of trouble and happy he'd gladly have them flown in from Brazil if he had to. "There are ten-year-old junkies," he reasoned to Nina. "There are ten-year-old children who hate their parents and run away and become prostitutes. Besides, it could be worse. She might be interested in Saint Francis and then she'd be asking for little peeps."

Ellen links her arm through Nina's. "Mother, last week in Sunday school Mrs. Del'Assandro said that when God is mad he puts out a contract on our lives. Jesus is the hit man. If blood clots move to your heart they can kill you."

"Mrs. Del'Assandro most certainly did not say that." Nina takes the bottle of perfume that Ellen is holding, says, "Clean your fingernails, Ellen, then go tell your father to come up and get dressed."

"Where are you going? Am I going?"

"No." Nina sprays a cotton ball with perfume and tucks it in her bra.

"Where are you going?"

"Just to the club for dinner and dancing."

"Then why can't I come?"

"No children tonight. Please go tell your father to come upstairs and get dressed."

Sometimes Ellen doesn't love her mother.

Ellen finds her father on the phone in his study. The room is cool, dark, though it is May and still afternoon. But her father is rich enough to have anything, even the night when he wants it and autumn air in spring. She sits on the desk in front of him, wraps the phone cord around her neck. "I am being hung in a public square! I am being persecuted for my belief in God!"

Sam swats her away, holds up a cautionary finger. She wanders about the room, picking up this and that, then shuts herself in the adjoining bathroom. She has been in here only a few times. The sunken tub is rimmed with candles, and beside it, a tangled pile of clothing. Some of Nina's makeup is scattered on the vanity and Ellen spritzes herself with perfume, dabs a little red on her lips. She lifts her long black hair off her neck the way she imagines a man might, and pretends the shiver at the nape is from a kiss so soft it is like a quiet she can feel. Something is different inside her; this whole day she has been restless, has felt something that is part like hunger, part thirst, and part like waiting for Christmas. She turns from the mirror when she hears from the tone of Sam's voice that he is nearing the end of his phone call. One of Nina's bras is hanging on the back of the door. Ellen holds it up to her chest, stands on the edge of the tub so she can see this part of herself in the mirror. The cups are as puckered and wrinkled as Grandma Chiradelli's mouth. If she ever has breasts this big, Ellen thinks, she will have them cut off; otherwise she wouldn't be able to sleep on her stomach at night. She puts the bra on her head, hooks the shoulder straps over her ears and fastens the hooks under her chin. This is how they look on Venus. All of the women on Venus have breasts on their head and are bald. All of the men are tall.

"Come out here, Elena," Sam calls to her now. She yanks the bra off her head and opens the door.

"How many times do I have to tell you not to come in here without knocking?"

"Mama sent me down to hurry you," Ellen says, and sits on his desk.

"Hurry me for what, pet?"

"Dinner and dancing at the club."

"Dancing? What dancing?"

She shrugs. "Mama says I can't go."

"Of course you can go. Are those your glad rags?" he says, looking down at her jeans and t-shirt.

She laughs. "I'll go and change."

"In a minute," Sam says. "Sit here with Papa for a while." He draws her onto his lap and she leans back against him.

"Papa, my carnation didn't come today."

"I know, Angel. Papa is fighting with the florist."

106

Sam strokes her hair, says, "*Bella. Bella,* Elena."

"*Te amo,* Papa."

"How much?" Sam whispers. "How much do you love me?"

Ellen answers out of ritual: "To the moon and back and twice around the world."

"For how long?"

"Forever and a single day."

It is nearing dusk when they get to the club, a sprawling, white-columned structure that the Italian Sons and Daughters of America bought from the township five years ago to use as a meeting place and family center. Sam, the vice-president of the ISDA since it was his money which imported the black and white marble and chandeliers from Sicily, had named it the May Club in honor of the spring birthdays of his wife and daughter. It has the requisite swimming pools, upstairs banquet rooms, gymnasiums and aerobics classes.

In the dining room Sam, Nina, and Ellen are given their usual window table that overlooks the bocci courts. Ellen likes to watch the players. Already the men are in their summer suits and fedoras. Ellen knows little of the game except that the brightly colored balls have to come close to the small white ball without touching it, and like church, the players must wear suits and ties.

"Stop. Stop that," Nina says, and puts a hand on Ellen's leg to still its swinging. "What's this?" She touches a bulge in Ellen's knee sock. Ellen pulls out a stack of religious tracts that she has taken from church, pamphlets with such titles as "The Road to Salvation," and "The Rewards of Piety." She carries them with her always and leaves them in restrooms wherever she happens to be. There are eight ladies' rooms in the club. Ellen has spent a good part of every dinner here visiting each of them twice: once to leave them, and a second time to see how many had been taken. She is sure Saint Teresa would have done the same.

"Haven't I told you about taking these things?" Nina says.

She has brought too many tonight; usually she carries just enough to lie smooth inside her sock. "Mrs. Del'Assandro told me I could have them. She says we should carry God wherever we go. Mrs. Del'Assandro says all God's angels would sleep next to me if they could."

"Mrs. Del'Assandro is a disturbed, unhappy woman." Nina holds out her hand for the tracts.

Ellen shakes her head, holds tight to them through her sock. "These keep the blood clot in one place."

"You make me tired, Ellen," Nina says.

"Everything makes you tired, Mama."

"Please," Sam says. "Let's have a nice meal tonight. Everybody pleasant and polite. If anybody is tempted to speak unkind words, chew ice cubes instead."

Ellen stuffs her mouth with three and crunches loudly.

Nina turns to Ellen, her face red. "Go. Go amuse yourself then if I'm so unbearable."

Ellen begins her usual tour of the restaurant, sitting down with strangers who most of the time neither welcome nor acknowledge her. Only once or twice has anybody complained and so Sam indulges her in this, too. The times he'd restrained her ended with Ellen ruining her mother's appetite to get back at him. Ellen frightens him a little. No one else can make him feel as she does. He spanked her once and promised himself and Nina never again. Ellen was four, too young to remember. She had done some small thing and when his threats had no effect, he spanked her. But the harder he hit her the more resolute she became in her refusal to cry. He had felt something beyond fury; it was as though she was mocking the impotence of his rage. It had ended with Ellen locking herself in the bathroom and Nina coming home to find Sam screaming crazy, threatening things about what he was going to do to Ellen when she came out: abandon her in a large, strange city where no one would ever find her. Nina had intervened and the next day Sam bought Ellen a pony. Thankfully, Ellen seems to remember nothing of this.

Ellen likes the darkness of the restaurant, the way the corners are so dim that unless she walks right up to the table the people are just shadows. She goes to the farthest corner where the aunts, Anna, Lena, and Lucia, usually are, the old, black-dressed women who do embroidery and talk of recipes and sorrow. And here they are tonight. Ellen sneaks up, crawls under their table and pretends she is Anne Frank, hiding from men who want to kill her. The veins in the old women's legs are maps for secret buried treasures. She sighs, draws her knees up. There is a nice breeze brushing across her cotton panties. All of the aunts wear the same thick black shoes with Catholic polish: shiny, but not glossy enough to reflect up when Sister Mary Margaret did a line check. Ellen knows which pair of shoes are Anna's. Anna always has her stockings rolled down around her ankles like sausage. Ellen loves Anna. After her papa and Grandma Chiradelli, she loves Anna best in the world. When Anna discovers Ellen under the table, her hands will reach for her, welcoming, as though it has been a thousand years since Anna last saw her and she will fold Ellen against her and her skin and clothes will smell like rubbing alcohol and lavender and grass. Anna is the only one who doesn't laugh or roll her eyes when Ellen tells her dreams of angels, and it is to Anna alone that Ellen has confessed her desire of becoming a nun or a saint.

There is dancing going on upstairs; Ellen hears the music of a tarantella, the stomping of feet.

"Wedding," one of the aunts says. "Sal Benedetti and Rosa, the last of Vito's daughters, God bless her." The other two murmur agreement and Ellen hears them put their forks down in order to cross themselves.

"Which one is Rosa?" Lucia says.

"The ugly one," Lena, the mean aunt, says. She once told Ellen she would go to hell for wearing so much jewelry and that in hell her necklaces and bracelets would turn into snakes.

"Lena, so what ugly? What's the difference when the lights are out?" Lucia says. "Rosa is a work of God but not his masterpiece."

"I had the most beautiful gown for my wedding night," Anna says.

"I also," Lena says. "The chair looked very nice in it. All that needlework my mother did on it, and for what? They all want you naked."

The aunts chuckle.

Ellen searches through her stack of pamphlets until she comes to the one with "La Pietà" on the front. She folds it into a tiny square and slips it beneath Anna's shoelaces. Anna will find it there later when she is undressing and say a prayer for her dead and for Ellen.

"I feel a little mouse at my feet," Anna says, and lifts the edge of the tablecloth to look at Ellen. Lena and Lucia peer down after her.

"*Buena sera*, Anna."

109

"Look the way she lies," Lena says. "*Puttana*. Good girls don't lie in public with their legs spread like crickets."

"I'm not a good girl. I'm spirited and tiring."

"*Si, spirito, e un valle di lacrime*," Lena says.

"No speaka, no *capische*," Ellen says and covers her ears, but she gets it anyway. *Spirited and tearful. A valley of tears.*

"Hopeless," Lena says, and continues eating.

"How is the future little novitiate?" Anna says, and hugs Ellen tight against her. "Oh, but it is good to see you."

Ellen whispers to Anna: "Something bad is going to happen to me, Anna. There is a blood clot in my leg from God. It might kill me. The next time you see me I might be dead."

"Why would God put a blood clot in your leg, dear?"

"He's mad at me."

"For what reason?" Anna says.

"He thinks I love Michael more than Him."

"Michael," Anna says dreamily.

Sometimes Anna drifts away when Ellen is speaking to her. Sometimes, Ellen thinks, Anna's head is stuffed with wet cinnamon that is hard like stone; words can't get past it. Grandma Chiradelli sometimes plays a game with Ellen to help her sleep: she makes Ellen imagine that her head is filled with cinnamon or sea water or night and then she says one word over and over and it makes changing patterns like a kaleidoscope: *Bella. Serenissima. Désolate.*

"Anna," Ellen whispers. "Help me, Anna. I don't feel good. I don't feel right."

"Papa seems to be searching for you, love," Lucia says.

Ellen looks up and sees Sam walking among the tables looking right and left. He might never find her. If she stays very still she is a shadow. She and the aunts are invisible as dreams.

When Sam turns back, Ellen goes up to him and he tells her it's time to eat.

Oh how Ellen hates peas! There are fifty-six of them. She arranges them into a circle in her flattened mashed potatoes. Now they are pills, like the pink ones her mother takes from a blue plastic case each morning. Ellen swallows them whole, one at a time, with water. When she takes them all she will be fifty-six days older. Inside each pea is a princess.

A man outside on the bocci lawn is smiling at her. Ellen has seen him several times before and he has never ignored her or given her mean looks. He is one of the players and though a little old—forty, Ellen guesses—he is very handsome. His eyes and hair are dark and he is tall. She watches. When it is his turn he throws the ball too hard and it knocks against the little white one. He looks over at Ellen again, smiling, and she dimples back.

"Who got married anyway?" Sam says, looking at two men in tuxedoes who have drifted outside to watch the bocci games.

"Vito Del Greco's daughter, Rosa, and Sal Benedetti," Nina says.

"Del Greco . . . with the six daughters?"

"That's right," Nina says. "They sit two rows ahead of us in church."

"Which one is Rosa?"

"The ugly one," Ellen says.

"Oh, yes," Sam says.

"Vito's wife is in my aerobics class. She said if we happened to be at the club tonight to stop in at the reception for a drink," Nina says.

"You said Mrs. Del Greco was a bitch," Ellen says.

Nina looks over at Ellen. "I most definitely did not say that."

"You said it last Saturday at the mall. You told Mrs. Genovese that Mrs. Del Greco was a ball-breaking bitch."

"I'd like to stop in and say hello," Nina says.

"No," Sam says.

"Why not?"

"Because I am fighting with Del Greco's pansy cousin, the florist."

"I insist," Nina says.

Ellen slips away while her parents argue to make her rounds in the ladies' rooms on the first floor and basement. She puts five or six tracts on the back of each toilet, a stack on the vanity, and slips one beneath each carefully folded towel. But she still has so many, even after leaving twice as many of them in all the usual places.

She pauses at the men's bathroom. Saint Teresa would probably do it. She puts her ear to the door and steals in when she doesn't hear anything. She stops and stares at the urinals. Planters, she guesses, except that there isn't any dirt inside. Artwork: standing back she sees that they are long faces, the jaws dropped

111

down in shock, the mouths with little pools of water inside. They are her parishioners, lined up and waiting. She moistens the edge of the pamphlets in the mouths, sticks one to each forehead. She is a priest. It is Ash Wednesday.

Nina and Sam are still at their coffee when Ellen returns. And the bocci players have come in. They are at a corner table opposite the aunts. The player who had noticed Ellen earlier is looking and smiling at her now. She saunters over.

There are seven players including the smiling one, who is the only one paying her any attention; the others are discussing something intently in Italian. She slides into the booth next to the one who smiles, sits as close to him as she dares. He asks her name.

Usually she invents a name for herself when strangers ask, but there is something about this man that makes her give her real name, as though she believes he will know if she is lying. She says, "Elena Serafina Capalbo Chiradelli."

"Those are a lot of names."

"Papa says I'll grow into them. My confirmation name is going to be Teresa. Then I'll have five names. When I get married I'll have six and if I get married twice I'll have seven then when I die I'll need a big headstone."

"Very true," the man says.

Ellen searches his salad for olives.

"Is that your papa over there?"

Ellen looks up and sees Sam motioning for her. "No. I never saw him before in my life."

Sam walks over. "Come, Ellen. It's time for us to go."

"Home?"

"Upstairs to visit the wedding celebration, then home."

"No."

"Come, Ellen, don't make Papa angry."

"No."

"Just for half an hour. Be an angel." Sam reaches for her hand. "No! No!"

"Have some work to do on this one, yes?" the man says. "Why not leave her here with me while you go upstairs? I'll be more than pleased to watch over her. We'll be here for hours yet."

Sam looks at Ellen. She smiles at him coyly, her eyes cutting around slowly to glance up at him. This is—was—Nina's expression, something he hasn't seen for at least ten years. Where did Ellen see it?

"You bought your car from us," the man says.

Sam looks from Ellen to the stranger. "What?"

"Your car. You bought it from us last year."

"Are you one of the Falconi brothers?"

The man nods.

"I'm afraid I don't remember you."

"Well, there are eight of us."

"Which are you?"

"Carlo."

"Carlo Falconi," Sam says, trying to stir his memory. "Well, it's a great car. Has never given me a minute's trouble, unlike certain little creatures." He winks at Ellen and she smiles so sweetly that it makes him heartsick. Sam turns to Nina. "Carlo Falconi," he says, but she is already moving away and heading toward the stairs. "Okay, then, I'll be back in half an hour or so. Be sweet, Elena."

"Always, Papa."

Ellen takes ice cubes from a water glass and rubs them over her eyelids. "Ice reduces swelling. I have hemorrhoids."

"You're a strange little bird," he says, and laughs.

Ellen draws her knees up and spreads them, so her panties are showing. From the dark corner across the room Ellen thinks she sees Lena's eyes flashing red and angry, Anna shaking her head, making the sign of the cross.

"What do you have there?" the man who calls himself Falconi says, pointing at her sock. She gives him the tracts. His eyes are so dark that when she looks in them she sees herself.

" 'The Road to Salvation,' " he says and laughs. "But where do the wicked go after death?"

"To hell!"

"And what is hell?"

"The absence of God and an everlasting pit of fire." Ellen has been trained in all the correct responses.

"And how does one avoid the torments of this pit?"

"By not dying."

"Ha! Pretty good," he says, and slips the tracts into his pocket.

"You can't keep those!"

He smiles at her. "Says who?"

"Says me. Give me," she says, holding out her hand.

113

But now the men at the table are quarreling about something and Falconi looks away from her. They are speaking argument Italian, something she has heard between her grandparents; it's like ordinary talk, as far as Ellen understands, but words mean more because you repeat everything twice in a shout and point at people while you say them. She sighs, drapes her legs over one of Falconi's and lies back. He glances down at her, rubs his hand over her calf. But there is a terrible tenderness there and she jerks her leg away and puts her crossed feet up on the table.

There is a pause in the conversation. "My God, whose *enfant terrible?*" somebody says.

Falconi looks down at her with his black eyes, says, "Just a little elf that wandered my way."

If she listens closely enough, Ellen can hear the aunts talking in the opposite corner. Their voices are like the cool side of a pillow. She stares up at the ceiling. And here are the aunts now, swinging on the chandelier, back and forth, back and forth, arcing out wide and high and fast so that their hair and skirts blow back. Anna, her favorite, straddles the center chain, her legs straight out in front of her, Lena and Lucia hold onto the sides. They drop words rolled in olives into the salads, contradict everything the men say as they swing over the table. Now the aunts and the men are repeating a little rhyme Grandma Chiradelli made up:

The moon is made of Swiss.
The aunts say:
It's made of fontinella.
The men say:
The angels waltz in heaven.
They do a tarantella.

Falconi pushes Ellen's legs off of his and slides out of the booth.

"Hey. Where are you going?" She follows him down a hallway where a yellow light from the lamps on the dark red walls throws a shadow. This is the corridor that leads to the conference rooms. She rarely frequents the bathrooms on this side because people in the restaurant don't use them; she left a stack of pamphlets in the ladies' room once, and when she checked back two weeks later they were all still there.

114

Falconi is sitting on a bench around the corner, smoking a cigarette.

"Are you trailing me, love?"

"My booklets. I want my booklets back now."

He flicks his cigarette ash into a potted palm and pats the bench beside him. "*Bella,*" he says. "You are a beautiful young lady. Sit here with me for a while and I will give them back."

"Do you promise?"

He nods. "Come closer. Sit close to me as you were doing out there."

She hesitates, then does so.

"Give me a kiss, and I'll give you your booklets back."

"You said I only had to sit here."

He laughs. "If you give me a kiss, I will give you five dollars."

"On the lips?"

"Right here," he says, touching his cheek.

Ellen kisses him and holds out her hand. He gives her the bill and she puts it in her sock. Ellen lets him touch her hair, her arms, her waist, and now inside her panties. This feels good.

Then it feels better.

Any place he touches becomes warm, tingly. She feels relaxed as nighttime in her grandparents' house. Feels like she does when she is spending a weekend with them and falls asleep on purpose in the living room so somebody will have to carry her upstairs. Then it feels like she is floating and she always hears Grandma Chiradelli's heavy step and voice behind her directing the invisible arms that bear her to the bedroom with the dark furniture and cool air that smells like cooking and leather and laundry bleach.

She is as relaxed as that now. The man's hands make her feel so good that she thinks there must be a little piece of God in them. Her skin is like breath on a cold window: thin and warm and shifting. She is in the center of a circle that swirls blue then white then blue again, and it feels like he is making the colors inside her out of her own heartbeats: bubbles rising up white through black and his hand rubbing them into blue.

I am dying, Ellen thinks, because when there is no place inside her that doesn't feel good, the circle begins to break from the center out, like layer after layer of glass. Anna's face appears smiling before her, her head covered with a white night cap. Her lips move without sound: *Michael.*

But then it stops and her skin fits tight to her again.

"Elena, Elena, you make me so sad," Falconi whispers. He turns her face up to his. "I want to tell you something you won't understand now, but I want you to remember. More than anything in life I want to be a father. But my wife can't have children. This is the closest I will ever come to witnessing the birth of anything."

He stands, walks around the corner to the men's room. Ellen follows him in, right into the stall. He looks surprised, then says, "Oh, I suppose you want your booklets back."

She shakes her head. "I want more."

He laughs. "Go find Mama, little girl."

Ellen wraps her arms around his waist. "I think I love you."

He looks down at her and is silent for a few minutes. "You are not afraid of me?"

"No," Ellen says.

This time it doesn't feel good; everything about him seems suddenly too big, too heavy. She feels as though she is being made to swim too fast, that his arms, tight around her, are holding her underwater so she can't breathe.

"You're hurting me," Ellen says.

"Look up. Look up at the light."

She does so. Years from now it will be this light that she remembers in detail, a dingy yellow bulb through an opaque frosted cover around the edges of which are moths in various stages of decay, and it will seem to belong more to seedy urban hallways than it does here.

Her heart is racing like someone is chasing her. With one hand Falconi pins her arms behind her back, the other hand is down there, pulling at her underpants. She hears silver clinking, and for a moment thinks he is counting his change. But it is a belt buckle making that sound.

"Don't be afraid," he says. There is a sharp, unexpected pain and Ellen thinks: this must be what it feels like to have your fingernails torn off. She screams for Anna and he puts his hand over her mouth. She is a face on a chimney in a picture where you circle what doesn't belong. Nobody will find her for years and

116

years. Her eyes and mouth are bricks that can't blink or speak. She might be here forever, staring at a light in the distance waiting for someone to look up and notice her.

But now she sees the faces of the aunts hovering around the light and knows from their expression that she is not going to die: they don't look surprised or frightened. Anna's face is ordinary and tired.

His body is still against her now. Ellen sits on the floor, and cries. The blood clot, instead of moving to her heart, is moving out of her.

"Elena," he says. "Elena, I want to tell you something." He pulls her to her feet. "I have never done this before. I have never hurt a child before. Do you believe me?"

She doesn't respond.

"I didn't mean to do this. I took advantage of you. I want you to say you can forgive me. Not now, perhaps, but someday."

She shakes her head. "I'm telling Papa. I am going to tell my papa."

He squeezes her face in his hand. "You mustn't. This has to be our secret."

"No," Ellen says.

"Sadly, if you tell your papa, I will kill him. I will shoot him tonight under a bridge. Do you want that? Do you want your papa to die because of you?"

Ellen cannot speak, is mute while he washes her face, combs her hair. "Your booklets," Falconi says, and puts them in her hand. "I want you to think of what happened as a game. Like bocci with our own rules. I know it doesn't seem so now, but in the long run that's all the importance it will have."

She stands by the sink a long time after he leaves. She is cold, feels as though she is dreaming and has to imagine her legs before they will work. She looks down at the tracts. Some angels look more real than others, some have wings that look stiff, made of plastic. It must be that some angels are not angels at all but ordinary men who bought their wings at Sears. God can't notice everything. Maybe some things are too tiny for him to see. Maybe he made children small because he doesn't like them. From heaven, she must look no bigger than an eyelash.

She puts the tracts in the garbage. What she wants more than anything in the world right now is a purple crayon so that she could write her name on every smooth surface she passes.

Anna is gone, the bocci players are gone, the tables all have new faces. Upstairs, the wedding guests are in a tarantella circle. Ellen weaves in and out of legs, bodies, trying to catch her father as he dances by.

Papa papa papa. But her voice can't reach him anymore than her hands can. Somebody steps on her feet. She sees Nina with her arm around Mr. Del Greco, and here is ugly Rosa with a big nose and a smile and too many teeth.

Then the music stops and Ellen feels hands reaching around her, a warm palm on her clammy forehead. She turns. Sam is smiling down at her and he seems to Ellen both too near and too far: as though his hand on her head weighs a thousand pounds but that if she called his name forever he wouldn't hear.

"You look worried," Sam says. "Did you have trouble finding us?"
She shakes her head.
"Did you see the bride? Too soon it will be your turn."
"Papa," Ellen starts.
"Yes? Why do you look like that?"
Ellen begins to cry.
"Elena, you're breaking my heart. Tell me."
"I can't," she says.
"Why? Has there ever been anything you couldn't tell me?" Sam strokes her hair and an image of herself with Nina's bra on her head—it seems so long ago now—flashes in her mind.
"You won't love me anymore if I tell you."
"That could never happen. Not in a million years."
"You will die if I tell you."
"I'll take my chances."
Ellen glances around. The room might be full of spies. "I know something," she says softly.
"What do you know?"
"God never wanted any children."
"How do you know that?"
"He killed his son. Jesus Christ is dead."
"Yes, but now he's in heaven," Sam says.
"He's in the men's room. He bled to death."
"Elena, Elena. Come now, dance with me like we always do," Sam says, and lifts her so her feet are on top of his. But even Sam's slow steps are painfully too wide. She feels a dragging

118

pressure in her lower belly, her own blood stinging against the places where her skin is raw. Tonight before she goes to bed she will stuff her panties behind the water heater in the basement.

The band is playing a slow song and people hold each other close. Ellen sees Nina dance by with Mr. Del Greco who is saying something to her that makes her smile.

"I have good news," Sam says. "I have settled with the florist and your carnations will start coming again."

"No," Ellen says, looking up at the musicians on the stage.

"No?" Sam says.

"Those things," she says, pointing. "I want those things that man has by the drum."

"Cymbals? What do you want with cymbals?"

Ellen looks at him. "I have to whisper it."

Sam bends down.

"I want cymbals in case I get lost. I could just stand still and crash them and you will always be able to find me."

"Elena, all you have to do is call for me and I'll find you."

"But what if I have lost my voice too?"

Sam draws her closer and Ellen concentrates on the warm pressure of his hand, his feet beneath hers moving slowly to the music. It is this image of herself she is already beginning to remember, the firm steps that lead her around and around through the confused crowd as though to tell her, Here is where you find yourself.

Nominated by Christina Zawadiwsky

VISITORS

by KATHA POLLITT

from GRAND STREET

The senile bat with nicotine-streaked hair
hefting and sniffing cantaloupes at Key Food—
where had I seen before
that look, shrewd, absorbed, like a bird with a seed?

Of course. And I almost cried out "Madame
Champrigand!" Who taught us girls *Topaze*
and the *belle logique* of the parimutuel system—
and there was a long pause

before I thought, *but she's been dead for years.*
This happens not infrequently—more often
too as I get older—the dead appear
not, as you might imagine,

to startle us with fear or guilt or grief
or the cold fact of our own mortality,
but just to take pleasure again in everyday life:
to walk the dog, or stand in line for a movie,

or pick up a quart of milk and the Sunday *Times.*
Why shouldn't they have an outing? All the same,
it must embarrass them to use their day
passes in such a modest way

which is why when we glimpse them they quickly
dart round the corner or step behind a tree
or cleverly melt into strangers. Only you,
loved shade, do I never see

across the traffic or ahead in the surge of shoppers
swept off into the just-closing elevator door.
Was life so bitter, then, that even these
innocent errands cannot lure you here

for just one afternoon? I would not speak
even your name, you would not have to see me
shadow you drifting down the sunny sidewalk
happy and idle, free. And when you came

at last to the dark and silent subway stairwell
I would not cry or insist. For I would know
you finally: separate, as you were, yourself.
I would not keep you. I would let you go.

Nominated by Francine Prose

SWEET RUIN

by TONY HOAGLAND

from HISTORY OF DESIRE (Moon Pony Press) and CRAZYHORSE

Maybe that is what he was after,
my father, when he arranged, ten years ago,
to be discovered in a mobile home
with a woman named Roseanne, an attractive,
recently divorced masseuse.

He sat there, he said later, in the middle
of a red, imitation-leather sofa,
with his shoes off and a whiskey in his hand,
filling up with a joyful kind of dread—
like a swamp, filling up with night—

while my mother hammered on the trailer door
with a muddy, pried-up stone,
then smashed the headlights of his car,
drove home,
and locked herself inside.

He paid the piper, was how he put it,
because he wanted to live,
and at the time knew no other way
than to behave like some blind and willful beast,
—to make a huge mistake, like a big leap

into space, as if following
a music that required dissonance

and a plunge into the dark.
That is what he tried to tell me
the afternoon we talked,

as he reclined in his black chair,
divorced from the people in his story
by ten years and a heavy cloud of smoke.
Trying to explain how a man could come
to a place where he has nothing else to gain

unless he loses everything. So he
louses up his work, his love, his own heart.
He hails disaster like a cab. And years later,
when the storm has descended
and rubbed his face in the mud of himself,

he stands again and looks around,
thankful just to be alive, oddly
jubilant—as if he had been granted
the answer to his riddle,
or as if the question

had been taken back. Perhaps
a wind is freshening the grass,
and he can see now, as for the first time,
the softness of the air between the blades.
Maybe then he calls it, in a low voice

and only to himself, *sweet ruin.*
And maybe only because I am his son,
I can hear just what he means. How
even at this moment, even when the world
seems so perfectly arranged, I feel

a force about to take it back.
Like a smudge on the horizon. Like a black spot
on the heart. How one day soon,
I might take this nervous paradise,
bone and muscle of this

extraordinary life,
and with one deliberate gesture,
like a man stepping on a stick,
break it into halves. But less gracefully
than that. I think there must be something wrong

with me, or wrong with strength, that I would
break my happiness apart
simply for the pleasure of the sound.
The sound the pieces make. What is wrong
with peace? I couldn't say.

But, sweet ruin, I can hear you.
There is always the desire.
Always the cloud, suddenly present
and willing to oblige.

Nominated by Michael Bowden, Carl Dennis, and Pamela Stewart

AGAINST THE TEXT "ART IS IMMORTAL"

by ALAN DUGAN

from AGNI

All art is temporal. All art is lost.
Go to Egypt. Go look at the Sphinx.
It's falling apart. He sits
on water in the desert and the water table shifts.
He has lost his toes to the sand-
blasts of the Saharan winds
of a mere few thousand years.
The Mamelukes shot up his face
because they were Iconoclasts,
because they were musketeers.
The British stole his beard
because they were imperialist thieves.
It's in the cellar of the British Museum
where the Athenians lost their marbles.

And that City of Ideas
that Socrates once had in mind
has faded too, like the Parthenon
from car exhaust, and from
the filthiness of the Turks
who used it as a dump.

If that city ever was
for Real in public works

and not just words he said:
No things but in ideas.
No ideas but in things
I say as William Carlos Williams said,
things as the Sphinx is our thing,
a beast of a man made god
stoned into art to guard the dead
from nothing, nothing and vanishing
toes first in the desert,
sand-blasted off into nothing
by a few thousand years of air,
sand, take your pick, picker,

go to Egypt, go look
at the Sphinx while it lasts.
Art is not immortal.
Art is not mortal.
All art is ideas in things.
All art is temporal. All art is lost.
The imperial desert is moving in
with water, sand and wind
to wear the godly native beast of man apart
back to the nothing which sculpted him.

And remember the Mamelukes, remember the Brits.
They were the iconoclasts of their own times,
primitive musketeers, primitive chiselers. This time
we can really blast the beast of man to bits.

Nominated by Laurie Sheck

THE BOX

fiction by SUSAN STRAIGHT

from AQUABOOGIE (Milkweed Editions)

THE BENCH AT the bus stop was covered with black spray paint. PB'S, it said, the squared letters making spidery, jointed patterns on all the buildings and walls in the neighborhood, even on the elephant-skinned trunk of the palm tree Shawan leaned against while she waited for the bus. When she had gone out into the yard this morning, she thought, her sisters had been scared. Nygia and Tanya held her shoulders, but she shook herself sharply and frowned. "Quit, y'all, I'm goin outside and tell them sorry-ass punks get out my yard. Mmm-hmm, in my robe and all." She walked out onto the step quietly, letting the wrought-iron screen door click into the lock.

Five of the Playboys stood on the sidewalk, leaning against the chainlink fence that surrounded the Johnsons' square of yellow grass. Shawan knew that they were watching the apartment house across the empty lot, waiting for the old man in the downstairs apartment to leave. He had a new TV, delivered in a box that anyone could have seen. Shawan stared at the boys, their arms draped over the fence casually, but the backs of their necks tight and wary. She had seen the short one run his palm, fingers spread, over the slight bulge made by a gun in his jacket. "Shawan, they packin, you know it," Nygia said through the screen.

"So. What y'all doin in front of my house?" she said loudly from the step. They all turned, heads swiveling like those submarines in the cartoons, she thought, and the short one said, "None a your damn business, bitch." He was maybe sixteen, three years younger than Shawan.

"I don't want you doin it in my daddy's front yard," she said. "And don't give me no trouble cause you think I ain't about nobody." She thought of V-Roy. These were young ones, who had probably forgotten V-Roy already.

"Nathan Thomas my uncle, and he be over here in two minutes if I call him. You know who I mean," she said, nodding her head at the only boy she recognized, with shiny-curled hair and a sliver of pink on his lip that looked to her like a tongue always poking out. They stood, hands in pockets, their eyes filled with hate and their elbows stiff as hangers; she kept her arms folded over her robe, afraid to move even backwards. The pink-lipped boy spat into the cool morning dirt and cocked his head toward the avenue. Nathan had been in the 102nd Street Crips years ago, and Shawan had known that they would recognize his name and his arsenal of weapons, even though he did nothing now. The Playboys moved slowly, pushing off the fence with their backs, keeping hands crushed to their thighs. "I'ma get that bitch," the short one said. Shawan was shaking, but she pressed each thumb hard against a rib and became calm. Nygia scratched the screen mesh and said, "Uncle Nathan still got his rep."

Now she was late. The deejay said it was 5:42, "Wake up with Willie G. Time," and Shawan usually caught the 5:30 bus. In the early morning cold, the avenue was nearly deserted. Them boys might be hidin out somewhere, she thought, waitin to jump me. Let em go head on. I'm tired of they mess, running the street like they own it. If they gon try and snatch my box out my hands, they better use the piece. Just kill me, cause I'll kill you.

Willie started a new song, the congas beginning the beat, and then the rest of the drums and bass pounding the rhythm. Shawan turned the knob on top of the radio all the way to "Bass." She loved the deep reverberations, the snap of the bass and its power under the surface of guitars and organ and, underscoring all, the cupped-palm handclaps. Church in the funk. She never turned the knob to "Treble" because it made the radio sound tinny, like white music.

Shawan leaned out over the curb. The bus was still several stops away. Drumming her fingers on the side of her thigh with one hand, she held the radio close to her body with the other, and the bass thumped in her chest. The ornate black grill cover-

128

ing Sims' Liquor became soft and pretty as lace when she looked at it with unfocused eyes.

With the hiss of opening doors, she had to turn the music off. Holding the box in her lap, staring at the black mesh and silver knobs, she felt the screaming of the brakes and engine pound her with noise. She needed the music, the box, each moment to calm her. When she opened her eyes every morning, she heard menacing silence, empty air without rhythm, for only an instant. She would reach out and turn the radio on, watching her own fingers grasp the lever. It never disturbed Nygia, sleeping next to her, and Shawan sometimes lay in bed for two or three songs, looking at the walls and the thin curtains. Some mornings, just after she woke up, things seemed sharp and unusually defined. She could see each thread and the square, regular weave of the curtains with the sun piercing them, and the hole in the plaster just below the window looked as if it was filled with tiny chalk beads.

With the bass sliding and changing in her ears, the steady clapping which made her imagine a line of people swaying, heads thrown back, she could think clearly and her thoughts slid along lightly on the sounds. Often at work she would tell her supervisor she was going to the restroom, and then she would stand in the tiled break room and listen to one complete song echoing from the walls.

They were putting the calls through rapidly, scattering voices all over the building. "We in the groove now," Mary T. said to Shawan. The calls finally slowed at lunchtime, and the switchboard operators sat back; Shawan felt the hollowness of her head with the earphones pressed in tightly.

Leonard was singing Diana Ross's song "Muscles" when no calls came through on his headset. "I want muscles, all over his body, from his head down to his toes," he sang in his falsetto, moving his shoulders delicately.

"You better stop dreamin, baby," Mary T. said. Leonard was six-four and weighed two-hundred-forty pounds. He shape like a tear, Shawan thought, the way somebody draw a tear, not like it really look if it's on a face. After it leave your eye and go down your cheek.

His head was small, with a bald spot at the crown, and his hips were square. He had to turn sideways to pass through the narrow spaces between desks. His desk was covered with pictures of Diana Ross, cut and pasted over carefully with pictures of him so that they stood close together, the way Mary T. said the *National Enquirer* had famous people secretly married when they hadn't even met. Taped to the backs of the operators' chairs were Xerox copies he had made, announcing "Diana Ross and Leonard 'Mr. Entertainment' Jackson appearing now at the Roxy." Shawan had brought him Diana's picture, from *Ebony*. He wanted to *be* just like her, he said, but he'd have to settle for singing like her.

"Girl, what do you think of the new song by Aretha?" Leonard asked Shawan. He turned to Mary T. and Cherie and said, "Note, I'm askin our resident music expert, y'all."

"Mmm hmm," Cherie said, hummed, in her high voice; it was the way she emphasized everything Leonard said. When the supervisor, Mrs. Badgett, left for a doctor's appointment or to run an errand, Cherie and Leonard would leave their seats, turn on Shawan's radio and do the new dances, looking over their shoulders at the office door. Shawan could measure the two years she had worked in the building by the first dances Cherie had done—the Smurf and the White Girl, long ago. Shawan never danced. She stayed in her seat and moved, not wanting anyone to see her from all angles, vulnerable.

Mary T. said, "Yeah, Shawan, what you think of Aretha's bad self? Is it the new jam?" Shawan dipped her shoulders and said, "It got potential." She snapped her fingers, and a call came through to her ears. When she had finished with the voice, she drummed softly on the table.

"She be doin all kind of stuff with her voice," Leonard said. "I personally have a different style. Mr. Entertainment, y'all!" He rocked his narrow shoulders. "But I still rather have a little butt like Diana's," he smiled. They all laughed, and Leonard's hand went up to the tiny patch of grayish hairs over his ear.

This was when she missed V-Roy the most, on a Friday afternoon, coming home from work. He would have been there at her house, waiting in his blue car with gray primer like camouflage. They'd be gone, riding for hours. V-Roy cruised, cool and slow, and Shawan deejayed, switching radio stations to keep only their favorite songs playing. They didn't stay in the neighborhood. V-Roy drove out to the beach, and along the coast past the airport. Sometimes on late summer evenings when the sun was just dropping they drove to Hollywood and watched the people. Or they went all the way down Sunset, starting from downtown, watching the neighborhoods change colors—Chinatown to Mexican to any-color Hollywood, to huge gates and houses and hedges, rich white neighborhoods near the hills and then blue, the ocean.

"Let me get a gangster lean," V-Roy would say, "so we can cruise right." He kept his lower body directly behind the steering wheel, shifted his shoulders toward the middle of the seat, curving his waist as gracefully as one of the samurai swords he wanted. "Say, baby," he teased, close to Shawan, looking out through the center of the windshield. "Do I got it now?"

She nodded, laughing at his exaggerated cool, his half-shut eyes. V-Roy had been her best friend since high school. He lived one street over, and when they walked together and people teased them, Shawan always said, "Nuh-uh, don't be thinkin that. He's my partner. We don't mess with each other." He wasn't in the Playboys, but his older brother Antoine had been, and V-Roy hung out with Rollo, who had been in for three years.

He was going to teach Shawan to drive someday. She was in no hurry. She liked him to drive so she could take care of the music, lean her head on the smooth vinyl seat, and watch people walk slantwise. Mrs. Badgett at work, with fine red veins in her nose like broken windshield glass, couldn't believe Shawan didn't drive. "Everyone drives," she said. "It's just impossible to get around in L.A. if you don't."

"Don't have a car," Shawan said. Her bus had been late, and Mrs. Badgett was disapproving. "I've seen a car key around your neck," she said to Shawan. Shawan pulled out the key V-Roy had made for her one day. "It belong to a friend," she said, her voice hard. After Mrs. Badgett left, Mary T. said, "White people think everybody born with a car under they ass."

"I heard that," Shawan said. "I'ma get me one someday, though. Watch me."

V-Roy had taken her downtown to buy the radio. It was her present to herself for her nineteenth birthday. They went to one of the Mexican-run stores where the radios crowded the windows and blared out onto the sidewalk.

"Girls don't never be sportin boxes like that," V-Roy had said, pointing to a black suitcase-sized radio. "Rollo got one a them."

"I know what he got. I could carry it if I wanted to," Shawan said sharply, walking into the store.

"Girls don't be jammin that much, period," V-Roy continued, smiling, waiting for her reaction. "That's for dudes."

"You gon quit with the 'girls' stuff?" Shawan said, "I ain't every girl, and I do what I please." She stared at the radios lining the wall.

"You know I'm just botherin you," he said, leaning on the counter. The way his legs crossed over each other as he stood made long, smooth folds in the silky material of his sweatsuit, Shawan remembered. His small teeth showed when he stuck his tongue in the corner of his mouth, the way he did when he smiled. She bought the silver radio because it was different from all the black ones, and it had a clear, strong sound. It was the size of a large shoebox.

V-Roy died three months later. He was sitting on a picnic table at Ninetieth Street Elementary School, with Rollo, just after the sun had set. Lemoyne Street Crips shot Rollo twice in the leg, and V-Roy in the head, once.

Shawan watched Nygia's stomach in their bedroom when Nygia undressed, imagining it hard and round and soon shiny as the domelike bald spot on Leonard's head. Nygia was three months pregnant and had quit her after-school job at McDonald's. "I'ma need some money to go to the store tomorrow," she said to Shawan. "Daddy ain't got paid yet."

Shawan went slowly to what had been her car money, hidden in a hairdress can. She had saved $420, with the smell of gasoline seeming to come from the bills, but now since Nygia wasn't working and needed so many things, the tight roll of money was spindly, thin as a cigarette.

She lay on the bed, listening as Nygia left with her boyfriend and Daddy rustled into his uniform. He left for work at 9:00 P.M., to guard a building only four blocks from hers downtown. Tanya would sleep, and the house would be silent but for the music. The shadows of the iron bars across the windows lay over her chest. Look like I'm on a barbecue grill, she thought. The moon must be bright.

It was full, she saw when she stood on the step, and it moved fast across the sky. The street was bright and silvery, the cars

132

glinting. She could see stars through the telephone wires. The radio played a slow saxophone and a caressing voice, and she changed the station until she heard the staccato beat of a Whodini rap, fast as a scary person's heart.

She walked down the street, toward the Ninetieth Street school, past the benches where V-Roy was shot. His blood, what she had been sure was the dark stain of his blood, was indistinguishable from the spilled wine and black circles of ground ash left by other people since. She watched two boys play basketball. The moonlight glared white on the cement wall behind them, where Shawan had been playing with Tanya's tennis racket several weeks ago. A teenage boy on a ten-speed had ridden up and tried to take the racket. He grabbed it from behind, jerking her arm up like a chicken wing, but she turned and swung her other fist into his chest. She ran forward to kick at the bicycle tire, and he fell. She kicked him, let him flail the racket at her like she was the thief, and trapped the netting against her thigh with the heel of her hand.

She remembered how she had told Leonard and Mary T. at work, and how they had laughed. "Ain't nobody takin nothin away from Shawan," Mary T. said, and Leonard pinched her biceps. "She *like* it when somebody try and dog her," he said. "Don't you?"

She turned up the music and walked away from the school. A lowrider cruised by very slowly, a car she didn't recognize, the same song on her radio pouring out through the car's open windows. The loud, uneven throbbing of the engine sounded like drums. She didn't look at the car, but kept her eyes straight ahead. Could be the dudes shot V-Roy, she thought. She saw the sharp flashes of gray-blue light from TV screens as she turned her head toward the houses, and the car's taillights drew away from her, the strong threads of song from the car and the box separating imperceptibly.

Walking in step to the beat, she dipped at the knees; this was V-Roy's street. She moved her eyes over the yards and looked into the alley next to his house. Three large trash bins, pale with white graffiti, stood against the fence, and Shawan walked past them cautiously, tensing. Come on, she thought. Where you at? She fingered her necklace, the key, the way she always did when

133

she walked; boys would run up behind people and snatch hard so that the clasps broke.

The blue Dart was parked far back against the fence; she couldn't see who was in the yard, but she heard Antoine's voice and laughter. "Let's book, cuz. It's time to go," he said, and Shawan saw him then, his blue bandanna tied around his head and knotted in the front. He stared at her. "What you need, now?" he called.

"Nothin from you," Shawan said. She didn't move.

Antoine got into V-Roy's car, and two boys followed. He turned the headlights on; they lit up the radio, made it shine. "Get outta the way," he yelled over the noise of the car. She walked past the driveway.

She was almost back to the house, her eyes blurred with staring at the sidewalk and seeing the gray primer of V-Roy's car, the one crazy hair that poked out from his eyebrow when she looked at the side of his face, and someone said, "Hey, girl, what you doin walkin around? You trying to get jumped?"

It was Marcus, whose aunt, Mrs. Batiste, lived next door. He had come to L.A. the month before, from Virginia, when the Navy transferred him to Long Beach. He opened the door of his car, a big Buick, and walked into the yard. "Why you walking? Ain't you got sense?"

"I got legs. I can walk," Shawan said, looking at his knees.

"Why you want to stay here and you could be with me, at a club?"

Shawan said, "Not if you act like last time." She lifted her chin and bit a tiny piece of her inside lip. He had taken her to his apartment and put his hands all over her. Like he own me already, and I don't have no say, she thought. He wanted all the say, not like V-Roy. Marcus looked at her with admiration, but it was mixed with admiration of himself, for picking her. He had run his hands over her buttocks, said he liked how she walked like a boy.

"You want to go driving, right now?" he said. Shawan looked down the street. The sidewalks, the cars, were brighter than in the day.

The seats were plush, light blue like the car. They drove down the avenue; the deep yellow light from a bar was a triangle of color in a block of dark doorways. Shawan reached down to turn

134

on the radio, but Marcus pushed her hand away and put in a cassette of love songs. "Why you don't sit over here?" he said, touching the seat beside him. His eyes were green, his skin the same gold brown as hers. Nygia and Tanya said he was fine. Shawan thought, he look good but he know it. He think too much when he smile.

"Cause I don't feel like it," she said. Facing out the window, she leaned her head back and saw herself in the glass when they passed streetlights.

"Where you want to go? Anywhere you say."

"Not to your apartment," she said. Her face faded and reappeared. "Just drive." They headed toward the ocean. She had gone to the beach once after V-Roy died. She took two buses, to Santa Monica, but the bus wasn't right. You couldn't cruise and listen to the music unless you had headphones like the boy several seats away from her. Every so often he sang out in a piercing voice, teasing her because they were songs she knew were playing on her station, and she was holding her silent radio.

Flames shot up into the sky outside the window, and Shawan sat up. "Natural gas," Marcus said. The fire released itself from a needle-thin white tower, reaching higher suddenly and then shrinking back until the flames were sucked into the opening, again and again.

He drove past the harbor, talking about the ship he worked on. Shawan watched his leg when he pressed the brake; the muscle was short and thick. He saw her. "Why you stay away from me so much? I ain't hurtin you," he said. "I want you to be my lady." She saw his tongue when he said "lady," just touching the underside of his teeth.

"I ain't nobody's 'mine'," Shawan said, looking past his face to the window. "Don't nobody own me."

She reached down and pulled out the cassette, listening to the deejay's familiar voice fill the car. Her voice could be smooth and beautiful as his when she wanted. V-Roy had recorded a cassette with her favorite songs, and she talked between each, using her low, sweet work voice, the one she had learned on the phones. V-Roy played her tape in his car whenever they went driving. He wrote "The Master Jam" on the case. Every time Shawan answered a call at work she practiced, making her voice sure and strong, not breathy. Mary T. and Cherie laughed at how quickly she could change, how assured she made herself sound. "My deejay voice," Shawan said. Leonard smiled and sang, "Last night a deejay saved my life from a broken heart."

Marcus stopped the car on the side of the highway. He turned to her and said, "Why you scared of me?"

Shawan felt anger rise in her chest. "I *been* told you I ain't scared," she said folding her arms. He turned the radio down, and his hand on the knob made her more irritated. "Why you do that?" she said.

"Cause I'm trying to get serious with you. When you gon let me do what I want? We could get married, I ain't playin with you."

"I don't want to get married. Why don't you teach me to drive?" Shawan said. He leaned forward and touched her breast, brushing his finger against the arm she kept over herself.

"Let me teach you something else," he said, pushing his chin forward. His hand stayed on her shirt, and Shawan felt the anger rise into her throat. She thought, Why it always what *you* want to do? She closed her hand around his wrist. She held it and squeezed as hard as she could, but he twisted his arm and fastened his hands around hers; his mouth was tight. Shawan looked at his hands. They were red, ruddier than hers. Hers were gold in the light from the streetlamp.

"Girl, you should see what old Spiros up to now," Mary T. said to Cherie, crumpling her paper bag from lunch. "He messin everybody up, evil man." Mary T. and Mrs. Badgett took lunch together now, because Mrs. Badgett had brought her tiny television to the break room so she could watch "All My Children."

"He kidnapped that girl, Shawan," Mary T. said. She slid into her seat next to Shawan. Leonard said, "You went and got hooked on them shows," laughing at her excitement. "Mmm hmm," Cherie said. "She know everybody's business."

"I know as much about Spiros and Brooke and them as Shawan know about deejays," Mary T. said, smiling, brushing against Shawan.

She didn't smile. "Don't nobody care about them white people," she said, looking away. "Don't even put them with the music."

Leonard clicked his tongue. "Ain't no need to go off on her like that, Miss Shawan," he said impatiently. "You been nasty all week."

"So. She the one want to live in ice-cream land, I ain't gotta go with her," Shawan said. She couldn't stop the words, or smooth her voice. It was thick and rough. Mary T. looked at her with lips drawn in at one corner.

"And who are you?" Mary T. said. "You somebody more than me?"

Shawan said nothing. She had always waited for Mary T. and Cherie to admire her voice, to ask her about music, when she came to work; now she felt herself wanting to shout at them for no reason. "I'm sorry," she said, looking at the gray metal desk. "But them people life ain't about nothin."

"They got some brothers and sisters on now," Mary T. said. Leonard came to stand behind Shawan's chair, and he touched the back of her neck. "Not no real ones," he said gently. "You want me to sing?"

"No. Diana's songs is all old," Shawan said coldly. She went into the break room, but while the drums and hands clapping bounced back at her, she cried instead of swaying.

She liked to see their suits, the elegant tailoring, how the coats made a sharp line from shoulder to hand as if nothing could soften it. Marcus had a suit like that, she thought, walking toward the bus stop. Two men who looked like bankers in her building approached, flicking their eyes over the radio quickly and then glancing away in disgust. "Everywhere you go," one of them said, and Shawan smiled, curling her arm tighter around the metal.

The only open seat was in the middle of the bus, just ahead of the rear door. Her foot was partly in the aisle, flat on the rubber floor, to steady her body when the bus lurched and swayed. An old man sat by the window, leaning his head against the yellowed glass. She stared at his clenched hands; they were black between the wrist and knuckles, ashy gray between the fingers and on the joints.

The bus stopped often in the downtown traffic, and soon the crowds of people waiting impatiently at the crosswalks and the crush of bodies standing in the aisles of the bus surrounded her.

137

Nearly empty buses with signs flashing for Santa Monica and Westwood passed like mirrors. She made her eyes blurry and dreamed until she felt the drag of stops much less frequently and knew they had left downtown and entered the long avenues of South-Central L.A. Her calf muscles relaxed, and she put one hand on her knee.

A young man stood up in the back of the bus and pulled a gun out of his jacket. Shawan had moved her head to the clear space by the door, and she saw him walk to the crowd's end and turn his back. "Everybody shut up," he said, not loudly. He faced the people in the rear of the bus, holding a shopping bag with brown-string handles, and the people near him began to drop their wallets and watches and rings into the bag. He held it with one hand, his wrist curving up and the bag falling open in front of the people he pushed it near. With the other hand he held the gun close to his waist, so that only the people he watched could see it.

He stood at the other side of the rear door for a moment, waiting as the long crush of people moved forward to leave by the front door. Shawan turned her head forward. Everybody always get off here, she thought. He gon get off, too. He moved just past the rear door and turned quickly, keeping his back to the driver and the passengers in the front. He looked down at Shawan and brought the bag close, pushing against her when the bus began to move. She took off her watch, and he still stared, the gun pointing downward. The watch cracked against something hard at the bottom of the bag. She saw the man look out the window at the streets, at the old man next to her. He was asleep, his mouth open. He wore no watch. The man with the gun looked at Shawan's radio, between her clenched legs. She slipped her hands up the sides and under the handle, curling her fingers around the smoothness. I ain't givin it up. The bag quivered, and he said, "The box, man," thrusting his head forward slightly, the way Marcus did when he talked. She sat still, staring at a point just past him and to the left, feeling the line of his body waver as the bus slowed. His knee pushed sharply into hers, and she made herself look up at his neck, round and dry, gray as a palm trunk, and then at his eyes. She didn't blink, only let her eyes shift out of focus so his eyebrows became one thick mustache over the trembling single eye she saw.

He yelled, "Open the door, man," as the bus stopped, and then he leaped out onto the street. No one moved. As the doors clamped together, in the moment before the gears shifted and roared, Shawan heard the gun fire. The bullet pierced the window behind the door, over the heads of the women in the long seat, and went out the other window. People curled their backs instinctively, putting their heads down. Shawan crossed her arms over the radio and leaned her head back against the metal frame of the seat. He had been shooting at her, she knew. She felt the cold iron on the nape of her neck, watched the buildings slide by, faster and faster.

When she stepped down at her stop, she turned on the music. Her heart felt out of rhythm, and her hands slipped with sweat against the metal handle. You chicken now? she thought. Too late to be chicken, too late to be gettin scary. She looked toward her house and turned to walk down the next street. She listened for the Playboys, for any voices, when she neared V-Roy's house. It was quiet, and the car had been backed into the yard. It looked far away, dark and indistinct in the gray light of evening. Shawan undid her necklace and pulled off the key. She opened the car door, touching the primer's roughness, and looked toward the house. When she turned the key in the ignition, the radio came on loudly.

I'ma just sit here and listen, she thought, but then the car smelled like weed and beer, not like V-Roy, and she saw the back door of the house open. Antoine looked outside. Shawan moved the gear shift the way she'd watched V-Roy move it; the car seemed to spin forward out of the driveway.

She stopped at the corner, watching the crowd of buses and cars on the avenue. Everything seemed too slow, just as it had on the bus when the man stared at her, and Shawan looked at the radio on the car seat beside her. She turned quickly onto the avenue, forcing another car to stop, and the radio fell forward. She remembered driving one night with V-Roy, watching two boys run from the sidewalk to smash the windows of the car ahead of them; they took the woman's purse and ran. There were no boys in the doorways now, but she pushed down on the gas pedal, and the car sped toward the light. Think I'm ignorant, huh? Me and V-Roy never stupid like that. Wait till the light red, then gon stop and show me your piece, say give up the ride or

139

give up your life. Antoine's boys. No, baby. She saw the yellow, then red, and only pushed harder. The bus driver saw her coming. He stopped in the intersection and honked as she flew over the rut in the street. Shawan looked up, higher than the street, and tried to see where she was, which way she should drive to go to the ocean, but she couldn't see, couldn't remember. Another red flash appeared in front of her, and when she sped up again, she hit the front of the car heading across her path. The steering wheel pushed hard at her ribs and collarbone, and then she sat back against the seat. She tried to breathe and couldn't. She locked the door and turned on her radio, which had fallen to the floor; she turned it up high, changed the car radio to the same station, and filled the car with music while people slapped the windows with the palms of their hands.

Nominated by Milkweed Editions

ONE THOUSAND WORDS ON WHY YOU SHOULD NOT TALK DURING A FIRE DRILL

fiction by MARK HALLIDAY

from THE NORTH AMERICAN REVIEW

FIRST OF ALL, I should point out that the topic of why you should not talk during a fire drill is such a large and complex topic that I cannot do full justice to it in only one thousand words. In only one thousand words I will only be able to scratch the surface of this very interesting topic which has so many important and sensitive aspects. There certainly is a great deal to be said about why a person should not talk during a fire drill, even when everybody knows it is just a drill and even if there is not a teacher talking to us at the time.

One outstanding reason for not talking during a fire drill is because the fire drill is a practice session for when there might be a real fire in which case all the students would certainly need to be very quiet so they could hear the instructions from teachers such as Mrs. DeMella who would be shouting out some important messages. She might be shouting about how we should stand in alphabetical order on the ballfield with the ninth grade closest to the flagpole. If you are talking when Mrs. DeMella shouts about this then you might not hear the instructions and possibly, with the black smoke billowing out the windows of the burning school, if this was a real fire and not just another drill, you might then become confused and forget where to stand, even though the whole school has practiced this entire thing about a thousand times, because at such a time your brain could become over-heated and you might run in circles like an insane dog. For this reason you would fail to stand in exactly the place where Mrs. DeMella wanted you to stand, in which case the teachers might count the students and come to the mistaken conclusion that you were absent and that you were roasting in the flames, running around trapped in the burning gym like a human torch, and as a result Mrs. DeMella might go insane with grief about her lost student, thinking that she should have shouted even louder about where everybody should walk and stand, all because you were selfish and kept on talking to your neighbor.

In a sense, the above explanation reveals very much of the es-sence of why a person should not ever talk during a fire drill, but of course there are further aspects of this interesting topic which can be explained and which will be explained. The concept of not talking during a fire drill is closely related to the concept of si-lence and to the concept of the value of silence or what we call quiet. In a quiet situation there is a great opportunity for people to hear what someone else may have to say, such as your teacher. In a sense this is the same idea as was studied in the preceding paragraph but there is definitely more to be said about silence or quiet or what we may call the absence of sound. Silence is a sit-uation which gives us the chance to rest our ears, and our minds, which are so busy during most of the day listening to words, words, words, and other noises, like the squeak of chalk on a blackboard (which is actually a green board) or Mr. Perkins clear-ing his throat which seems to involve a remarkable amount of phlegm or mucus or what have you. After a few hours of hearing so many sounds, some of which are remarkably unpleasant, not to mention the voices of our teachers helping us to understand the Constitution and the methods for determining whether two trian-gles are congruent (side-angle-side, angle-side-angle, and side-side-side) (but not angle-angle-angle), there is a need for silence, or quiet, and it is a very human need. Thus if a student is talking during a fire drill, that student is ruining a golden opportunity to experience silence, because after all a fire drill is a time when silence is golden, and mandatory, except of course for a teacher such as Mrs. DeMella who has the job of shouting instructions to everybody very loudly just in case someone may have forgotten the fire drill procedure from the last fire drill which took place one month ago.

At this point the important issue of why you should absolutely not talk during a fire drill has certainly been clarified in more than one way. However, there is no doubt in my mind that more can be said on this issue which has fascinated the minds of various thinkers since mankind became civilized and outgrew the habits of apes and related primates. If a tribe of monkeys were to participate in a fire drill they would probably go right on chattering and scratching their armpits and hopping on each other no matter what Mrs. DeMella said, and this would be terribly upsetting for her and the other teachers because the high noise level would make them think all the monkeys would get burned to a crisp in the event of a real fire. But fortunately thanks to Charles Darwin and his assistants mankind has evolved and has discovered the concept of self-control which is very beautiful. Surely we can feel proud of the human species when we see the entire ninth grade standing in alphabetical rows by the flagpole with nobody saying a single word, standing there in a condition of total and complete silence and pretending that something important is going on even when everybody knows there is no fire and we could all do the entire drill in our sleep.

In conclusion, possibly a few words should be said on the question of why a person might make the mistake of talking during a fire drill. Here is an example. Bryce Carter grabbed my Screaming Blue Messiahs tape and I had to get it back fast before he wrecked it.

Nominated by Lynda Hull and Lloyd Schwartz

MIGHTY FORMS

by BRENDA HILLMAN

from ZYZZYVA

The earth had wanted us all to itself.
The mountains wanted us back for themselves.
The numbered valleys of serpentine wanted us;
that's why it happened as it did, the split
as if one slow gear turned beneath us . . .
Then the Tuesday shoppers paused in the street
and the tube that held the trout-colored train
and the cords of action from triangular buildings
and the terraced gardens that held camellias
shook and shook, each flower a single thought.

Mothers and children took cover under tables.
I called out to her who was my life.
From under the table—I hid under the table
that held the begonia with the fiery stem,
the stem that had been trying to root, that paused
in its effort—I called to the child who was my life.
And understood, in the endless instant,
before she answered, how Pharaoh's army, seeing
the ground break open, seeing the first fringed
horses fall into the gap, made their vows,
that each heart changes, faced with a single awe
and in that moment a promise is written out.

However we remember California later
the earth we loved will know the truth:

that it wanted us back for itself
with our mighty forms and our specific longings,
wanted them to be air and fire but they wouldn't;
the kestrel circled over a pine, which lasted,
the towhee who loved freedom, gathering seed
during the shaking lasted, the painting released
by the wall, the mark and hook we placed
on the wall, and the nail, and the memory
of driving the nail in, these also lasted—

Nominated by Rita Dove, Jane Hirshfield, Dorianne Laux, Sharon Olds, and ZYZZYVA

LONG, DISCONSOLATE LINES

by JANE COOPER

from THE IOWA REVIEW

in memory of Shirley Eliason Haupt

Because it is a gray day but not snowy, because traffic grinds by
  outside,
because I woke myself crying help! to no other in my bed and
  no god,
because I am in confusion about god,
because the tree out there with its gray, bare limbs is shaped
  like a lyre,
but it is only January, nothing plays it, no lacerating March
  sleet,
no thrum of returning rain,
because its arms are empty of buds and even of protective snow,
I am in confusion, words harbor in my throat, I hear not one
  confident tune,
and however long I draw out this sentence
it will not arrive at any truth.

It's true my friend died in September and I have not yet begun
  to mourn.
Overnight, without warning, the good adversary knocked at her
  door,
the one she so often portrayed

146

as a cloud-filled drop out the cave's mouth, crumpled dark of an
    old garden chair. . . .
But a lyre-shaped tree? yes, a lyre-shaped tree. It's true that at
    twenty-four
in the dripping, raw Iowa woods
she sketched just such a tree, and I saw it, fell in love with its
    half-heard lament
as if my friend, in her proud young skin, already thrashed by the
    storm-blows ahead,
had folded herself around them,
as if she gave up nothing, as if she sang.

Nominated by Sigrid Nunez

THE DREAM

by WILLIAM MATTHEWS

from ANTAEUS

A bare hill. Above it, the early evening sky, a flat,
blue-gray slate color like a planetarium ceiling
before the show's begun. Just over the hill and rising,
like a moon, the stuttering thwack of helicopter rotors

and then from behind the hill the machine itself
came straight up and stood in the air like a tossed
ball stopped at its zenith. It shone a beam of light
on me and a voice that seemed to travel through

the very beam intoned—that's the right word,
intoned—*We know where you are and we can find
you anytime. Don't write that poem. You know the one
we mean.* Then all was gone—the voice, the beam,

the helicopter and the dream. I'd lain down for a nap
that afternoon and slept through dusk. Outside the sky
was flat, blue-gray and slate. I'd no idea what poem
they meant. I lay swaddled in sweat five minutes

or an hour, I don't know. I made coffee and walked,
each muscle sprung like a trap, as far as the bridge
over the falls. I'd have said my mind was empty,
or thronged with dread, but now I understand

that in some way I also don't know how to say
I was composing with each trudge these words.
Until I steal from fear and silence what I'm not
supposed to say, these words will have to do.

Nominated by Richard Jackson, Arthur Smith

THE HAIR

fiction by JOYCE CAROL OATES

from PARTISAN REVIEW

THE COUPLES FELL in love but not at the same time, and not evenly.

There was perceived to be, from the start, an imbalance of power. The less dominant couple, the Carsons, feared social disadvantage. They feared being hopeful of a friendship that would dissolve before consummation. They feared seeming eager.

Said Charlotte Carson, hanging up the phone, "The Riegels have invited us for dinner on New Year's," her voice level, revealing none of the childlike exultation she felt, nor did she look up to see the expression on her husband's face as he murmured, "Who? The Riegels?" pausing before adding, "That's very nice of them."

Once or twice, the Carsons had invited the Riegels to their home, but for one or another reason the Riegels had declined the invitation.

New Year's Eve went very well indeed and shortly thereafter—though not too shortly—Charlotte Carson telephoned to invite the Riegels back.

The friendship between the couples blossomed. In a relatively small community like the one in which the couples lived, such a new, quick, galloping sort of alliance cannot go unnoticed.

So it was noted by mutual friends who felt some surprise, and perhaps some envy. For the Riegels were a golden couple, newcomers to the area who, not employed locally, had about them the glamour of temporary visitors.

In high school, Charlotte Carson thought with a stab of satisfaction, the Riegels would have snubbed me.

Old friends and acquaintances of the Carsons began to observe that Charlotte and Barry were often busy on Saturday evenings, their calendar seemingly marked for weeks in advance. And when a date did not appear to be explicitly set Charlotte would so clearly—insultingly—hesitate, not wanting to surrender a prime weekend evening only to discover belatedly that the Riegels would call them at the last minute and ask them over. Charlotte Carson, gentlest, most tactful of women, in her mid-thirties, shy at times as a schoolgirl of another era, was forced repeatedly to say, "I'm sorry—I'm afraid we can't." And insincerely.

Paul Riegel, whose name everyone knew, was in his early forties: he was a travel writer; he had adventures of a public sort. He published articles and books, he was often to be seen on television, he was tall, handsome, tanned, gregarious, his graying hair springy at the sides of his head and retreating rather wistfully at the crown of his head. "Your husband seems to bear the gift of happiness," Charlotte Carson told Ceci Riegel. Charlotte sometimes spoke too emotionally and wondered now if she had too clearly exposed her heart. But Ceci simply smiled one of her mysterious smiles. "Yes. He tries."

In any social gathering the Riegels were likely to be, without visible effort, the cynosure of attention. When Paul Riegel strode into a crowded room wearing one of his bright ties, or his familiar sports-coat-sports-shirt-open-collar with well-laundered jeans, people looked immediately to him and smiled. There's Paul Riegel! He bore his minor celebrity with grace and even a kind of aristocratic humility, shrugging off questions in pursuit of the public side of his life. If, from time to time, having had a few drinks, he told wildly amusing exaggerated tales, even, riskily, outrageous ethnic or dialect jokes, he told them with such zest and childlike self-delight his listeners were convulsed with laughter.

Never, or almost never, did he forget names.

And his wife, Ceci—petite, ash-blond, impeccably dressed, with a delicate classically proportioned face like an old-fashioned cameo—was surely his ideal mate. She was inclined at times to be fey but she was really very smart. She had a lovely whitely glistening smile as dazzling as her husband's and as seemingly sincere. For years she had been an interior designer in New York

151

City and since moving to the country was a consultant to her former firm; it was rumored that her family had money and that she had either inherited a small fortune or spurned a small fortune at about the time of her marriage to Paul Riegel.

It was rumored too that the Riegels ran through people quickly, used up friends. That they had affairs.

Or perhaps it was only Paul who had affairs.

Or Ceci.

Imperceptibly, it seemed, the Carsons and the Riegels passed from being friendly acquaintances who saw each other once or twice a month to being friends who saw each other every week, or more. There were formal dinners, and there were cocktail parties, and there were Sunday brunches—the social staples of suburban life. There were newly acquired favorite restaurants to patronize and, under Ceci's guidance, outings to New York City to see plays, ballet, opera. There were even picnics from which bicycle rides and canoe excursions were launched—not without comical misadventures. In August when the Riegels rented a house on Nantucket Island they invited the Carsons to visit; when the Riegels had houseguests the Carsons were almost always invited to meet them; soon the men were playing squash together on a regular basis. (Paul won three games out of five, which seemed just right. But he did not win easily.) In time Charlotte Carson overcame her shyness about telephoning Ceci as if on the spur of the moment—"Just to say hello!"

Ceci Riegel had no such scruples, nor did Paul, who thought nothing of telephoning friends—everywhere in the world; he knew so many people—at virtually any time of the day or night, simply to say hello.

The confidence born of never having been rejected.

Late one evening the Carsons were delighted to hear from Paul in Bangkok, of all places, where he was on assignment with a *Life* photographer.

Another time, sounding dazed and not quite himself, he telephoned them at 7:30 A.M. from John F. Kennedy Airport, newly arrived in the States and homesick for the sound of "familiar" voices. He hadn't been able to get hold of Ceci, he complained, but they were next on his list.

Which was enormously flattering.

Sometimes when Paul was away on one of his extended trips, Ceci was, as she said, morbidly lonely, so the three of them went out for Chinese food and a movie or watched videos late into the night; or impulsively, rather recklessly, Ceci got on the phone and invited a dozen friends over, and neighbors too, though always, first, Charlotte and Barry—"Just to feel I *exist*."

The couples were each childless.

Barry had not had a male friend whom he saw so regularly since college, and the nature of his work—he was an executive with Bell Labs—seemed to preclude camaraderie. Charlotte was his closest friend but he rarely confided in her all that was in his heart: this wasn't his nature.

Unlike his friend Paul he preferred the ragged edges of gatherings, not their quicksilver centers. He was big-boned with heavy-lidded quizzical eyes, a shadowy beard like shot, deep in the pores of his skin, wide nostrils, a handsome sensual mouth. He'd been an all-A student once and carried still that air of tension and precariousness strung tight as a bow. Did he take himself too seriously? Or not seriously enough? Wild moods swung in him, rarely surfacing. When his wife asked him why was he so quiet, what was he thinking, he replied, smiling, "Nothing important, honey," though resenting the question, the intrusion. The implied assertion: *I have a right to your secrets.*

His heart pained him when Ceci Riegel greeted him with a hearty little spasm of an embrace and a perfumy kiss alongside his cheek, but he was not the kind of man to fall sentimentally in love with a friend's wife. Nor was he the kind of man, aged forty and wondering when his life would begin, to fall in love with his friend.

The men played squash daily when Paul was in town. Sometimes, afterward, they had lunch together, and a few beers, and talked about their families: their fathers, mainly. Barry drifted back to his office pale and shaken and that evening might complain vaguely to Charlotte that Paul Riegel came on a little too strong for him, "As if it's always the squash court, and he's always the star."

Charlotte said quickly, "He means well. And so does Ceci. But they're aggressive people." She paused, wondering what she was saying. "Not like us."

153

When Barry and Paul played doubles with other friends, other men, they nearly always won. Which pleased Barry more than he would have wished anyone to know.

And Paul's praise: it burned in his heart with a luminosity that endured for hours and days and all in secret.

The Carsons were childless but had two cats. The Riegels were childless but had a red setter bitch, no longer young.

The Carsons lived in a small mock-Georgian house in town; the Riegels lived in a glass, stone, and redwood house, custom-designed, three miles out in the country. The Carsons' house was one of many attractive houses of its kind in their quiet residential neighborhood and had no distinctive features except an aged enormous plane tree in the front which would probably have to be dismantled soon—"It will break our hearts," Charlotte said. The Carsons' house was fully exposed to the street; the Riegels' house was hidden from the narrow gravel road that ran past it by a seemingly untended meadow of juniper pines, weeping willows, grasses, wildflowers.

Early on in their friendship, a tall cool summer drink in hand, Barry Carson almost walked through a plate glass door at the Riegels'—beyond it was the redwood deck, Ceci in a silk floral-printed dress with numberless pleats.

Ceci was happy and buoyant and confident always. For a petite woman—size five, it was more than once announced—she had a shapely body, breasts, hips, strong-calved legs. When she and Charlotte Carson played tennis, Ceci was all over the court, laughing and exclaiming, while slow-moving premeditated Charlotte, poor Charlotte, who felt, in her friend's company, ostrich-tall and ungainly, missed all but the easy shots. "You need to be more aggressive, Char!" Paul Riegel called out. "Need to be *murderous!*"

The late-night drive back to town from the Riegels' along narrow twisty country roads, Barry behind the wheel, sleepy with drink yet excited too, vaguely sweetly aching, Charlotte yawning and sighing, and there was the danger of white-tailed deer so plentiful in this part of the state leaping in front of the car; but they returned home safely, suddenly they were home, and, inside, one of them would observe that their house was so lacking in imagination, wasn't it? So exposed to the neighbors? "Yes, but you wanted this house." "No, you were the one who wanted this house." "Not *this* house—but this was the most feasible." Though sometimes one would observe that the Riegels' house had flaws: so much glass and it's drafty in the winter, so many queer elevated decks and flights of stairs, wall-less rooms, sparsely furnished rooms like designers' showcases, and the cool chaste neutral colors that Ceci evidently favored: "It's beautiful, yes, but a bit sterile."

In bed exhausted they would drift to sleep, separately wandering the corridors of an unknown building, opening one door after another in dread and fascination. Charlotte, who should not have had more than two or three glasses of wine—but it was an anniversary of the Riegels: they'd uncorked bottles of champagne—slept fitfully, waking often dry-mouthed and frightened not knowing where she was. A flood of hypnagogic images raced in her brain; the faces of strangers never before glimpsed by her thrummed beneath her eyelids. In that state of consciousness that is neither sleep nor waking Charlotte had the volition to will, ah, how passionately, how despairingly, that Paul Riegel would comfort her: slip his arm around her shoulders, nudge his jaw against her cheek, whisper in her ear as he'd done once or twice that evening in play but now in seriousness. Beside her someone stirred and groaned in his sleep and kicked at the covers.

Paul Riegel entranced listeners with lurid tales of starving Cambodian refugees, starving Ethiopian children, starving Mexican beggars. His eyes shone with angry tears one moment and with mischief the next, for he could not resist mocking his own sobriety. The laughter he aroused at such times had an air of bafflement, shock.

Ceci came to him to slip an arm through his as if to comfort or to quiet, and there were times when quite perceptibly Paul shook off her arm, stepped away, stared down at her with a look as if he'd never seen the woman before.

When the Carsons did not see or hear from the Riegels for several days their loneliness was almost palpable: a thickness in the chest, a density of being, to which either might allude knowing the other would immediately understand. If the Riegels were actually away that made the separation oddly more bearable than if they were in fact in their house amid the trees but not seeing the Carsons that weekend or mysteriously incommunicado with their telephone answering tape switched on. When Charlotte called, got the tape, heard the familiar static-y overture, then Paul Riegel's cool almost hostile voice that did not identify itself but merely stated *No one is here right now; should you like to leave a message please wait for the sound of the bleep*, she felt a loss too profound to be named and often hung up in silence.

It had happened as the Carsons feared—the Riegels were dominant. So fully in control.

For there was a terrible period, several months in all, when for no reason the Carsons could discover—and they discussed the subject endlessly, obsessively—the Riegels seemed to have little time for them. Or saw them with batches of others in which their particular friendship could not be readily discerned. Paul was a man of quick enthusiasms, and Ceci was a woman of abrupt shifts of allegiance; thus there was logic of sorts to their cruelty in elevating for a while a new couple in the area who were both theoretical mathematicians, and a neighbor's houseguest who'd known Paul in college and was now in the diplomatic service, and a cousin of Ceci's, a male model in his late twenties who was staying with the Riegels for weeks and weeks and weeks, taking up every spare minute of their time, it seemed, so when Charlotte called, baffled and hurt, Ceci murmured in an undertone, "I can't talk now, can I call you back in the morning?" and failed to call for days, days, days.

One night when Charlotte would have thought Barry was asleep he shocked her by saying, "I never liked her, much. Hotshit little Ceci." She had never heard her husband utter such words before and did not know how to reply.

They went away on a trip. Three weeks in the Caribbean, and only in the third week did Charlotte scribble a postcard for the Riegels—a quick scribbled little note as if one of many.

One night she said, "*He's* the dangerous one. He always tries to get people to drink too much, to keep him company."

They came back, and not long afterward Ceci called, and the friendship was resumed precisely as it had been—the same breathless pace, the same dazzling intensity—though now Paul had a new book coming out and there were parties in the city, book signings at bookstores, an interview on a morning news program. The Carsons gave a party for him, inviting virtually everyone they knew locally, and the party was a great success and in a corner of the house Paul Riegel hugged Charlotte Carson so hard she laughed, protesting her ribs would crack, but when she drew back to look at her friend's face she saw it was damp with tears.

Later, Paul told a joke about Reverend Jesse Jackson that was a masterpiece of mimicry though possibly in questionable taste. In the general hilarity no one noticed, or at least objected. In any case there were no blacks present.

The Riegels were childless but would not have defined their condition in those terms: as a lack, a loss, a negative. Before marrying they had discussed the subject of children thoroughly, Paul said, and came to the conclusion *no*.

The Carsons too were childless but would perhaps have defined their condition in those terms, in weak moods at least. Hearing Paul speak so indifferently of children, the Carsons exchanged a glance almost of embarrassment.

Each hoped the other would not disclose any intimacy.

Ceci sipped at her drink and said, "I'd have been willing."

Paul said, "*I* wouldn't."

There was a brief nervous pause. The couples were sitting on the Riegels' redwood deck in the gathering dusk.

Paul then astonished the Carsons by speaking in a bitter impassioned voice of families, children, parents, the "politics" of intimacy. In any intimate group, he said, the struggle to be independent, to define oneself as an individual, is so fierce it creates terrible waves of tension, a field of psychic warfare. He'd endured it as a child and young adolescent in his parents' home, and as an adult he didn't think he could bear to bring up a child—"especially a son"—knowing of the doubleness and secrecy of the child's life.

"There is the group life, which is presumably open and observable," he said, "and there is the secret inner real life no one can penetrate." He spoke with such uncharacteristic vehemence that neither of the Carsons would have dared to challenge him or even to question him in the usual conversational vein.

Ceci sat silent, drink in hand, staring impassively out into the shadows.

After a while conversation resumed again and they spoke softly, laughed softly. The handsome white wrought-iron furniture on which they were sitting took on an eerie solidity even as the human figures seemed to fade: losing outline and contour, blending into the night and into one another.

Charlotte Carson lifted her hand, registering a small chill spasm of fear that she was dissolving, but it was only a drunken notion of course.

For days afterward Paul Riegel's disquieting words echoed in her head. She tasted something black, and her heart beat in anger like a cheated child's. *Don't you love me then? Don't any of us love any of us?* To Barry she said, "That was certainly an awkward moment, wasn't it? When Paul started his monologue about family life, intimacy, all that. What did you make of it?"

Barry murmured something evasive and backed off.

The Carsons owned two beautiful Siamese cats, neutered male and neutered female, and the Riegels owned a skittish Irish setter named Rusty. When the Riegels came to visit Ceci always made a fuss over one or the other of the cats, insisting it sit in her lap, sometimes even at the dinner table, where she'd feed it on the sly. When the Carsons came to visit, the damned dog as Barry spoke of it went into a frenzy of barking and greeted them at the front door as if it had never seen them before. "Nice dog! Good dog! Sweet Rusty!" the Carsons would cry in unison.

The setter was rheumy-eyed and thick-bodied and arthritic. If every year of a dog's age is approximately seven years in human terms, poor Rusty was almost eighty years old. She managed to shuffle to the front door to bark at visitors but then lacked the strength or motor coordination to reverse herself and return to the interior of the house so Paul had to carry her, one arm under her bony chest and forelegs, the other firmly under her hindquarters, an expression of vexed tenderness in his face.

Dryly he said, "I hope someone will do as much for me someday."

One rainy May afternoon when Paul was in Berlin and Barry was in Virginia visiting his family, Ceci impulsively invited Charlotte to come for a drink and meet her friend Nils Larson—or was the name Lasson? Lawson?—an old old dear friend. Nils was short, squat-bodied, energetic, with a gnomish head and bright malicious eyes, linked to Ceci, it appeared, in a way that allowed him to be both slavish and condescending. He was a "theater person"; his bubbly talk was studded with names of the famous and near-famous. Never once did he mention Paul Riegel's name,

158

though certain of his mannerisms—head thrown back in laughter, hands gesticulating as he spoke—reminded Charlotte of certain of Paul's mannerisms. The man was Paul's elder by perhaps a decade.

Charlotte stayed only an hour, then made her excuses and slipped away. She had seen Ceci's friend draw his pudgy forefinger across the nape of Ceci's neck in a gesture that signaled intimacy or the arrogant pretense of intimacy, and the sight offended her. But she never told Barry and resolved not to think of it and of whether Nils spent the night at the Riegels' and whether Paul knew anything of him or of the visit. Nor did Ceci ask Charlotte what she had thought of Nils Larson—Lasson? Lawson?—the next time the women spoke.

Barry returned from Virginia with droll tales of family squabbling: his brother and his sister-in-law, their children, the network of aunts, uncles, nieces, nephews, grandparents, ailing elderly relatives whose savings were being eaten up—invariably the expression was "eaten up"—by hospital and nursing home expenses. Barry's father, severely crippled from a stroke, was himself in a nursing home from which he would never be discharged, and all his conversation turned upon this fact, which others systematically denied, including, in the exigency of the moment, Barry. He had not, he said, really recognized his father. It was as if another man—aged, shrunken, querulous, sly—had taken his place.

The elderly Mr. Carson had affixed to a wall of his room a small white card on which he'd written some Greek symbols, an inscription he claimed to have treasured all his life. Barry asked what the Greek meant and was told, *When my ship sank, the others sailed on.*

Paul Riegel returned from Berlin exhausted and depressed despite the fact, a happy one to his wife and friends, that a book of his was on the paperback bestseller list published by *The New York Times*. When Charlotte Carson suggested with uncharacteristic gaiety that they celebrate, Paul looked at her with a mild quizzical smile and asked, "Why, exactly?"

The men played squash, the women played tennis.

The Carsons had other friends, of course. Older and more reliable friends. They did not need the Riegels. Except they were in love with the Riegels.

159

Did the Riegels love them? Ceci telephoned one evening and Barry happened to answer and they talked together for an hour, and afterward, when Charlotte asked Barry what they'd talked about, careful to keep all signs of jealousy and excitement out of her voice, Barry said evasively, "A friend of theirs is dying. Of AIDS. Ceci says he weighs only ninety pounds and has withdrawn from everyone: 'slunk off to die like a sick animal.' And Paul doesn't care. Or won't talk about it." Barry paused, aware that Charlotte was looking at him closely. A light film of perspiration covered his face; his nostrils appeared unusually dark, dilated. "He's no one we know, honey. The dying man, I mean."

When Paul Riegel emerged from a sustained bout of writing the first people he wanted to see were the Carsons of course, so the couples went out for Chinese food—"a banquet, no less!"—at their favorite Chinese restaurant in a shopping mall. The Dragon Inn had no liquor license so they brought bottles of wine and six-packs of beer. They were the last customers to leave, and by the end waiters and kitchen help were standing around or prowling restlessly at the rear of the restaurant. There was a minor disagreement over the check, which Paul Riegel insisted had not been added up "strictly correctly." He and the manager discussed the problem and since the others were within earshot he couldn't resist clowning for their amusement, slipping into a comical Chinese (unless it was Japanese?) accent. In the parking lot the couples laughed helplessly, gasping for breath and bent double, and in the car driving home—Barry drove: they'd taken the Carsons' Honda Accord, and Barry was seemingly the most sober of the four of them—they kept bursting into peals of laughter like naughty children.

They never returned to the Dragon Inn.

The men played squash together but their most rewarding games were doubles in which they played, and routed, another pair of men.

As if grudgingly, Paul Riegel would tell Barry Carson he was a "damned good player." To Charlotte he would say, "Your husband is a damned good player but if only he could be a bit more *murderous!*"

Barry Carson's handsome heavy face darkened with pleasure when he heard such praise, exaggerated as it was. Though afterward, regarding himself in a mirror, he felt shame: he was forty

160

years old, he had a very good job in a highly competitive field, he had a very good marriage with a woman he both loved and respected, he believed he was leading, on the whole, a very good life, yet none of this meant as much to him as Paul Riegel carelessly complimenting him on his squash game.

How has my life come to this?

Rusty developed cataracts on both eyes and then tumorous growths in her neck. The Riegels took her to the vet and had her put to sleep, and Ceci had what was reported to the Carsons as a breakdown of a kind: wept and wept and wept. Paul too was shaken by the ordeal but managed to joke over the phone about the dog's ashes. When Charlotte told Barry of the dog's death she saw Barry's eyes narrow as he resisted saying Thank God! and said instead, gravely, as if it would be a problem of his own, "Poor Ceci will be inconsolable."

For weeks it wasn't clear to the Carsons that they would be invited to visit the Riegels on Nantucket; then, shortly before the Riegels left, Ceci said as if casually, "We did set a date, didn't we? For you two to come visit?"

On their way up—it was a seven-hour drive to the ferry at Woods Hole—Charlotte said to Barry, "Promise you won't drink so much this year." Offended, Barry said, "I won't monitor your behavior, honey, if you won't monitor mine."

From the first, the Nantucket visit went awkwardly. Paul wasn't home and his whereabouts weren't explained, though Ceci chattered brightly and effusively, carrying her drink with her as she escorted the Carsons to their room and watched them unpack. Her shoulder-length hair was graying and disheveled; her face was heavily made up, especially about the eyes. Several times she said, "Paul will be so happy to see you," as if Paul had not known they were invited; or, knowing, like Ceci herself, had perhaps forgotten. An east wind fanned drizzle and soft gray mist against the windows.

Paul returned looking fit and tanned and startled about the eyes; in his walnut-brown face the whites glared. Toward dusk the sky lightened and the couples sat on the beach with their drinks. Ceci continued to chatter while Paul smiled, vague and distracted, looking out at the surf. The air was chilly and damp but wonderfully fresh. The Carsons drew deep breaths and spoke admiringly of the view. And the house. And the location. They

161

were wondering had the Riegels been quarreling? Was something wrong? Had they themselves come on the wrong day or at the wrong time? Paul had been effusive too in his greetings but had not seemed to see them and had scarcely looked at them since.

Before they sat down to dinner the telephone began to ring. Ceci in the kitchen (with Charlotte who was helping her) and Paul in the living room (with Barry; the men were watching a televised tennis tournament) made no move to answer it. The ringing continued for what seemed like a long time, then stopped and resumed again while they were having dinner, and again neither of the Riegels made a move to answer it. Paul grinned, running both hands roughly through the bushy patches of hair at the sides of his head, and said, "When the world beats a path to your doorstep, beat it back, friends! *Beat it back for fuck's sake!*"

His extravagant words were meant to be funny of course but would have required another atmosphere altogether to be so. As it was, the Carsons could only stare and smile in embarrassment.

Ceci filled the silence by saying loudly, "Life's little ironies! You spend a lifetime making yourself famous, then you try to back off and dismantle it. But it won't dismantle! It's a mummy and you're inside it!"

"Not *in* a mummy," Paul said, staring smiling at the lobster on his plate, which he'd barely eaten, "you *are* a mummy." He had been drinking steadily, Scotch on the rocks and now wine, since arriving home.

Ceci laughed sharply. " 'In,' 'are,' what's the difference?" she said, appealing to the Carsons. She reached out to squeeze Barry's hand, hard. "In any case you're a goner, right?"

Paul said, "No, *you're* a goner."

The evening continued in this vein. The Carsons sent despairing glances at each other.

The telephone began to ring, and this time Paul rose to answer it. He walked stiffly and took his glass of wine with him. He took the call not in the kitchen but in another room at the rear of the house, and he was gone so long that Charlotte felt moved to ask if something was wrong. Ceci Riegel stared at her coldly. The whites of Ceci's eyes too showed above the rims of the iris, giving her a fey festive party look at odds with her carelessly combed hair and the tiredness deep in her face. "With the meal?" she asked. "With the house? With us? With *you?* I don't know of anything wrong."

Charlotte had never been so rebuffed in her adult life. Barry too felt the force of the insult. After a long stunned moment Charlotte murmured an apology, and Barry too murmured something vague, placating, embarrassed.

They sat in suspension, not speaking, scarcely moving, until at last Paul returned. His cheeks were ruddy as if they'd been heartily slapped and his eyes were bright. He carried a bottle of his favorite Napa Valley wine, which he'd been saving, he said, just for tonight. "This is a truly special occasion! We've really missed you guys!"

They were up until two, drinking. Repeatedly Paul used the odd expression "guys" as if its sound, its grating musicality, had imprinted itself in his brain. "OK, guys, how's about another drink?" he would say, rubbing his hands together. "OK, guys, how the hell have you been?"

Next morning, a brilliantly sunny morning, no one was up before eleven. Paul appeared in swimming trunks and T-shirt in the kitchen around noon, boisterous, swaggering, unshaven, in much the mood of the night before—remarkable! The Riegels had hired a local handyman to shore up some rotting steps and the handyman was an oldish gray-grizzled black and after the man was paid and departed Paul spoke in an exaggerated comical black accent, hugging Ceci and Charlotte around their waists until Charlotte pushed him away stiffly, saying, "I don't think you're being funny, Paul." There was a moment's startled silence; then she repeated, vehemently, *"I don't think that's funny, Paul."*

As if on cue Ceci turned on her heel and walked out of the room.

But Paul continued his clowning. He blundered about in the kitchen, pleading with "white missus": bowing, shuffling, tugging what remained of his forelock, kneeling to pluck at Charlotte's denim skirt. His flushed face seemed to have turned to rubber, his lips red, moist, turned obscenely inside out. "Beg pardon, white missus! Oh, white missus, beg pardon!"

Charlotte said, "I think we should leave."

Barry, who had been staring appalled at his friend, as if he'd never seen him before, said quickly, "Yes. I think we should leave."

163

They went to their room at the rear of the house, leaving Paul behind, and in a numbed stricken silence packed their things, each of them badly trembling. They anticipated one or both of the Riegels following them but neither did, and as Charlotte yanked sheets off the bed, towels off the towel rack in the bathroom, to fold and pile them neatly at the foot of the bed, she could not believe that their friends would allow them to leave without protest.

With a wad of toilet paper she cleaned the bathroom sink as Barry called to her to please hurry. She examined the claw-footed tub—she and Barry had each showered that morning—and saw near the drain a tiny curly dark hair, hers or Barry's, indistinguishable, and this hair she leaned over to snatch up but her fingers closed in air and she tried another time, still failing to grasp it, then finally she picked it up and flushed it down the toilet. Her face was burning and her heart knocking so hard in her chest she could scarcely breathe.

The Carsons left the Riegels' cottage in Nantucket shortly after noon of the day following their arrival.

They drove seven hours back to their home with a single stop, silent much of the time but excited, nervously elated. When he drove Barry kept glancing in the rearview mirror. One of his eyelids had developed a tic.

He said, "We should have done this long ago."

"Yes," Charlotte said, staring ahead at dry sunlit rushing pavement. "Long ago."

That night in their own bed they made love for the first time in weeks, or months. "I love you," Barry murmured, as if making a vow. "No one but you."

Tears started out of the corners of Charlotte's tightly shut eyes.

Afterward Barry slept heavily, sweating through the night. From time to time he kicked at the covers, but he never woke. Beside him Charlotte lay staring into the dark. What would become of them now? Something tickled her lips, a bit of lint, a hair, and though she brushed it irritably away the tingling sensation remained. What would become of them, now?

Nominated by Richard Burgin and Robert Phillips

164

WRITERS AND
THEIR SONGS

by WILLIAM KENNEDY

from THE MICHIGAN QUARTERLY REVIEW

I WAS WORKING as a newspaperman when I was drafted into the army during the Korean war, and I decided to write a continuing column about it called This New Army, which was what everybody was calling that same old army in those days. I wrote about how unbelievably stupid sergeants and corporals were, how unspeakably dreadful army food was, and how very peculiarly the general behaved when he noticed I was marching out of step.

When these columns were published back in Glens Falls, New York, enlistments in this new army dropped to zero, the first time I changed the world with my writing. This change was testified to by the local doomsday recruiting sergeant, who packaged off my clippings, along with a formal complaint, to Fort Benning, Georgia, where I was taking basic training in a heavy-weapons company of the Fourth Infantry Division. Because I could type, somebody had made me the company clerk, and so I also got to answer the phone. A call came in one day and guess who it was for? Me. The major who ran the Division's public information office was calling.

"Kennedy," he said to me, "that was a funny column you wrote the other day about the general."

"Thank you, Major," I said. "I'm glad you liked it."

"I didn't say I liked it and don't write any more." And then he added, after a pause, "Come up and see me and maybe I'll give you a job."

Well I did, and he did, and for the next two years I spent my days writing for army newspapers in the U.S. and Germany— Germany because our Fourth Division became the first American troop unit to go back to Europe after World War II. I was also thrown in with the literate and subliterate malcontents who populated the public information section, most of them also draftees and ex-newsmen, and four, including me, aspirants to writing of a different order—short stories, novels, films, plays; we weren't particular.

These years were seminal for me, the period in which I dove head first into literature. One of my great pals was a brilliant newsman from Mississippi who had not only seen and talked to Satchmo, he had actually attended a lecture by William Faulkner. Closer than that to the Empyrean no man I knew had ever ventured. Four or five nights a week we would gather in our enlisted men's club in Frankfurt, arguing, over heilbock and doppelbock, the relative merits of Sherwood Anderson, Hemingway, Dos Passos, Steinbeck, Caldwell, Fitzgerald, Mailer, Algren, Katherine Anne Porter, Flannery O'Connor, James Jones, Irwin Shaw, Thomas Wolfe. "Wolfe said it all but Faulkner said it better," was the youthful anthem from Mississippi.

I tried then and since to read everything that all these writers ever wrote and I have succeeded, perhaps by half, though I'm still working on Faulkner. I also began writing what I thought of as serious short fiction. I had written stories in college, all derivative and blithering, but now I was beginning to match myself against these maestros I'd been reading. At first I was such an amateur I couldn't even imitate them, but in the year or two after I left the army I managed to write dialogue that sounded very like Hemingway and John O'Hara, I could describe the contents of a kitchen refrigerator just like Thomas Wolfe, I could use intelligent obscenity just like Mailer, I could keep a sentence running around the block, just like Faulkner. But where was Kennedy?

I came to loathe the stories, as did my family, my friends, and fiction editors from coast to coast. Nevertheless, by diving into literature I had baptized myself as a writer. I have since come to look upon this as a religious experience; not because of its holiness, for as a profession it is more profane than sacred, but because of its enmeshment with the Catholic Church's supernatural virtues of faith, hope, and charity—as I had learned them.

Charity, of course, is what the writer supports himself with while he is finishing his novel.

Hope is the virtue by which he firmly trusts that someday, somewhere, somebody will publish his novel.

But it is in the virtue of faith that the writer grounds himself (or herself) in the true religious experience of literature; and faith was defined early on for me as a firm belief in the revealed *truths*—truths of God as religion would have it; truths of the writing life, as I would have it.

"How may we sin against faith?" the catechism used to ask itself, and then it provided four answers:

Sin number 1: "By rashly accepting as truths of faith what are not really such." I take this to mean that the writer should learn how to tell the difference between literary gold and dross. Michelangelo said a work of sculpture is created by cutting away the unnecessary part of a block of marble. Georges Simenon removed all words from his work that were there just to make an effect. "You know," he said, "you have a beautiful sentence—cut it." But it was Hemingway who forever codified this issue when he said: "The most essential gift for a good writer is a built-in, shock-proof shit detector. This is the writer's radar and all great writers have had it."

Sin number 2: "By neglecting to learn the truths which we are bound to know." This is a large order. It means you should read the entire canon of literature that precedes you, back to the Greeks, up to the current issue of *The Paris Review*; and if you have any time left over, you should go out and accumulate an intimate knowledge of politics, history, language, love, philosophy, psychology, sex, madness, the underworld, soap opera, your cholesterol level, and whether the Beatles will ever have a reunion.

Sin number 3: "By not performing those acts of faith, which we are commanded to perform." This means you should write even on Christmas and your birthday, and forswear forever the excuse that you never have enough time.

Sin number 4: "By heresy and apostasy." This means writing for the movies.

167

You see here before you a heretic and an apostate. My life after the army was a tissue of muddle, a pilgrimage through ignorance, anxiety, and innocence, but a pilgrimage with some discernible milestones. Five years after leaving the army I would get married, write my first and last play and my twenty-fifth short story, then quit journalism to write a novel. I would write the novel and it would be awful. Seven years after the army I would become managing editor of a daily newspaper. After nine years I would quit journalism again to finish another novel. I would be showing improvement in novel writing, but not much. After fifteen years of work as a half-time journalist, half-time fictionist, I would become a movie critic. After seventeen years I would publish my first novel. After nineteen years I would become a book critic. After twenty-two years I would become a teacher. And then, after thirty-one years, I would write my first movie script, may God have mercy on his soul.

I was not always a heretic. For a time I was a true believer in journalism, lived it passionately, gained entry to worlds I had no right to enter, learned how to write reasonably well and rapidly, was never bored by what I was doing, found it an enduring source of stimulation, met thousands of the crazy people who inhabit it and learned madness from most of them. I loved the tension, the unexpected element of the news, the illusion of being at the center of things when you were really at what approximated the inner lining of the orange peel.

Also I learned who I was, in certain small but significant ways. I became, as I mentioned, a managing editor, a position to which I had been obliquely gravitating since the beginning; for in wanting to learn all there was to learn about writing, I also wanted to learn all there was about what you did with writing after you wrote it. I became an escalating figure in the editorial room: from lowly slug in the sports department, to army columnist, to inquiring reporter and rewrite man. I harangued myself onto the police beat, became Saturday city editor, feature writer, substitute night city editor, general reporter; city editor when the reigning figure went to lunch and never came back; acting managing editor when the boss infarcted myocardially. And then, at long last, managing editor.

When this happened to me—over the objection of my second self, which had always wanted to be a daily columnist until the

seductive muse of fiction deflowered my pencil—I contemplated
the new condition and wrote to a contemporary of mine who had
also become a managing editor. He'd been a youth page writer
for a local daily when I was still in college, and I always envied
him that head start. Now here we were in perfect equanimity,
managing editors both, he in Albany, I in Puerto Rico, and I ap-
prised him of this, also reminding him of what Mencken had once
written: "All managing editors are vermin."

I remained verminous for two years, for we had started this
newspaper from scratch and it was a challenge unlike any other
I'd known. I never worked harder, never found more pleasure in
the work, yet always longed to be out of it, for the job had interrupted my novel in progress, and I yearned to return and see
how it would turn out. It took me those two years to accumulate
the courage and wisdom to quit a lucrative, fascinating job, live
off my savings and a weekend editing job, and work five full days
on fiction. What I had finally come to realize was that I'd learned
all I wanted to learn about newspapering, and that I could never
learn enough about how to write fiction; for the more I learned,
the more difficult writing became; and that is still so today. I
don't mean to be simplistic about journalism, which is mired in
the complexity of randomness. It was a great training ground for
a writer; but I'd reached my limit with it and knew in my soul
that I was a committed novelist, whose work is grounded in the
complexity of unconscious logic.

The problem then became the quest for the elusive Kennedy
voice. I had ceased to be consciously emulative of anyone in my
work, but what I was left with was what I now think of as the
voice of literary objectivity, a journalistic virus, an odious mi-
crobe that paralyzes the imagination and cripples the language.
"Cut, cut, cut," counsels Simenon; but what is left after all the
cuts? Is there something new on the page? Something original? Is
there energy in the sentence, power in the scene? In the interest
of curbing excess, has the heart been cut out of the story? In the
relentless quest for realistic action and surface, has the intellectual dimension been excised, or avoided?

In recent years a number of very good young writers have
been, and are still being castigated, even vilified, because of the
brevity of their styles and content. This is the critical assault on
so-called minimalism, that word a critic's invention that is not a

new subject for assaulting purposes. Forty years ago the critic Philip Rahv looked around and found the novelists of that day excluding the intellect in favor of depicting life on its physical levels (which is the journalistic way, of course). Rahv accused the American writer of "a disinclination to thought and . . . an intense predilection for the real," and found also that less gifted writers following Hemingway's method were producing "work so limited to the recording of the unmistakably real that it could be said of them that their art ended exactly where it should properly begin."

The transition from journalism to fiction is always a precarious trip, for journalism foists dangerous illusions on the incipient fiction writer. The daily journalist is trained, for instance, to forget about yesterday and focus on today. There is also a car parked downstairs, ready to carry him off into tomorrow, and so every new day becomes, for him, a tabula rasa. This is deadly. The fiction writer who puts little or no value on yesterday, or the even more distant past, might just as well have Alzheimer's disease; for serious fiction, especially novelistic work, has time as its essence and memory as its principal tool.

The journalist is also under pressure to believe that merely his presence at the great moments—whether he be first on the scene after a murder of passion, or witness to the fall of an empire—gives him the stuff of fiction. This is true to a point, but the stuff in question is merely raw material. The writer who believes he has a ready-made work of fiction spread out before him in his notes, needful only of a bit of sprucing and spicing, is deluded. He is a victim of the cult of experience, the impulse that sends writers who can find no value in the quotidian off to wars and revolutions to find something to write about. More than experience is called for.

In recent months in this country we have witnessed a rather tub-thumping, hog-stomping, name-calling literary argument on this subject, begun by our contemporary, Tom Wolfe, a notable tub-thumper and baroque hog-stomper of high journalistic achievement and repute, who moved into the realm of fiction with an extraordinarily successful first novel, *Bonfire of the Vanities*. Having succeeded, he now would like others to succeed also by writing novels like his. The debate over this has flourished in the pages of *Harper's* magazine and the *New York Times Book*

Review, among other places, and Mr. Wolfe has had his say twice on the subject. Also, his argument has been deconstructed by some notable figures in contemporary literature, Philip Roth, Mary Gordon, John Hawkes and Robert Towers among others, and its parts have been handed back to Mr. Wolfe, somewhat the worse for wear. Even so, there is merit in his point of view. I mentioned to him last month that I'd followed the exchange with great interest and had heard several arguments on both sides of the issue. That surprised him. "If there's anybody on my side," he said, "I haven't heard from them."

The essence of Mr. Wolfe's side of the argument is that American literature in the last half of this century has gone down the tube of privacy, inversion, neo-fabulism, magical realism, absurdism and so on, and that the only way to rescue it is through a return to realism of a nineteenth-century order, writing akin to that of Dickens, Trollope, Thackeray, Zola, and Balzac. The means of achieving this movement back to the future of the novel, says Mr. Wolfe, is reporting.

He writes: "I doubt there is a writer over forty who does not realize in his heart of hearts that literary genius, in prose, consists of proportions more on the order of 65 percent material, and 35 percent talent in the sacred crucible."

Mr. Wolfe also believes that, because of the way fiction has been written in the past twenty-five years, "Any literary person . . . will admit that in at least four years out of five the best nonfiction books have been better literature than the most highly praised books of fiction."

This latter notion has at least two memorable antecedents, one an essay by Norman Podhoretz, the editor of *Commentary* magazine, written some thirty odd years ago. As Mr. Wolfe does today, Mr. Podhoretz back then found fiction wanting in imagination, in disciplined intelligence, and also lacking a "restless interest in the life of the times."

Discursive writing, argued Mr. Podhoretz, had taken over the province that the novel had voluntarily surrendered—that province being the criticism of morals and manners. In short, the novel had no contemporary social relevance, he said, and the real art form of the age was the magazine article.

Similarly, the critic Leslie Fiedler, the great doomsayer of our era, all but exulted back in the early 1960s that the novel as a form was just about dead, that the public for novels had become sub-literate, that the artistic faith that had sustained writers was dead and, what's more, America never had an unequivocal avant-gardist among novelists of the first rank anyway.

In a sub-literate era, he wrote, who needs fiction? For, what *documentary realism* once promised to give people in *novel* form, non-fiction was providing more efficiently, more painlessly. As to the myths the sub-literates always look for—boy gets girl, good guy kills bad guy, etc.—television and film were providing them more vividly than the novel, and at less intellectual cost.

Some truth there, alas, in Mr. Fiedler's argument. Even so, it's very troublesome being a novelist when critics with a license to kill keep saying you're dead. Such complaints also cheer up *serious* people who do not find their own predilections and prejudices reflected in the novels they read. They see instead a hostile fiction that supports dangerous ideas and does not strike sufficiently critical attitudes toward the social forces and institutions that oppress certain multitudes, or certain elites. They see the literature of the age being written by the disengaged, the alienated, the untalented, the Philistines, the dropouts, the solipsists, the anarchists; and who will save us from drowning in all this irrelevance? these serious people wonder.

I could join Tom Wolfe's argument happily and point out my own black beasts of contemporary literature; but I am more inclined to defend this literature and its creators for several reasons.

What is fundamental to the counter-argument is the number of great books that have been written that did not directly concern their own time, but have prevailed as classic works nevertheless.

Consider only three of these books written out of their own age: *Benito Cereno* by Melville, written in 1856 of an event from 1797, but emblematic of the racial conflict that prevailed throughout the long era of slavery, and relevant even today; *The Red Badge of Courage* by Stephen Crane, written thirty years after the Civil War had ended, but a masterpiece of that war that speaks to all soldiers of any war; Hawthorne's first novel, *The Scarlet Letter*, written in 1850, probing the conflict between the Puritan culture of the seventeenth century and the privacy of love, but a cautionary tale of secrecy and shame whose meaning has endured, will endure.

Should we have told these writers that their choice of time was out of joint? Clearly their books are relevant not only to their own time, they are relevant to all time. I don't believe it matters whether a writer crisscrosses continents in search of today's material. I believe that what Alfred Kazin wrote is the truth: " . . . every writer criticizes life and society with every word he writes. The better the writer, the more this criticism and his imagination will fuse as one."

Or consider Tolstoy on the same subject:

> An artist's mission must not be to produce an irrefutable solution to a problem, but to compel us to love life in all its countless and inexhaustible manifestations. If I were told I might write a book in which I should demonstrate beyond any doubt the correctness of my opinions on every social problem, I should not waste two hours at it; but if I were told that what I wrote would be read twenty years from now by people who are children today, and that they would weep and laugh over my book and love life more because of it, then I should devote all my life and strength to such a work.

How can anyone have the audacity to tell a writer what and how to write? The writer, of necessity, is the sole judge of that, for the making of these decisions is evolutionary, a process of trial and rejection, of finally choosing among infinite possibilities the method, and story, and characters that allow the work to be written at all. I could never fault any writer for not writing about the age, for in my own experience it has been extremely difficult; and I offer only one example.

My time in the army represented two years of my life, and not merely life lived, but life reported on through a newsman's eye— reporting on the army, on Germany, on the cold war getting hot, on an innocent abroad, on fraternization with frauleins, on the black market, on army skulduggery, on leftover Naziism, and much more. I had, and still have some of that world at my fingertips; and also I've gone back twice to Germany to rekindle my memory.

Why? Well I wanted to write about it all, and did write about it—in short stories over a decade; and all those stories died. I

173

also wrote about two hundred pages of a novel about it, and that too died. Why do my stories die when clearly I have at least 65 percent of them living right there in the file cabinet? Obviously, in my case, because it is not the *material* that makes a work of fiction come to life. It is, in fact, almost impossible to say what it is that does that. Material can begin a piece of work, emotion and ideas can keep it going, but in order for the work not to self-destruct along the way, something else must happen. The writer must find himself in a strange place full of unknowns, populated by characters who are not quite strangers but about whom little is certain, everything is to be discovered. There must be a transformation of the material, of the characters, of the age, into something that is intriguingly new to the writer. "Art," wrote Boris Pasternak, "is interested in life at the moment when the ray of power is passing through it."

The writer, when he is functioning as an artist, understands when this power is at hand, and he knows that it does not rise up from his note-pad but up from the deepest part of his unconscious, which knows everything everywhere and always: that secret archive stored in the soul at birth, enhanced by every waking moment of life, and which is the source of the power and the vision that allows the writer to create something never before heard or seen on earth.

This creation of the new is what a good reader seeks and will recognize. Listen to Seamus Heaney, for instance, on what he expects from good poetry: "You want it to touch you at the melting point below the breastbone and the beginning of the solar plexus. You want something sweetening and at the same time something unexpected, something that has come through constraint into felicity."

Or E. M. Forster trying to define *Moby Dick*. He calls the book a yarn about whaling interspersed with snatches of poetry, also a battle against evil conducted too long or in the wrong way, also a contest between two unreconciled evils; and then he throws up his hands: "These are words," says Forster, "a symbol for the book if we want one, but . . . the essential in *Moby Dick* is prophetic song, which flows athwart the action and the surface morality like an undercurrent. It lies outside words."

Prophetic song. Nice work if you can get it.

Almost, but not quite, just by the nature of Melville's effort, one might conclude he was striving for that song from the outset. But to think that is to believe in creation as nothing more than conception; that the song, the achievement, was already present in the embryo. If this were true, what then can we say of Melville's years of gestation among whales, his months of research ("I have swam through libraries," his narrator writes in *Moby Dick*, and the same was true of Melville) and his year and a half of writing and rewriting the text? One of his biographers pointed out that although seventeen months seems a short time for the composition of such a book, it would have been an unusually *long* period given the manic pace at which Melville was writing.

An ancillary note: Nathaniel Hawthorne, with whom Melville became soul-mates during the writing of *Moby Dick*, had taken ten years for his own literary embryo to mature into the form and substance that became *The Scarlet Letter*.

Writers (and their songs) grow like plants, like trees, like children, like disease, like love. They go through stages of fragility, woodenness, pubescence, death, and passion. You'll note that I have put death before passion. This corresponds to the crucifixion, burial, descent into hell, and resurrection that befalls all literary careerists who keep the faith. Fitzgerald's noted line, "There are no second acts in American lives," was cockeyed and trivializing. He was talking about stardom. Resurrection has come to many American writers—Melville, the most egregiously belated case, and Faulkner, and Henry James, and Kate Chopin and Willa Cather, and Edith Wharton, and Fitzgerald himself, (though he was dead at the time); and it is now happening with Hemingway. It even happened to Faulkner when he was still alive, the problem being that no one knew he was alive, his books all out of print. Then suddenly they were *in* print and still are, along with those of the other writers in this group, who have all been elevated to a cosmic status that will long outlast the stars as Fitzgerald perceived them.

Not all of these writers wrote of their own age, though most did; and most of them were realists; but not Melville, and not always James, who wrote romances and took excursions into the world of ghosts. In the words of Maupassant, they each made themselves "an illusion of a world," each according to his or her sex, knowledge, style, talent, joyful or melancholy disposition, mythic or mordant mind.

So whose realism is this anyway?

And what of dreams? Are they part of realism?

And what of the surrealistic episodes that all of us have gone through but try not to accept as real? Kafka and Borges and García Márquez have made them real, without doubt, just as they were supposed to; because they found it necessary. "The great artists," said Maupassant, "are those who impose their particular illusion on humanity."

I am delighted to report to you that pursuing my own particular illusion I have just finished a section of a new novel in which I use—at long last—that experience I had in Germany so many years ago. I am also pleased to report that I have transformed it to such a degree that it no longer resembles anything I lived through. The character who inhabits this transformed experience is forever doing things that are wild and illegal and outrageous; not at all like me, which may be the reason I could never before write about the place. Yes. Absolutely. That last possibility is so clearly accurate that I hereby aver its truth: that I couldn't write it *because* I had lived it; because I knew it *too well*; because I knew *how it would come out*: boringly, as it always had.

The writer usually feels that any successful transformation of the work is a form of personal growth; but also that he's transformed his chosen art form, the novel, a micromillimeter or two, as well. Mr. Fiedler and other undertakers who have come after him, tend to think otherwise. As the novel replaced narrative poetry as the reigning form, so the movies and television will replace the novel, is their view. Since the form of the novel no longer progresses, they argue, since it doesn't redefine itself beyond what the modernists—Joyce, Proust, Mann, etc.—were able to do, then it is doomed to repeat itself, grow moldy, and become an esoteric genre only antiquarians will pursue henceforth.

Maybe it is all too true that the attention span of the reading audience is now at the level of a manic Siamese cat, and that the future of the word lies with magazine journalists and screenwriters; but I don't buy it. I've worked in those usurping forms and will work in them again. I love them both. But I live for the novel and will never believe it is less than what Henry James called it—the great form, in which *anything* is possible.

Back in the late 1950s, when I was trying to read the complete shelf of William Faulkner, I kept coming across speeches or interviews in which he talked of uplifting man's heart. In his Nobel speech he said it was the writer's "privilege to help man endure by lifting his heart." In a literature class at the University of Virginia he said: " . . . the artist believes what he's doing is valid in that it may do something to uplift man's heart, not to make man any more successful, but to temporarily make him feel better than he felt before, to uplift his heart for a moment."

This uplift business baffled me. I was reading and re-reading *The Sound and The Fury* and *Sanctuary* and *Light in August* and *The Wild Palms* and *Absalom Absalom*—tales of incest and whoring and rape and dying love and madness and murder and racial hate and miscegenational tragedy and idiocy—and saying to myself, "This is uplift?"

But I kept reading and found I couldn't get enough; had to reread to satisfy the craving, and came to answer the question in a word: yes. I felt exalted by the man's work, not by reveling in all the disasters, but learning from his language and his insights, and his storytelling genius, how certain other people lived and thought. I was privileged to enter into the most private domains of their lives and they became my friends, or people I'd keep at least at arm's length, or people I pitied, or feared, or loved. This was truly an uplifting experience, something akin to real friendship, and I began to understand the process by which writing reaches into another person's heart.

Now let me mention two letters I received from a man who had read my novel *Ironweed*. About four years ago he wrote the first letter. He was moved by the book and had to write and tell me. Two years later came the second letter in which he hinted he might have known the street life, the drinking life of a bum, just as *Ironweed*'s hero, Francis Phelan, knew it. The letter writer was now living with his sister, doing handyman's work for her, and staying out of trouble. His sister didn't like drunks, and would even cross the street to get away from a wino. Then her brother pressed *Ironweed* on her, got her to watch a home video of the film of it, and got her to read the book. At the end she

177

found herself crying, and she said to her brother, about Francis, "You know, he wasn't such a bad guy."

That would be quite enough for me, but the story has a coda. The sister no longer fears winos, no longer crosses the street to get away from them. She now gives them her loose change. And at Christmas she passes out to them, one and all, half-pints of muscatel.

This is a true story. It is a realistic story of our age. It has been transformed somewhat by the writer, who is very glad to have written it.

Nominated by Ellen Wilbur and The Michigan Quarterly Review

STRONG POMEGRANATE FLOWERS AND SEEDS OF THE MIND

by LINDA GREGG

from BLACK WARRIOR REVIEW

You ask about the men in my past and it makes me think
of Rome falling. "After a thousand years (Saint Augustine
said) during which no foreign invader had penetrated
the walls." You and I start at the end, begin with smoke
and rubble, ruin and death. You must imagine those walls,
one and then another, as if the city were a labyrinth.
And at the center, not a bull, lion or nest of snakes,
but women and the folds of their garments which "fall
in glory" over and over after. Women who know about god
and love, about the house with colonnades looking out
one way to the sea and the other way to the ocean,
with smells of their birthplace among the trees. You must
climb over the wreckage of walls and continue on with beggars
and the wounded. Must learn about shadows and about rape,
of cleansing with water. Augustine said many attributed
the fall to a loss of faith in the pagan gods, and something
about suppression by the emperors, Gratian and Theodosius.

It is true that I have worshipped trees. I have been praying
to whatever I can get. I have found fragments of stone,
one with the breasts of a woman on it and the name Elythia
as Greek letters cut into the marble. I tell you this
because you love me and have such a serious mouth and eyes.

Nominated by Li-Young Lee and Black Warrior Review

WHEN THEY LEAVE

by GEORGE KEITHLEY

from THE AMICUS JOURNAL

When they leave the world will be at peace
forever. A room with wide windows
shut against the weather. Wind
beyond the glass bending the brilliant maples.
Will we hear wings beating out of those trees?

Who can inhabit the unholy sleep
of the soul once they wander
silently away? Who'll bark, howl,
bray, croak, whirr, whinny, all
together raise their joyful noise? None

of these creatures who breed and birth
their young and feed
so near to us
a man forgets
the grace granted to each one—

Cattle
because they are convenient—

Coyotes
because they are not—

The cats
which remind us of our debts—

The sentimental dog who swallows his pride
and happily prevails
by licking plates.

Ordinary horses
who carry their ancient hearts under ours.

Also the bristling hog we dread and eat.

The customary spotted goat we know
will never acknowledge its guilt—

Black clouds of crows who strut
among the muddy furrows
at seedtime. Hosts of locusts
floating like smoke over the fields—
The brown bats in love with our streetlamps.

Droves of animals who mate and thrive
and swarm before our eyes only
to disappear when we dream
because they are too innocent
to survive.

Nominated by Vern Rutsala

WOMAN WHO WEEPS

by ELLEN BRYANT VOIGT

from THE ANTIOCH REVIEW

Up from the valley, ten children working the fields
and three in the ground, plus four who'd slipped like fish
from a faulty seine, she wept to the priest:
> Father, I saw the Virgin on a hill,
> she was a lion, lying on her side,
> grooming her blonde shoulders with her tongue.

Six months weeping as she hulled the corn,
gathered late fruit and milked the goats,
planted grain and watched the hillside blossom,
before she went to the Bishop, kissed his ring.
> Father, I saw Our Lady in a tree,
> swaddled in black, she was a raven,
> on one leg, on one bent claw
> she hunched in the tree but she *was* the tree,
> charred trunk in a thicket of green.

After seven years of weeping,
not as other stunned old women weep,
she baked flat bread, washed the cooking stones,
cut a staff from a sapling by the road.
The Holy Father sat in a gilded chair:
> Father, I saw Christ's Mother in a stream,
> she was a rock, the water
> parted on either side of her,
> from one stream she made two—

two tresses loosened across her collarbone—
until the pouring water met at her breast
and made a single stream again—

Then from the marketplace, from the busiest stall
she stole five ripened figs
and carried her weeping back to the countryside,
with a cloth sack, with a beggar's cup,
village to village and into the smoky huts,
her soul a well, an eye, an open door.

Nominated by Marianne Boruch, T. R. Hummer

NOSOTROS

fiction by JANET PEERY

from SHENANDOAH

IT WAS ALWAYS hot in the little house, her mother's house, even in December. Licha, lying on the floor, arms above her head and braced against the mirrored bedroom door, thought how cool it was here, in Madama's house where the big air conditioners hummed, pumping cold air through all the louvered vents in the spacious rooms. Madama's son Raleigh strained above her, drops of his sweat pooling on her breasts and belly like warm coins, his movements grinding her hips into the wool carpet until they stung, but it was cooler. Licha drew up her knees and curled her toes; even the carpet was cool, and she wondered how far down the coolness went.

All the houses in the Valley were slab houses, built on concrete. There were no basements; hurricanes came this far inland. Few peaked roofs: there was no snow here. Ever. Under the slab, Licha knew, and in the space between the walls, lived thousands of lizards: stripebacks, *chalotes*, green anoles. They came out to bask on the hot packed dirt around the foundation, to crawl up the screens. Madama hated them. If she saw too many she called the exterminators down from McAllen. Then Licha's mother Camarena was set to draping the furniture in sheeting, removing dishes, food and clothing from the house so the pesticide wouldn't contaminate Madama and Raleigh. When the exterminator's immense plastic tent was pulled from the house and all the lizard carcasses were shoveled into bushel baskets, her mother would come back in to give the house a thorough cleaning:

185

Pine-Sol the terrazzo, scrub the pecky cypress walls, shampoo the carpets. Then she would move everything back in, washing each dish and glass and fork in hot detergent water while Madama supervised, giving orders in her tight rough voice.

At the little house behind Madama's, her mother's house, lizards entered and departed through the gap between the screen door and the flagstone sill, unremarked. Geckos made their way around the walls, eating insects, spatulate toepads mocking gravity. But it was so hot there. Licha thought about the house she and Raleigh could have when she finished high school and moved from the Valley, a little college house with a peaked roof and an air conditioner in the window, a Boston fern hanging above the table, her biology texts and notes spread out beneath it.

"Squeeze your titties together," Raleigh said. "I want to see them that way."

She braced her feet against the floor and took her hands from the door. She tried to place them on the sides of her breasts, but his movements inched her too far up. "I can't. I'll hit my head."

Raleigh balanced on one arm, pushing his glasses farther up on his nose. She didn't understand how he could sweat so, when it was as cool in the room as it was in the stores downtown. The lenses of his glasses were fogged. She wondered why he wore them, what he saw as he watched, if he saw the two of them as a watery image, the edges of their bodies blurred and running together. She wondered what it was he wanted to see in the mirror, with his glasses. She looked up at him, under the rims, at his eyes, and their blue startled her. It was an uncommon color, she thought, a surprise of a color, a color she marveled the human body, with its browns and tans and pinks, could produce. She couldn't look at it long without imagining it was from another place—foreign, vaguely holy, like the blue of the Blessed Virgin's mantle at the church of San Benito; cool and infinite, like the blue of the sky when the heat lifted and the haze that sealed the Valley blew away in the wind of a norther. It was a blue like ice and snow.

It snowed sometimes in Austin, even in San Antonio. Where her brother Tavo had gone—to Fort Dix, New Jersey—it was probably snowing now, great fat flakes floating and floating, covering the barracks until they looked like rows of sugared cakes, and Tavo, inside with other soldiers, maybe some from other warm places, laughed from the surprise of it. As much as she hoped Tavo wouldn't have to go to Vietnam, she envied him his chance to be away, to open a window and draw the coolness in. She closed her eyes and imagined she could smell the snow. It must be sweet and powdery, she thought, like coconut. She looked again at Raleigh, his neck cords straining, watching in the mirror. "Have you ever seen snow?"

"Don't talk," he said. "I'm almost there." He clenched his jaw, and Licha knew her question had irritated him.

Raleigh went to school in Tennessee, to Vanderbilt. He was home for winter break. Madama had picked him up at the Brownsville airport, taking the yardman Perfilio along to drive the big car. She refused to drive the road alone. Raleigh's father, called Papa by everyone in the little towns along the highway, had been killed on this road, on an inspection tour of his groves. As he pulled out of the Donna off-ramp, he was struck by one of his own trucks, the driver drunk and running with no lights, a load of stolen television sets concealed by cotton bales in the truck bed. On the day of Raleigh's return Licha had seen Perfilio pull the car into the driveway, Raleigh and Madama in the back seat. When Perfilio piled Raleigh's red plaid luggage on the *porche* beside the tall white poinsettias, Licha thought they looked like Christmas packages from another country, from England or Scotland, not like they should belong to Raleigh, whom Licha and Tavo had grown up with, the three of them playing in the shell-flecked dirt around the roots of the live oaks in the backyard, none of them wearing a shirt, Raleigh's hair bleached almost white with the sun, tanned until he was nearly as brown as Licha and Tavo.

Licha was nine when she overheard Madama's order: the children were not to play together any longer. Madama stood by the laundry shed, her mother at the clothesline. "Camarena," she said, "that girl of yours isn't mine to boss, but she's about to bust out of herself."

Her mother pretended she didn't understand Madama's English, and it irritated Licha; her mother smiling, nodding, an impassive, half-comprehending look in her eyes, wiping her hands on a dish towel or patting little balls of dough into flat round tortillas: pat-pat-pat, smile, nod, shuffle around the big *cocina* in her starched blue work dress and apron, her backless sandals.

187

She had lived in the little house eleven years, since Licha was five, but still she pretended she didn't understand, or understood only dimly, forcing Madama into a fractured mixture of languages: "Camarena, *deja* all that laundry *sucio en el* whatchamacallit."

Licha and Tavo had laughed about it, about their mother getting the best of bossy Madama in such a sly, funny way, but it made Licha angry that her mother could let Madama think she was stupid; her mother understood everything Madama said. After Madama's bridge-club meetings she entertained Tavo and Licha with stories and imitations until they collapsed on their beds in the little house, wrung out from laughing at the dressed-up stupidity of Madama and her henna-rinsed friends. On the day of Madama's order, she had pretended not to understand, but she complied, keeping Tavo and Licha from Raleigh. Licha remembered how unfair it seemed, and that Madama saw it as her fault: *that girl.*

"Hurry, Raleigh," she said. "They'll be back."

"Maybe if you did something more than lie there," he said. "Move a little."

She tried moving her hips in a small circle. She wasn't sure if it was the right way, the way he expected or was used to, or if there was a right way. Their first time, two days before, when they stood behind the closed door of Raleigh's bedroom, she hadn't had to move at all, and it had been over sooner. Madama and her mother had gone to the grocery store. Raleigh came around the side of the big house to the clothesline where Licha was hanging towels. He held a radio to her ear, as though the years they spent avoiding each other had been no more than a few weeks. She heard a raspy female voice.

"Janis Joplin," he said. "Great, isn't she?"

He lowered the radio when Licha nodded. "Bobby McGee," she said. "I heard it at school."

Raleigh looked the same as he had in high school, when Licha would see him in the halls or at a football game, surrounded by other boys in the same kind of clothing: madras shirts, wheat jeans, loafers they wore without socks. They dressed as if they were already in college, and everyone knew it was where they would end up. The other Anglo boys—those who would stay in the Valley to work and marry, to hunt whitewing dove in the fall, *javelinas* and coyote the rest of the year—wore blue jeans and white T-shirts. Raleigh's hair was still cut in Beatle bangs, but he had grown sideburns, the earpieces of his new wire-rim glasses cutting into them. "Are you at Consolidated?" he asked.

She looked at him, trying to decide if he was joking. She reached for a clothespin to clip the corner of a towel over the line. He should know she wouldn't be at Blessed Sacrament; she was the daughter of a maid, and the public high school was her only choice. When she nodded, he asked her what she was taking.

She wanted to tell him about the frog dissection they had done the week before in biology, how she had cut into the pale, pearlescent belly to expose the first layer of organs, the ventral abdominal vein like a tiny, delicately branching river, the torsion of the small intestine giving way to the bulk of the large intestine and how both of them, when held aside, revealed the deeper viscera, the long posterior vena cava, the testes, kidneys and adrenal bodies; how the heart and lungs lay over the perfect fork of the aortic arch; how surprisingly large the liver was, its curves, its fluted edges, and how she could hardly catch her breath, not because of the formaldehyde or out of revulsion, like some of the other students, but from awe, for joy at the synchrony and mystery of the workings of the body laid out before her, its legs splayed on the cutting table, the fragile mandible upturned and yielding to her touch. She wanted to tell him how she felt as her probe and scalpel moved through the frog's body, about the sacred, almost heartbreaking invitation of it, but she couldn't. "I'm taking biology," she said.

"Does Mohesky still teach it?"

She nodded. "I really like him." She became aware of Raleigh looking at her breasts, and when she stooped to pick up another towel from the basket she checked the buttons of her blouse. She hoped he didn't notice the downward glance that meant she knew he was looking at her.

"Come in the house a minute," he said. "I want to show you something."

When they were just inside his bedroom he closed the door, telling her how beautiful she was, how sweet. She was all he thought about his first semester away at school. Her breasts were beautiful; titties, he called them, and he'd bet they'd grown— would she show him? She was surprised to feel her nipple tighten when he took it into his mouth, the whole breast seem to swell

189

around it. He lifted her skirt and eased his fingers past her panties until the middle one was inside her. "You know all about it," he said. He unzipped his pants.

"It hurts," she said, and he stopped moving his fingers. "A little."

"You don't act like it," he said. He slid his fingers out and guided himself into her, knees bent, his hand pressing against her hip.

"That doesn't mean it doesn't."

"You like it, though." It wasn't a question, and Licha didn't bother to answer. She did like it. She liked it that he wanted her. She liked the push of it, the tip of him pushing past the part of her that felt like a small, rugate tunnel into a bigger part that had less feeling, more like a liquid cave that seemed to swallow him. She worried that she was too big. Anglo boys said Mexican girls were built for breeding. She wondered if Raleigh was small. She had seen other men; several times she had surprised Tavo, and she had seen *braceros* relieving themselves in the groves after *siesta*. She hadn't looked closely, but it seemed that most of these were more substantial, their color fuller, more nearly like the rest of their skin. Raleigh's was the color of sunburn, almost purple at the tip.

When it was over he had gone into the bathroom. She heard the tap running, a flush. She cleaned herself with her panties, not wanting to use the lacquered box of tissues beside Raleigh's bed. She noticed only a slight pink tinge, no more blood than from a paper cut. She tucked the panties into the waistband of her skirt and pulled down her blouse to conceal them.

Now, two days later, he had come up behind her as she emptied trash from the little house onto the burn pile at the back of the property. "*Nalgas*," he said, patting her bottom. She laughed at the *pachuco* word for buttocks, at the growling, mock-salacious way he said it, the furtive waggle of his eyebrows behind his glasses, and she had gone with him again to the big house, this time to Madama's bedroom where he locked the door and showed her the full-length mirror behind it. Facing it, with Raleigh behind her, Licha watched his hands, nervous and more intent this time, move up her body, the tips of his fingers tapered, almost delicate, nails bitten to the quick. She could see ragged cuticles and dark flecks of dried blood as his fingers

190

worked at buttons, at the elastic of her shorts. He pressed himself closer, sweating already, his breathing shallow and uneven, and when they were on the floor, Licha on her hands and knees, Raleigh upright, kneeling behind her, she looked at their image in the mirror, at Raleigh watching, his head thrown back and arms extended so his hands grasped her hips, his movements regular and insistent. She thought of the mice they had mated in biology lab, of the male, a solid black, his motions powerful and concentrated in mount, of the female, a pink-eyed white, hunched and holding her ground to help him, her neck at an angle of submission, and she knew they were more alike than different, the mating mice, herself and Raleigh; that this impulse shot through all of life, through male and female, and made them do the things they did, made men and women lie down together. We are mating, she marveled.

He seemed to go deeper this time, deeper than when they stood against his bedroom wall. She felt her belly swell from him, a soft, cramping fullness like her menstrual cycle, pleasant at first, then almost painful. She asked him to stop, and he had waited while she turned over to face him, her arms braced against the door. Then he had continued. Again she tried to hold her breasts for him and to move her hips at the same time. "You have to take it out," she said. "Before." She had forgotten to tell him the first time.

He said nothing, concentrating on their image in the mirror. Finally he moaned, withdrawing, and Licha felt slow, warm spurts against her thigh. She squirmed beneath his weight, and when he rolled over she got up. "We'll leave a spot."

She went into the bathroom, looking for a cloth for the carpet. She didn't want to use the pale yellow towels folded in a complicated way across the bar, so she tore a length of paper, setting the roller spinning, and hurried to dab at the wetness where they had lain. The paper pilled and shed, leaving lint on the close shear of the wool. She tried to pick it off with her fingers, but it stuck here, too. Raleigh laughed and got up to go to the bathroom. "Don't worry so much," he said. He closed the door. "Camarena will get it."

His mention of her mother startled Licha; she and Madama would be back soon from McAllen. She dressed quickly, tucking the wad of paper into her pocket. She was halfway down the

191

galería to the stairs when she heard the bathroom door click open and Raleigh call out, but she didn't want to risk the time to answer.

The little house felt hot and close after the expanse of the big rooms. Even before she opened the door she smelled the heat inside, the dust, warm *cominos* simmering into the beans in the big cast-iron *olla* on the hot plate. As she crossed the room to her bed she compared what she had seen upstairs in the big house with her mother's attempts to brighten things: a scattering of secondhand bathroom rugs across the dull linoleum, knickknacks cast off from Madama, paper flowers at the single window. Licha's bed was the lower bunk of a government-issue set, curtained with a sheet tucked under the mattress of Tavo's top bunk where boxes of clothing and household things were stored now that Tavo had gone. The beds were white, but the paint had chipped, exposing leopard-spots of army green. At the head and foot the letters US were carved into the wood. When Licha was learning to read, she thought the letters meant herself and Tavo; us, *nosotros,* and she felt special, good, tracing the letters with her fingers, with a purple crayon, lucky: no one else had a bed that told of herself and her brother, of their place in the world. She didn't want to believe Tavo when he laughed and told her what the letters stood for. Her mother slept on a daybed in the opposite corner, behind a partition made of crates and a blue shower curtain with a picture of an egret wading among green rushes. Licha lifted her sheet curtain and lay down, letting the heat and dimness envelop her.

She heard the car pull into the driveway, the sound of its doors closing and Madama's voice telling Perfilio to wash the car. She heard the slap of her mother's sandals on the flagstone path, coming toward the little house. She wished she had washed; the girls at school said other people could tell by your smell if you had been with a boy. In the stuffiness of the room her mother would notice it. She lay still and hoped her mother would think she was asleep.

Through the thin sheet Licha saw her come in, silhouetted in the light streaming through the doorway. She could see well enough to tell her mother still wore her apron. Madama insisted on it, especially when they went to town. Licha watched as she took it off and folded it over a wooden chair, then began taking dishes and pots and pans from the crates stacked to form shelves, wisps of hair springing from the bun at the back of her neck.

She tried to remember how her mother looked when her skin wasn't glistening with sweat, when her hair wasn't escaping from the bun: Saturday before church, sometimes for whole days in winter if a norther came in and work at the house was light. Even through the screen of the sheet Licha could see the patches of darker blue under her mother's arms, around her waist, between her shoulder blades. They were as much a part of her mother as the starched workdress, as the apron, as the low song she sang while she worked, a song that irritated Licha for its persistence, its quality of being a song yet not a song, more a droning, melodic murmur made low in the throat that had the power to remove her mother, lift her beyond Licha's reach and back into the time before Licha, a song from her mother's earlier life in the *barrancas* of the East Sierra Madre, the place she had left to come here, first to work for Papa in the fields, then for Madama in the house, a place she never talked about.

When Tavo and Licha asked about it she said little. All they knew was that Papa had found her walking along the road, fifteen, pregnant with Tavo, on one of his trips below the border to find workers. He didn't like the migrant teams, preferring whole families who wanted to come across, to live in the block houses at the bend in the levee until they found something better, or even asked about something better, and then he would help them, with papers, by getting their children into school, with medicine and food. Her mother had been alone on the road, in the last months of pregnancy, but Papa had idled the truck alongside her, asking questions in Spanish, inviting her to join the families in the truck bed. Tavo had been born in the block house by the levee. Licha was born three years later. Her father was a *Latino* from Las Cruces working a few months with the Army Corps of Engineers on an irrigation project before he moved on. This was all she knew. She and Tavo had stopped asking; their mother didn't welcome questions about the other life.

A stack of Melmac plates clattered to the floor, causing Licha to jump. Her mother stooped to pick them up, her eyes on Licha's curtain. *"¿Estás aquí?"*

Licha swung her legs over the edge of the bed. "I'm here, Mama." She made it a practice to answer her mother's Spanish with English, as though she were talking to a toddler just learning the words for things. "What are you doing?"

Her mother ignored her and continued picking up the scattered plates. Licha sighed and repeated the question in Spanish. Her mother was stubborn enough to ignore the question all day if it was a matter of will.

Her mother smiled at her, setting the stack of plates on the wooden table. She told Licha she and Madama had gone to an appliance store in McAllen. She described the shining rows of silver and white, and a new color for stoves and refrigerators called avocado green. They had picked out a new stove for the *cocina* in the big house. It was to be delivered tomorrow. And guess who, as a gift for Christmas, was to have the old one? Licha smiled in spite of herself. "We are!"

Her mother crossed the room and stood behind the big chair next to the window. "*Ayudame, chica.*"

Licha helped her move the chair. They placed it at an angle by Licha's bed, then lifted the table from the corner where the new stove would go. They put it by the window. While her mother dusted the tabletop, Licha went outside to get one of the potted aloes that lined the step. She arranged it in the center of the table.

"*Mira*, Mama," she said, gesturing grandly toward the plant. "*Better Homes and Gardens.*" They laughed, and Licha felt good, good and happy, like Licha-nine-years-old, Licha-of-no-secrets, her mother's *chula niña* in a ruffled skirt and braids stretched tight for church. She watched her mother poke the broom into the cleared corner and shoo a lizard along the baseboard toward the door, her throaty song rising in the heat, happy with so little, and suddenly she was angry.

"A stove," she said. "An old stove. How much did the new one cost?"

Her mother continued sweeping, the hem of her work dress swaying stiffly with the motions of the broom. "*No importa.*"

She felt like grabbing the broom away and forcing her mother to listen. "We don't need a stove. Let her sell the old one and give us the money. Let her buy us an air conditioner. She has enough. She has everything." She thought of nights in the little

194

house, trying to sleep with only the old black fan to cool her, its woven cord stretched from chair to chair, tripping her if she got up to get a drink of water, the frayed fabric encasing it reticulated like the backs of the water snakes she sometimes saw in the arroyo. "It will only make it hotter in this place!" She pushed against the screen door hard enough to wedge the flimsy frame against the bump on the far edge of the step and walked out.

She cut through the live oaks, through the rows of oleander set out like railroad tracks to shield the little house from view, around to the back of the property to the overgrown area she and Tavo and Raleigh had called the jungle when they were little. It was mostly scrub pecan choked with ololiuque vines, avocado trees, crotons and yucca, but a few banana and papaya trees survived, making it seem exotic and lush. Saw palmetto slashed her legs as she ran past the boundaries. She looked down to see the thin lines like razor cuts across her thighs. She darted through the algarroba thicket and came out on the other side, to Grand Texas Boulevard. A fine name, she thought, for the rutted road that led to the highway toward Reynosa.

She slowed down, thinking about what had just happened, thinking that she now knew what made people run away. It wasn't a simple matter of not liking home, it was far more complicated than that, and at the point when things became too complicated to even think about any longer, people ran away. For whatever reasons they had that were too entwined to sort out. She imagined her mother, a pregnant girl from the *barrancas*, walking along a road, and she imagined a man in a truck, a man in khaki workpants and a Panama hat, a smiling, red-mustached man. She would have climbed inside the truck bed, too. She saw herself riding away from the Valley to a different place, any place, maybe a place with snow. To Fort Dix where Tavo was, a soldier in uniform, able to be what he was without people thinking they *knew* what he was just by looking at him, by knowing where he came from, where there was more to get excited about than avocado appliances, where he made his own money and didn't have to depend on a bossy old woman like Madama, where he didn't have to care what such a woman thought of anything he did. Tavo would understand how she felt. He had been glad to leave the Valley.

She picked up a stone and threw it at an irrigation pump. She knew what Tavo would think of what she and Raleigh did. He would spit, and make the jerking, upward jab with his wrist, like stabbing. He would stab Raleigh if he knew. He wouldn't see that Raleigh wasn't like the others; he was more like Papa. Tavo would see only his side of it, the *pachuco* side that hated all Anglos. He wouldn't see that it was different with Raleigh, that they were what they were, male and female, Licha and Raleigh. He wanted her, he found her beautiful. The feeling made her stomach tighten as she walked along, slower now. She held her shoulders straighter and began to sway her hips the way she had seen other girls do, feeling the heads of her femurs articulating deep in her pelvis. She knew now why those girls walked like this: a man wanted them.

She stopped to watch the sun go down behind a grove of Valencias. The heavy fruit hung full and brilliant, orange as the sun, as the bright new tennis balls Madama kept in canisters on the laundry-shed shelf. She heard the big trucks start up, loading *braceros* for the trip back to the *colonia*. Traffic on the highway quickened and Licha turned to go home, the trucks rumbling by. When she heard the clicking noises the men made, their high-pitched yips of appreciation, she toned down her walk, but she thought: let them look, let them want.

He didn't come for her the next day, or the next, though she made many trips between the house and the laundry shed, the laundry shed and the burn pile, watching the back door of the big house. She began to think she had been a fool, that Tavo's version of the way things were with Anglo boys and Mexican girls might be right. She could hardly bear her mother's excitement about the stove, and she snapped at her to stop polishing it so often—she'd polished it every day for eleven years—to speak English, to pick up her feet when she walked and stop shuffling around like a cow. Her mother stared at her when she said this, and Licha had seen her face close down.

On Saturday Perfilio brought two chickens and her mother baked them, filling the house with a rich yellow smell that made Licha queasy. She couldn't touch the chicken and she didn't go with her mother to church. She knew it was far too early, improbable, given the dates of her cycle, but she began to worry beyond reason that she was pregnant.

196

At sundown Saturday a norther blew in, rattling the rickety door and filling the house with random pockets of cold air. Licha pulled a sweater from the box under her bed and put it on. She slid the shutter panel across the window and shut the heavy storm door. She sat at the table in the dark, not bothering to pull the string on the overhead light. When the first knock came she thought it was the wind, but it kept up and finally she opened the door.

Raleigh wore a zippered red windbreaker and his hair blew up behind his head like a rooster's tail. He was smiling. "Did you miss me?"

She wanted to slap his glasses away so they skittered across the flagstone into the potted plants and he would never find them. She wanted to tear off her blouse and sweater and show him her breasts, press them into his chest so hard they burned him. "No," she said.

"You're mad at me." He tried to look around her to see inside the house. "Can I come in?"

She looked behind her into the dark room, at the silly rugs and the shower curtain and the stove in its corner like a squat white ghost. "I'll come out.

They walked around the house to the jungle, Licha with her arms folded across her chest, her hands tucked into the sweater sleeves, Raleigh with his hands jammed into the pockets of his windbreaker, neither of them speaking. Licha sat on the rim of a discarded tractor tire where Tavo had once found a coral snake. She shivered, glad it was too cold for snakes. Raleigh sat beside her, quiet. He bent to flick an oleander leaf from the toe of his loafer.

Alarm surged through her. He had found someone else, she wasn't good enough. Madama had found out. She wanted Licha gone—that girl, her mother, gone.

"I'm busted at Vanderbilt," he said. He looked at her. "Kicked out."

Licha hoped she kept a straight face, kept from smiling: this is *all?*

"Mother's been hauling me all over south Texas for the last two days, throwing her weight around." He laughed, but Licha could tell he didn't think it was funny. "She thinks she can get me into

197

San Marcos or Pan American. They're piss-poor schools, but I guess it's better than getting drafted." He laughed again.

Licha waited to see if he had anything else to say, but he was quiet, drumming his knuckles on the thick black tread of the tire. "Maybe it's not so bad," she said. She thought about telling him what Mr. Mohesky had told her—that if she continued to work hard he would help her apply for a scholarship to San Marcos—but she didn't.

He shrugged, then pulled a jeweler's box from his pocket. "Anyway, I got you these." He handed her the box. "For Christmas."

"Not yet," she said.

"You don't want it?"

"I mean, it's not Christmas yet." She held the box, stroking the nap of the black velveteen.

"Soon enough," he said. "Open it."

Inside was a pair of earrings, tiny gold chains with filigree hummingbirds at the ends, red stones for each eye. In the moonlight she could make out the store name on the inner lid: Didde's of San Marcos. She imagined him on the streets of the college town, going into the jewelry store while Madama waited in the car, poring over hundreds of boxes until he chose these, for her. "Thank you," she said, and when he stood and held his hand for her she went with him through the jungle to the laundry shed. He waited while she removed the silver hoops she wore, then he inserted the posts of the new earrings into her lobes. She tilted her head to each side to help him, and she was reminded of the female mouse. The thought came to her that staying still was just as powerful an act as moving, just as necessary, and she again felt linked to the everlasting, perfect cycle of things.

They made love on the floor of the laundry shed, her hips lifted, supported by a pile of towels. They were damp against her skin and smelled of Lifebuoy soap and Clorox. Her carotid artery throbbed from the rush of blood to her head, but she didn't complain, and she didn't tell him to withdraw. She wanted to give him this, a sign of trust, of utter welcome. It would be all right, no matter what. What they were doing, this act, was a promise of that, a pact. She felt the earrings slide back and forth against her neck.

She made it back to the little house and into bed before her mother returned from church, and when she woke up Sunday morning, the first things she felt were the hummingbird earrings. She thought of Raleigh. Was he waking up just now in his room in the big house, remembering what they had done? She moved her hands down her body to the warm pocket between her legs and wondered how she felt to him. How could they ever know, male and female, what each felt like to the other? She heard her mother stirring and she sat up to part the curtain. Her mother was tying her apron on over her work dress.

"¿Café?"

"Coffee," Licha repeated automatically. Sunday mornings they usually sat at the table drinking coffee. It was her mother's day off. "Why are you wearing that?"

There was no answer. Licha sighed, repeating the question in Spanish. Her mother explained that Madama needed her to help with a party. She had to clean, prepare food, set things up. She would come home in the middle of the afternoon to rest, then she would go back in the evening to serve.

"On Sunday?" Licha pulled out a chair and sat down at the table, pouring coffee into a Melmac cup, adding sugar.

Her mother shrugged, and the helpless gesture irritated Licha.

"Why didn't you tell her no? You always do everything she says. 'Sí, Madama, no, Madama, ¿algo más, Madama?'" She rose from her chair and went to the small refrigerator for the milk.

Her mother stood at the sink, calmly tucking wisps of hair into her bun with bobby pins, her back to Lichà, saying nothing. Licha thought she may as well have been talking to the stove, for all the effect it had. Even her mother's back looked obstinate, her hips wide and stolid, square and stupid, the apron bow at her back as ridiculous as the daisy garland around the ear of the cow on the milk carton she took from its shelf. She stirred the milk into her coffee and looked at the older woman. She knew her mother's life would always be the same, shuffling back and forth between houses, going to church, easing her knees and elbows with salve she made from Vaseline and aloe, waiting on others, obsequious, stubborn in her obsequiousness, forcing Madama into pidgin silliness, and all of it because of stubbornness, because she wanted nothing more, because she thought no further

199

than the day after tomorrow. Licha banged her cup onto the table, sloshing coffee over the edge and onto her cotton shift. "Why didn't you get papers when Papa offered? You could get a better job."

Her mother turned, and Licha saw her face, hurt, defiant.

"You could *learn* to read, Mama." She felt suddenly defeated; there was nothing she could do. "It's your only day off," she said weakly.

She watched her mother rinse her own cup and dry it; she took it with her to work because Madama believed disease was spread by sharing dishes with the help. She left the house, closing the screen door gently, leaving Licha alone at the table sipping coffee she could barely swallow for her welling sense of injustice. Licha got up and ran after her mother, catching up with her along the flagstone path. "Don't do it, Mama. Say no. Say it for once in your life. Show her what you think of her."

Her mother shook her head. "I think nothing. I only work." She resumed her walk.

"You work for nothing. For a house too little and too hot. For a stove!" She grabbed her mother's arm and shook it. Her mother looked away, across the yard toward the laundry shed.

"*Dejame en paz.*"

"English, Mama, your English is good. Use it. Make her *see* you!"

Her mother looked at her hard, and Licha felt suddenly exposed in her cotton shift, as though she was standing naked on the path. Her mother shook off Licha's hand. "No."

Perfilio came around the corner of the house with a wheelbarrow full of sand and a box of candles. He began placing the *luminarias* around the patio. Licha stood still, watching her mother walk toward the service entrance. Her mother had almost reached the door when she whirled, throwing her coffee cup to the ground. She started back down the path toward Licha, her face dark and angry. She reached out and with a violent flick at Licha's ear set one earring spinning wildly. "*Éstos son de Madama!*"

Licha's hand flew to her ear, to the sting. She was dumbfounded by her mother's anger until she realized she thought Licha had stolen the earrings from the big house. "They are mine," she said, proud that they were, glad her mother was wrong. "Raleigh gave them to me."

Her mother's eyes widened. Licha watched as she took in the information, as she looked at her daughter for clues. She felt her mother's eyes on her body, looking through the thin shift at her breasts which seemed in that moment huge and bobbing, giving away her secret. Her mother slapped her.

"Fool!" She slapped her again and Licha reeled. "It is worse!"

Licha ran to the little house, to her bed, where she cried until her eyes were red and swollen and her throat was raw. She got up to dress. Her hands felt limp as she pulled her skirt up over her hips. She didn't want to be home when her mother returned for her nap, but she didn't know where to go. She didn't want to go for a walk, and the few girls at school she could call her friends were just that, school friends; they rarely saw each other outside, and if they did they only teased Licha about studying so hard and taking everything so seriously. When she opened the refrigerator to look for something to eat she realized it was Raleigh she wanted to talk to. She sat at the table most of the afternoon, pushing cold rice around her plate with the tines of a fork, watching the activity at the big house, Perfilio arranging the *luminarias*, raking palm trash from the drive, pulling the car around. When she saw her mother come out the service entrance, she left the house and hurried to the laundry shed.

The pile of towels was still on the floor, flattened slightly from the weight of her body and Raleigh's. She fluffed them up with her foot to make them look more natural. She looked out the window to see her mother going into their house, then she took a tennis ball from the shelf. She planned to stand behind the poinsettia bush outside Raleigh's window and throw the ball against the screen.

Her first throw fell short of the window, and her second, thumping against the wire mesh, was louder than she imagined it would be. The ball bounced into a plot of white azaleas. Its presence there looked miraculous and unreal, like one fully ripened orange in a grove of trees still in blossom. Licha thought of leaving it there and giving up, but she wanted to see Raleigh. As she crossed the front yard to retrieve the ball, she heard the heavy, carved door swing open on its wrought-iron hinges.

201

Raleigh stood on the *porche*, the fingers of his right hand kneading his left bicep, the blue stone in his class ring glinting in the sun. He stepped from the *porche* and walked toward her. His face looked fuller, younger, somehow; he had shaved his sideburns. She remembered her mother's slap. She couldn't make herself meet his eyes.

"What's the matter?"

She still couldn't look at him. "My mother knows," she said. She felt bad and stupid, as though she alone was responsible for what they had done. It was her fault her mother knew. "I'm sorry." She hoped he would tell her it was all right, that he didn't care, that he was glad: now they could be together.

He laughed. "Is that all?"

She looked at him, relieved beyond words.

"It's not like she hasn't done the same thing," he said. "She's been around the block."

She was puzzled. "What?"

He waved his hand, dismissing it. "It was a long time ago." He winked at her. "You know. When we were kids."

Licha never thought of her mother in that way. Her mother was just what she was—aproned, blue-dressed, patting tortillas, sweeping: working. She started to ask him what he meant, but all of a sudden she knew. She remembered when they had first come to live in the little house, her mother—younger, thinner— had sat on the floor with them, showing them how to cut circles of colored paper and twist them into the shapes of bougainvillea, oleander, the blue trumpets of jacaranda, her hair loose and fragrant from the Castile shampoo she kept on the shelf above the sink. Laughing, she had tucked one of Licha's flowers behind her ear, and in the hollow of her throat a small vein pulsed. Licha had reached up to place her fingers on it, moved to joy, to longing at the happy mystery of her mother's beauty. Her mother had scooped her up and hugged her with a strength that surprised her. In the hot still nights after she and Tavo were in bed, her mother would leave the house. Just for a walk, she said, just to cool off. Licha would try to stay awake until she came back in, but the hum of the fan would always put her to sleep. In the morning her mother would be at the sink, running water for coffee, draining the soak water from the beans, and Licha would forget. But it was Papa who brought the fan, Papa with the red mustache that fascinated her, taking off his Panama before he entered the little house, patting the top of her head, "*Qué chula niña.*" Papa who brought the beds.

"Come inside," Raleigh said. "You can see the preparations for Mother's big to-do." From his tone Licha could tell what he thought of Madama's party, but she hesitated.

"She's not here. She's at the club getting a bag on."

She followed him into the house. As they passed through the big hall she caught a glimpse of the *sala* with the grand Spanish windows she had seen only from the outside. At the far end of the room stood an enormous fir, its branches flocked with white, shimmering with gold and silver birds. She thought of the plastic Santas she and her mother would hang on the potted Norfolk pine they brought in from its place among the other plants that rimmed the little house, the red suits nearly pink from sun and age, the white of the beards and fur trim gone yellow.

"She's got it all decked out," he said, starting up the stairs to the *galería.* Licha followed him. She nodded though she knew he couldn't see her. When they were inside his bedroom he locked the door and took a mirror from the wall. He propped it on the floor against the bed. He fingered one of her earrings. "Beautiful," he said.

She pushed his hand away, but then stood still, her arms lifted as he pulled her blouse over her head. He kissed her, unhooking her bra. She felt her nipples draw and tighten. "My mother isn't what you think," she said. The words surprised her; she felt her knees weaken, almost buckle.

He eased himself down and took her nipple in his mouth, but she drew it back. "She speaks English. She only pretends she doesn't so your mother will look like a fool." She felt the beating of her heart, shuddering and rapid, almost hot, astonishing as sudden anger.

He laughed, nuzzling her, pulling at the elastic of her skirt. "I know," he said. "It's been a joke for years. I used to spy on Mother's bridge club just to hear her do the Camarena imitation."

Licha stared at him as he unbuckled his belt and stepped out of his jeans. "Lie down, *chula.*" His hands on her shoulders, he pressed her down with him until they were kneeling beside the mirror. She looked at him, at the dark triangle of pubic escutcheon against his pale skin, at his penis rising, then to the mirror where she saw the flexion at the side of his buttock where the gluteus inserted, where she saw herself, smaller, a fool looking up at him, a fool somehow more beautifully made, browner, smoother, more round. She tried to meet his eyes, fixed on his own, but couldn't, and she had the feeling each of them was seeing something different in the framed rectangle, like two people looking at the same slide under a microscope, trying to adjust the focus to accommodate both their visions, failing. She removed his hands from her shoulders and stood up, gathering her clothes. "I have to go," she said.

She walked out into the early dark of December. Light shone from the little house, and as she got closer she saw her mother's form moving back and forth against it. Licha knew she would be eating her supper, standing over the *olla* eating beans rolled into a flour tortilla, alternating beans with bites of pepper, waiting to go back to work. She looked up when Licha entered, but didn't meet her eyes.

"Café," she said, gesturing toward the pot on the stove. Licha saw that the light came from behind the pot, from a small bulb under the hood of the stove that cast the shadows of the *olla* and the coffee pot onto the floor. She sat down at the table. Her mother took cups from their hooks, poured them full and placed them on the table. She sat down across from Licha, and Licha looked at her, at the crease from her nap across the smooth brown of her cheek, her hair freshly brushed and fastened back, in her eyes the sleepy distance of the saints, the prophets. Her mother lifted the lid of the sugar bowl. "*¿Azúcar?*"

Licha nodded. Her mother spooned the sugar into their cups. They were small things—not objecting to her Spanish, letting her mother serve her—but Licha could tell they pleased her. The low song began in her throat, obscuring for a while the faint metallic buzz of the stove light rattling under its enameled hood. Then it trailed away. They sat for a long time at the table, speechless, beyond apology. Even the presence of a small green anole emerging from behind the stove to skitter across the top and bask briefly in the harsh white glare, the ruby throat it expanded when threatened now a flaccid sac, was not enough to disturb the silence between them. When her mother scraped her chair back on the linoleum and left for work Licha sat for a long time afterward, drained and still, stunned by the complex living heart of grace.

Nominated by Shenandoah

BOOKS OFT HAVE SUCH A CHARM: A MEMORY

By WILLIAM J. SCHEICK

from THE NORTH DAKOTA QUARTERLY

> *All that mankind has done, thought, gained or been: it is lying as in magic preservation in the pages of books.* —Thomas Carlyle

IT WAS JUNE, 1953, the summer I would turn 12, and my mother had given me an order. A short, somewhat roundish woman, my mother was raised in an orphanage, but somehow she had instinctively found her heritage as an Italian mother without having benefited from a parental model. It was not just particularly the tone of her commands that was so Italian, but especially the hand gestures, in this case a pointed finger, signing forth the meaning of her spoken words. I especially needed signs to accompany words, it seemed. I was a wretched failure when it came to language, whether written (which I could not read or spell) or spoken (which I apparently did not hear). My abysmal ineptitude with language was something which my elementary school teachers knew to distraction, which I knew to my silent utter despair, and which my mother knew too but refused to accept. I pretty much sensed the meaning of a few words, such expressions as *der Dummkopf* (blockhead) and *der Dummerjan* (simpleton), spoken without hand signs by my German father and his brother, my favorite uncle. But the words fundamentally troubling me were in English, a language I could not master even though I had always lived in the United States.

So that June my mother gave me a verbal order, which she also signed with her hand: I was to walk to the public library, eighteen blocks away, and borrow at least one book for the summer.

206

This was not a desperate decision on her part, a final attempt to break through what others considered to be my obstinacy. Rather, it was the arbitrary addition of one more weapon to her arsenal for her campaign to defeat whatever it was that accounted for her son's bizarre problem. (Heaven forbid that it might be something congenital.) Combating my inability to read, she was worrying herself to heaven, and nothing could defeat her faith, particularly the belief that some magical combination of tactics would exorcise her son of the demon of perversity. Concerning her frail son, she did not share the conclusion of dying, battle-weary Talbot in Schiller's *Die Jungrau von Orleans:* that "Mit der Dummheit kämpfen Götter selbst vergebens" (the gods themselves contend in vain against stupidity). "Don't worry, you will read," she would say. It was a promise, and it was a command.

I wanted to believe too. But I could not. Day after horrible day since the age of five I had been on the frontlines of the Sisters of Notre Dame. I was miserably entrenched there, as traumatized as were some combat soldiers in the Korean War, which would end that summer. I had my orders, I was laden with equipment, I was informed of my higher mission; nevertheless, as knowledge burst open in language all around me, all I could do was duck for cover into dreams of escape to vernal pastures, to another possible existence, if not on this planet, then on another. So I went through the paces, if not a good soldier, a dutiful one who now and then took painful strafing silently.

Such rote training brought me to the library that summer day. I had been there before—it was a converted automobile service station—but I did not know my way around the stark building very well. Soon, however, I found my way into the "Children's Room." Like the soldier who quickly learns the importance of appearances, I tried to give an impression of knowing what I was doing, and so I merely entered an aisle at random. I sat down on the floor of that aisle and pretended to look through some books on a bottom shelf. The spines of most of these books were so skinny that they bore no titles—not that I could have read the titles had they been there. I pulled a few books off the shelf with the intention of letting them sit next to me on the floor while I evasively feigned a knowing perusal of them.

The cover of the topmost book of that small pile caught my eye. It presented a picture of a beagle. My attraction to this picture at that time, well before Snoopy made beagles popular, was embedded in a personal memory. I had recently had a beagle for a friend, for about six months or so. It was the first and only animal companion I ever had as a child. He was my secret sharer, but in the five-room flat in which we lived he did not work out for my family. He was trouble for my mother when he broke free of restraints, expensive for my father when he was hungry, terrifying to my sister when he barked; and he sneaked into my bed at night to sleep by my side, which was *Verboten.* One morning I awoke, and he was gone, given away to someone who had the space, the time, the money, and the energy to care for him. I was sure, in my sadness, that he was running with wagging tail through the very fields where I always wished to be, away from the mind-numbing cement shards of Newark, New Jersey, away from the relentless terrors of school, and away from the alienating disappointment in myself. I never forgot my beagle, a fellow silent chaser of dreams who was to me much more than a symbol of country freedom.

There on that book's cover was a beagle which looked, to my child's eye, identical to my dog. I touched that book, picked it up, and placed it on my lap. I ran my fingers over the picture of the dog on the cover, as if it might have fur or might respond to my touch. My eyes ran across the title, *Amos, The Beagle with a Plan.* Without realizing it, I had read the title. I had read it with some trouble that I somehow had hardly noticed. Without opening the book, I borrowed it from the library for the entire summer, and brought it home to an approving mother. This was a book, I was sure, that could be judged on the basis of its cover.

I do not recall how long I waited before undertaking what I knew would be the arduous task of beginning this book. Never before in my life had I wanted to read a book. Reading was for me a frustrating encounter with the inexplicable because for me language was dauntlessly unpredictable. Certain combinations of letters could not be relied upon to sound the same way in any given situation, a problem worsened by the fact that in my school intensive phonics had been displaced by the look-and-say method. When I closed my eyes (as instructed) to picture a word in my mind, I saw nothing at all; and if I kept my eyes shut long enough, I imagined myself and my dog running over green fields. This method, we now know (though little is done about it), fails frequently with boys generally. And in my case, the deficit of not having any inner picture of words and of not fathoming the various patterns whereby similar combinations of letters have different pronunciations was compounded by another problem: a curious tendency on the part of my eye and mind to scramble letters in words, making these words utterly chaotic and unrecognizable.

The last problem is today considered a symptom of dyslexia, a disability totally unknown as such in the 1940s and 1950s. The victim of dyslexia typically confuses the orientation of letters. He or she may reverse the left-to-right direction of eye movement when reading, may transpose words in a sentence and letters in a word, may fail to see (and sometimes to hear) similarities or differences in letters or words, and may be unable to work out the pronunciation of unfamiliar words. I knew these dreadful patterns firsthand from years in the trenches of elementary school. That there might be a group of children who shared my condition and that my problem might not be my fault were unknown to me in my lonely unspoken despair, which I concealed from the face of my mother's patient faith.

Under the shade of a fugitive lilac bush, with no one around to measure my progress, to critique my failures, to patronize me, I started to read about Amos, the lost, forlorn beagle. I read very, very slowly, moving from word to word the way a baby waddles forward with its first steps. I fell over a word here and there that I could not decode, and I had to reconstitute groups of words into sentence units as best as I could. But ever so slowly pages were turned, and I got the gist of the story about a dog who, like mine, had been separated from its family and who, against all odds, found his way back home. That dog was my dog, and I was the little boy in the book. I read, increasingly so absorbed in the story, in the fantasy of my own involvement in the narrative, that I lost all consciousness of the reading process. I was one with the story, as if I were experiencing it firsthand. At times during Amos' trials my heart ached and I cried; but my heart burned in delight at the end, when Amos ("full of the joy of morning" and of a sense that "the world was new") found his home and the waiting little boy. And even though the words had literally trailed off into white space at the end of the 157-page book, my mind continued the final scene of reunion, on and on, until my own lost dog and I were, in my mind, running together across vernal pastures on a cool day with a bright sun and a friendly wind.

At some point this daydream ended. Perhaps my mother called me for dinner. Returned to the real world, I suddenly realized something: I had read a book. Actually, I had read a book, *and* I had *loved* reading that book. I had shared in an amazing adventure, a marvelous escape similar to what I had always imagined in my own mind. How could I love a book, I wondered. Everyone—*everyone*—knew I could not read. But I had read it, and I wanted to read something else just like this book about Amos. The following days I read this book again and again, its magic working every time, and that was that: books could be incredibly wonderful, and I was going to read them, secretly, no matter what might be required of me.

By today's standards, John Parke's *Amos, the Beagle with a Plan* (Pantheon, 1953) is a rather old-fashioned book forgotten even in the annals of children's literature. But as my mother intuited, books (like music) oft have such a charm because they contain magic. Like her, I learned never to underestimate the power of a book. As a conduit of her faith in me and as a catalyst at a certain juncture in my life, the story about Amos fired some instinct in me. I was now determined to read writings which would similarly transport me into imaginative realms. Somehow, and equally mysteriously, this determination coalesced with a steady abatement of the most extreme symptoms of my dyslexia. I read, and read, and read throughout my teenage years as if I were a fatigued veteran of charred longing who had finally found the glowing "green thought in a green shade." One now-forgotten children's book had rekindled, transformed, and redeemed my life.

I never told my mother about my "miraculous" experience that summer, but she saw a remarkable, slow but enduring, improvement in my classroom performance during the next year. Nor did she ever say anything to me about the change, as if in fear that some spoken word by her might dispel the cryptic exorcism she had somehow managed that summer of 1953. Her incantatory "Don't worry, you will read," she doubtlessly worried, might prove finally to be only a frail verbal counter to the curse that had plagued her son. A time would come, however, when she would look at her son, place her hands on her hips, and simply say with a diagnostic nod, "Well." She no longer held her breath or crossed her fingers. Her son had read (and bought) thousands of publications, was awarded a PhD in literature, talked about writings in university classrooms, edited a literary journal, and authored his own books, articles, poetry and fiction. The power of the words had held.

Perhaps the grudging gods tend only to half-grant any of our wishes, and possibly for good reason. Amos, the beagle, had found a way home, and my dog had not. I watched for him as long as I could. In time, however, I discovered that I had been not only the waiting little boy in the story, but also the battle-weary and alienated beagle himself; I discovered that I had been waiting to return to myself. I too had, amidst trails, followed some instinctive plan, a nurturing order and promise, and I too had mysteriously, magically found a way home.

Nominated by Naomi Clark

CHINESE FIREWORKS BANNED IN HAWAII

by ERIC CHOCK

from BAMBOO RIDGE

for Uncle Wongie, 1987

Almost midnight, and the aunties
are wiping the dinner dishes
back to their shelves,
cousins eat jook from the huge vat
in the kitchen, and small fingers
help to mix the clicking ocean
of mah jong tiles, so the uncles can play
through another round of seasons.
And you put down your whiskey
and go outside to find your long bamboo pole
so Uncle Al can help you tie on
a ten foot string of good luck,
red as the raw fish we want
on our plates every New Year's.
As you hang this fish over the railing
Uncle Al walks down the steps
and with his cigarette lighter
ignites it and jumps out of the way.
You lean back and jam the pole
into the bottom of your guts,
waving it across the sky,

whipping sparks of light from its tail,
your face in a laughing Buddha smile
as you trace your name in the stars
the way we teach our kids to do
with their sparklers.
This is the family picture
that never gets taken, everyone
drawn from dishes and food and games
and frozen at the sound
of 10,000 wishes filling our bodies
and sparkling our eyes.
You play the fish till its head explodes
into a silence that echoes,
scattering red scales to remind us of spirits
that live with us in Hawaii.
Then, as we clap and cheer,
the collected smoke of our consciousness
floats over Honolulu, as it has
each year for the last century.
But tonight, as we leave,
Ghislaine stuffs her styrofoam tea cup
full of red paper from the ground.
This is going to be history, she says.
Let's take some home.

Nominated by Bamboo Ridge

1989 GILLETTE, OUR NAVY

by DAVID ROMTVEDT

from THE SUN

THE U.S. NAVY recruiter in Gillette answers the phone, "Ahoy there, shipmate," and concludes his conversation by wishing to all "Fair seas and fresh winds." Or else, "Fair winds and fresh seas."

But the seas departed Wyoming millennia ago and in this land of almost 100,000 square miles only 366 are water. Of the Platte they say a mile wide and one inch deep. And the Powder isn't named such for capricious reasons. Mostly, there isn't enough water here to float a duck, and a battleship would make a nice windbreak for sheep. So eight recruiters sit in offices and polish their shoes until they reflect the sky a watery blue.

Far away in Puget Sound, the Navy attempts to train bottle-nose dolphins. Never mind that these bottlenose are Atlantic dolphins unable to live in the North Pacific's cold water. The blood vessels in the skin contract to retain heat, the skin disintegrates and sloughs off, and the dolphins are vulnerable to infection. And never mind the family and social life of the dolphin. Here, each animal is placed in a twenty-five-square-foot tank fourteen feet deep.

Dolphins can protect the Navy's submarines from Russian frogmen; dolphins can learn to fire poison pellets, or CO_2 cartridges, or bullets; dolphins can learn to kill.

But so far the dolphins have learned to kill only themselves. Some bash themselves against the walls of their pens until they

214

pass out and, unconscious, drown. Some die of stomach ulcers. Some refuse to eat, starving themselves to death.

For those who do not kill themselves, help is close at hand. They are "destroyed." The Navy says they only kill those who "go insane." One dolphin is blind—she has been beaten across the face with a bucket by her trainer. Another dies of open wounds— he has been kicked in the head until he bleeds, and the bleeding will not stop.

No one knows how many dolphins the Navy has. No one knows how many dolphins have died, have been murdered, have committed suicide, have "gone insane."

"Ahoy there, shipmates," Ron says with a smile. And on the billboard above scrub desert the U.S. Navy jets scream sweetly toward the sea, toward the dolphins.

The U.S. Navy in Wyoming has eight sailors and an officer, all recruiting. When they snap to attention, dust flowers around their heads, obscuring their eyes. When they speak, dust billows around their mouths, and mixed with their saliva, muddies all their words. When they walk, dust rises from their feet and mixes with the snow to form a gray wall reminiscent of a fog bank settling on a dock.

In Wyoming the U.S. Navy is silly and superfluous but the world is small and one. Though the cottonwoods, the aspen, the willow, all the trees of this quiet dry land are rooted, though they would be terrified by the sea, though they have never felt the touch of a dolphin on their bark, though everything that a person could say of them about ignorance and distance is true, still, they know. The trees of Wyoming know the lives of the slave dolphins of Puget Sound. The trees refuse to fight so they weep. And in this driest of lands, we too commit that ultimate act of excess; we weep.

Nominated by Kent Nelson

JANE ADDAMS
(September 6, 1860—
May 21, 1935)

by GWENDOLYN BROOKS

from BELOIT POETRY JOURNAL

I am Jane Addams.
I am saying to the giantless time—
to the young and yammering, to the old and corrected,
well, chiefly to Children Coming Home
with worried faces and questions about world-survival—
"Go ahead and live your life.
You might be surprised. The world might continue."

It was not easy for *me*, in the days of the giants.
And now they call me a giant.
Because my capitals were Labour, Reform, Welfare,
Tenement Regulation, Juvenile Court Law (the first),
Factory Inspection, Workmen's Compensation,
Woman Suffrage, Pacifism, Immigrant Justice.
And because
Black, brown and white and red and yellow
heavied my hand and heart.

I shall tell you a thing about giants
that you do not wish to know.

Giants look in mirrors and see
almost nothing at all.

But they leave their houses nevertheless.
They lurch out of doors
to reach *you*, the other stretchers and strainers.
Erased under ermine or loud in tatters, oh
moneyed or mashed, you
matter.
You matter. And giants
must bother.

I bothered.

Whatever I was tells you
the world might continue! Go on with your preparations,
moving among the quick and the dead;
nourishing here, there;
pressing a hand
among the ruins,
and among the
seeds of restoration.

So speaks a giant. Jane.

Nominated by Bruce Weigl

THE STUFF MEN ARE MADE OF

fiction by FELIPE ALFAU

from CHROMOS (Dalkey Archive Press)

Memento homo, quia pulvis es, et in pulverem reverteris.

A FAMILY LIKE THAT OF COELLO would be inconceivable except in two places: Spain, where they came from, and New York, where anything goes. This is not intended as a play on words but as a preparation for the incidents preceding the demolition of a building in Harlem, where this family lived, incidents which some members of the Spanish colony in that neighborhood considered incredible, while others considered highly significant and which, not having taken the trouble to doubt, I pass along to those enjoying the same lazy distaste for systematic disbelief.

The story might open on the day when Mr. Robinson called on the Coello family with the unselfish and civilizing purpose of illuminating the darkness in which this foreign family undoubtedly existed, of preaching to them some good modern sense, of rescuing them from their foolishness and of rendering them an invaluable service by, incidentally, selling to Don Hilarión Coello a life insurance policy.

Mr. Robinson did not know that day when he took derby, umbrella and briefcase and departed on his way to the Coellos, that his visit would be fateful and the starting point of events which he never suspected and never learned. He walked in one of those New York spring showers that last all week. As he crossed Lenox Avenue, the wind blowing caused him to lower his umbrella, blocking his view of traffic and he nearly walked in the path of a fast-moving taxicab and came close to putting an abrupt ending to

218

many subsequent events. He heard the noise of brakes forcibly applied and of English forcibly used, all of which he disregarded with professional philosophy.

He turned into 123rd Street where Don Hilarión Coello lived.

The Coellos were a very proud and very mournful family. They lived in one of those apartments with an endless narrow corridor onto which small rooms open like cells and one cannot walk through without instinctively accelerating one's steps for fear that something may be lurking in one of the treacherous rooms, ready to spring, to snatch, as one passes.

If Don Hilarión called out authoritatively from one end of the house to his wife at the other end, she would have to journey that long corridor looking into every room repeating: "Where are you? where are you?" and she always grew a little afraid.

It was sad to look that way for a person, it was like one of those melancholy fairy tales or a dream, and yet it was an everyday affair.

That apartment, with all windows overlooking a court that was in itself a nightmare, could have turned the happiest person into the most helpless hypochondriac, let alone a family with the propensities of this one.

Black garment encased, somberly proud families like the Coellos, whose poverty has gone to their heads and are intoxicated with failure, were common in Spain and this was the paradox of the Coello family as of so many others. Unable as they would have been to remain themselves under changed conditions in a country of which they were a typical, if old product, they could be unmolested in New York and even contribute to its typically heterogeneous population. Here they could mourn the glad tidings about their country brought by the newspapers, they could wail and deplore to their hearts' content, remain in their pure unadulterated state, like calamares in their own black sauce, with all their militant, though aesthetically justified defensive chastity, worshiping traditions which dictate to cover the greatest possible area of human bodies. Don Hilarión Coello sported an abdomen like a balloon, and his wife one like an apron which would have permitted her to remain chaste even in a nudist camp.

As one of their friends said—an individual who having arrived here six months before them felt entitled to become their spiritual cicerone in the labyrinth of American life:

"That is the convenience of New York, Don Hilarión. On one side you have progressive Nordics who do gymnastics and read science, and on the other you have retrograde Latins who procreate behind shut windows and read the catechism."

"You have said it." Don Hilarión spoke with a very profound and important manner: "On one side you have one thing and on the other you have the other thing. On one side the wrong and on the other the right."

Don Hilarión felt very important, and his family thought that he was and therefore they also felt very important. Don Hilarión was a notario, not a notary, mind you; that does not quite convey the meaning, but a notario. A notario in Spain, at least in Don Hilarión's day, was a title given to a man having achieved the summit of his career in the field of law. It was the coronation of every law student. When parents addressed good children showing particular brilliance, they always said: "Study law, my boy. It has many applications, among them the diplomatic service, and you may even someday be a notario and always be respected and looked upon as an important citizen, not to speak of the good profits you will derive." And the good children always imagined themselves with beard, silk hat and a frock coat, walking along the street acknowledging the deferential greetings and respectful salutations of the admiring crowds.

Don Hilarión had been one of those boys.

He had studied law.

He did not enter the diplomatic service because he only had studied two dead languages.

He did not wear a silk hat and a frock coat, because his friend and spiritual guide had advised him that in this country one did not have to be ceremonious, but do as one pleased; a somewhat exaggerated statement, but safe where Don Hilarión was concerned.

He did not have any greetings to acknowledge, except occasionally those of the janitor and of one or two acquaintances, because the rest of the population did not know him from Adam.

But Don Hilarión was a notario. He felt important. His family felt important. But they were Spaniards of the old school and therefore were gloomy.

Their obvious reason was that Don Hilarión could not practice law in New York because he was not a citizen and besides, his knowledge of English was very limited. However, he had set up one of his rooms as an office, with all his law books, solid cabinets, large imposing desk and heavy chairs. The room was small, Don Hilarión fat, and consequently it was difficult to move about the place. Once he succeeded in sitting at the chair behind his desk, it was not easy to induce him to abandon his post and leave the room, and Don Hilarión sat there all day, reading newspapers from Spain, and it made him feel like a very busy man. This room was at the end of the long corridor and it was from there that Don Hilarión, finding it difficult to extricate himself, called out to his wife who was most of the time with Vicenta, the servant, in the kitchen, unfortunately located at the other end, and she had to look in every one of the rooms, when she very well knew that he could be but in one, held there at the mercy of his furniture.

Donã Dolores arrived breathless: "What is it, Hilarión?"

"Nothing, woman, what can it be? The usual thing. Can you lend a hand? I want to get out of here and I am in a hurry. Where did you think I was?"

By this time she had already got hold of his hand, heaved and given him a good start. "That's enough now, woman. I can manage the rest by myself."

"Such small rooms in this country! In Spain this furniture was lost in that office you had, remember?" Her voice was very throaty, very weepy.

"No use complaining, woman. Nothing gained by that," Don Hilarión finished, heading for the bathroom, newspaper in hand.

Doña Dolores walked back swiftly along the corridor wailing at her memories, at her wretched present: "Those were rooms! At least one had that in one's poverty." She assumed a very resigned air, very brow-beaten. "But when one is so poor one does not even have the right to complain . . . " She reentered the kitchen and ably turned her lingering remarks into a fitting continuation and confirmation of her interrupted talk with Vicenta:

"I should say one has no right to complain. With sufferings, one finally does not mind anymore. But still there are things that reach your marrow. Don't think I don't notice, Vicenta. I did not want to say anything the other day about the incident of the shoes of Hilarión—but the procession goes on inside."

She referred to her husband having had a patch placed on one of his shoes. Then he had met some friends and they had walked. One of them was a Spanish writer who wrote chronicles about New York for South American papers and was always making bad suggestions. This time he suggested that they all examine their feet, right where they were, on Seventh Avenue, to determine who had the largest.

Don Hilarión suspected that the writer had spied his repaired shoes and was calling attention very indelicately to the fact. He had arrived home feeling very depressed and had discussed the incident with his wife in front of Vicenta. The matter had gradually diminished in his mind, but in Doña Dolores's it had behaved like a rolling snowball, reaching the phenomenal proportions of a unanimous world confabulation to vex them, to mock their honorable poverty.

Vicenta tried to soothe her with the usual speech: "Don't think about it, Doña Dolores. A writer! Like all the rest of them. They are always talking for the sake of talking. Who takes writers seriously?"

But Doña Dolores persisted. She relished such experiences that made her feel like a martyr. She resented Vicenta's lightly discarding the matter, simply because she had no appearances to maintain, robbing this succulent humiliating morsel of all its imagined seasoning. She skillfully misinterpreted:

"All right, Vicenta, you let it go at that. It does not hurt you. When one is poor, one does not even have the privilege of complaining. Being poor is the worst sin I suppose, which must be constantly expiated, paid for, when one can pay for nothing else." She compressed her lips and a wistful smile sent her eyes in search of remote places of mournful reveries.

Vicenta, whose salary had not been attended to for the last six months, misunderstood sincerely: "Doña Dolores, you know very well that I am not one to think of certain things and I am very happy to work for you as it is. But what you do is like someone stabbing you and then you take the knife and twist it around."

"Now I twist it around! When one is in my position, one must be even accused, held to blame for one's own sufferings." She shifted to the other section of her servant's speech which offered opportunities too tempting to pass over: "And as for the other matter, Vicenta, you will be paid. Don't worry." Her voice rose to eloquent heights: "You will be paid even if I have to tear the flesh off my bones like that famous merchant of Italy, and you can have the blood too."

"Please! Doña Dolores! I am not worrying—" Vicenta gave up in hopelessness and turned to proceed with her chores and made an attempt at changing the conversation: "What shall we order from the grocer's today?"

"Anything," said Doña Dolores, disgusted with her servant's reluctance to continue her pet type of talk. "You know better than I. That is, if they want to send it. We also owe them money and—"

An interruption was advancing tumultuously along the corridor and invaded the kitchen. It was her two children, a boy and a girl, Jeremias and Angustias, both thin, sallow-complexioned and darkly sad-eyed. Both spoke with the same tearful throatiness of their mother and showed already strong-inherited and well-encouraged tendencies to gloom, contrasting with their noisy if not cheerful behavior. This last strange and unexpectedly inconvenient attitude for Doña Dolores was resignedly explained in her mind by what she considered the vulgarizing influence of the environment. Superficially, both children had become thoroughly Americanized in an amazingly short time. They were even called Jerry and Angie in school, a thing which extracted most devilishly from their names all the glorious, tragic implications.

"We want lunch!" Jerry shouted brutally, but with elegiac overtones.

"And in a hurry!" Angie completed with even worse manners and heart-rending harmonics.

Their mother withered them with a well-planted look: "I don't know what has come over these children since we came to this country. They were never like this in Spain. They have changed so!" In Spain they were half their present age, and never left home.

The children had sat at the kitchen table with drooping mouths and heads humbly to one side, to eat the lunch that Vicenta was preparing for them.

"Mama, can we have some money for carfare?"

"Yes, teacher is taking us to the Museum of Natural History and each one is supposed to provide his own carfare."

223

"Now you want money for carfare. When it is not one thing, it is the other. In that school they are constantly demanding money. We are poor and can't afford it."

"Oh, Mama! All the other children are going. Must we always be thus humiliated before others?" Their chins quivered, their voices shook effectively.

"Yes, I know. You have begun to suffer privations early, but you must be resigned. Being poor is no shame when one is honest. You go back to school and tell that teacher that your father cannot afford these luxuries like the rich parents of other children, but that you don't mind, that your father is a respectable notario and that in our poverty we base our pride." Her voice was decidedly damp.

"But Mama, you know they won't understand all that." They appeared to have given up melancholic displays as useless.

"Well, they should. It is high time someone woke them up to the fact that this life is not a novel. In this country they have no consideration. All they think of is money and good times, always telling one to be gay and keep smiling." She made an effective pause. "Smiling! Yes, while the procession goes on inside. These women teachers here never marry, never have children, they don't know what suffering is, what privation, what life is."

"All right, Mama, but can we have the money?"

"Go on now," Vicenta stepped in: "You have enough museum pieces with those bespectacled old hens who teach you—"

"Miss Finch is not an old hen and she does not wear spectacles," Angie charged.

"Never mind that. You go back there and tell them that you did not get the money. Come on! Finish that omelet. You have appetites like millionaires. We can't be throwing food away in this house. Your father—" Vicenta checked herself. This pessimism was contagious. "Go ahead now, hurry! Run along and take an umbrella. It is raining."

And so it was and at this time, under another umbrella, Mr. Robinson was fatefully walking toward their house.

No sooner had the children left than Doña Dolores resumed her interrupted litany: "I suppose I should also laugh at the question of the cream puffs. I should be very cheerful about it."

"There you go talking about that again," Vicenta said while looking into the icebox and kitchen closets to see what was needed. She knew the incident by memory. For some reason it was one of the selected tear-jerking, bitter-smile-squeezer pieces in Doña Dolores's repertoire.

It seems that a friend, knowing Don Hilarión's precarious financial condition, had given him some matter to investigate concerning Spanish law. It turned out to be a very simple matter and Don Hilarión felt that it detracted from his importance as a notario to do a piece of work that could have been attended to by any law apprentice, any law office amanuensis. However, when he was paid, he made his grand gesture. He went to a pastry shop run by another Spaniard in the neighborhood and bought some cream puffs.

"To sweeten the bitterness left by this humiliating job," he said as he laid them on the table before his wife.

That night they had dinner accompanied by the usual lamentations all around. When time for dessert arrived, the children greeted the appearance of the cream puffs with vociferous sadness.

"You must be grateful for this little luxury, my dears. It has cost your father very trying moments, but do not be common. Poverty is no excuse for bad manners."

Angie was the first one to make the nefarious discovery. She held up the puff she had opened, under the overhanging lamp, for all to see: "This pastry is bad. Look, it is green inside."

Doña Dolores looked, they all looked. Vicenta had appeared at the dining-room door and also looked. This was a real crisis and Doña Dolores rose to it:

"Rotten!" she exclaimed in piercing tones. "Even that! Poor people must be given rotten things, because they have no money to buy at the right places—" She was beside herself. "That is too much. We may be poor, but too proud to permit such insolence!" The children's mouths were already drooping and trembling at the corners. "Take them back immediately, Hilarión!" Angie began to bawl shamelessly, a true Desdemona, and her brother bit his lip and cast his eyes down, a little man in distress. Doña Dolores fell prone upon the table, wiping aside the guilty puff: "Mockery, Hilarión—rotten mockery!" she wailed prostrate by the shock.

Vicenta surveyed the scene in perplexity. Don Hilarión gathered the offending puffs back into their box of shame and left like one walking to his doom, muttering between his teeth: "How long, my Lord, how long?" He returned the pastry, got his money back, and bought himself some cigars instead.

That incident had been one of the high, cherished moments of the Coello family.

"Just when poor Hilarión, happy at having earned some money, wanted to celebrate by giving his children something sweet, which they so seldom have." Doña Dolores concluded: "I am supposed to dance a fandango for sheer happiness."

At that moment the doorbell rang. Mr. Robinson had arrived.

Vicenta walked the length of the corridor wiping her hands on her apron and opened the door. Mr. Robinson introduced himself and in that roundabout manner which every salesman considers deceptive and enticing, he hinted at the purpose of his call. Such linguistic subtleties were beyond Vicenta's neglected knowledge of English and she called her mistress:

"Doña Dolores, please come and see what this man wants."

Doña Dolores was slightly more successful than her servant and understanding that the man had something good for her husband, she led Mr. Robinson, who had not removed his derby, into her husband's office: "Hilarión, this gentleman has come to see you."

Don Hilarión removed his gold-rimmed spectacles and regarded the gentleman. He assumed his most important manner, meanwhile trying to rise unsuccessfully: "Please have a seat, sir. In what can I serve you? Forgive me for not rising, but as you see, this furniture—"

"Don't bother. It's perfectly all right," said Mr. Robinson, squeezing past some furniture and into a chair. "My name is Robinson of the ——" he gave the name of some insurance company, and with that he opened his briefcase and spread his subject's literature before the prospective client, right over the newspaper that the latter was reading. Then in a speech not too short to be unimpressive and not too long to be wearisome, he stated his case, being careful to make himself clear to this foreigner.

Don Hilarión and his wife, who stood in the doorway, listened, the former pompously, the latter politely. Then when Don Hilarión thought naively enough that Mr. Robinson had finished, he cleared his throat and began: "You see, Mr. Robinson, I do not believe in life insurance policies, I—"

The other took ready advantage of Don Hilarión's halting English to lunge confidently onto well-trod ground: "What do you mean you don't believe? I don't care how rich you are. No one can afford to be without this protection. What about your wife, your children? Suppose you die one of these days. If you have the policy I have been speaking of, your wife won't have the added expense of your funeral, and she will get some money besides—"

"Holy Virgin!" Doña Dolores cried on the verge of a faint. "Listen to what this man is saying. He is talking about your death, and he dares to suggest that I profit by it." Her face had gone from pallor to deep red. "Listen, mister. We may be poor, but we are no ghouls and when anyone dies in this family, God forbid, we shall obtain the money somehow to give them a decent, Christian burial. Listen to him!"

"Please, woman! Let me bear this cross alone," Don Hilarión said, while Mr. Robinson looked from one to the other endeavoring to make out these foreigners. "Pardon, Mr. Robinson, but as I said before, I do not believe in life insurance. No one can insure his life. One never knows when one will die and therefore there is no use—"

"Listen, brother. You don't know what you are talking about. If you would let me explain—"

Don Hilarión had succeeded in rising: "I don't know what I am talking about? Did you say I don't know what I am talking about?" He smiled a superior smile and deliberately placed his gold-rimmed spectacles upon his nose. "Perhaps you don't know whom you are talking to, sir. I happen to be a notario. Do you hear? A notario."

"So what? What's so wonderful about that? I am a notary also, and I can prove it."

There was a silence. Doña Dolores approached, Don Hilarión removed his glasses and leaning on his desk scrutinized his visitor, hat and all.

"You are also a notario?"

"Sure! What's wrong with it? Anyone can be one. All you do is pay a few dollars and you are a notary."

Don Hilarión staggered and, holding on to the arms of his chair, he slid down into his seat slowly, dejectedly, like one crushed to dust that settles gradually. Another silence followed, a longer one, like the kind that comes after an explosion.

227

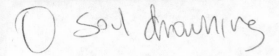
Soul drowning

"For a few dollars—anybody—a notario—" he managed to whisper hoarsely.

Doña Dolores precipitated herself forward and reached across the desk, a hand gripping her husband's shoulder: "Hilarión, Hilarión! Oh my God!"

"What did I do now?" questioned Mr. Robinson, puzzled. These foreigners were too much for him.

"What have you done?" Doña Dolores had turned on him like a lioness: "You have killed him!"

"But madam, I only—"

"Go away, please. Can't you see that he is ill? Go away!"

"All right, lady." Mr. Robinson picked up all his papers. "I'll be back when he is feeling better." He walked out hurriedly despite the furniture. He had nearly sold his best policy to a man who could die at the slightest provocation.

Doña Dolores was hovering over her fallen husband: "What is it, Hilarión? Speak to me."

Don Hilarión heaved a sigh that was like lifting a ton of bricks: "Nothing, woman, nothing—I prefer not to speak now," and then he began to talk. That man usually of so few chosen words began to talk rapidly, carelessly, in a manner his wife had never heard before. He poured out his soul. He spoke of his life, a subject he had always skipped with dignified reticence. He spoke of his hopes and illusions, of his disappointments and subsequent pessimism.

"Forgive me," he ended. "I have been talking a good deal and one should not burden a woman with one's troubles, but sometimes a man talks as he swims: to save himself from drowning. Talking is for the soul what motion is for the body. The body moves, does; the soul speaks, explains. I had to talk, but now I have to rest. I feel very tired. You go about your things and let me rest awhile." And Don Hilarión leaned his head on a hand that also shielded eyes no longer adorned with gold-rimmed spectacles.

"My poor Hilarión! What a blow!" said Doña Dolores, or rather, her lips formed the phrase silently, and silently she left the room, and once in the corridor she walked with more resolution to the kitchen.

Don Hilarión remained in the same position for a few moments. Then his eyes opened and he noticed once again the

Spanish paper he had been reading. In sudden rage, he crumpled it up into a shapeless ball and hurled it against the walls lined with his law books. Then he sat back, his breath coming in gasps, and his eyes roved over those books. For only a few dollars anybody could be a notario!

He felt an uncontrollable desire to tear those volumes from the shelves where they reposed, to trample them, to smash them. He made an effort to rise and something snapped inside of him sending a sharp pain from his chest along his arms. Everything reeled, everything went dark: "Dolores—Dolores—!" he cried with despair.

Doña Dolores was rushing along the long corridor, looking into every room: "Where are you? Where are you?" She finally reached his room: "Hilarión, what is it, Hilarión?"

Don Hilarión did not answer. He was leaning back in his chair, his head drooping on one shoulder, his arms hanging lifelessly down the sides.

"Hilarión, are you sick? Hilarión, speak! Hilarión—! Vicenta! Come!" she howled.

Don Hilarión was dead.

To try to convey in words the extremes to which Doña Dolores went in displaying her just, unquestionable sorrow, would be impossible and if possible, useless, since no one could conceive of it more than of the stellar light-years in a book of astronomy. One can conceive possibly the feelings of a panhandler who is seeking five cents for a cup of coffee and suddenly finds himself owning the treasures of Ali Baba, then one could raise that to the nth power, but it would do no good. One cannot conceive that, and yet this is but like an orange compared to the earth if one considers the sorrow of Doña Dolores, the full measure of her bereavement.

Even she felt that it was quite impossible to do complete justice to her position, and like a clever actor fearing that a role may lie beyond his dramatizing potentialities, she wisely and conveniently for the surrounding world chose to underact her part. In all her sympathy-acknowledging answers she was sober and introduced simple phrases such as: "No, nothing, my dear. He left us nothing but his good name and the honor of bearing it," and "Yes, my dear, quite unexpected, but those who live honestly in spite of their poverty are always ready when the moment

229

arrives," or "That is right, my dear. Death is the common leveler and no amount of money can pave the road to the kingdom of heaven and it is easier for a camel to pass through the eye of a needle—" But her expression was a thing to behold and she always ended with the same words: "Ay! They did not baptize me Dolores for nothing!"

But throughout all this Doña Dolores smiled wisely, sadly and to herself, as one who is keeping a secret. She was preparing her great coup, her fitting and masterly stroke. When words failed, it was time for action, and since tears, sobbing, nervous attacks and bellowing could do no justice to the situation, she, Doña Dolores, the champion mourner, would not be caught napping. She would do something, she would do something that would show how she could feel such a thing, something that would break all previous records set by the loudest mourners in this world, something memorable that would put to shame the most rabidly unfortunate characters in history.

Two days after the death of Don Hilarión, Doña Dolores summoned a Spanish undertaker by the name of Zacatecas. They remained a long time closeted in Don Hilarión's office, where the body lay in state. When they came out, enigmatic phrases were heard:

"You must reconsider the price, Señor Zacatecas. We are poor. He left us nothing but his good name and—"

"I know, madam, but this is a special job and besides, I may get into trouble and the least that could happen would be losing my license. Also remember that you would have had to buy a coffin."

"Very well, Señor Zacatecas. Please hurry and do your best."

"Oh, don't you worry about that. I will do my best. Now I am going for lunch and to my office to get some things and will be right back."

The Señor Zacatecas having left, Doña Dolores walked up and down the corridor several times, an unfathomable and resolute smile upon her lips.

When the Señor Zacatecas returned as promised with a large black case, she ushered him again into her husband's office and left him there behind the closed door. After that she had to perform what she called the painful duty of taking some nourishment to remain alive for the children's sake and then she sat sur-

230

rounded by friends and acquaintances like a queen on a throne to bask in their admiring sympathy and discuss and comment at length with undisputed authority upon the exemplary past actions and never well-praised virtues of the illustrious and important defunct, while some black-attired guest summed up matters with a deep remark such as: "The real trouble with life is death."

Time passed and a few close and dejected friends sat at her sadly regal, if materially poor table to "do something for life, since one can do nothing for death" by eating a hasty supper prepared and served by Vicenta with red swollen eyes and unsteady hands.

The children sat through all this together, their thin faces paler than ever, Angie crying intermittently under the protective arm of her brother.

"Vicenta, please see that the children eat something."

"Yes—Doña Dolores," she said shakily and she went to the children and, holding them tightly with trembling arms, she disappeared with them into the kitchen, sobbing.

The mournful gathering remained repeating the same words, singing the same praises until well into the night. The children also remained up, Doña Dolores affecting an adequate disregard for anything not connected with her bereavement.

And then the Señor Zacatecas emerged from Don Hilarión's office where he had been all that time and called Doña Dolores, who responded immediately, reentering the room with him.

They remained there mysteriously with the door closed quite a while and then she reappeared, followed by the Señor Zacatecas and closing the door carefully behind. Then she summoned everybody.

All the guests walked in single file along the corridor, Vicenta and the children bringing up the rear. They arrived as the Señor Zacatecas was taking his leave noiselessly like a shadow, and standing in front of the closed room, they met Doña Dolores, arms folded, beaming upon them her despair, her tragedy:

"I have summoned you all to witness the proof of my devotion." She quoted the old saying cryptically: "Things you will see of the Cid, that will cause the stones to speak." And she flung the door open.

The grief-stricken gathering crowded in the doorway and gasped.

231

Don Hilarión was sitting at his desk, in typical pose, pen in hand resting on a sheet of foolscap, his gold-rimmed spectacles balanced on his nose. There was even a frown clouding his noble brow as if it were laden with the problems and responsibilities of justice. The Señor Zacatecas had done a good job.

The wall behind his chair displayed a Spanish flag, adding to the sad arrangement a touch of glorious brilliance. It was a perfect picture of dignity, sacrifice and important futility. Doña Dolores had risen to unsuspected heights of genius to meet the challenge of the occasion:

"From now on," she said throatily but with appropriate self-control and an edge of fatigue in her voice, "this will be his shrine, his sanctuary. He will sit among his legal books and papers, in the atmosphere that was his life." She grew stern with the assurance of the cruelly wounded person before an appreciative, almost envious audience: "They shall not take him away from me. He was our only and most precious possession in our poverty. He was all we had. His exemplary life, his important achievements, no longer appreciated in these materialistic days, shall guide us in our dark hours of sorrow. He was a notario as you all know and he will remain one. Indeed death is the common leveler and all dead notarios are equal. In the new fields he is conquering, his well-justified ignorance of a vulgarly modern language will no longer stand in his path to glory. Here you behold Don Hilarión Coello, Notario."

"Doña Dolores—" came from every mouth like a murmur in response to her funeral oration. It sounded like "ora pro nobis," and involved an admiring recognition that was worth living for. The children hung on to Vicenta's apron, their faces a deathly white, their eyes like saucers. Doña Dolores raised a hand in the classic mob-stilling gesture.

"I propose to pay him homage once a year on the anniversary of his departure. He shall remain here, where he can be respected and honored as he deserves, but I appeal to your honorable sense of secrecy to keep this from misunderstanding outsiders as it would be very sad to have him who was a respected and important man of law involved in legal complications." There was a strange leer on her face as she lighted two candles which had been placed on the desk and knelt in front of it.

"Doña Dolores—" The murmur rose again, and again it sounded like "ora pro nobis," which smoothly turned to general prayer trailing among the kneeling figures along the corridor. Then Doña Dolores rose, and all, knowing that the audience was over, filed out silently, still crossing themselves with reverent fear.

When they had all departed, Doña Dolores put out the candles and locked the door of the shrine. Vicenta was standing in front of her, the children still grasping her apron. They looked like a petrified group and Vicenta said hollowly:

"I wouldn't do that, Doña Dolores. It does not seem right."

"Let anyone try and take him away," Doña Dolores responded with threatening finality as she pocketed the key.

The next two days Doña Dolores spent several hours enclosed with her dead husband. On the third day she only stayed a few minutes and when she came out she telephoned the Señor Zacatecas to come immediately.

As soon as he arrived she took him into the room: "Look here, Señor Zacatecas. There seems to be something wrong with your work. There is a strong smell and then also stains in the face and hands. I have not looked further because I did not want to disarrange anything until you got here. Come and look for yourself. Don't you notice the smell?"

They struggled past the furniture. The Señor Zacatecas bent close to the figure, he looked, he sniffed, he finally straightened up: "That cannot be helped, Madame, the job is good. I worked for hours on him. If you had called me sooner it would have been easier, but when you called me, he was already in pretty bad shape and it was hard work to get him in the position you see him now. I had to use special chemicals and after a while they react that way. But this is nothing. You keep the windows open for a while and it will wear off. I really don't want to know any more about this affair. I may get in trouble. I only did it because we are both Spanish and must stand together, but I want no more of it." The Señor Zacatecas departed.

Doña Dolores opened the window and looked into the pallid abyss of the court. Her gaze then remained suspended in space for a long time and then she also left the room.

The first year went by slowly at first and then it gathered speed uneventfully. In the beginning Doña Dolores's visits to her husband were frequent and the children lived in constant fear, stayed away from the house as much as possible and at night insisted that Vicenta sleep with them. Then after a few months the visits of Doña Dolores grew more scarce. She seemed to prefer to pour her eternal lamentations enriched by this magnificent new addition into the faithful, though inattentive ears of her servant. Then a few days before the anniversary, it was decided to pay a call on Don Hilarión to see that everything was as it should be.

They discovered that all the furniture had accumulated an alarming amount of dust, as had Don Hilarión. They considered the matter at length and finally arrived at the conclusion that everything had to be dusted, including the old notario.

"I thought it might be disrespectful," said Vicenta, "but what can one do?"

"It is more respectful to clean him, to perform that duty instead of allowing him to accumulate dirt. After all, Vicenta, cleanliness is next to holiness."

They left the room and Vicenta returned to it with duster and broom. She swept the floor as well as the furniture permitted and then dusted every piece with expert hand. When she came to Don Hilarión, she remained a while, duster in hand poised in mid-air, and then with a shrug of the shoulders, she began vigorously.

At the first stroke the duster caught the gold-rimmed spectacles and sent them crashing against the desk, one of the lenses breaking.

"Now I've done it!" poor Vicenta said in distress. She picked up the spectacles and with some effort she managed to balance them upon Don Hilarión's nose, which seemed to have shrunk. Indeed, the whole figure appeared slightly shrunk and distorted out of position, and then she also noticed Don Hilarión's face. It had also changed, for it seems that time passes even for the dead. His lips had receded somewhat and began to expose his teeth, with the suggestion of a macabre smile. The frown in his forehead was a bit accentuated. The whole face and hands looked much darker. Vicenta studied the whole thing for a while shaking her head and then left the room closing the door.

When the anniversary arrived Doña Dolores invited a few friends. They arrived endeavoring to cover their curiosity with an

234

air of great reverence and when Doña Dolores opened the door of the sanctuary, they all crowded in with almost abject hurry.

Doña Dolores was about to deliver the speech she had presented for the occasion when she caught sight as well as all the others of the expression on her late husband's face. The lips now fully exposed the teeth in a decided broad smile and the frown had become marked to the point of ferocity. The contrast was, to say the least, disconcerting.

Doña Dolores approached the sitting figure and eyed it. She overheard snickers and giggles and even a remark or two from a couple of American guests about the skeleton in the family closet. They all seemed nervous, fidgety. A young lady became hysterical.

And then Doña Dolores's eye fell upon the broken spectacles: "What is the meaning of this? Vicenta, come here. Explain!"

The dejected servant advanced twisting her apron in embarrassment: "Well, madam, the duster caught the spectacles and they fell and—" She broke down and rushed from the room crying, her apron already a sausage in her hands, to seek refuge in the kitchen.

Doña Dolores looked at her husband's face again and mused: "I wonder what chemicals that Zacatecas used?"

The guests seemed unable to restrain their risibilities. Their rampant fear had created a nervousness which found only this outlet. They gulped, inflated their cheeks, coughed applying their handkerchiefs to their faces, and grew purple.

Doña Dolores turned upon them, the livid image of righteous indignation: "Shooo, imbeciles!" she emitted with all her might.

And this was too much for the guests. With howls and roars, they stampeded out of the house, convulsed by loud, open, ribald laughter.

The ceremony had ended.

The second year went by even faster than the first. The family activities had progressively invaded the room. There were things there which had to be used. At first Doña Dolores or Vicenta entered on tiptoe and left silently, but later they hurried and forgot to close the door on their way out and the door was open most of the time. The children appeared to have lost their fear. They played in the corridor and once when their ball rolled into

235

Don Hilarión's office, Jerry walked in boldly, retrieved it, and as he was leaving, he stopped to study his father.

"Come over here," he called to his sister and when she came: " 'S funny, but doesn't he remind you of someone, with that mustache and all?"

Angie looked carefully, her head to one side: "That's right! That portrait in the principal's office in the school."

"Doesn't it though?" They both laughed and then, forgetting all about it, resumed their play right in there.

Doña Dolores, who saw them as she came in from shopping, scolded them that time, but the scene was repeated often later and she minded it less each time and eventually noticed it no more. She was going through that critical age in which women sometimes become slightly stupefied.

Vicenta dusted Don Hilarión regularly like another piece of furniture. Once while thus occupied, she noticed that the pen had fallen out of his hand. She tried to replace it but the fingers had contracted or separated and wouldn't hold it. She tried to press them together and one of them came off in her hand. Vicenta contemplated this minor disaster stoically. She remained undecided with the finger in her hand looking for an adequate place to deposit the relic. At last she dropped it in the wastebasket. When Doña Dolores eventually spotted the missing finger, she simply sighed and said: "That Zacatecas—that Vicenta—!"

More time passed and one day when Doña Dolores had to use the desk, she discovered that her husband was in the way: "Come over, Vicenta, help me with this."

Together they shoved Don Hilarión and chair and when Doña Dolores finished whatever she had to do at the desk, they forgot to replace the throne and master, and he remained in that position, on the side of the desk, like one applying for something to an invisible provider.

The family moved and lived about that corpse as if it were but an object, one more useless object which Vicenta had to attend to protestingly. One could often see Doña Dolores sitting there writing a letter or one of the children doing homework, with the vigilant, immobile figure next to them, frown, spectacles, mustache, smile, teeth and all.

The third anniversary passed unnoticed and when Doña Dolores remembered, she realized that it would have been an anticlimax to open a door which had been open already for such a long time. Besides, her friends were already completely familiarized with the presence of Don Hilarión. He had been very often included in their visits and two friends left the house once talking like this:

"But how is it that the authorities have not found out about this irregularity? Or if they have found out, why have they done nothing?"

"Well, you know. These foreign families can live in New York in their own colony, completely isolated from the rest of the town, like in an independent state. As long as they do not bother the rest, the city does not bother to find out. The thing remains among the group, but if anyone outside their circle has learned of it, it has been probably discarded as an old Spanish custom."

This explanation was as good as any, and as for the children, they were entering that age in which they felt ashamed of being connected with anything different from the rest and they did not mention it. Perhaps they did not give it enough importance anymore.

Don Hilarión was still holding together in spots, but on the whole, he looked quite bad and threatened to disintegrate completely at any moment. Every time he was moved, one could feel something snap, crush and roll down to accumulate in the folds of his clothes, in small particles, like crumbled fragments of old cork that sometimes found their way to the floor and had to be swept up.

One day Vicenta said to her mistress: "You know, Doña Dolores? This thing is falling apart, and it is only in the way here. I think we could put it in a trunk and send it down to the basement. Then we will have more room and we certainly need it with all this heavy furniture."

Doña Dolores pursed her lips and looked her husband up and down: "Yes—I suppose so. The purpose would be the same. I only promised not to let them take him away, and I am a woman of my word, but I suppose he will be better off that way."

And Don Hilarión, in the collapsible condition he had reached was easily crammed into a trunk and sent down to the basement.

Time moved on to the melancholy accompaniment of Doña Dolores's lamentations, seasons followed seasons, and years pursued years with gradual acceleration, and the story might close one day when Mr. Goldstein, the landlord, called on the Coellos, thus saving them from perishing under the ruins of the building which had to be demolished, and incidentally to render them the service of another apartment in another building which he also owned. Mr. Goldstein did not know that day, when disregarding coat and hat he left his office on the other side of Mount Morris Park, that his visit would bring to an end the incidents of which he fortunately had never learned. He walked on one of those splendid New York summer days that last about an hour and was thinking big, generous, humane thoughts. His heart was warm toward his fellow man. That building had developed a weak spot and was unsafe. He might as well tell the tenants to move, since the building had to come down anyway. He wanted to keep a clear conscience.

As he reached the park's sidewalk, he was nearly run down by a speeding car and one wonders what he thought of worrying about other people's troubles.

At that moment Doña Dolores was speaking with bitterness to Vicenta: "I suppose I should be happy enough to sing, after all the misery I have known, after all the misfortune that has piled upon my head. I did not want to say anything the other day about the incident of Angustia's party dress, but the procession . . . "

The usual, unavoidable interruption was advancing loudly along the corridor.

Jerry entered the kitchen and suggested in comically deep tones: "What about food, Mama? I have to rush back for the meet." His voice was changing and his gloom only seemed increased by his puberty.

"It is high time you thought of something else besides playing. If your poor father were alive . . . "

The bell rang. Mr. Goldstein had arrived.

The moment he explained the object of his visit, Doña Dolores put her hands to her head. "Ay Dios mio! Vicenta! Listen to what this man says. The house is going to fall down. This is the very dregs in the cup of bitterness which has been my life. Even the house where I live is going to fall on me, all because poor people cannot afford to live in solid buildings. Oh my God, my God, my God! When a person is as unfortunate as I am, she has no reason for living. I may as well die right now. Let's get out of here this minute!"

238

The magnanimous offer of Mr. Goldstein to move to another of his houses was accepted as soon as he had reassured Doña Dolores that all his other buildings were sound, solid as a rock, and the preparations for moving were begun at once.

The next day as Doña Dolores stood on the sidewalk and saw the two moving vans drive away packed with their belongings and heavy furniture, she turned exhausted on Vicenta: "Did we forget anything?" she asked feebly.

"I don't think so, Doña Dolores," the servant answered through a yawn that nearly turned her inside out.

"Well; it would make no difference anyway. We are too poor to own anything of any value. . . . How tired I am!" She addressed her two children who stood there looking very bored and dutifully sad. "All right then, let's go."

The group walked slowly in the direction of the new house.

And the last incident one may accept since one has accepted so many others is that one day after the old unsafe building had been duly demolished and nothing remained but abandoned foundations replete with debris, a tramp was rummaging through and came upon a bundle of dark clothes covered with dirt and dust. He picked it up, shook it and more dust dropped from it, mixing with the other. Having found the clothes acceptable, he walked away still brushing and shaking from them the last traces of dust, without bothering to think whether it was the stuff houses are made of, or the stuff men are made of.

Nominated by Dalkey Archive Press

MAINTENANCE

by NAOMI SHIHAB NYE

from THE GEORGIA REVIEW

THE ONLY MAID I ever had left messages throughout our house: *Lady as I was cleaning your room I heard a mouse and all the clothes in your closet fell down to the floor there is too many dresses in there take a few off. Your friend Marta Alejandro.* Sometimes I'd find notes stuck into the couch with straight pins. *I cannot do this room today bec. St. Jude came to me in a dream and say it is not safe.* Our darkroom was never safe because the devil liked dark places and also the enlarger had an eye that picked up light and threw it on Marta. She got sick and had to go to a doctor who gave her green medicine that tasted like leaves.

Sometimes I'd come home to find her lounging in the bamboo chair on the back porch, eating melon, or lying on the couch with a bowl of half-melted ice cream balanced on her chest. She seemed depressed by my house. She didn't like the noise the vacuum made. Once she waxed the bathtub with floor wax. I think she was experimenting.

Each Wednesday I paid Marta ten dollars—that's what she asked for. When I raised it to eleven, then thirteen, she held the single dollars away from the ten as if they might contaminate it. She did not seem happy to get raises, and my friends (who paid her ten dollars each for the other days of the week) were clearly unhappy to hear about it. After a while I had less work of my own and less need for help, so I found her a position with two gay men who lived in the neighborhood. She called once to say she liked them very much because mostly what they wanted her to do was shine. Shine?

"You know, silver. They have a lot of bowls. They have real beautiful spoons not like your spoons. They have a big circle tray that shines like the moon."

My friend Kathy had no maid and wanted none. She ran ten miles a day and lived an organized life. Once I brought her a gift—a blue weaving from Guatemala, diagonal patterns of thread on sticks—and she looked at it dubiously. "Give it to someone else," she said. "I really appreciate your thinking of me, but I try not to keep things around here." Then I realized how bare her mantel was. Who among us would fail to place *something* on a mantel? A few shelves in her kitchen also stood empty, and not the highest ones either.

Kathy had very definite methods of housekeeping. When we'd eat dinner with her she'd rise quickly, before dessert, to scrape each plate and place it in one side of her sink to soak. She had Tupperware containers already lined up for leftovers and a soup pan with suds ready for the silverware. If I tried to help she'd slap my hand. "Take care of your own kitchen," she'd say, not at all harshly. After dessert she'd fold up the card table we'd just eaten on and place it against the wall. Dining rooms needed to be swept after meals, and a stationary table just made sweeping more difficult.

Kathy could listen to any conversation and ask meaningful questions. She always seemed to remember what anybody said—maybe because she'd left space for it. One day she described having grown up in west Texas in a house of twelve children, the air jammed with voices, crosscurrents, the floors piled with grocery bags, mountains of tossed-off clothes, toys, blankets, the clutter of her sisters' shoes. That's when she decided to have only one pair of shoes at any time, running shoes, though she later revised this to include a pair of sandals.

Somehow I understood her better then, her tank tops and wiry arms . . . She ran to shake off dust. She ran to leave it all behind.

Another friend, Barbara, lived in an apartment but wanted to live in a house. Secretly I loved her spacious domain, perched high above the city with a wide sweep of view, but I could understand the wish to plant one's feet more firmly on the ground. Barbara has the best taste of any person I've ever known—the best khaki-colored linen clothing, the best books, the name of the best masseuse. When I'm with her I feel uplifted, excited by life; there's so much to know about that I haven't heard of yet, and Barbara probably has. So I agreed to help her look.

We saw one house where walls and windows had been sheathed in various patterns of gloomy brocade. We visited another where the kitchen had been removed because the owners only ate in restaurants. They had a tiny office refrigerator next to their bed which I peeked into after they'd left the room: orange juice in a carton, coffee beans. A Krups coffee maker on the sink in their bathroom. They seemed unashamed, shrugging, "You could put a new kitchen wherever you like."

Then we entered a house that felt unusually vivid, airy, and hard-to-define until the realtor mentioned, "Have you noticed there's not a stick of wood anywhere in this place? No wood furniture, not even a wooden salad bowl, I'd bet. These people, very hip, you'd like them, want wood to stay in forests. The man says wood makes him feel heavy."

Barbara and her husband bought that house—complete with pear-shaped swimming pool, terraces of pansies, plum trees, white limestone rock gardens lush with succulents—but they brought wood into it. Never before had I been so conscious of things like wooden cutting boards. I helped them unpack and stroked the sanded ebony backs of African animals.

Then, after about a year and a half, Barbara called to tell me they were selling the house. "You won't believe this," she said, "but we've decided. It's the maintenance—the yardmen, little things always breaking—I'm so busy assigning chores I hardly have time for my own work anymore. A house really seems ridiculous to me now. If I want earth I can go walk in a park."

I had a new baby at the time and everything surprised me. My mouth dropped open, oh yes. I was living between a mound of fresh cloth diapers and a bucket of soiled ones, but I agreed to participate in the huge garage sale Barbara was having.

"That day," Barbara said later, "humanity sank to a new lowest level." We had made signs declaring the sale would start at nine A.M.—but by eight, middle-aged women and men were already ripping our boxes open, lunging into the back of my loaded pickup to see what I had. Two women argued in front of me over my stained dishdrainer. I sold a kerosene heater which we'd never lit and a stack of my great-uncle's rumpled tablecloths, so large they completely engulfed an ironing board. One woman flashed a charm with my initial on it under my nose, saying, "I'd think twice about selling this, sweetheart—don't you realize it's ten carat?"

Afterwards we counted our wads of small bills and felt drained, diluted. We had spent the whole day bartering in a driveway, releasing ourselves from the burden of things we did not need. We even felt disgusted by the thought of eating—yet another means of accumulation—and would derive no pleasure from shopping, or catalogs, for at least a month.

While their new apartment was being refurbished, Barbara and her husband lived in a grand hotel downtown. She said it felt marvelous to use all the towels and have fresh ones appear on the racks within hours. Life seemed to regain its old recklessness. Soon they moved back to the same wind-swept apartment building they'd left, but to a higher floor. Sometimes I stood in their living room staring out at the horizon, which always seemed flawlessly clean.

My mother liked to sing along to records while she did housework—Mahalia Jackson, the Hallelujah Chorus. Sometimes we would sing duets, "Tell Me Why" and "Nobody Knows the Trouble I've Seen." I felt lucky my mother was such a clear soprano. We also sang while preparing for the big dinners my parents often gave, while folding the napkins or decorating little plates of hummus with olives and radishes.

I hungrily savored the tales told by the guests, the wild immigrant fables and metaphysical links. My mother's favorite friend, a rail-thin vegetarian who had once been secretary to Aldous Huxley, conversed passionately with a Syrian who was translating the Bible from Aramaic, then scolded me for leaving a mound of carrots on my plate.

"I'm not going to waste them!" I said. "I always save carrots for last because I love them best."

I thought this would please her, but she frowned. "Never save what you love, dear. You know what might happen? You may lose it while you are waiting."

It was difficult to imagine losing the carrots—what were they going to do, leap off my plate?—but she continued.

"Long ago I loved a man very much. He had gone on a far journey—our relationship had been delicate—and I waited anxiously for word from him. Finally a letter arrived and I stuffed it into my bag, trembling, thinking I would read it later on the train. Would rejoice in every word, was what I thought, but you know what happened? My purse was snatched away from me—stolen!—before I boarded the train. Things like that didn't even happen much in those days. I never saw the letter again—and I never saw my friend again either."

A pause swallowed the room. My mother rose to clear the dishes. Meaningful glances passed. I knew this woman had never married. When I asked why she hadn't written him to say she lost the letter, she said, "Don't you see, I also lost the only address I had for him."

I thought about this for days. Couldn't she have tracked him down? Didn't she know anyone else who might have known him and forwarded a message? I asked my mother, who replied that love was not easy.

Later my mother told me about a man who had carried a briefcase of important papers on a hike because he was afraid they might get stolen from the car. The trail wove high up the side of a mountain, between stands of majestic piñon. As he leaned over a rocky gorge to breathe the fragrant air, his fingers slipped and the briefcase dropped down into a narrow crevasse. They heard it far below, clunking into a deep underground pool. My mother said the man fell to the ground and sobbed.

The forest ranger whistled when they brought him up to the spot. "Hell of an aim!" He said there were some lost things you just had to say goodbye to, "like a wedding ring down a commode." My parents took the man to Western Union so he could telegraph about the lost papers, and the clerk said, "Don't feel bad, every woman drops an earring down a drain once in her life." The man glared. "This was not an earring—I AM NOT A WOMAN."

I thought of the carrots, and the letter, when I heard his story. And of my American grandmother's vintage furniture, sold to indifferent buyers when I was still a child, too young even to think of antique wardrobes or bed frames. And I also thought of an-

244

other friend of my parents, Peace Pilgrim, who walked across America for years, lecturing about inner peace and world peace. A single, broad pocket in her tunic contained all her worldly possessions: a toothbrush, a few postage stamps, a ballpoint pen. She had no bank account behind her and nothing in storage. Her motto was, "I walk till given shelter, I fast till given food." My father used to call her a freeloader behind her back, but my mother recognized a prophet when she saw one. I grappled with the details. How would it help humanity if I slept in a cardboard box under a bridge?

Peace Pilgrim told a story about a woman who worked hard so she could afford a certain style of furniture—French Provincial, I think. She struggled to pay for insurance to protect it and rooms large enough to house it. She worked so much she hardly ever got to sit on it. "Then her life was over. And what kind of a life was that?"

Peace Pilgrim lived so deliberately she didn't even have colds. Shortly before her death in a car accident—for years she hadn't even ridden in cars—she sat on the fold-out bed in our living room, hugging her knees. I was grown by then, but all our furniture was still from thrift stores. She invited me to play the piano and sing for her, which I did, as she stared calmly around the room. "I loved to sing as a child," she said. "It is nice to have a piano."

In my grandmother's Palestinian village, the family has accumulated vast mounds and heaps of woolly comforters, stacking them in great wooden cupboards along the walls. The blankets smell pleasantly like sheep and wear coverings of cheerful gingham, but no family—not even our huge one on the coldest night—could possibly use that many blankets. My grandmother smiled when I asked her about them. She said people should have many blankets and head scarves to feel secure.

I took a photograph of her modern refrigerator, bought by one of the emigrant sons on a visit home from America, unplugged in a corner and stuffed with extra yardages of cloth and old magazines. I felt like one of those governmental watchdogs who asks how do you feel knowing your money is being used this way? My grandmother seemed nervous whenever we sat near the refrigerator, as if a stranger who refused to say his name had entered the room.

I never felt women were more doomed to housework than men; I thought women were lucky. Men had to maintain questionably pleasurable associations with less tangible elements—mortgage payments, fan belts and alternators, the IRS. I preferred sinks, and the way people who washed dishes immediately became exempt from after-dinner conversation. I loved to plunge my hands into tubs of scalding bubbles. Once my father reached in to retrieve something and reeled back, yelling, "Do you always make it this hot?" My parents got a dishwasher as soon as they could, but luckily I was out of college by then and never had to touch it. To me it only seemed to extend the task. You rinse, you bend and arrange, you measure soap—and it hasn't even started yet. How many other gratifications were as instant as the old method of washing dishes?

But it's hard to determine how much pleasure someone else gets from an addiction to a task. The neighbor woman who spends hours pinching off dead roses and browned lilies, wearing her housecoat and dragging a hose, may be as close as she comes to bliss, or she may be feeling utterly miserable. I weigh her sighs, her monosyllables about weather. Endlessly I compliment her yard. She shakes her head—"It's a lot of work." For more than a year she tries to get her husband to dig out an old stump at one corner but finally gives up and plants bougainvillea in it. The vibrant splash of pink seems to make her happier than anything else has in a long time.

Certain bylaws: If you have it, you will have to clean it. Nothing stays clean long. No one else notices your messy house as much as you do; they don't know where things are supposed to go anyway. It takes much longer to clean a house than to mess it up. Be suspicious of any cleaning agent (often designated with a single alphabetical letter, like C or M) that claims to clean everything from floors to dogs. Never install white floor tiles in the bathroom if your family members have brown hair. Cloth diapers eventually make the best rags—another reason beyond ecology. Other people's homes have charisma, charm, because you don't have to know them inside out. If you want high ceilings you may have to give up closets. (Still, as a neighbor once insisted to me, "high ceilings make you a better person.") Be wary of vacuums with headlights; they burn out in a month. A broom, as one of my starry-eyed newlywed sisters-in-law once said, *does a lot*. So does a dustpan. Whatever you haven't touched, worn, or eaten off of in a year should be passed on; something will pop up immediately to take its place.

I can't help thinking about these things—I live in the same town where Heloise lives. And down the street, in a shed behind his house, a man produces orange-scented wood moisturizer containing beeswax. You rub it on three times, let it sit, then buff it off. Your house smells like a hive in an orchard for twenty-four hours.

I'd like to say a word, just a short one, for the background hum of lesser, unexpected maintenances that can devour a day or days—or a life, if one is not careful. The scrubbing of the little ledge above the doorway belongs in this category, along with the thin lines of dust that quietly gather on bookshelves in front of the books. It took me an hour working with a bent wire to unplug the birdfeeder, which had become clogged with fuzzy damp seed—no dove could get a beak in. And who would ever notice? The doves would notice. I am reminded of Buddhism whenever I undertake one of these invisible tasks: one acts, without any thought of reward or foolish notion of glory.

Perhaps all cleaning products should be labeled with additional warnings, as some natural-soap companies have taken to philosophizing right above the price tag. Bottles of guitar polish might read: "If you polish your guitar, it will not play any better. People who close their eyes to listen to your song will not see the gleaming wood. But you may feel more intimate with the instrument you are holding."

Sometimes I like the preparation for maintenance, the motions of preface, better than the developed story. I like to move all the chairs off the back porch many hours before I sweep it. I drag the mop and bucket into the house in the morning even if I don't intend to mop until dusk. This is related to addressing envelopes months before I write the letters to go inside.

247

Such extended prefacing drives my husband wild. He comes home and can read the house like a mystery story—small half-baked clues in every room. I get out the bowl for the birthday cake two days early. I like the sense of house as still life, on the road to becoming. Why rush to finish? You will only have to do it over again, sooner. I keep a proverb from Thailand above my towel rack: *"Life is so short / we must move very slowly."* I believe what it says.

My Palestinian father was furious with me when, as a teenager, I impulsively answered a newspaper ad and took a job as a maid. A woman, bedfast with a difficult pregnancy, ordered me to scrub, rearrange, and cook—for a dollar an hour. She sat propped on pillows, clicking her remote control, glaring suspiciously whenever I passed her doorway. She said her husband liked green jello with fresh fruit. I was slicing peaches when the oven next to me exploded, filling the house with heavy black smoke. My meat loaf was only half baked. She shrieked and cried, blaming it on me, but how was I responsible for her oven?

It took me a long time to get over my negative feelings about pregnant women. I found a job scooping ice cream and had to wrap my swollen wrists in heavy elastic bands because they hurt so much. I had never considered what ice cream servers went through.

These days I wake up with good intentions. I pretend to be my own maid. I know the secret of travelers: each time you leave your home with a few suitcases, books, and note pads, your maintenance shrinks to a lovely tiny size. All you need to take care of is your own body and a few changes of clothes. Now and then, if you're driving, you brush the pistachio shells off the seat. I love ice chests and miniature bottles of shampoo. Note the expansive breath veteran travelers take when they feel the road spinning open beneath them again.

Somewhere close behind me the outline of Thoreau's small cabin plods along, a ghost set on haunting. It even has the same rueful eyes Henry David had in the portrait in his book. A wealthy woman with a floral breakfast nook once told me I would "get over him" but I have not—documented here, I have not.

Marta Alejandro, my former maid, now lives in a green outbuilding at the corner of Beauregard and Madison. I saw her recently, walking a skinny wisp of dog, and wearing a bandanna twisted and tied around her waist. I called to her from my car. Maybe I only imagined she approached me reluctantly. Maybe she couldn't see who I was.

But then she started talking as if we had paused only a second ago. "Oh hi I was very sick were you? The doctor said it has to come to everybody. Don't think you can escape! Is your house still as big as it used to be?"

Nominated by The Georgia Review

GIFT SHOP IN PECS

by LEN ROBERTS

from PARTISAN REVIEW

They paint yellow and red flowers
    on the white vases,
with pale green leaves and stems,
some with dark blue centers,
three dark blue circles with X's.
The embroidery, too, and the small,
    carved walnut boxes,
flowers jutting out everywhere, not
    one Jew on the train
to Auschwitz, which is not so far
    from here,
not one young wife with two children
    dragged from her side. And
African masks, the death mask, the
    life mask, the mask
of love chisled in a jade-like stone,
so heavy I could hardly pick it up
to see the naked bodies, the veils
    covering and uncovering
them. I almost bought the many-armed
    Lady from India, the Wise Fool
from Vietnam, I almost paid the full
    thousand forints
for the handsome Polish moccasins
    with the pointed toes
and small, beaded white horses, smaller

men with sabers drawn
as they rode off the stitched edges.
I had to lift them all to feel their weight,
I had to bring them close so I could see
   the tiny hands and feet, the
curve of an arm, the straight nose, the
   buckle on his shoe, the gillyflower on hers, I had to feel the heaviness
   of their dreams, the foolishness
of their hopes as they dipped thick bread
   into the bowls, as they
snuffed out the candles name by name
by the tiny carved altar, I had to bend
   to hear their silence
as they bowed from the waist and curtsied,
   stiff-legged, without
a single moan, not one face turned
   away, not one hand raised
as they began their strange dance
   on the dustless shelves.

Nominated by Hayden Carruth and Sharon Olds

SESAME

by JACK MARSHALL

from ZYZZYVA

Delectable little seeds
freckling the round cookies' crown—
kaa-iik, in Arabic, strands of skin-
smooth dough pinched together
end to end, each a circle
fitting in the palm of the hand;
speckled with anise seeds, baked
in the oven, golden brown.

Weeks later, I still have the shoebox
filled with them you left for me.
These last years, each new batch made
smaller, thinner,
by your hands that near the end
had to see for you
instead of your eyes that saw,
you said, "only smoke."

After each visit I'd bring my stash
on the plane back to San Francisco
and in my kitchen dip one,
then another into coffee, lingering
over them—hard, edible
chunks of dust; inside, a horizon
taste of anise, after-
taste of the black licorice

252

we were addicted to as kids. Daily
dust we used to munch on
for hours, without their giving out,
kept in the battered tin can on the stove.

Over dishes piled with them,
women gossiped, planned weddings;
men discussed business and argued
the minutest variations of religious law.

Now I ration and savor
each one, since they're growing scarce,
and the recipe has disappeared
along with the maker.

*

Her cooking pots and pans—dented,
discolored, burnt black—
over the years took on
character, each taking on
a different face and shape,
like friends I'd recognize
in her small apartment. Kitchen folk,
who'd served her more than 50 years.
Friends of the family, in
and out of the fire.

*

Having arrived too late,
coffin already closed,
I missed seeing you
a last time.
Later, took a keepsake
from your dresser—
the old pair of scissors,
handles' black enamel
wearing off—I now use
to cut the manuscripts

you never saw, and trim
the beard you made a face at
on first seeing.

Make another face. Any
of your many mocking ones . . .
I wouldn't mind.

*

Laid in ground, July's end
evaporating, in slow-
motion recall: her never asking
"What's on your mind?"
but "Ish fee elbak?" Arabic for
"What's in your belly?"—question
whose grasp of the real
does not depend on any answer.

"Phish elbak" ("Satisfy your belly.")
she'd urge me to
go out into the street
when she'd find me poring over
my microscope and slides,
staining an insect wing, or after
one of my successful chemistry experiments
which stunk up the house . . .

              But I was already
happy, like the roaches
inside the walls
with a little garbage.

*

Excess honey
crystallized in the aluminum foil
lining the can of baklava
she'd urged on me and I'd protest, having

254

too much luggage for the plane-ride back . . .
and now, late as usual, remorse
a near miss,
am glad I brought it.

        Shaved slivers, thick
sugar chunks like coarse silver-streaked
quartz, sticky, fragrant with rose-water . . .
I pinch out
and melt under the hot tap
from the kitchen sink.

I have no use now
for so much sweetness.

*

Long distance
calls I used to make to you Sundays . . .
I'll miss them,

and, as they say, regret
my lower phone bill.

*

She used to tease me:
"If you lost your mind
you wouldn't be losing much."

*

At the cemetery, nodding
toward the expensive pink marble
headstones among rows of grey slabs,
Louie says, "When you're alive
people are not so good to you,
but after you're dead
they're very good. In death,
they're terrific."

255

*

September sun, lower
earlier each day,
and a hard soughing
wind high in the trees . . .

Summer, which did not come,
is not going to.

*

After 80 years, she still cannot read
nor write a word in English or Arabic,
not having been to school, neither
in Beirut or Brooklyn.

In more than 50 years, she absorbs
a few simple words in English in the way sand
absorbs water, and peppers her Arabic
with mockeries of the language
in which she feels herself a reluctant
refugee.

Mimicking Pop's "Don't give me a lecture,"
with "Don't give me a rupture."

*

Another moon shot.
After the first man was landed,
she said, "Let's see them land a man
on the *sun!*"

*

After managing to scratch her name
in English (lower case, predating e.
e. cummings), a painstaking
scrawl, barely

legible enough to qualify
for citizenship papers back when,
she promptly put pen and paper down
ever after.

Her illiteracy, a kind of stubborn
immobility.
         Obstinate
power of the old
         to say *No*.

*

Sad, the way old faces change so much
we can no longer detect in them
any similarity to our own.

*

In the absence of a tape, impossible to reproduce her speech.
Spoken Arabic comes from far deeper
in the throat than English, or what she often scornfully referred
     to as
"Frenjy": all that is quaint, mannered, and ultimately
worthless.

Hawked, gargled, spit: Arabic,
arid and vivid at once. Desert parched
down to a mineral grit where dryness hones things to an edge.
Gutturals and consonants grind stones,
pulverize enemies into a pinch of snuff;
the stuff old Arab men stick up their noses.

*

Odd, from that place you did not see to here,
but from this place you see to there. If so, where
go to be seen

here?

*

In the Koran, "Paradise
is under the feet
of your mother."
Paradise may be
all lust. If so, then aren't we already in paradise . . .

*

At times now, absently turning on the afternoon TV soaps
and game shows. Like you, watching without seeing,
listening without watching, leaving on without listening,
colored flicker, canned laughter.

At your grave we joked
about putting in with you your beloved
TV.

*

You keep coming back
to her whom you came from and fed on
and left.

            She herself is gone. Now
you are not *from* any more, but *to.*

*

Passed on. But not gone? O.K. then,
withdrawn—as God
is that which we have
to do without. For the faithful, God
becomes all
the dreams one
never acted on.

All fresh grows
old. God

or word, what-
ever you cannot live or face,
you're told.

*

Pop used to chide me: "You want things easy
and want to find things out for yourself."
Both true.
And what I have found out for myself is that
things are not easy.

*

Curses in Arabic are like a secret weapon,
incendiary
burrs attaching to the hated one and burning
through the genetic
channel of assholes descending in time
back to his ancestors.

Founded not on feast or famine,
Islam is a fire in the bowels,
extinguishment of the senses.
No wonder, Rimbaud's
headlong
rush into that inferno.

Curses' portable
stream of fire
to annihilate
an enemy's traces
as surely as the desert
wipes out footprints.

We ought to study curses
to know what lies in store for us.

What would have become of Rimbaud in reverse?—
After Africa, poetry . . .

*

How tired of speaking, how exhausted
from appearing you must have been.

The older people become, the more their faces have
to carry the weight
of their entire body.

*

Ike telling about his father:
how in the hospital after a massive heart attack,
the old man (an avid cardplayer) in a coma
kept repeating, "Give me an ace, give me
a king, a queen,
give me a heart, give me a heart . . . "

an hour later, gone.

*

A certain logic of feeling?—
that what we hear leads us to want to hear more?
Forms a pattern oddly familiar
yet alluringly strange; leaps on us
in welcome
surprise or fearful dread, words that must be
made to flow as easily as water; aqua
architecture, going through
you back to the beginning
before taking a next step forward.
Words that can sometimes rescue
if you're lucky
enough to be surprised by them.

*

On TV, the young woman in Istanbul,
after terrorists had gunned down worshippers in a synagogue,

quips, "My mother is Jewish, my father is Muslim;
we have our own Mideast
crisis at home."

*

Yehudi Arabi.
Arabic Jew.
Ox-
      ymoron.

*

In the future
slum or kingdom
come, never
mind the doves, the
wolves will do
fine.

Only let
streets and alleys
not be just wide
enough for one,
in which no two
can meet.

*

Lately am getting practice in peering
into people's eyes at 8 in the morning
at the clinic, putting in Mydriacil drops
to dilate their pupils.

Patients call me "Doctor."
I don't correct them.

Most people squirm in their seats, flinch at the drops
that sting. But the old Asian women from Vietnam and Laos,
slender as young girls in their long, flower-print skirts,

are quiet and still when I lean forward with the dropper;
not blinking, they stare straight ahead.

Photos of the eyes' interior
show light pockets of fluid and dark craters,
nerve webs, blood vessels, like the moon's surface.
Or solar coronas, helical patterns like the rings of Saturn.

Any of them could be your
cataract eyes.

*

Passing the cemetery, an elderly woman on the street
greets a neighbor and her two small boys.
Passing them, croons, "My, my, how you boys are growing fast!"
then turns away, muttering under her breath, "To what,
I don't know."

*

Under blue sky, red-breasted robin standing on funereal land-
      scaped grass . . .
as if these colors, day's variation of the rainbow, delectable
little seeds, could heal once.
And for all.

Nominated by Dorianne Laux, Stanley Lindberg

SEEING YOU

by JEAN VALENTINE

from AMERICAN POETRY REVIEW

1. MOTHER

I was born under the mudbank
and you gave me your boat.

For a long time
I made my home in your hand:

your hand was empty, it was made
of four stars, like a kite;

you were afraid, afraid, afraid, afraid,
I licked it from your finger-spaces

and wanted to die.
Out of the river sparks rose up:

I could see you, your fear and your love.
I could see you, brilliance magnified.

That was the original garden:
seeing you.

2. LOVER

Your hand was empty, it was made
of four stars, like a kite;

blessed I stood my fingers
in your blue finger-spaces, my eyes' light in

your eyes' light,
we drank each other in.

I dove down my mental lake fear and love:
first fear then under it love:

I could see you,
Brilliance, at the bottom. Trust you

stillness in the last red inside place.
Then past the middle of the earth it got light again.

Your tree. Its heavy green sway. The bright male city.
Oh that was the garden of abundance, seeing you.

Nominated by Henri Cole

RAISIN FACES

fiction by HELEN NORRIS

from THE VIRGINIA QUARTERLY REVIEW

THERE WERE NIGHTS when she had a humming bird sleep as she hovered above the bloom of oblivion, dipping a moment to suck its sweetness, then hover again. But there were the nights, black holes of Calcutta, from which she emerged with a weight on her chest, her limbs in chains, and a weariness that was deep in the bone, as if she had labored the livelong night. After such nights she would sit in her chair in the breakfast nook, still a bit in chains, her mind a blank, and let the sun creep over her hands, and slowly she would begin to think, pushing her mind like a grocery cart from one thing to another thing, gradually filling it up with the children, the long afternoons they had spent in the park, the beach, the sand, and the flash of waves . . . till she had a paper sack full of things to feed upon for another day. When this was done, she removed the blue plate from the bowl of cereal Hattie had poured her the night before. She rummaged around with her finger for raisins and ate them slowly, one by one, remembering the water, the children, the sand. Till Hattie came in and found her there and exclaimed, "Miss Coralee, honey, how come you eatin' that dry old stuff?" And then she would carefully drown it in milk. Hattie came smelling of scouring powder and ever so faintly of bacon and corn. During the day it would all wear off. Or Coralee got used to it.

"Hattie, you ate up my raisins again." And the two would have them a wonderful laugh. There was nothing better than Hattie's laugh. It was gingerbread-colored like herself and full of spice, all

265

kinds of it. And she would say, "I must of forgot to shake up that box. They sinks to the bottom, they bad about that." Then she would get down the box of raisins and shake a handful into the bowl, and she would say, "You the raisin-eatinest woman I know." And she would add, "They good for you. They full of iron, how come they black. They put the stiffenin' in your bones."

To encourage Miss Coralee to eat, she would pour herself a handful of raisins and eat them thoughtfully, one by one. And the two of them would remember the children. Hattie had never known them of course. She had come to work eight years ago. But she knew everything that Coralee knew, even things Coralee had plain forgot. Often she said she dreamt of the children. Sometimes in her dream she was struggling against the undertow and snatching Billy by the tail of his shirt and knocking the water out of his lungs. For it was she who had saved the child and not some stranger who happened along. "He was a chil' you got to watch out for ever minute."

"Yes, he was," said Coralee, shaking her head, "but bright as a button, that he was."

"Bright as a shiny blue button," said Hattie.

"You remember the way he would screw up his face when somebody cornered him and kissed his cheek?"

"Sure do," said Hattie. "He was a sight."

"He got away from us once, you know. We were headed some-where. . . . " She stopped and puzzled. "You remember where we were headed, Hattie?"

"You was headed for Mississippi that time. To see your cousin lived in the Delta."

"That's right, we were. We certainly were. We had a wonder-ful time that year. The whole long trip was one big picnic. . . . Do you think we could have a picnic today?" As soon as she said it she knew they would. The weariness went out of her bones. She was full of glistening leaves and sky. The children were run-ning beneath the trees. But she waited for Hattie:

"Don't see why not. Ain't fixin' to rain. What kind a san'wich you got in min'?"

"Any kind as long as you fix it with olives. But I want it to be a surprise."

"Well, it ain't that time. I got to straighten up. You be all right settin' here till I through."

266

Then she brought the album with all the pictures and found the ones of the Delta trip. She opened it beside the cereal bowl. "You set here and study it while I finish up."

Coralee would turn the pages, savoring each, while Hattie, moving from room to room, would sing to herself snatches of song she had learned in church. She made heaven sound like a happy land with a life as happy as life with the children ages ago. When Hattie came close, Coralee would say, "You remember Mindy's first bathing suit? She wanted to sleep in it all night long."

"Sure do. It was pink, real pink. And when it got wet it turn plum' red."

"Wasn't she funny outrunnin' the waves?"

"And all a time shriekin' fit to kill. . . . It's like I birth them chirren myself."

Coralee sighed. "Where did they go?"

"Where did who go?" And when Coralee didn't answer, she said, "Your chirren growed up, that's the trufe of it. Ain't even move off and lef' you, now, like mos' chirren takes a min' to do. I reckon they prob'ly comin' by today." She brushed up the crumbs at Coralee's feet. "My baby lef'. But not for good. One day I looks up and he be there. He stay long enough to git what he want. And then no tellin' how long it be."

"Hattie, my babies left for good."

"Now, who you think come by las' week? Got the same name. Talked like he growed up here to me."

"The ones comin' by are not the same."

Hattie shook her head. "I better he'p you on with your clothes. Case they takes a notion to see 'bout you."

"I don't want to wear that dress with the jelly."

"That jelly dress done put in the wash. I gone find me somep'n bright for you. Summer done got here all the way."

And Coralee thought, Is it summertime? Summer was children and happy time, the world of water and sun and sand. Summer had waited for Hattie to say it.

In the late afternoon Mindy came by. "Knock, knock," she said, bursting into the hall, not knocking at all. Coralee was sitting in the living room. She had gone to sleep over television plays and didn't wake up when they went off the air. Mindy switched the damn thing off. She wandered around the house for a bit, as she always did whenever she came. She skimmed the mantel with her pink-nailed fingers. Her hands were plump. "I'm checkin' on Hattie," she said when asked. "Hattie, I'm checkin' up on you," she called aloud in a jolly voice.

"Yes, ma'am. I know you checkin' on me. You have a nice trip?"

"Oh, that was over a month ago."

"Yes, ma'am, but we ain't seen you since."

Mindy was large, with lively hair. Gold with a rapturous streak of white that swept her brow and was up and away, her sole concession to middle age. Coralee watched her, half asleep, as if she were peering at a curious fish inside a tank. Mindy stayed a while in the dining room, opening drawers and cabinet doors, slamming them shut. Coralee watched her and wished her gone. Whoever she was, she had no business rummaging around. Coralee hadn't let her own children play in the dining room. Mindy called Penny up on the phone in the hall and said she had something to talk about. "Well, pretty soon. I'm leavin' now."

"Mama, be good," she said as she left. But Coralee was dozing again.

"What did she want?" said Coralee, startled out of her sleep when the front door shut.

"Nothin' much. Jus' checkin' on us."

"I wish she'd tell me what she wants."

Then Hattie brought her an early supper. She stuffed some pillows at Coralee's back and rested the tray on the arms of the chair and stayed with her in case she spilled.

"Eat somethin', Hattie," said Coralee. "You know I do better when you eat along."

"Well, maybe I sip some coffee," said Hattie. "But I got to feed my baby at home."

"Is he here for long?"

"No tellin'," said Hattie. The skin beneath her eyes went dark. Her eyes grew older than 38.

"My children are gone," said Coralee. "But they were a pleasure for many years. I think of Penny and how she hated to have her food cut up for her. She wanted to cut it up herself. The fuss she made! You remember that?"

"She'd snatch the knife right out'n your hand. Try to grow up fast. Like to cut herself."

"Oh, my! I remember that. She was such a lively child. We have a picture of fourth of July and barbecue all over her face."

"You want me to find it?"

"Let's have a look. I forget just who she was sittin' next to."

"She was settin' nex' to her Uncle Dave. But you can study it while you eat."

She got the album and found the place. And Coralee ate and sipped her tea, while Hattie fed her bits of the past. The children were with them and nourished her.

The next day Penny came with Mindy, and the two of them went through her things, through all her closets without asking her. They even pulled down the attic stairs, and Mindy climbed while the rungs cried out beneath her weight. Penny stood at the foot and called, "My girdle says I'm stayin' here," and Mindy replied in a voice too muffled for them to hear.

They had left the front door wide to summer and filled the house with air still chilly to Coralee. They said the house needed airing out. The ceiling creaked. The woman in the attic sounded like a squirrel got in from the roof, but bigger than that.

"What do they want?" asked Coralee.

Hattie muttered grimly, "They ain't said yet." She seemed to feel the chill herself. Her hand shook dusting a china doll.

They stared at Penny out in the hall with her high heels and her slender form in a yellow silk and her short brown hair in a stylish cut. She was like a girl high-strung with youth till she turned around. A torpor was in her olive face, which looked like something stored away. Coralee one time had said in a wondering voice, "She doesn't look familiar to me." And Hattie replied, "I reckon a doctor done made that face." But a doctor had never made her voice, which was deep and vacant, to match her face. It tended to wander away from thought.

They went away. Hattie swept the hall of the attic dust and swept their footprints off the porch. "How 'bout a picnic, Miss Coralee? It warmin' up outside real good. You rather have music on the stereo? Them songs you was singin' that time you was all campin' out at the lake."

269

"Why don't we have both?" said Coralee. She was past the age when you had to choose. Hattie understood and gave her choices, then gave her both.

But Mindy and Penny struck next day. They had Billy with them out of the bank. Hattie went to the kitchen and shut the door, but they sent her off to the store for food. They opened windows to let in air. Coralee couldn't think who they were or why they were always coming by. Whenever they came they made her cold. She pulled her sweater across her chest.

Mindy came right down to the point. "Mama, we've got a situation here. You're fond of Hattie. She's good to you. On the surface she is, but she's stealin' you blind behind your back."

Coralee heard the words like so many stones that were dropped on her.

"Mama, your silver is just about gone. Now, where did it go? Did you put it somewhere and then forget? I don't think you're able to carry that stuff. You don't see well, and Hattie's been stealin' it from under your nose."

Coralee was staring into their faces, trying to think what right they had to accuse her of stealing. For it seemed they were accusing her. She said at last with dignity, "Why would I want to take my own silver?"

"Not you, Mama! Hattie's been takin' it, robbin' us all."

"Robbin' you?"

"Mama, that silver goes to me and Penny after you're gone. Grandmother told us before she died."

"I never heard that."

"Well, she said so, Mama. You just forgot. She's robbin' us all. Billy says it must be reported and we go from there."

"The police," said Billy. He was short and stout, with minimal hair, but sideburns the color of weathered granite came to a point like inverted tombstones framing his face. Coralee thought they looked pasted on. There was something about him she didn't trust. "The thing is, Mama, we could get it back if she hasn't done something untraceable with it. And that may be. It well may be. We'll have to dismiss her in any event. That works a hardship on all of us. We'll take turns staying here with you until we can find somebody else."

She listened, dumbfounded. "I don't want somebody else."

270

They said at once, "You don't have a choice."

She was thinking in the depths of her bewildered mind that Hattie always gave her a choice.

Mindy said in a placating voice, "Wouldn't you like to have your children come stay with you for a little while?"

She looked at them, at their stranger faces. "No," she said.

Their faces tightened and then relaxed. "You don't mean that, Mama."

Her mind grew dappled with flecks of fear. "You can't take Hattie. She's all I have."

"Nonsense, Mama. She's just a maid, and we'll get another."

"I don't care what she did. If she did anything."

"But we care, Mama," Penny broke in.

"She has broken the law," Billy said with decision.

She was almost in tears. "It's not a law if it isn't stolen."

"You're not being rational," Penny said.

And Mindy said, "Where is it, then? Where has it gone?"

She closed her eyes to shut them out. "I put it away. I can't remember."

"Where?" Penny said. In her deep, vacant voice the word was like God's.

"We have searched the house. Tell us where," said Mindy.

"I can't remember." They had her at bay. She began to cry.

They circled the room. They walked to the window and bunched together like a flock of birds. Their thin legs waded knee deep in sun. "Here she comes," they said. "Comin' up the walk. Why doesn't she ever use the back?" They turned to Coralee. "Mama, we'll give you till tomorrow to remember. And if you can't, then she'll have to go. Mama, don't tell her why we came. Don't tell her, Mama."

They went away.

Hattie laid the groceries on the kitchen table. Then she put them away. Coralee, weeping, could hear her stashing them on the shelves. She could hear milk sliding to the coldest part of the refrigerator. She could hear water running into the kettle. She was trembling all over and willing herself to have taken the silver and put it somewhere that she couldn't recall. She was willing herself to recall where it was, to recall long enough to tell Hattie where. She was saying, Please, God, let me be the one did it. I want to be the one, please, God, please, God.

271

By the time Hattie came with their cups of tea, God had let her be the one.

Hattie looked at her hard. "Miss Coralee, honey, them chirren a yours done made you cry?"

Coralee sobbed aloud.

"Honey . . . honey . . . don't you fret none about 'em. They done gone down the drive and outa your sight." She drew up a chair and stroked Coralee's arm. "Sometimes chirren can aggravate you so you got to let it out. My baby can git me so mad at him."

"These people don't seem like my children to me. The things they say. They don't like me, Hattie."

"Honey, it jus' the way chirren can be."

Coralee took the tea and drank a little. It made her feel better and even more sure she had taken the silver and put it somewhere and then forgot. She grew almost happy to think how her memory had played her a trick. "Hattie, I know you'd rather have coffee. You don't have to drink the tea for me."

"I likes 'em bofe. And it don't seem right to be drinkin' different. My husband was aroun', I took to drinkin' whatever he said. Exceptin' his likker. I didn't like that."

"You think he's ever comin' back to you, Hattie?"

"No'm, I don't. He gone for good."

Coralee sighed and sipped her tea. It seemed to her that a darkness waited. She thought it had something to do with the silver. Maybe she wouldn't be able to recall. But she wouldn't try to remember yet. "I get to thinkin' they can't be the same. They look so different."

"Your growed up chirren? They the same, all right."

"Penny was sweet with her little curls. For the longest time she didn't know how to give you a kiss. She would just touch her little tongue to your face. . . . They can't be the same."

"They *is* the same. Ever'thing that be gonna change some day. Some way."

"Change to worse, you mean?"

"Ain't for me to say."

"Look at *me*," said Coralee. "I couldn't be worse than I am today. They say I can't manage by myself. I guess I can't."

"You a fine, upstandin' woman," said Hattie. "Your mem'ry ain't good, but it could be worse. And mostly what all you disremember ain't worth the trouble to call it to mind."

"I could get it back if I tried hard enough."

"Sure you could. But it ain't worth the trouble. It mostly trash."

Coralee's hand with the teacup shook. Hattie took the cup. "Hattie, you got to help me remember what I did with the silver. They want to know."

Hattie got up and took away the cups. Coralee could hear her rinsing them out. When the water stopped running, "Hattie," she called, "you gotta help me remember."

"Right now I gotta fix your dinner. Then I goin' home. But I fix you up for bed 'fore then."

Coralee was frightened. When she tried to think she came to a wall that stopped her mind. "Don't leave me," she said, "not knowin' what to say when they come tomorrow."

Hattie came then and stood in the doorway. Her face was dark. "You tellin' me you done took your own silver and put it somewhere and cain't recollec'?"

"Yes, yes. But I don't know where. If you could look in some of my things. . . ."

"I he'p you tomorrow. Soon's I come."

"But they're comin' tomorrow. They said . . . they said . . . if I can't remember they know it's you."

Hattie put a strong, firm hand on the door. "I seed it comin'. They 'cusin' me?"

"If I can't remember. . . . " She began to cry. "I got nobody but only you."

Hattie's voice was cold. "You got them chirren that 'cusin' me."

"No, I don't. The children I had are lost and gone."

"Jesus, I wisht I could be like you and see my chil' as someun' different what he was long time ago. I know he be the same one chil'. All that time he stay so sweet, this troublesome was growin' there. No way, no way to weed it out. Sweet and troublesome. Sweet and bad."

Coralee was struck with fear. "I want to go bed," she said.

"You ain't the onliest one want that. Pull the cover up over my head and when I wake it all be gone. . . . I took it," she said, "to keep my baby outa jail. He owed a man gone git him put in jail for good. And now they gonna git me first. Serve him right he got no mama come runnin' to, keep him outa the trouble he make. 'Cause this trouble ain't gone be his last."

Coralee pled, "If you brought it back. . . . "

"It gone already. My baby done sold it off for cash. He stole some money had to pay it back."

Coralee cried, "I'd a give you money. All you had to do was ask."

"Miss Coralee, I couldn't take your money. Them chirren a yourn don't give you hardly enough to count. But you never looked at them silver things. I thought you'd never come lookin' for them."

"I didn't. I wouldn't. I never cared about things like that. Those people who came here said it's theirs. . . . I don't know. I can't think."

She rocked in despair, the rocker creaking, leaving the rug, slapping the floor till Hattie grimly pulled her back. "Don't git nowheres a-travelin' in that." Her face was darker than ever now. "I bes' clear out and head on home."

"Hattie . . . I'm gonna call that lawyer. He made me a will long time ago. What is his name? Started with 'B'."

"Don't know nothin' 'bout no lawyer."

"He made me a will long time ago." Coralee rocked with her eyes closed, and the tears seeped from under the lids. "Get the telephone book and read. . . . Read the names till I say to stop. Look up lawyers and read the names. Just keep on till I say to stop. . . ."

Mr. Barnhill said he was much too busy and couldn't come. It was out of the question. Not today.

"Then come tonight. You have to come before tomorrow."

"My, my," he said, and was she sure it couldn't wait? At last he agreed to come at four. "I hope you have a good-sized piece of that gingerbread left." And he had himself a good-sized chuckle, because it had been some 20 years. Lately his memory had sprung a leak, and he was pleased to recall details.

"Fix me a cup of coffee, Hattie, and make it double, double strong." While she sipped she was trying to find her mind, where she had dropped it along the way. Beneath her breath she recited the multiplication tables—the twos, the threes. She found she couldn't finish the fours. The fives had wholly disappeared. She tried to name the capital cities, but they had gone with the tables she'd lost. She wept for them. I used to think straight. What happened? she asked. She recited the 23rd Psalm aloud. She whispered the rhymes the children had loved.

"Bring the children, Hattie," she said.

And Hattie, looming like doom in the doorway, laid the album in her lap. "What good they gone do us now? You rummage aroun' and pickin' 'em outa the book like raisins. Raisin faces is all they is."

"I remember things when I'm with them. I touch their faces and think of things."

"Things done happen long time ago ain't gonna he'p us none today."

Coralee drank the bitter brew. "I let my mind get away from me."

When Barnhill came—he was running late—she didn't know him, he had changed so much. He seemed too old, no match for the people she had to fight. And had to beat. She peered from her chair with anxious doubt at his bushy white brows, at his pink cheeks as pink as a brick, his creamy moustache like a piece of pulled taffy scissored off. He hadn't had any of this before. Even his voice had a sandiness that sounded old. She was afraid he was as old as she, and if he was, then he wouldn't win.

He patted her shoulder in a knowing way and, sitting before her, fixed her with an indulgent eye. "Now, what can I do for you?" he said.

She was conscious of Hattie harbored in the kitchen, sounding each word for a prison ring. "Did you make me a will?" she asked in a voice as firm as she could make it sound, and just to be sure he was the same.

"Miss Coralee, I made you an excellent will. I reckon it was twenty years ago."

"Did I sign it?" she asked, for something to say.

"Of course you did. And got it witnessed. All of that."

She gazed into space. "I want it changed."

He pulled his watch chain, slid his thumb and finger down it, dropped his eyes. "I wouldn't think there'd be a need."

"People change their wills. I want it changed." Then as he made her no reply, "The telephone book is full of people who can change a will. All it takes is run my finger down the page and stop when I come to the best in town. I want it changed and changed today."

275

He smiled at her. "Well, now." he said. "I see it's a matter of some concern. . . . You tell me how you want it changed."

She pulled her sweater over her chest. "I have this maid who looks after me."

He inclined his head. "I believe you have children in town," he said. "Perhaps they should. . . ."

"I don't have any one but her."

"Surely. . . ." he said.

But she hurried on. "She took some silver to sell for me. I didn't have any use for it. I never have company in to eat. Most of my friends have moved away. Some have died. . . ."

He listened to her with his bushy eyebrows slightly raised and his fingers touching across his vest.

"Certain people . . . have got the notion she sold the silver without askin' me."

"I see," he said with a knowing nod, and he seemed to be looking at rows of cases, similar ones.

"They want to make trouble. . . ."

"Prosecute?" he said. "On your behalf?"

She grew confused. "Make trouble," she said. Her hands were shaking. "I thought if you would change my will and let it say I leave it to her. . . ."

He interrupted. "That wouldn't do." He seemed to consider. "If she broke the law . . . if she took the silver when she shouldn't have, and that would be easy to prove, you know, then willing it now wouldn't make it right with the law, you see. . . . A lot of silver? What value?" he asked.

Her mouth was dry. "I don't recall."

"You don't recall what you told her to sell?"

She shook her head. Her mind was beginning to slip away. Into the threes and then the fours. . . . She began to tremble. "I just don't want any trouble," she said. "Please, no trouble. I just don't want her taken away." Her voice choked. "I can get the money to pay your bill." And then she was thinking how little she had, and how did she know what it would take.

"Well, well," he said. It was plain to see he had counseled a thousand old ladies before and knew at what point they began to cry and knew at what point he would say, "Well, well." He drew out his watch and studied it. "This watch belonged to my father," he said. "Haven't had it worked on in 20 years. Wonderful the way they made them then." He put it back and fingered the chain. "Miss Coralee, I see you've got strong feelings here. There *is* a little something we could do. It might be a little . . . but in this case. . . . You could sign a deed of gift dated back to a time before she took the silver. It would mean you had already given it to her. So who is to say what she does with it?"

She couldn't help crying with joy and relief. "Can I sign it now?" she said through tears.

"Hold on," he laughed. "I have to draw it up, you know."

"I'll have to have it before tomorrow."

"Well, what if I send my girl from the office around real early? You can sign it then. She can witness it."

He stood up then and patted her shoulder. "You dry your eyes. It's gonna be fine." At the door he added, "I hope she's grateful to you for this." And then he let himself out the door.

"Hattie," she called with joy in her voice, "did you hear what he said? He's goin' to make it all right for us." When Hattie came toward her across the room, it was as if she had lost and found her all at once. She hadn't ever seen her before, not really seen how fine she was, tall enough for the highest shelf, her skin the color of fresh-brewed tea and her gingerbread laugh that was full of spice.

"Miss Coralee, honey, you done so good. You spoke right up to that lawyer man."

"I did, didn't I, Hattie?" she said.

But it wasn't going to be right at all. The girl from the office never came. Coralee sat before her cereal. The raisins in it were hateful to her. When Hattie arrived, she was full of tears. "Did you call that office place?" asked Hattie.

Coralee had never once thought of that. "Hattie, you dial." He had seemed too old to remember things. She tried to recall the things that were said the day before. She only recalled it would be all right.

But the line was busy and busy again. When Mr. Barnhill was finally there, he said, "Good morning, Miss Coralee. Well, well. I've given it thought. It won't be possible to proceed as we said. I'll have to get back to you later on." She heard the never in his voice.

277

She could scarcely report his words to Hattie. Betrayal was all she could recall. Hattie was grim. "Them chirren a yourn has got to him. I heerd in his voice he got a mind could be changed for him. It don't matter none how they done it. Lord, Lord, what I gonna do?"

"Maybe another lawyer would do it. That one seemed too old to me."

"Ain't no time, no time for that. Your chirren be here any time."

Coralee began to cry.

Hattie said in a high, tight voice, "How'm I gone think with you carryin' on?" Coralee choked down her sob. "You got some kinfolks lives outa town?"

Coralee closed her eyes to think. She remembered the capital city of Maine. She whispered a line of the 23rd Pslam. . . . "There's a cousin a mine . . . in Jacksonville. I never did like her all that much.

"Never min' that. You tell 'em how you done recollec' you sent that silver along to her. You tell 'em you give her a piece at a time. I wrop it and took it down to mail. And you done sent her that gifty deed. It hold 'em off for a little spell. Till I can git myse'f outa here." She picked up her purse.

"I won't say it right. You know I won't."

Hattie laid her purse down with a joyless cry. "You tellin' the trufe. I got to fill in what you forgits." She sat in a rocker facing the door. "I mostly skeered a that banker man. Anything money they cain't turn loose. . . . I gits to dreamin' it was me done fished him outa the water that time. Shoulda lef' him to drown hisse'f."

"That was my Billy. It's not the same."

And suddenly they were on the porch and letting themselves in with a key they had. Billy and Mindy were in the room. They seemed to fill it with Judgment Day. They stared at Hattie as if they thought she had her nerve.

"Well, Mama," said Mindy, "did you remember?" It was plain she had not remembered her girdle. The streak in her hair fell across her cheek.

Coralee sobbed a single breath. "Remember what? If you're talkin' about the silver, I did." She told it all, her fingers clutch-

278

ing the arms of her rocker. When she had finished she shut her eyes and asked God please to forgive her lie.

"A gifty deed?" said Mindy to Billy.

"I think she means a deed of gift."

"Well, what about it?"

"I don't know how she got the thing, if she got it at all. But she knows the term. I don't think Barnhill would draw it up."

They spoke as if she were not around or couldn't hear or had no sense.

"The whole damn thing is just insane. I don't think I believe a word. I'll have to check with Cousin Mabel. I haven't heard from her in years. I have her address somewhere at home. Or Penny has it. We'll try to call. What if Mabel does have the silver?"

He ruffled a sideburn and smoothed it flat. "We'll talk about that when we know the facts."

Without even saying goodbye they left. Hattie raised the curtain and peered outside. "Sweet Jesus, they got the po'lees! They talkin' to him. And now they bofe of 'em drivin' off." She turned to the room. "But they be back, direc'ly they speak to that cousin a yourn. Merciful Jesus, they be comin' back!" She sat abruptly, unable to stand. "They comin' to git me pretty soon. I got to git outa town real fast. I got to leave. I got to go."

"Where? Where?" said Coralee.

"Jus' git me a bus ticket somewhere fur. Fur as I got the money to pay."

"Take me with you," said Coralee. The words came out as if they had been in the roof of her mouth for a hundred years. And she was back to a little girl saying them to her black mammy that time whenever it was she left. Nobody told me why she left. She had to go was all they said. Coralee climbed the gate and screamed. Screamed to go and was left behind. Nobody ever took care of me and rocked me to sleep the way she did.

"You crazy?" said Hattie. "You talkin' crazy. I got no time for studyin' you."

"Take me with you," said Coralee. "I got nobody but only you."

"You got them chirren is causin' this trouble."

Coralee cried, "My children are lost and gone for good. How many times do I have to say? You're the only one remembers them and knows what page to find 'em on."

279

Hattie stood and grabbed her purse. She looked around the room they were in, at fine chairs backed with linen squares and the table with china dancing dolls and curtains of lace and picture frames of shining gilt. "You got in your min' to leave all this? You mighty crazy to swap all this. What you think you swappin' it for? Ride on a bus no tellin' where."

"What good is it? What good to me?" She began to rock. "It's like . . . it's like I get to losing who I am and when you come I know again. . . . I rather lose this than who I am. In the night it's like I lose my name. It's like I'm born all over again and all they say is stuff me back inside again. At night you're gone off home but here. I need someone gone home but here and comin' closer all night long."

"Ain't no way it can be that way. Things done changed the most can be. You be nothin' but trouble to me. White and black don't mix no way. I got no money comin' in. The work I gits, it might be long time comin' my way. You ain't do nothin' but slow me down, so likely they cotch us and bring us back and claim I done stole you 'long with the silver."

Coralee was shivering, winter cold. Too cold to climb the gate and scream. She held her handkerchief pressed to her eyes, pressed so hard that her eyeballs ached. She heard no sound, nothing at all, till Hattie was whirling about the bedroom, opening drawers and slamming them shut. Then she was back, saying, "Take that handkerchief down from your face. I brung the money, what little you got."

Hattie was standing there holding a suitcase, holding her purse and Coralee's. "We got to hurry. I brung them raisins for you to eat."

But in the doorway Coralee turned. "We have to take the children," she said.

Hattie gave her a look of bleak despair. "We got no room for that heavy thing. I got your grip here packed to the brim."

"We can't go off and leave them here."

Hattie stood still and shut her eyes. "Jesus, give me strength," she said. She put down the bag and opened the album. She ripped the pages out of the binding and stuffed them into her own handbag. . . .

Nominated by Andrew Hudgins, Joyce Carol Oates

RIVER GIRLS

fiction by JEANNE DIXON

from NORTHERN LIGHTS

THEY WERE LATE this spring because of the cold. But every year when school lets out and the weather warms up, those pale young girls with stringy brown hair or blond, freckles maybe, their cotton-blend dresses hanging straight to the knee, those country girls with lunch box and thermos—Donna, Ardella, Delphina, and Joyce, and Tootie (if she's not too grown-up), dark-eyed Debbie, tall shy Johanna with her braces and glasses—all those see-through girls the boys never notice, shed school clothes like snakeskins and take to the rivers on horseback.

Donna rides a pinto, a stocky black and white. Ardella has a common bay, Delphina a blaze-faced sorrel. Tootie's horse is part Belgian, black as soot at midnight. He pulled a loaded stone boat to victory in a pulling match at the Hamilton Creamery Picnic one year, "broke his wind" doing so, and was sold to a canner for dog food. Tootie's dad bought him back. "A darn good kid's horse," her dad said. "Slow and steady. Can't get him out of a trot." The man could not have guessed what wild currents the old horse would swim, what heights he would scramble to, how he'd pace like a hound to the hunt through the quivering light of the river-lands.

Appaloosa, buckskin, mouse-grey—they gather speed at the first scent of river water. And all the dogs for a mile around hear the clatter of hooves on the gravelled lanes and bark to get out and go with them—fat black labs that slept through the winter by the heater-stove, water spaniels, springers, a wire-haired fox

281

terrier, two red dachshunds, Babs (the postmistress' old Pomeranian with bulging eyes), Donna's German shepherd and its pup, Ardella's black poodle, Tootie's three-legged Airedale that got caught in a trap set for wolves. Ranchers' dogs, too, will run with the river girls. No master's voice can hold them.

The girls take short-cuts down to the Clark Fork, to the Musselshell, to the Yellowstone, Flathead, Whitefish, Blackfoot, Stillwater, Tongue. Montana rivers belong to the river girls. They don't care what they have to do to claim them. They will rip fenceposts straight out of the ground, hold the barbed strands flat so the yelping, galloping horde can jump over. Landowners shoot at them—rock salt, buckshot—but no one can hit them. River girls will do what they want to do. Not even their mothers can stop them.

Tootie and her bunch belong to the Flathead. They tear across fields that used to hold steers or alfalfa, now contain trailer-house occupants. They ride at full gallop over new-seeded lawns, topple tubs of petunias, scatter trailer-house cats and trailer-house children in their rush to get down to the river. A trailer-house woman shakes a fist at them. "I know where you're going, you bad, bad girls! I know what you're up to!" But river girls are already gone, down through the buckbrush and feathery grasses, down through the silver-dimed aspen, down to the willows that shelter them, to the cottonwood trees that love them.

Fishermen don't love them.

Fishing the Flathead, Dutch Anderson and his slow-witted son heard the yelps of the dogs, the whinny and splashing of horses. Dutch dropped his fishpole and tackle, turned for home, and ran. Ever slow, the boy waited on the river bank, astonished in place, as the girls came swimming through the thick green shade. River girls speak softly of this, how the boy reached out to catch them, how he shouted a foul obscenity at them, how Ruth Ann on Dark Hunter scooped up river water and threw it at the boy's face. Dutch and his wife still search the river-lands, looking for him. All they've ever found is a mountain ash twisted in the shape of a fisherman, fishline ingrown in the bark of its branches.

Ruth Ann isn't with them anymore. She became a cheerleader, and Joyce has heard that she's gone all the way with three different members of the Flathead Braves. (Ardella *will* not believe this, Delphina swears it is true!) Tootie will be the next to leave, though she would never say so. Her breasts have grown to the size of the small green apples on the tree by the homesteader's falling-down cabin. She's unbraided her hair and has combed it out in a kinky mass of marshgold or tansy. The last day of school, Pinky MacHarris asked if she'd go out with him when he got his new car, and she said no, not in ten million years.

She leads the way to the place they will go. She jumps the black Belgian from a white clay bank and into the river. The others follow. Smoothly as carousel horses, the sorrel, the pinto, the buckskin, the bay, go up and down, their legs reaching out under water, drawing together, galloping under water as they gallop on land, heads thrust out, ears forward, nostrils red with effort. The dogs form a V-shaped flotilla behind them: the Airedale, the spaniels, the brave little Pom—its fur fluffed out like dandelion puff keeps it afloat. Sun slants across the surface of the water like fire, white fire, flaming around them, subliming them all into gold.

This is what they are up to:

They swim to an island in the middle of the Flathead. They will come ashore on gravel banks or sandbars, sand thick with river mint and hoptoads. And they will turn the horses inward, follow a streambed through wolf willow, wild blue iris, pink roses, through sumac implicit—poison or true. The mothering trees watch over them. They are going to the Place of the Dragon.

They tether their horses to thin green saplings and they run through the river sand to the edge of the deep blue pool edged in snakegrass and waterlilies. All together, the girls will jump in, climb out, jump in. They dive for gold flakes at the bottom of the pool, gold that will always avoid their grasp. Showers of gold rise up around them until they are swimming through clouds of shimmering gold, suspended in water as clear as the vapors of heaven. They weave garlands for their necks, they sing what river girls sing. And they talk, they talk about the time when they will have bosoms, and will walk like Madonna, and sleep in the arms of the boys from their school. But they *won't* have babies, on this they're agreed. No matter how the boys bug them, they won't give in.

Think how the forest has fallen to silence. The smallest of leaves will not tremble. Tootie is chosen this year, so she stands up, steps up to the edge of the pool. She dusts the sand off one shoulder and thigh, hipless, her long legs coltish and dancing. She glances back at the others, at the horses on their tethers, at the dogs beneath the trees, then she calls out across the pool and into the shadows of the cottonwood grove, and waits for the echoing answer.

"Dragon?"

. . . dragon, dragon, dragon . . . "Are you home?" . . . home, home, home . . .

The horses stand in the shade, hooves cocked, eyes closed. Even the dogs are quiet, hardly panting, hidden in the tall green grasses and rushes, waiting in the green leaves of willows.

"Tell me, Dragon, who will I love?"

. . . love, love, love . . . Tootie gasps and covers her mouth with her hands.

Debbie whispers, "Don't be scared, go *on*, ask the question!"

Tootie calls out to the darkness moving through the trees. "Dragon, will anyone love me?"

. . . me, me, me . . .

"Dragon, will I marry?"

. . . marry, marry, marry . . .

At this, the girl falls over backward, laughing and laughing on the river sand. The river girls fall down beside her. They tease her and tickle her. They rub her breasts and her belly with willow leaves. They struggle to hold her, then let her go. She flees. The girls chase after her, shrieking through the river brush, and the dogs jump up—the dachshunds, the Airedale, the German shepherd and its pup, are barking and chasing her, too. The girls free the old Belgian from its tether, drop the halter rope, have to chase it through the undergrowth, weaving through the trees. They catch the old horse and lead him to the pool, lead him in. They climb on his back, bring him irises and roses to twine in his forelock and mane, white daisies for his tail, water lilies—both pink and white—and they want him to know how they love him, how they cherish him, how they're going to miss him, the big black brute.

By the end of summer the Belgian will be put out to pasture, but only for the winter. He will always belong to the river girls— if not Tootie, to someone else, maybe Alice Starbuck, or Daphne

Winters out on Fox Farm Road, maybe Kim or Cara will ride him next summer, maybe Starla.

Sometimes we see them on their run to the rivers, or watch them walk their horses across a high trestle—careful, setting each hoof down just so across the cross ties—or hear the yelping of the dogs late at night, sight the girls beneath the moon in autumn gardens, working their changes, doing what river girls do.

Nominated by Sandra Alcosser, and Northern Lights

THIRD DUNGENESS SPIT APOCALYPSE

by NELSON BENTLEY

from BELLOWING ARK

It was the morning of January 10, in the seventh year of Bonzo,
As Beth and I sauntered the deck of the ferry *Yakima*, under
    radiant
Blue sky. The *Yakima's* wake trailed churning back to the
    Edmonds
Dock, and still echoing in my Irish ears was the short blast,
Pause, long blat that signalled departure for Kitsap. On the
    scuba
Diving platforms with their weathered, sea soaked planks,
    reposed
Half a dozen sea lions, blouaghing like Dante Gabriel Rossetti
    after
A holiday meal. A freight train rolling the Sound edge gave forth
Its Diesel moan. Islands rose in the mists of morning like
    recumbent
Whales, or large sheep that needed shearing on the slopes of
    Gilead

About 1000 B.C. I leaned on the *Yakima's* rail and watched
The sea lions who sprawled on the slippery boards that still
    tossed
In the foaming swirls of the wake. To the west lay the wooded
    slopes

Of Kitsap. I noticed about fifty seagulls flapping with an infinite
Leisure, imperturbable and resigned as Buster Keaton, as they
Soared and dipped, near the railing. It was then I realized
The gulls were led by a six foot oyster who flapped with a slow
Waltz rhythm and resembled the giant roc from the *Adventures*
Of Sinbad the Sailor. His purple, grey and white shell, full of
   ridges
And convolutions, looked like a relief map of the Olympic Range.

Behind him, doggedly winging the fresh Sound wind, came a
   twelve
Winged Olympic Elk, astride whom sat W. C. Fields, dressed as
   he was in
Poppy, holding his tall hat with his right hand, the elk's reins
In his left. "Moose," growled the oyster, doing a mid-air shuffle
Like Ted used to do on a stage, "Your orders are to meet us on
   Dungeness
Spit, in two hours. Have a Moosehead in Sequim, and tune up
   your
Ears with some Yeats trimeter. Recite a chunk of 'Song of
   Myself.'
Think about Emerson by the Musketaquit. Get in touch with
The muskrats of Michigan." At this point, Fields' elk bugled, like
A 1927 Buick passing a plowhorse on Middlebelt Road. Fields

Grabbed his hat with both hands, remarking "Godfrey Daniel!
   Are you
An elk or a sea lion? Keep those antlers steady." He looked like
Barney Google astride Spark Plug in the T-Bone Stakes. I stared
At him as Zachariah must have at the dappled grey horses God
   sent
To patrol the earth after the Babylonian exile. As the ferry
   floated in
At Kitsap, one gull stood on each piling, looking as if he'd just
   read
Schopenhauer, followed by the 148th Psalm. Some were brown,
   some
Gray, with white patches. They looked as though they'd been
   following
Me since I was four. After the prescribed Moosehead in Sequim,

I drove Kitchen Dick Road to Dungeness Spit, and sauntered
  with

Beth through the rainforest ferns, moss, and pine fragrance,
  angling
Slowly down to the spit past nurse logs, crumbled and lined with
  moss
And small trees. I was wearing my Russian hat, and looked like
A cross between Gorbachev in Ireland and Cucullin just after
He flattened a thunderbolt by one blow of his fist and kept it in
His pocket, in the shape of a pancake. As a matter of fact,
  Dungeness
Spit was full of pancake-shaped rocks. Huge logs lay slumbrously
In the surf like stranded dragons. Rocks of a hundred colors and
  sizes,
Muted in color and shaped by centuries, lay above the high
  outgoing tide
That lapped against ancient stumps. Gulls rode bobbing the
  waves

Just beyond the breaker line. Waves tumbled and foamed up the
  gravelled
Slant of beach. Sand and rocks glistened from the tide. Along
  the spine
Of the spit, logs piled like a wall, roots jutting up like Ezekiel's
  hair.
I stopped to meditate on Ezekiel, actually a Douglas fir log.
  Downbeach,
Beth ambled the tidal edge. The sound of churning breakers was
  hushing
In the gravel. Westward toward the ocean, the Strait of Juan de
  Fuca's
Shore curved in toward Port Angeles. Across the strait, dim in
  mist,
Vancouver Island was mostly lost among blue cloudbanks. Sun
  illuminated
Dungeness Spit as I saw, riding in from the north, across the
  strait,
What appeared to be a fine kettle of fish, on the back of a
  rhinoceros

Disguised as an elephant, ridden by Oliver North and Admiral
Poindexter, who held an American flag and a carved sign
    reading
"White House Basement." At this point Roethke, still incarnated
As a giant oyster, settled with a flutter of his six wings on a
    cedar
Stump the size of our old kitchen table at Elm, and spoke with
A growling, gritty, rumbling, gravelly bellow. I thought to
Myself, "Beware the words of an infuriated oyster." "Moose,"
    roared
The oyster, fingering his convoluted top with a gray, gull-like
Wing. "What do you see?" "Well, Ted, I see, behold, a
    rhinoceros
Posing as an elephant, and Oliver North holding a fine kettle

Of fish." "What does that remind you of, Moose?" "Well,
    Oyster, I mean
Ted, it makes me think of Jeremiah." "Right on the nose, Moose.
When Jeremiah saw the boiling pot from the north, the Lord
    said
To him 'Out of the north evil shall break forth upon all the
    inhabitants
Of the land.' " The oyster hopped, like a rather ponderous
    ostrich,
Onto another cedar stump which was festooned with pebbles
    and about
A hundred jelly beans. "What are these on the stump, Moose?"
"Red, white, and gray pebbles, and red, white and blue
    jellybeans,"
I replied. "What do they signify, Moose? Come on, make it
    snappy.
Never try the patience of an oyster." "Reagan's pseudo-American

Viewpoint?" "Gillyflower ho. You've got it." I was perched on a
    dry
Douglas driftlog on the crest of the spit. In the inner harbor,
    waterbirds
Sailed like an armada. At the end of the spit the lighthouse was
    barely

289

Visible, white in the sun, floating on the misty blue shoreline. The rhinoceros
Stood snorting and glowering as the tide washed around his ankles,
And Oliver North sat grinning on top of him, looking like Reagan
In an early role, or Alfred Newman on a Mad Magazine cover.
I could see he was the embodiment of Reagan's faulty ideas of
America. About him in the White House was his pantheon of nationalists:
Reagan, Meese, Buchanan, Regan, circumventing congress and our laws.

Above North hovered the sleepy presence of Calvin Coolidge, Reagan's
Guardian Angel. "Over here, Moose," the oyster growled grittily,
And I walked gingerly past the grim grunts of the rhinoceros,
To a gravelly slope, shell-and-kelp-strewn, on either side of which
Lay fir-logs that looked as though they'd been tossed in ocean waves
For decades. On one log sat Cotton Mather, Douglas MacArthur, Rambo,
Bonzo, Jerry Falwell, Oliver North, and Zane Grey. On the other sat Walt
Whitman, Abe Lincoln, Jeremiah, Buster Keaton, Emerson, who was waving
A huge transcendental eyeball, Mark Twain, and Frank Baum, who
Wore a hat featuring a map of the Land of Oz. Two cheerleaders

Pranced forth onto the pebbles: first, Richard Nixon, who began trudging
Gravel like Roger Chillingworth among the kelp, or like Poe's Raven
Shifting his claws on the Bust of Pallas, or like Senator McCarthy entering
An Un-American hearing, or like Al Capone pondering his next move,

And growled rather like a rhinoceros, looking Bonzo, North and
    Falwell in
The eye, "Give me an N." "N." "Give me an I." "I." "Give me
    an X." "X."
"Give me an O." "O." "Give me another N." "N." "American."
    "American." In
Front of the other log, Vachel Lindsay and the oyster were doing
    a waltz,
Followed by the Charleston and a Bunny Hop. As they passed
    me, Ted
Grunted, "I studied this with Lewis Carroll." Then Ted, Vachel,
    and Fields

Picked up megaphones and called toward Abe, Buster, Twain,
    and Baum,
"Give me a W." "W." "Give me an A." "A." "Give me an L."
    "L." "Give me
A T." "T." "American." "American." The oyster rolled around in
    surf
For a minute, emerged fresh and dripping on the gravel, and
    growled
"Remember, Moose, what Moses said just before climbing Mt.
    Pisgah
In Deuteronomy. 'I call heaven and earth to witness against you
This day, that I have set before you life and death, blessing and
    curse;
Therefore choose life.'" And there they joyously hoofed the gravel.
The rhinoceros watched glumly, weighed down by the White
    House basement;
Ted and Vachel danced weaving the tideline, singing "Yankee
    Doodle Dandy."

Nominated by Harold Witt

STORIES

fiction by F. L. CHANDONNET

from THE THREEPENNY REVIEW

I

THIS IS A PRESENTATION of some entries in the diary of a boy—
my son—who died of pneumonia and, I think, exhaustion recently.
I say "some entries" for a number of reasons, not the least of
which is that an entire body of anyone's personal rumination can
be tedious to contemplate. And the boy was sixteen years old, an
age that forgives itself too many confusions. I think a reader
ought not to have to suffer through such dense idiosyncrasy.

I have made changes for the sake of brevity and clarity.

Edward was very dear to me.

I had, myself, kept a diary as a boy and know only too well the
terrible prospect of disclosure that threatens every young diarist.
And so I've deleted the egregiously personal from his notes. (I
stopped keeping a diary at about the age Edward did, and when
I tried to read my entries a couple of years later I found I
couldn't: They were terribly embarrassing, the perceptions utterly self-conscious. Even with the log entries—the quotidian—
there was this fraud.)

And of course there are the awkward composition and incom-
plete representations that challenge the editor (I suppose that is
what I am) to conclude either that they are not worth finishing,
or that they are worth the moral and intellectual demands of ex-
trapolation.

I present the boy's sentiments because they're interesting. He
was articulate, and at the same time able to apprehend what was

292

in an interlocutor's heart, no matter the energy or plausibility of the misrepresentation.

His talents, such as they were, grew out of the meager soil of the family's peasant stories—he always listened closely—and his reading, a boy's reading when everything is seminal.

I will recount a couple of these stories—some of them merely scenes—so that the reader may establish what congruence he can between what Edward heard and what he wrote.

My Brother or sister told the story of the great-uncle who worked as caretaker in an insane-asylum and who was witness to a variety of behaviors. (Each element was related in an inviolate series, as with the alphabet. If a scene or event should be described out of its customary position in the sequence, one of us corrected the mistake, and the litany went on. There were no thematic priorities that I remember. One simply observed the protocol of rote.)

A young man—they were all men and, for the most part, young—was an extraordinary pianist: there was a grand piano in his cell and he played it beautifully. But, invariably, in the midst of one of his isolated recitals, he stopped, stood, and raged. At no particular object. He waved his arms, shouted and cursed, and otherwise alighted from his short flight of reason. (A half-dozen scenes later, a young man sang—in an extraordinary baritone— selections from Verdi operas. The description of the singer introduces a violent dynamic to the sequence: initially, there is verisimilitude lent the two cases because they are diagnostically corroborative—the singer stops singing and rants. Then the mind settles on the coincidence, always suspect. And, finally, the detail that could not have been invented gels our certitude: He sang not solos but only his part from duets and trios. It was Verdi, and so the part was melodic—but not sufficiently melodic to have testified to the young man's sanity.)

In the next scene, or cell, a man prays to God for deliverance, for the key that will let him out of his cell. There is no interruption of the prayer: it is understood that what is unlikely, what rounds off his craziness, is that in or out of his cell there is no change in his disturbed nature. The key means nothing.

Edward occasionally asked for clarifications and for information that might attach more substance and form to what he heard. (In

293

another time, perhaps, he might eventually have repeated the stories.) He asked, "What made these men crazy?"

It was not the fashion, then, that many were born so. And my brother, after a pause, replied, "Venereal disease."

The young Edward, "What's that?"

His aunt, opaquely, "Filth."

One man in his cell hunched over an escritoire for most of the day. If this seemed obsessive, that he should write continuously with a pencil on a plain tablet, one ought to consider, said the narrator, that there wasn't much else to do, after all. He was particular in his dress and civil to the attendants. The great-uncle never discovered why this man had been incarcerated. The orderlies were close-mouthed. But the man was deferred to in the way that we defer to the violent, and so those who weren't privy to his history supposed that he had committed some awful crime for which there could be no satisfactory explanation.

Edward asked, "What did he write?"

The answer, "He wrote about his family, himself, some travels in Europe, observations on and commentary about justice in the United States. There was nothing remarkable, nothing that pointed to the reason he was in the asylum."

Once, Edward wondered aloud about what seemed to be fictive additions to the narrative, or even bald ratiocination. Why were these explanations not in the body of the story?

In fact, Great-uncle had been an astute observer and had addressed all probable concerns. If some seemed after-thoughts now, it was because a destructive boredom would have resulted from the exact retelling.

With each account came a large store of explanations. And the stories became more stylized with the passing generations. (Until, one supposed, they disappeared. I am of a mind that useful information—lore, for example—is no less a physical phenomenon than is some bit of matter, and is, correspondingly, at once mutable—who is to say where ideas go or what they do?—and eternal. To be sure, such a view relegates accuracy and the process of authentication to the moral sphere, relatively unimportant in these times. But these are rather fine concerns and come to little, imbued as stories so often are with the unseeing urge to obeisance by one generation to another. I admired Great-uncle and the others. Who among us tells of his life and not of himself?)

Another story involved my father. (I can't think of him without adding to his name "an expert machinist." It was the custom in his time to append skills and achievements to a name just as in earlier times one's birthplace was thought to be of consequence.) He was poor, as the story goes, and had social and intellectual pretensions. On Wednesday nights, one of Father's fellow workers came to the tenement flat to declaim. Two or three neighbors might be there, along with my mother and the six children.

The program was invariable and consisted of a half-dozen poems. Two were narrative: "Evangeline" and a translated abbreviation of "La Chanson de Roland." One was a pastoral. The rest were religious poems of the pietistic sort that was popular then.

As children will, they strewed themselves around the parlor, preferably out of their father's line of vision, in the most unlikely and, probably, comfortable positions. The rhetorical presentation was nothing if not pompous—it was the style, then—and was thought to be "accomplished."

The children listened, rapt, to the history. They began to fidget during the pastoral and to transmit covert simian grimaces to one another. (Father maintained that this deterioration was due in no small part to his co-worker's inability to vary his stagey delivery.) The man postured and puffed for the "mottled light beneath a beech" precisely as he had for Roland when the latter, in effect, blew his brains out. And the recitation of "Roland" itself had lasted twenty minutes.)

After the pastoral came the first of the religious poems, announced as "A Dissertation, in Verse, on the Theological Virtues of Faith, Hope, and Charity." The performer roared along, his face a tumid mask, blank—or inured—to the sacrilege at his feet. The children's detritus became missiles and their titters choking and coughing sounds whenever a member of the adult company looked their way.

Father appeared insensible to this little rebellion, and the children were thus encouraged to continue to flout decorum during "An Ode to Saint Sebastian."

The grotesque and horrible death inspired a general hilarity in the children, even in the face of certain, brutal retribution. (My father was not above leaving welts and bruises on the faces and backs of his children.)

The last piece, "Lying in the Arms," was a kind of de-Christing of the Pietà. The audience was asked to place *itself* in the arms of the Virgin, instead, and to imagine thereby her grief and love. This poem, although it was part of an unvarying repertoire, never commanded the attention of even the adults, and was considered a kind of dénouement of the evening. Its conceit was impossible and bore repetition only by reason of the importance of its protagonists.

During the opening lines of "Lying in the Arms" the children recognized the impending end to their liberty and therefore gave even more play to their chaotic instinct, until at last there was barely-controlled flatulence and even the odd escaped guffaw. Very soon, before the poem (of some hundred lines) was half through, their exclamations and movement abated; their faces lost the pink of sublimation. At the end, his arms hanging parallel at an angle that nicely balanced his upward gaze, the performer uttered the final refrain and repeated the last lines, "Lying in the Arms, Lying in the Arms."

Now the children were quiet, attentive, lending weight to what must surely be a unanimous suspicion that Father's memory was defective.

Edward expressed concern that his grandfather was too easily dubbed a brute. In the story, the children's behavior was as predictable as the program, which suggests that their father was not nearly as severe in his retribution as the story implies. In an—I admit—odd defense of the soubriquet I reminded Edward that he himself had not infrequently laughed in my face as I applied the strap to him.

"There's something blasphemous about the last poem," he said.

I'm afraid that no sampling of Edward's reading could be considered representative. Like most young readers, his ability to discriminate or even to categorize was not well developed. And so he would read through what was conveniently available (loose books from my library, from the public library, inexpensive paperbacks, found books) what was conveniently available of a category that caught his fancy.

He would, for example, develop an interest in the dystopian novel, and soon exhaust his own patience with that narrow genre.

For a time he read biography and asserted that the study of history was properly the study of personality. Historical fiction interested him, and then history. His last enthusiasm was for philosophy, the analysis of which was beyond his ability, really. It was to his credit, however, that he plodded through many a dense or abstruse treatise without understanding much. It seemed enough that a work was alien to his experience, or that its vocabulary was new. The difficult, even the impossible, held a fascination for him that is commonly reserved for the bizarre.

I want to mention, finally, an interest—which is not to say a fixation—Edward developed in a series of books by a popular writer named Castañeda. The consideration is not impertinent to Edward's final interest.

At least one of the books was given to Edward by a friend. I, myself, read one or two, as I had an interest in sampling Edward's reading.

Castañeda's stories dealt with the preternatural. (Although uncomfortably, I thought: The incoherence and the improbable in aboriginal behavior he could barely address except through the agency of hallucinogenic drugs and plants. The opus is a great effort to conciliate—through facile and popular means—his own understanding with the experience of a people who barely speak his language, and whose customs and traditions he must present with the ancient and simpleminded metaphor of transmutation.)

Birds and dogs communicate complex thoughts. Human beings become animals. And over all, there is that impenetrable Caste of the Aware defining and disseminating its imprecise arcanum.

Edward was concerned that what took place was impossible. He asked why, then, would anyone write about such things (the intimation being, therefore, that such things as happened were not impossible. Men, quite literally, became crows). I suggested— weakly (the alternative was to draw the convenient parallel with, and the strength from, the impossible, the nonsense that is so much of Art)—that such stories would earn money for the author, as would engaging descriptions, or depictions of the tension that is inherent to the ordinary.

Edward asked, "What makes the stories convincing?"

I offered that Castañeda was a madman; that he was offhand; that he was, in the magical sense, charming.

Here are some of Edward's notes.

II

The focus of my attention was reciprocating between the snippets of odd religion I could hear and my own musings about the received correlation between cold granite and piles when I heard the thumping in the tenement. I was frightened at first because I couldn't see what it was—the way violence on the periphery of a sense frightens us in a dream. But I rose and turned. His head was lower than the rest of his body—good for healing, I thought. He stood abruptly, brushed himself, stepped past me, and sat down.

Quite the gentleman: His skin was pink. It was clear, too, like the skin of a shopkeeper. I thought it must be protesting the sun on it—braying in some inaudible frequency—and the blood on it as well, an enameled rill coursing down his high cheek along the jaw to a drop on the chin.

He sat on the wide granite stoop as if he knew what stoops were about. This was no fool, for all his theology. He knew my father wouldn't pursue him here. The landing at the door was a kind of gate beyond which everything was permitted: he might sit on the stoop, just as he might urinate on the wheel-less automobile he now studied, or he might lie there and bleed undisturbed.

I liked him and wanted to give him credit for negotiating the stairs on his neck and shoulders—and the 180 degree turn between the two small flights, a complex and dangerous carom. And credit for standing up straightaway to perform a comic self-dusting (there was no dust: my mother kept the decaying stairs and landing paintless with her scrubbing). But what could I say? You fell with, you were thrown with, you caromed with grace?

He looked at me now with round yellow-brown eyes, close together and intelligent. A nose like a rudder swept down to a full or fat lip (it was hard to say which). (I understand now why soldiers who have been injured, somehow, are given medals. It is for love and curiosity: Generals want to know more about the ambience of injury.)

"Do you really think that Christ came to the United States?" I asked. I thought he couldn't be serious.

A barely audible "America" percolated out of his throat, the "m" a ventriloquist's miraculous "m." And the gold eyes caught my face. (To the missionary, a question is an oath of allegiance.)

298

But he grew sullen again. Was he skeptical about the motivations of a potential convert? Or was he only in pain? What could I, a boy and the son of a fool, know or feel about extraordinary revelations of the sort he possessed? "Do you have Hell?" I asked. I was being selfless; It was for my father that I asked. I was helping the missionary in his work, goading him into vengeful and positive action.

"Are you angry?" But of course that dissipated his anger and he favored me with an expression which ought to have been charismatic (after all, slights—of whatever magnitude—are slight, and one reacts no doubt to the larger stimulus always, which is to say, to God) but which was only intense and, further parsed, both febrile and hangdog.

From a trouser pocket he produced a paper towel and applied the stanch to his cheek, dabbing vaguely as if at perspiration. From inside, a door scraped open and, after a second, slammed shut. He dropped the dotted paper between his feet and said, "What is really true is obvious and doesn't require much evidence. What requires a lot of evidence and proofs is at least suspect." Gesturing to the stairs with his head, he continued, "Is this a good life for you?"

There was a prickle on my nape. My father did not throw me down stairs, it's true. But he did other things, evidently. I struck out, "Next we're gonna levitate. Am I right?"

He pointed to the wreck.

The automobile had been there for months. The complaint to city authorities had been mistimed, lodged as it was when the car still had tires on it, and appeared to belong to someone. In time its windows had been crazed and broken. A neighborhood sidewalk lawyer inquired about printed guidelines that might describe the degree of decay that initiates municipal concern.

"This is a bad neighborhood for you," I said. "Catholic. Are you going to go up and give it another shot?"

He ran his fingertips down a lapel.

"My father doesn't trust people who wear suits. You look like you come from City Hall."

"Did you ever wonder why I would put up with this kind of abuse?" He kicked the paper towel away. "Do you really think there are that many crazy people around? Do you want a ham-

299

burger?" He rose and dusted the seat of his trousers, stopped in mid-brush, and looked down as if to reprimand me for staring at his ablutions.

Across the street was the Luncheon Spa. A sign above the entrance read, "Where the Elite Meet to Eat." The place sold food and magazines. We sat in a booth.

"You have to admit it's pretty exciting," he said, with a real warmth on his face, bruised now around the forehead and one eye. (Two weeks after I'd left home and come to live with him— the missionary—my father had caught him on the street.) The idea of owning his own planet was central to his enthusiasm.

Of course it *was* exciting. I said, "If you're an Arab and you die," this was a gift, some supporting evidence, "women wash your feet. And you get to sit in the shade. They bring you figs." (I wondered why one man's apotheosis was humble and another's so ambitious.)

His name was Bob, his church's a tautonym. Green plants, hanging and on pedestals, colored his small apartment so that there was nowhere for the eye to rest that was free of the blue of garden.

His eschatology was preposterous, but he didn't carry on about his own excellence or mine, and that pleased me. And he presented the insolent, strange physics of translation-from-revelation with such straightforwardness and lack of zeal that the impertinence of an inquiry into the peculiar necessity for translation seemed obviously that: an impertinence. I would have, quite naturally and often, presumed something even sillier than what preoccupied me now, he suggested. And he furnished examples enough, silly and true, to have stirred resentment and admiration in any sixteen-year-old: I love my father; I assumed that something financially fortuitous would happen to me someday; I thought that bears hibernated and that all men shall be brothers.

When he posited something difficult (on the first day on the stoop I should have said something difficult-to-swallow) I searched the set of his face for the humor of the skeptic or the cynic's calm.

He said that a young man had visited him—in this apartment—, a young man with shoulder-length hair and wearing a cinched

300

white gown. Adhering to the gown were a number of glowing balls, iridescent balls, of the size used in ten-pins, he said, all along the upper and lower edges of his arms and to either side of his body. Bob couldn't see the feet of the apparition.

I asked, "Was it an apparition?" As a little boy, I imagined that babies "appeared" in cribs. "How adhesive would the balls have been, rubbing against the doorframe? Did he come through the door? Did he knock? Were the balls an aide to propulsion? What would be the purpose of exhibiting these phenomena? Marveling at the extraordinary is only a manifestation of ignorance. How does that promote a sense of conviction?"

Bob continued, "What he said seemed to flow from his hands to me. The spheres rolled out of his head and up from below to his hands. His hands spoke to me."

These declarations left me confused in the same way a popular writer had left me, with his matter-of-fact claims of transmutation induced by drugs and aboriginal rites. Imagine becoming a crow or a wolf! How simple it was!

What the apparition conveyed—it *was* an apparition, Bob said—was millenialist: There would be meted out portions of land, and so on, the diminishing reserves of which was not an obstacle when one considered the innumerable planets that existed in the universe.

I'm reminded of an unlikely story my father or one of his siblings recounted at the kitchen table. It was of a man who had been a brilliant pianist and who had suffered some kind of mental breakdown. Thereafter, the pianist, when he attempted to play, found it difficult or impossible to finish a piece. As the story went, the technical demands of his art caused him some considerable strain. He was left with a profound paralyzing anger and spent much of his time, when he was not in the midst of some soon-to-be-truncated prelude, shouting wild, detailed imputations and ascriptions of responsibility for his condition. (What seems implausible is that he should have started a piece at all: it is a commonplace among performing artists that the "butterflies" are at their most disruptive before and at the beginning of a performance. And yet the pianist could not have been wholly fantastic. There was talk of Debussy and Schubert, and our family had

301

neither musicians nor intellectuals in it. And the episode was not obviously didactic. There was no contravention—by the pianist or any other—of the family's moral sense, which is to say its usual way of doing things. Further, the story was ascribed to someone whose credibility was unquestioned.)

I know my digressions often materialize as my father's stories. It's because I think of him so frequently, about his too frequent incursions into my life. I have in mind the assault on Bob two weeks after I'd left home.

Bob prospected for converts in a variety of ways. I've already mentioned that he went to individual residences and spoke to people there. Once a week, if the weather was good, he walked three blocks from his apartment to a large intersection of five streets. One of the corners was known as a place where orators held forth—crackpots, it was said by some, and by others men and women who sought to legitimate their delusions by publishing them.

It was the custom—the corner was prominent but narrow—that the speakers stood in a queue. On that day, Bob followed two speakers, one who averred that world peace would follow the universal outlawing of military conscription, and another, the man before Bob in the queue, who alleged that certain kinds of food promote peace of mind.

Later, Bob told me that his presentation had been met not only with the usual curiosity but with genuine interest as well. He told of the substantial rewards that would come to those who converted—I've mentioned the meting out of parcels of land, and even planets. He explained that his goal was simply to proselytize and to have converts proselytize in turn. And he said that there was no cost for membership in the church, financial or emotional.

"Hey! Who wants to go to Mars?" A shout from the gathering audience.

A calm Bob. "You have only to read astronomy to know that our own solar system is dust; that there are uncountable billions of planets; that it is probable that life on many of them is immeasurably better than ours on Earth. What I offer is the solid scientific sentiment—discovered by Darwin—that the improbable is less so with the passage of time."

302

Bob himself was not excitable, and this calmed his listeners. Now the heckler was silent.

Bob went on, "Do you think that God, with all time on His hands, could ignore the needs of mankind? And if He did, with all of Time mixing the elements, could He prevent the accident of human happiness from coming to pass?" Surely they could not attribute indifference or arrogance to God.

Now he described the manner of revelation, after which the heckler responded, "A guy with glowing balls wearing a dress?"

Someone shouted, "AIDS!" which initiated a rolling chuckle. The crowd had grown enough that pedestrians negotiating the corner remained in the street.

"Do you joke about burning bushes?" They quieted. "What about flaming chariots?" Bob's voice rose, "What about strange dreams and silver stones?"

He appealed to their credulity as if it were a quality, something they could be generous with.

"Hey! Hey!" A fat man whose pale nose grew out of an inflamed red base threw glances to his right and left and contended, "Hey! The guy was deaf, right? He talked with his hands!"

"Wy'ent you get a job?"

"Wait! Let him talk!"

At the rim of the group, now numbering thirty or so, a reedy whine intoned a Low-Church melody:

FATHER we THANK Thee FOR the NIGHT,

"Hey! Lady! Wait your turn!"

"He spoke with his hands and said what was already in my heart."

AND for the PLEAsant MORNing LIGHT;

"He is the same 'angel' who will come to you on the day of reckoning, to settle accounts. How many here are ready to settle?"

"Fucking bitch!"

FOR rest and FOOD and LOVing CARE

It was an old woman. Someone shouted, "Shut up!"

AND all that MAKES the WORLD so FAIR.

There was a soft thud, and the voice became a bleat for a second.

"Those among you who have sought to explain your convictions to others will be transported to planets where you will rule absolutely!"

"Will we have glowing balls?"

"Wait! Let him . . . "

"Many of you are poor, and so are halfway to sainthood. What have your churches done but take . . . "

"At least they're not crazy!"

" . . . your money! You're poor and you're nothing! Your families are poor! Your families have been nothing for a thousand years!"

"Hey! Do we hafta die to get the planet?" The fat man's eyes darted to the faces around him.

It was then that my father materialized in the front rank. Which put a quick fright into Bob, so that he paused (to all outward appearances because his response to the fat man's question would be noteworthy). "No. It's important to understand that *every* day is a day of reckoning. I'm not talking about some wild war that will announce a new order, some Armageddon in the vague future." (Here I commended him for laying siege to the suspect. But he didn't respond, and continued with the story.) "You could be judged at any time. What is important is that you *do* good, not how *much* good you do. If you are good *now*, in a moment your misery could be gone."

The lids half-covered half my father's eyes. His thin frame hung loose in an old suit. His left hand held the right forearm behind his back. "What about families?" he asked. "If people are to be rewarded as you say, families will disintegrate."

Bob raised a hand to signal to all the quality of the question, or to quiet the susurrus of impatience the question stirred, or to protect his head from the short piece of two-by-four lumber that missed his hand and clattered against his chin and cheek and forehead.

Bob saw, all at once, the grain of the sidewalk, upturned or downturned faces, and two or three hands that clutched carelessly at the buttons and material of his suit-jacket, condemning the poor quality. Then he stood on the wooden box (could even seconds have passed?) feeling grateful. My father was gone; the eyes he looked into were stunned and expectant.

He fairly shouted now, half his face burgundy-stained, "Consider that the most successful among you will have millions of others to do your bidding! Brothers and Sisters! Please give what you can to this mission!"

304

Bob took a cloth cap from inside the jacket and demonstrated its lining.

I asked, "When you speak on that corner, do you recognize anyone?"

"Yes," he said. "There are four or five who come there regularly. And they will ask the same questions every week, if they see the crowd is good."

"I wonder if you dressed well, if you wore obviously expensive clothing, if that wouldn't lend more credence to what you say. The most successful chiliasts dress well and are elaborately coiffed."

Bob said, "I've thought about it."

My father sent me a long letter.

My dear Edward,
Since you seem to have been avoiding me (in fact, avoiding everyone: your friends say they haven't seen you since you left home) I thought I should write you, for no more complex reason than that your disappearance saddens me. Your aunt and I were chatting at home recently—she was telling the story of the pompous poet (it's the one you found amusing)—when she asked about you. She remarked that the phrase "mottled light beneath the beeches" had intrigued you. It *is* a peculiarly flat phrase, isn't it? And you don't have actually to have been at the recital to see how much flatter it was made by the stiff poses and elocution.

Your aunt and I disagree about the declaimer's name. I know it is Dunham. She is equally sure it isn't and sought to convince me with a mnemonic device she had fabricated as a girl: His name was Smith, she said, and he forged literature.

Anyway, his name was Dunham, and the religious poems were his. I suspect that he had written the pastoral as well. Although he had a job—worked with my father, in fact—he never seemed to have any money. His clothing was threadbare and his wife and children were, from all appearances, ill-fed. I suppose he was glad for the couple of meals his neighborhood recitals fetched him every week.

Our family thought of him as a preacher and therefore accorded him—as was our custom—both respect and ridicule. The

305

former by way of an invitation to address us, the latter in the children's demeanor.

My father was not a religious man and had read a good deal of theology. It is difficult to know why he entertained the simple-minded, formulaic verse that Dunham peddled. Your aunt suggests that he was sorry for the dissipation of the stories of his own childhood, and felt ill-at-ease with the idea of progress. (And of course he could hardly have had a bishop or an academician come to our flat.)

But I rather think that he saw himself as a failure: He was a machinist, after all, and had read a great deal. And so he sought to lend the same legitimacy to the silly as to the sensible. (Is there another rescue for the failure?) At supper he would point to the silliness of the philosophers. And he would go to great lengths to explain to us the meanings of martyrdom. If he lived today, he might want to "go back" to farming.

But back to Dunham for a moment. We're accustomed to the unbearably pious and smug expression of the doomed saint. And Dunham never failed to incarnate the cliché: arms extended and supplicating, head rolled back, whites of eyes displayed, mouth in ecstatic rictus. I reckon that Dunham didn't know Saint Sebastian *didn't* die of his arrow wounds (difficult to believe, that: can you imagine a third-century puncture wound *not* putrefying?).

A good poem would have been a meditation on Sebastian's convalescence and his pointless re-confrontation with Diocletian. S. S. was condemned, originally, for his proselytism. Why should he check his career by throwing his miraculous survival in the tyrant's face?

My father, in one of his dissertations on martyrdom, contended that life in the third century probably wasn't very pleasant. Under such circumstances the extreme action isn't extreme, he said. And it is always possible that S. S. simply wasn't very bright (we tend to forgive the perfervid a certain mediocrity of intellect). Sebastian, overwhelmed by his good fortune, is certain that his emperor—never mind the persecutions—will suffer a fit of empathy. Picture Sebastian ambulatory, just, his brow damper than his normal zealot's brow. Imagine his shock when he hears, now, that they will beat him to death.

You know, I think that artists' preference for death-by-archery is understandable: compare the delicate pricks of Renaissance ar-

306

rows with the alternative bludgeoning. (Did you know that Sebastian is the patron saint of pin-makers? It seems comic, doesn't it?)

As for the franchised Pietà, I don't know that it was blasphemous. I mean, I think it's a bit late in the day for that, for blasphemy. (Primitive religionists, you know, consider the rendering of the human—or divine—form blasphemous. And I remember hearing as a boy that you blasphemed—officially—if you struck a priest. Something like killing a policeman today. I thought it a weak business, and un-American.)

Father seemed to like the first of the religious poems, the one about faith, hope, et cetera. He said Dunham lent a kind of rough strength to virtues that hadn't breathed since the eighteenth century. (Of course, Dunham did nothing but orate, and Father was being sentimental.) He thought the theological virtues an important convention, one that had been burdened in recent times with the cowardice and indolence of the tenured. Years before, one of the last sermons he had submitted to was on Faith, Hope, and Charity. The preacher was a humorless man, his face—paralyzed with age—flat and, except for the nose, gray. He spoke a special, nearly technical language to define the virtues, and made use of the kind of abstract reference to authority that would appeal to reactionaries. There was no effort to authenticate, to please, to stir; there was only a recitation of what was true, in a tongue that was as dead as Latin.

As he told the story, Father would get red in the face and gurgle, "The man was pissing from the parapets!" (I think your grandfather would have been less bitter about the twentieth century if America had anointed its rebels with a little boiling oil. Now there were so many—and so many who proclaimed they were willing to pay some large price for their rebellion—as to make the "great lies," as he called convention, attractive.)

I mentioned that your aunt and I had disagreed about Dunham. It's peculiar that whenever a story deals with our time or, later, yours, there's little that we—my brothers and sister—agree on. I think that time and generations are sieves that leave us with truth, or maybe agreement. A grand piano in a madman's cell is no less improbable 75 years ago than it is now. And yet, it is not anything that you or we ever would contest. And what would orderlies or a janitor know of Verdi? These are questions that we

307

ask of the present—we can't tolerate the absurd in the present—but which may betray an opacity of spirit when we ask them of Great-uncle.

(One supposes that, therefore, one would inquire about the severed art, or the mindset of a beaten orator, or the eternity of repetition. But one doesn't ask. I don't know why.)

I saw your missionary preach on the street recently. He has a low-key approach to the extraordinary (!) which captures the attention. But he strikes me as a weak fellow. Someone in the audience taunted him and threw a sliver of wood at him. He suffered a scratch and immediately became incoherent.

I know the conventional wisdom is that assault does not convert. And that I'm going against it. But *really*, Edward.

As do your uncles and aunt, I look forward to hearing from you.

Your father

For some three weeks, Bob instructed me in matters of revelation and doctrine. I was especially anxious about addressing strangers and explaining to them what must initially seem ridiculous. But, Bob said, some would listen politely, even confess curiosity and want to know more about me and my religion. Others would not, and were of no consequence.

My first call was to a woman who might have been fifty years old or so. She listened with a bemused expression and at the end of my talk, as I handed her my card, identified me as my father's son. She asked if I was well. (I had been perspiring heavily during the presentation. It was nerves and some fever.)

During the next few days I met with rejection, mostly. Many rudely shut the door in my face. Others were more or less successful in containing their smiles. And there were those who affected a caring way, and heard nothing.

It didn't help matters that I was experiencing some congestion in the chest and a fever which might betray (falsely) a certain fear of contradiction. (I remember my aunt's effrontery, the answers that relied on my intentions; on her view of my perspicacity; on the sudden appearance of some moral qualm, surfacing at odd moments like an intermittent malfunction. How could she, or anyone, assume that I wouldn't remember my own questions years hence? And her appalling answers? I can see her black irises, intending that I should know the family history, as if that involved what the family had done.)

Some were quick to anger and warned me not to return.

This infection leaves me without much energy. I'm able to knock on doors for a couple of hours every day. At home, as I rest, Bob teaches me how to answer this or that question (never counter, always absorb, he says). And I think that I must know someone utterly when I face him for the first time. What I have to say is peculiar enough so that everyone thinks it contentious. Bob says that if I am to relate what I know (and relate it with an air of truth) I must love everyone, without regard to who or what they are.

III

Edward returned home some two months after he had left, and died of pneumonia and exhaustion two weeks later.

In point of fact, the family was unaware that his was a death-bed. Throughout his life, Edward had contracted viral infections that laid him up, sometimes for a week or even more. When we finally understood how seriously ill he was, it was too late to reverse the effects of the congestion.

Interestingly, on his last day, Edward unburdened himself with a full recantation. His aunt had been enormously upset at his straying, as she called it. And so she was heartily pleased that he had disavowed the silly incantations and the ghosts that peopled his new creed.

I submitted an obituary notice to the local newspaper, outlining, among other things, Edward's fascination with the bizarre and his eventual conversion to a chiliastic sect. But the editor saw fit to print only Edward's vital statistics, and information pertaining to the family members who survive him.

Nominated by Sigrid Nunez

TEXT

fiction by MELINDA DAVIS

from THE QUARTERLY

It was by brick he died, they decided—what else?—a young bridegroom, married only the seven nights of the *sheva brachos,* not a *trefah* mark on the body, money in the wallet, hands and clothes clean. A cigarette they find in his beard, burning. Books on the ground. A bag of soft peaches. A brick, spent, at rest, such a brick as could kill a person, plumbing the air above a head without even a whir, a clean plummet, a clean kill, *kerplunk,* dead, finished. The young wife takes off her shoes and tears her clothes and goes to the kitchen, cutting cakes for faces, for mouths. Two men from the camera store come and bring another— the accountant? the carpenter? the one who sells hats?—and they take ladders from the back of an automobile (ah, you see, the carpenter) and they place the young bridegroom in the back where the ladders had been and they take him to a place where such a bridegroom as this is taken and they say to him, listen, you are only dead. You are dead only, *nisht gerferlich,* not so terrible, it happens. Relax. Take it easy. Do not be afraid. You are in our hands. We will lift you up. You do not have to lift a finger. We will take care of everything, all of those things that are done for the dead. We will take away the evil that remains on your skin, the last traces of evil that cling to your lips as your soul leaves your body through your mouth to the mouth of God. We will explain it all for you. We will give you time to adjust. We will use warm water while it lasts. We will hold you in an upright position. We will not allow the flow of water to stop during purification. We will not allow your hair to stick to your eyes. We will do things for you now you may think are too sad to mention, but these things are the right things to do, these things we are doing, with all of this nice clean white cloth and these buckets of water and this white of an egg and this bag of sand. And listen, by the way, do us a favor, we mean only respect, we do not expect from you even a thank you, so forgive us, please, if we leave something out.

We are only human.

We are all going to die.

> In the night, I hear frozen wings battering the ceiling, shards of ice and brick and plaster falling on the sheets, a siren, men shouting, a baby crying in a wall, large metal cans, a bus, a clock, nothing. In the morning, I see tea towels on my mirrors and people in my chairs, a woman cutting cucumbers, checking lentils, boiling eggs . . . men huddled, hidden in fringes, speaking in words for winged instrument and flute, a psalm, a song for a lyre, a low stool, no one answering the phone. This may all be true, all of it. Do I know? It has been a shock.

They keep coming to me with their questions. They keep coming to me wanting all the things that people want . . . they should find a house, a husband, their keys. They should know only *simchas*. It should be for the good. There should be a nice family to rent the basement. It should be, please God, not that word we do not say, that they find tomorrow morning, with their tests, in his gut. There should be a *bocher* to cross the children at the corner? There should be (you could help?) a little money for the wedding. There should be no harlots among the daughters of Israel. There should be rain for our land at the proper time, the early rain and the late rain, and we should gather in our grain, our wine and our oil. It should happen in our day that a redeemer should come to Zion. There should be resurrection of the dead.

> I dream that I am carrying him in water, water whirring between my skin and his, water-marked skin, the

*color of onions, smelling of wood, scenting the water,
water fluttering, dry, feathered, lifting him up as I
hear him breathing, lifting him away until the hearing
stops. I wake up and I see that I have dirty hands.*

What can I do, do I have control over bricks? This brick they
found, they brought me, this brick that did the deed. A red
brick, a brick not so different from the bricks I have that hold
together my house, my rooms, my life. Here it is, this brick, this
brick that got past the code: a crumble in my hands, red, redder
where it hit him, worn, worn down by what, the wind? The sun?
The moon? The stars? A government inspection? The hand of a
child? From bricks I know nothing. Nothing is what I know from
bricks. These are the prayers we say for the dead. *Tehillim, kepittel chof gimmel. Tehillim, kepittel tzadik aleph. Tzidduk ha'din.
Av harachamim. Tehillim, kepittel mem tes. Tehillim, kepittel yud
zion. Tehillim, kepittel chof bais. Tehillim, kepittel koof yud tes.
Keil Malei Rachamim. Kaddish.*

*There is meaning here and I will find it. Something
in the hour, the weekly portion, the seventh day . . .
the number that derives from joining our names together, the names of our fathers and our father's father's father . . . a movement of spheres, a concealed
light, a correction in the world for holy purpose: a tikkun. A tikkun, they tell me. A tikkun, a brick, a blooding. Do you remember how the first blood was mine? A
separating blood, a first showing on the sheets, opening me, a knife in me, a sacred blooding before separation. A blooding, a brick, an unspeakable blooding. I
sweep the floor while the living men watch me, before
they lower you to the floor, before they close your
mouth with a string and lower you to clean straw,
clean sheet . . . a bed overturned, the smell of a
match, a spilling of water on the floor. I had not seen
the whole paleness of you as you breathed.*

No no no no no no no no no no no no no no. A Jewish person
does not worship the dead. For this we have the rest of the
world. For this they have a world of dead Jews. For this they

312

have the dead Yoshka. I can say this to her? I can tell her now, enough, finished? I can look at her, a child just, I danced with her on my shoulders, waving flags? I can look at her and say my darling, my *maidel*, the daughter almost of my almost daughter? Have we not seen death before, even of our littlest tiniest babies, our tiny babies? Do you think I do not also have pictures of death that come to me also in the night? That come to me over my fish . . . on the bus, in the toilet, in the mirror? My *maidel*? Do you think I do not have to push myself also from my sheets? To make a living, a cup of tea, what to give to the Brooklyn Union Gas? To show my face to God three times each day in *shul*? The IRS?

To what extent does one rend his garment? To exposing his breast down to the region of the navel; some say only down to the region of the heart. Although there is no authentic proof on this point, there is some allusion to it from the *Navi'im*, as it is written: *Kiru l'vavichem v'al bigdeichem.* Having reached to the navel on hearing another evil report, he moves away a space of three fingers from the former rent and rends afresh. If the forepart of his garment is become full of rents, he turns the garment front to back and then rends it again; if it becomes full of rents in the upper parts, he turns the garment upside down; but one who rends the lower part or on the sides of the garment has not discharged his duty, save the *Kohen Gadol,* who rends his garment below.

> *There is no new blood from me. There is to be no more sweeping away of life. I will be the mother. You will be the dead father. The child within me quickens and says kaddish at the appointed time. The child is surely a boy and should be standing nearer the ark.*

There is a madness here, a madness. I must go over the text. It is all of it in the text, everything. Everything is in the text. There is a brick. It is written. It was by brick he died, they decided. Books on the ground. A bag of soft peaches. It is all written down.

She says she looks at the sky and can see the destruction of the wicked. She says the time has come for the coming of the *moshiach,* for bread to grow on trees, for women to give birth without

313

labor. She says the time has come for the dead to awake in their graves and to roll underground until they reach *Yerushalayim*. She says redemption is here, in the merit of her bridegroom, in the merit of his death as our final sacrifice to God.

The *shochet* slaughters it, and the first *Kohen* at the head of the line receives it and hands it over to his colleague, and his colleague to his colleague, and the *Kohen* nearest the altar sprinkles it once toward the base of the altar. He returns the empty vessel to his colleague, and his colleague to his colleague, receiving first the full vessel and then returning the empty one. There were rows of silver vessels and rows of golden vessels, and the vessels did not have flat bottoms lest they set them down and the blood become congealed. Afterwards they hung the offering, flayed it completely, tore it open, cleansed its bowels until the wastes were removed, and the parts offered on the altar were taken out, namely, the fat that is in the entrails, the lobe of the liver, the two kidneys with the fat on them and the tail up to the backbone, and placed in a ritual vessel, salted and burned by the *Kohen* upon the altar, each one individually. The slaughtering, the sprinkling of its blood, the cleansing of its bowels and the burning of its fat override the Sabbath, but other things pertaining to it do not override the Sabbath.

I do not believe the world. I do not believe how the world is going on, going to business, roasting chickens, boiling nipples, making beds. I have told them to gather their children, to clean their houses, to pack a bag, so that all will be prepared when the clouds come to lift them. I have told them to sound the sirens. I have spoken to a man from TV.

I have looked down on the men as they daven, as they dance, in great hammered waves of black and beard . . . their singing and their swaying, their egg and onion, their schnapps, their shoving for a place in the eyes of the Rebbe, their cries for redemption, their service of the heart. Until when? they shout with their children on their shoes. Until when? they shout with their fists full of bread. Can they not believe what they believe? Have they not read what is written?

Can they not write what must be written now?

314

Which of us is mad, then? Which of us? Am I to be the voice of the other side? Am I to speak for the evil inclination? I must go over the text from the beginning, *taka*. I must find the meaning in the words. It was by brick he died, they decided—what else?—a young bridegroom, married only the seven nights of the *sheva brachos*, not a *trefah* mark on the body, money in the wallet, hands and clothes clean. A cigarette they find in his beard, burning. Books on the ground. A bag of soft peaches. A brick, spent, at rest, such a brick as could kill a person, plumbing the air above a head without even a whir, a clean plummet, a clean kill, *kerplunk*, dead, finished. I look up and I see bread growing from the trees. I look down and I see the ground open beneath the bridegroom and I see his body begin to roll. On the street, the bricks of our houses are turned to sparks. I look up at the sky and I see the face of God.

Speechless.

Nominated by The Quarterly

PORTABLE PEOPLE

by PAUL WEST

from THE PARIS REVIEW

JOHN WILLIAM POLIDORI

LORD BYRON'S DOCTOR and traveling companion, John Polidori, was dead by his own hand at twenty-six, having taken a potion he himself had brewed, based on prussic acid; but then, all through his time in Europe as part of Byron's entourage, he had been trying out one form of suicide or another. He was a man perpetually on the edge, almost a *maudit*, and his manner—alternating between sulks and effusive silliness—early on began to provoke Byron beyond endurance (he several times thought of killing him off, either by drowning or in a duel). Polidori was a prodigy, the youngest man ever to receive a medical degree from Edinburgh University, and he came from an artistic family: his father had translated *The Castle of Otranto* into Italian, and he was the uncle of the future Dante Gabriel and Christina Rossetti. At first he amused Byron and had so earned the honor of traveling as a near-equal with the most famous man in England. He had also been promised five hundred guineas by Byron's publisher, John Murray, for a full diary of Byron's doings while abroad. Polidori kept that diary, but was dissuaded from publishing it. After his death, his aging sister ripped out of it what she thought the obscenest pages and allowed it into the world (it came out in 1911), but it is clear from what such initiates as William Michael Rossetti said that Polidori had set down every instance he had witnessed of Byron's sex life (Rossetti remembered a chambermaid raped in Ostend, for instance).

It is odd to think of a doctor in such a constant ferment of emotion, as full of malice and masochism as Polidori was, always bringing to the fore Byron's latent sadism. He used Polidori as a butt and Polidori seethed. He ridiculed his amours, his verse, his ideas, and even gossiped that something unholy was going on in Polidori's medical career: all his patients died, and he seemed more interested in dissection than in prophylaxis or cure. At one point, perhaps to get away from a medical scandal threatening in Italy, Polidori planned to go to Brazil, to make a fresh start on fresh meat, as Byron quipped, and it was clearly dangerous to entrust one's body to his flighty, devious hands.

An image builds of a man who, despite his levity and charm, was too highly strung for his own good: a plagiarist, a hanger-on, a climber, a satanist who was also a klutz and a social menace. The novelist Stendhal watched him getting arrested at the Milan Opera and left a long, detailed account of it, and Byron's table-talk leaves one in no doubt as to the bickering that went on between the two of them. Eventually Byron had to let him go and paid him off. Polidori became a gambler and took his own life in August, 1821, upon which event Byron commented, "Poor Polly is gone."

IMELDA MARCOS

Miss Manila calling. She hears a dream, when it was wartime in the doghouse of the heart, although a garage is where she started, only nine, jammed in with Mamma Remedios and the other kids, next to the fumey clapped-out car, whose metal was a foretaste of the corrugated iron prefab in Leyte.

In one painting, where an oily tropic sky walks the full moon out from under its epidermis like a tumor of shrapnel, she just touches his hand: the nail of her little finger taps his third knuckle, receiving the current. In the end, Manila's Four-Hundred accepted her, but never with the homesick fervor of the GI's to whom she crooned. Tried for Miss Manila. Sounds like an offense. Lost, having no money with which to win votes. So, as they say, she intervened personally with the mayor, and it was all right after that, apart from the weird games he liked to play with leeches. Then Ferdinand the Bull, the sawn-off nouveau riche living down a trial for murder, underpacked the rugs with so much moolah their heads rode ever nearer the ceilings. They were the only patients to whom doctors offered *quantity* of life. Retinue of seven hundred at the White House.

Fifty-seven, she competed for Miss Manila all over again, purring how contestant Aquino had no make-up, no manicure, whereas "Filipinos are for beauty. Filipinos who like beauty, love, and God are for Marcos." Could Cleopatra be a klutz? Never in all her lovely life did Miss Manila have a thousand breasts or six thousand feet.

FEODOR CHALIAPIN

My voice was such a Volga orgy, lardies unt gentleschnitches, zat, ven I sprang a title role, no longer ze burly peasant I once was, but *really Boris,* I could turn toward the wings and without breaking cadence or tone command my offstage servant "Go-oo to-oo thee Haut Elle art vance and breeng me the Vine Ay Four Gott." *Da.* They were listening to my face, much as, later, they worshipped at Stalin's mustache. On waxen cylinders I still rise from the mud like an Egyptian pharaoh, basso profundo dell tutto mondo. Yet where is my Chaliapinograd? Whose is my voice now?

AUGUSTE RODIN

God's dong, if such a thing can be, is a velvet hammer made of love that thumps the stars home, where they belong, in the moist pleat of the empyrean. Surely he needs no goading on, unlike myself, finger-dipping each and every cleft of every model, and all that a mere preliminary to what goes on after the day's work is done, and we twist the big key clockwise. That is when I get my girls to tongue one another before my very eyes. It is almost as if the sculpting is mere prelude to the venery. By midnight, they are all going their ways, about their business, with Rodin syrup dribbling from them as they walk, like molten marble. Those who pose for me must taste my will, upended like ducks on a pond.

318

When my Balzac, now, strides forth with upright phallus in his fist, from behind he must be read as a giant lingam marching to India. I mean these burly semblances to stun, my Lord, as when, for Becque and sundry appreciative madams, I turn actor and behead with a sword the plaster statues arranged in front of me. Those who cry out, in abuse, "Rodin is a great big prick" are right. I am always and ever the policeman's son, neither peasant nor poet.

I receive on Sundays, as my copy of *The Guide to the Pleasures of Paris* says, married to that carthorse, Rose, who gave me a son with a broken brain, abandoned by Camille, who once adored me and now in the asylum murmurs, "So this is what I get for all I did." At least she, unlike my Yankee heiress Claire, fat and daubed and drunk, never kept leaving the dinner table to go and throw up, as now, or play her creaky gramophone while my public sits around me, hearing me tell them yet again that it was indeed I who stove in Isadora Duncan, pommeling that little earlike hole between her lively legs, and it was also I who, like the milkman delivering, brought her weekly orgasm to little sad Gwen John in her rented room. I snapped her like a wineglass stem, but made her coo all the same.

When I get Upstairs, His Nibs and I are going to go on such a masterful rampage the angels will cry to be raped, neuter as they are, and none shall contain us, we shall be so massive in our roistering, from the hand-gallop to the common swyve, with our humpbacked fists banged deep into the soft clay of eternity.

NIKOLAI POLIKARPOV

We showed them off first in the May Day fly-past over Moscow in 1935, loud and stocky, their bodies like tapered barrels. The Polikarpov I-16 was a reasonably fast and swift-climbing fighter, capable of 323 m.p.h., and in the Spanish Civil War it often outmaneuvered the Messerschmidt Bf109B's. *Ishak*, we named it: Little Donkey, its thick back strong for the rod. Twenty thousand little donkeys we had, all told, and I am proud (though not exactly gibbering with delight) to have designed it. Whenever I see the plan view of it, I see not an airplane but the constellation Cygnus, with the same stubby nose, straight leading edge to the wings, forward-curved trailing edge as if plucked voluptuously after it, except that the constellation has a longer, narrower fuselage, between Eta and Albireo anyway. Is Cygnus the plane of my dreams, not quite attained in my own design, but designable somewhere by someone? Am I thinking of the Thunderbolt or Spitfire, instead, whose trailing edges had that half-elliptical, rapturous curve? What I have forgotten is that there is no need, not even a reason, to draw Cygnus so beautifully, a crude simplistic cross would link up the stars. There is no swan up there, no little donkey down here. It is all in our minds where, when we fly, we are truly being flown.

EDITH SITWELL

Once upon a train her father lowered his copy of the *Times*, looked at her, shuddered, and shut her out again. As an adolescent she wore what she called her Bastille: one piece, both brace and corset, to remedy a curvature of the spine and weak ankles; the other a facial brace to straighten out her long tuber of a Plantagenet nose. Her specialist, a Mr. Stout, looked like a statuette made in margarine then frozen stiff. Perhaps she felt much the same when out walking in Eckington woods, made to wear a veil lest the locals see how like a leper she was. Truly hurt into poetry (and into witty sarcasm), she had pale gold hair that sometimes looked green and decided she must have been a changeling left behind by pranking fairies who took a human baby away with them. She was our first mutant muse. Those same locals she hid from in the woods decided she slept in a coffin and was really a vampire, flying with wings made from old umbrellas and the lost kites of little local boys. Her father wrote a famous history of the two-pronged fork, but made a point of asking Sargent the painter to emphasize Edith's crooked nose when he painted her, but Sargent straightened it instead and omitted her pet peacock, thus giving her the confidence later on, when pushed to go to local balls with her hair all frizzed and hauled down along and over her nose, to spurn the white tulle dress chosen by her mother and buy herself one of long black velvet. She was six feet tall. If you looked like a greyhound, she said, why try to look like a Pekingese?

320

At her most crocodilous, as she called it, she said of one poetaster critic that he examined the nature of groundsel and the sexlife of the winkle and told someone else that she had just been defending him: "They said you weren't fit to live with pigs, but I said you were." Her histrionic acuity rarely faltered, perhaps because she warmed her head with a turban. Virginia Woolf said she looked like an ivory elephant. She herself, after meeting Marilyn Monroe and Zsa-Zsa Gabor and the international stud Porfirio Rubirosa, said she felt she had been made for physical love, but wept at never having known it. Her first love was an unresponsive Guards officer, her last the homosexual painter Pavel Tchelitchew; but her truest lover was the photographer Cecil Beaton, who made her lovely, finding her complexion fresh as that of a convolvulus, her eyebrows like tapering mouse-tails, the noble forehead like tissue-paper, her wrists like delicate stems, and her visage entire flooded with the mad moon-struck ethereality of a ghost.

VIRGINIA WOOLF BY THE RIVER OUSE

I am going to flush myself away, an Ophelia of the middle class. Suttee voce. Odd how the mind never deserts you, even at the very last, when it is the thing that has condemned itself to go.

No more picnics, no more sun-mulled shrimp or heavy sherry trifle. No more peeking into the windows of London, when the saffron lamplight beckons and we stand on tiptoe, ogling the linoleum and the big pot rabbits full of fairground feathers. They eat with their sleeves rolled up, their elbows in the fingerbowls. They pick their noses while buttering their bread. They masticate from side to side, sliding the wodge of food across.

Well, here lies one whose books were writ in water. How may a flow appraise a flow? I would have been better off at the bottom of the Arno or shipwrecked with Shelley off Spezia. The mind is a surf, ladies. All else is a railway compartment full of Arnold Bennett. That is what has done me down, done me in: too many Brussels sprouts, too few visionary flight lieutenants.

I wanted a wedding cake made of snow, ice cream made from yaks' milk and pink. I wanted the bright beautiful refulgent day, not the sullen undertow that told me only: You are a woman and you will have to die. I do not thus like the initiative twisted from my hand. I go down the field with today's *Times* in my hand, to do something rich and strange to myself, and back I come, burbling for tea and scones, a yak, a crested warbler, a Beethoven with breasts, a Debussy with a womb, a Rodin with his period thick and musky on him, a Wagner in full flying menopause.

SOPHIE SCHOLL, 22 FEBRUARY 1943

One last cigarette, my Lord, as if tobacco were *your* sacrament, and they will manacle my hands behind me and lead me up a few stairs to the big locked door with the bulbous brass handle. As if I were being taken to the headmaster for a dressing-down. For chatter, or cheating in the Latin test. It will not be long now. All I hear is a rattle of keys. The tall narrow door opens inward, pulled, and two men with faces impersonal as raffia tug me toward them as if they have been waiting for me all their lives. Seven seconds is all it takes from the door's opening to the end. Now, lifted aloft, I fly like Saint Joseph, a thought-out sentence per second. Two. I am laid face down on the rack. Three. A small bridge of wood comes down over my neck. Four. What have I done? Five. I insulted the Führer. Six. Who was *he?* Seven. I have been misinformed. Eight. I feel quite well, waiting. Nine. It will be more than twelve. Ten. I saw the hose, the lidded basket. Eleven. I have been misinformed. Twelve. Thank God it never happened. I am aboard the train from Ülm, a daisy in my hair and carrying a wicker basket that holds a spice cake and one bottle of Mosel wine. I draw the blackout curtains and see a jar of marmalade, two hundred and fifty grams of butter, some strudel. I am still in my student skirt and blouse.

HERMANN GOERING, NUREMBERG, 1946

Fat men are the wisest dreamers. I always ate up sleep, on my back or side virtually weightless, and here in a cell on the lip of oblivion I still munch the same creamy finitudes, doting on sleep's huge maternal billow, lurching downward only to heave myself back among the living for a final hug. That wind chime from on high is the tinkle of a hundred medals airing. Inert I lie, half-swooning, lifting an eyelash, or rather the baby muscle that guides it, but the exertion kills me.

So, this is the final sleep. I have often wondered at the rough handling meted out by executioners and their ilk to the corpses they have only just made, crudely slinging the sack of potatoes onto the wheelbarrow, shoving the floppy leg into the waiting truck and slamming it home behind the door. They do not even hose you down. Before the deed they affect a coarse civility of nods, head-lifts, tight lips, while the drums roll, the trap creaks, the dynamo whines. Then they belabor you about like a sewer made of cloth.

Well, you deathsheads, this is Hermann having his last little schlaf at his own bidding. Fat men make the best nodders-off. I will not wait for Keitel and the rest. To Keitel I said: "Never confess. Be a man. Shout an oath when they spring the trap. Curse them for scuttling the *Graf Spee*. Damn that little spirochete, Goebbels. Yell to hell with that *amateur* fat man, Churchill."

This is the sternest hemlock of them all, but it makes me purr just to think of the burly master sergeant from Utah coming to take me to the rope, and looking forward to his eggs and ham afterward, or whatever these bogeymen eat, and finding the big paunch has slipped ahead of them like a new-calved island, pink with poison, or a freshly barbered hog. Oh that I could have been wearing antlers at this moment, just for show.

VLADIMIR NABOKOV IN CAYUGA HEIGHTS

A day of purest Arizona, this: dry, calm, and blue, tempting me to stroll abroad in the Arts quad of our famous university, where an open-necked shirt is formal enough if sheathed in a tweed jacket. When I first came here, I bought my clothing at the military surplus stores and have never felt closer to people than then. It was here I used to skulk behind the trees, then pounce upon passing (or failing) students to ask them if they knew what kind of tree it was. They never knew. I had almost no friends, American men having no gift for friendship (Swiss cuckoos are more cordial). Yet I was not looking for friendship today, or the names of trees, or even the dilatory afterbirth of the *Zeitgeist*, hovering like stratocirrus above Goldwin Smith; I was hunting no butterfly either, but the pensive silence for which universities are known. Amid which tenured geniuses think. All I could hear, however, was a barrage of uncoordinated drums and, raised in agony garbed as song, the unsorted voices of those who clearly cannot read. I was lone witness to the latest variant of Hottentot, who needs to bounce and twitch, deafened and barbarically exhorted, not to re-read *Madame Bovary* or the fiction of the neglected Hellens, but to Swing Out, Sister, or something such, doubtless from a branch of some tree the simians cannot name. I had always wondered at the pigskin cult, but now I see the link to drums. The young come here to shove and shout. Or, rather, to watch others shove and shout. Is it for lack of a civil war that American universities are so physical? Their syllabi swell with boys' books, Hemingway and Conrad, for instance, and the subdominant hemispheres of almost all brains obey the nonstop music. I am glad that the bruited move to rename The Corners Community Shopping Center *Le Petit Coin Nabokov* failed because of the suddenly revealed erotic connotation involved. "Why," said one tweeded worthy, not having made love to a Lolita—*Loh-lee-ta*—"it would be the same as saying Cooch Corner. Imagine a bus stop called that." Had I been there I would have directed his etymological lobes to the derivation of Grove Street, in the Oxford of England and not that of the Mississippi windbag, couching the earlier word (if I may) in the headline phrase: Carnal Ukase, No Thoroughfare. Sea. Yew. En. Tee. (As Quilty might say.) 'Twas there, in the old days, Community Corners et cetera, I bought my liquors, when I could afford. What a dismal privilege this Outre Tombe revenance has become. As if I am having my career all over again, I yearn for another, warmer lake, God (or royalties) permitting. I miss only the little ironing boards that swivel down. I miss the mucilage, the correction fluids, the misspelling of *pyjamas,* and the now-lost euphemism: comfort station. I even miss the petty Antarctica of the stomach as ice-cubes go sledding endlessly through. I miss all the No-Tell Motels. The view from up here is ridiculous: one sees only the tops of closed books, gilt or tinted, mottled or plain. All Open Sesames have closed.

HENRY M. NEELY

In the sky, apple-pie, at least in Henry M. Neely's *Primer for Star-Gazers*. When he looks at Cygnus, he sees a baseball game: *The batter has hit a fly to center. Albireo is running to get it and second-baseman Phi is also out after it. Shortstop Eta has run over to cover for Phi and left-fielder Vega is running in to back-up third in case of trouble.* He not only wants you to get it, he wants you to say it right too; Eta, he says, is *Ate-a*, Phi is *fie* (rhymes with pie and rye), Vega is *veega*, and, oh yes, Albireo is *al-beer-ee-oh* (accent on *beer*). Not only that: in some of his constellation maps, a neat amputated hand appears with an inch of cuff on show, the forefinger drooped to indicate where, say, Orion is. For other textbooks you have to be as grown-up as possible. You never get baseball and you may flounder for years when you wonder how to say Dschubba (*jub-a*, he says, rhyming it with *tub* and *rub*), though he adds that classicists disapprove of the name and that the government list of navigational stars ignores the classicists. The universe, when you look up at it, and so cramp the basilar arteries in the back of your neck, is so infantilizing anyway that Henry M. Neely seems to be doing it right, treating us in its presence as the children we in fact are. Gone back into his beloved universe since 1963, is he getting close to one of those hands? Will he one day soon show up in one of the diagrams, complete with head and trunk and legs, re-attached to his hand at last?

NIXON IN CHINA

Here in the library, one can tinkle the ivories ad lib, cracking a smile at the chinks in between. It is good to get away from them. In their old, naïve way they are too sly for the likes of me. The two of them love to hear a foxtrot, and when she breaks into a dance, does the actual step, he restrains himself but looks quite horny. They belong in an opium parlor, both of them. But they have that oily skin and you always know they are doing their damndest to screw you out of something. Thank the Lord for a wily old negotiator like me, heart of Irish oak, most of all when they get this tong-war look and you get dizzy looking into their hardly open eyes, as if you were falling backward off the Great Wall into the eye of the tiger. Dizzy, sweaty, that's how I get when they start to stare me down, and, wouldn't you believe it, I start to fumble and look sideways as if I am not who I am, plenipotentiary of decency. Of the power that came my way, let it never be said I wasted it, but without getting too formal, too much of a man in the golden chair, too unhusbandly, unfathering. This is a real country, even if you have to say it behind your hand, whereas ours, well ours is a bit of an easy mark especially for young crazies. I like to think a country keeps its rear-end tight, all apucker, like this China. Does them good to see a turned-up nose like mine, but they don't go running all over the place to change the Chinese nose. No sir, you could bomb pretty well any species of slants into submission, but you could never bomb them into changing their noses, their eyes, their ways with children's feet. A virtuous man needs something to fight against. That's why there is evil. Always another war to win out here.

That is why we have dragons.

That is why their women, from Madame Mao on down, have these twat-like slits in their dresses, to make you half-believe that what should be between their gams has slid around their thighs and is ready there for servicing, like a wound from that ritual of the thousand cuts. I have not studied Chinery for nothing.

Never mind how closemouthed they are, there is always a way in, past the silks and the red-faced lions, past the gingerbreadmen soldiers and the plump sentries with their fur hats and their dreadfully kept nails. How come the country that gave us gunpowder and spaghetti needs a few thousand manicurists?

I am summoned. Mister President has been away far too long just to have washed his hands. Back I go to the foul and febrile element I work in: the vice of others, their vile buyability. As Pat says, the men in suits have no suits. Here is a yellow peril that needs a good tailor too. See the supple bend of my threads as I move. Watch this old fox trot, watch me make these madams drool.

ROY HARRIS

Yup: Grandpaw drove the pony express, he and Paw went off to Oklahoma, built them a cabin there with just an ax. We had a

326

phonograph, a Edison, with those sigh-lindrical records, yknow. I read and read, Shakespeare and Greek philosophy. I ran my farm real good. I do most things well. Then I trucked butter and eggs to places off the beaten track. In California, that was. I went to Rochester and stayed five years, bust my spine, wrote a string quartet, stayed true to Bach. By 1935 a national poll had placed me first among American composers and an international one put me just behind César Franck. It had begun all right. During the blitz on London they chose a hundred works to be saved, and my *Third* was the only one by an American.

Well, iffen I was a cornball, I got to Cornell anyway, as Composer-in-Residence, just about self-taught by them sigh-lindrical records. I just wrote all the time, I was on earth to do it, and I raced a fast car whenever I could. Open-air music, mine, of the prairies. Bury me there or in the streets of Laredo. I excel at the Passacaglia. Contrary to Virgil Thomson, I was never awarded by God or the US of A a monopolistic privilege of expressing our nation's deepest ideals and highest aspirations. I came right on the heels of César Franck, breathing down his neck. My pieces do not always begin alike. Boy, you sure lose buddies fast in this game. Old Virgil, he wrote right under my photo: "Roy Harris, in youth squarely a charmer, in middle age a businessman, later prone to anger," but he did add "at all ages clearly a star," so it's okay, Virge, I ain't agoing to slug you from up here. Just you keep away from my beans and flapjacks, let me hear the clank and jingle of the old corral, the clap-clap sound of steaming hoss-flop, the pounded triangle that says Come And Get It. Should I have smoked a foot-long pipe like Ruggles or worn a dicky-bow like you and Aaron, with one of them boiled shirts?

Just you give me the strong silent sun and keep your Pulitzers to yourselves.

WILLIAM EMPSON

"Slops," this poet and critic answered when asked what food he preferred, and he cooled his soup by squirting it back into his plate as if trying to cool his whistle. In the dead of winter he walked through slush and snow in ordinary shoes, from his apartment to his office, about a mile, so I found and, at the kneel,

fitted to him a pair of rubber overshoes, which he never afterwards seemed to remove. Before succumbing to his daily mon-
soon of cognac, he spoke in lively fashion of Newton, China, and
Yorkshire, usually in that order, and then students used to creep
up on him and gently spin him around in his office chair as if he
were an astronaut being tested for vertigo. He never woke up
during these rotations. He went back at night to a place full of
rotting oranges, used tissues, and odd socks. *Don't you know
who he is?* his South African wife kept saying. She was the eighth
type of ambiguity. Off he set, to visit Wallace Stevens, who had
died twenty years earlier, and back he came, saying with his best
military-colonel-cum-Tory look, "We are none of us getting
younger." If he made the journey, who knows what he found at
the other end. A palm, perhaps. He wrote the best poem in the
world about a woman slipping off her nylons. He once, for some
minutes, watched my neighbor's door lamp through my telescope, thinking it Mars.

GEORGE GERSHWIN

I gotta get it, I'm gonna get it, I got it. Read it in the newspaper
that Mister Paul, Mister Whiteman, Mister Paul Whiteman and
I, I, I, I, we gonna do a piece together, a piece so different it will
make the world stop and spin the other way, east-west. Well,
Mister Whiteman and I, I, I, I, know nothing about this newsy
little news item. We have no plans, though we do seem to have
talked man to man some time or other. So I gotta take the train,
see, I hear the rhythm of the rails—the word said *riddem*—and
it is all there anyway, that long dizzy ascent on the clarinet
included. All I gotta do is write it down, syncop-syncop-ated.
Cat-screech among the honored brownstones. An epileptic's gen-
tleness with the balls of his feet. Three weeks only in the work,
and it is a riot. Thank God for newspapers that have the brains to
tell us what to do, to do, when we can't think of it. When in
doubt as to where to go, even if destined to die young, go decide
on a train, a train, and the train will tell you. And when you read
in the newspaper that you died young, died young, you don't
have to believe it, like that nice Mister O'Hara said. If you gotta,
you gonna. If you gonna, then, then, you don't always gotta. Get
it?

A BORGESIAN BEAST

Imaginary being, he called me, that silvery, dapper Argentine whose favorite word was *dim*. As if I were some volume in the infinite, darkling library of his mind. Why did he never call me what I truly am? I was never a white panther with black rosettes, the beast too blurred to be seen, too shy to look blind men in the eye. According to him, I looked down, too fierce to be seen at all. Only when I did would other beasts approach, and when they did (said my Argentine) I fell upon them and devoured them. Never. No, dearest folk, I could have been a rainshower chasing a white sheet, a burst of shellfire pitting a snowy plain. But I was not. I was never cinders in milk. I was a Dalmatian, named for islands, and only a legally blind man could have seen my apparition in such black-and-white opposites: I was the beast made by the figure his shadows cut into his glare, I was the ghost his penumbra pocked with craters, I was the black night of the soul mended with balled-up white hankies. I was all imagery. I was a deposed chicken inspector dreaming of a panther who imagined a leopard in the act of devising a dog.

FRITZ ZWICKY, ASTRONOMER

Over the years I guess I wore those bastards down. I called them spherical bastards because they were bastards whichever way you looked at them, the diners at the smarty-pants Atheneum Caltech dining club. Down on the floor I'd land, challenging them all to one-arm pushups, and I never had a single taker. I got away with it, in a profession in which as always the plums go to the sleek, because I and I alone discovered supernovas. I also found the missing mass that holds the universe together. Among the great zooming minds, I am not such a little shit myself, even if, in the final years, they did shove me off down to the basement where the graduate students make love to their constipation. "Who the hell are you?" I'd yell at any of them. "I am Zwicky, the explosive, flat-faced pale-eyed Bulgarian raised among the cuckoo clocks and the slotted cheeses. Tell them you have seen the great Zwicky at his most Bulgarian. I am the klutz who got it right." I never told them, though, my head was full of stars exploding long before I knew they could. With the gentle, timid, utterly neurotic cripple, Baade, I invented the word for them. Baade was a cretin, but others invented that word for him: not I. Baade used to go around asking, "What if Zwicky goes mad? He's going to murder me." Baade and I sat at opposite ends of the dining table, but I never attacked. One evening I said, to them all, "We should launch a rocket to the moon to recover rocks for study." But all they said was "Aww, Fritz, leave the god-damn moon to the lovers." No vision, those fuckers. It was I who first thought of mixing explosive chemicals with the emulsions used in photography. Point the scope and the film would fry. You'd hear it. It was I who stuck a charge on the nose of an Aerobee rocket and fired a bit of metal off into deep space when the rocket reached its apogee. It was I who had a night assistant fire a rifle bullet straight past the Hale telescope and out the dome to knock a hole through the air to make seeing better.

Those bastards in their smoking jackets, worrying about which fork to use. I am still at the little Schmidt in the cluster of carrasco oaks, and the universe I am still such a boor in is wilder than they think. And more boorish. I myself contain the missing mass. I am an asteroid named Zwicky. So is Baade. In the Main Belt. Will we never collide? Will we never arm-wrestle? I wait for all those bastards down there to come up here to be asteroids. Good evening, gentlemen. Now you are through, say hello to your favorite bull seal.

DUKE ELLINGTON

Aiming not to be too smooth, too downtown chic, when the wet-eyed band began to play, I made up music for a shaggy world full of mules and homeless dogs, dirty plates and air-shaft shut-ins. Our moles had hairs growing out of them. We played the grapefruit rinds, the empty cans, the ghettos of ebony. Something cumbersome and roughcut was vital: tans, grunts, hiccups, washboards, and muted shrugs came with the indigo, the velvet. Our music lurched from rubato to showdown. We were cats yowling at the moon, not so slick or sharp as lumped together under shagbark. We growled our prayers into metal cones, making back-street nocturnes that said nothing was flawless, not even the booksmart harmony of the old-time Greeks.

And yet, for all the hotsteps, and beats syncopated until there was nothing left but in-between, I was always yearning for that grander something: the symphony, the suite, making me, even if only for one evening, the lynx of *Nachtmusik*, his forte something contrapuntal to the point of mayhem, his weakness the old habit of, when the band cranked up, heading for the low-down tune, when all the time there were battlements and esplanades, boulevards and plazas. I took the A-train once too often. In my wide pliable mouth there lurked a nightjar's blistered tongue.

COUNT BASIE

Unstrung by noise amid which hid a chime, a ring that sang, I saved one finger for the note that sealed a chorus. Black *embonpoint* hunched over a fairy's wink, I must have seemed dumber than ebony. *He plays so few notes*, they said, unable to spot a picky high-wire artist when one came along. Pink, link. Pinkety-plink.

I was Bill, I was William, I the Count who eased his way in on there as of then, oh yair, somebody between lyric simpleton and chromatic oaf. I did not so much tickle ivories as caress them half to death, cunning linguist of the grand. The yachtsman's cap gave me tons of extra class.

Watch that ruby on his little finger, they said when I laid the keyboard open just a crack after all the rest had done and the melody was dying in the air in front of us, its energy newgone. And then I did my Countly thing: never stretching a riff too far. I had a small and brassy band, a touch of cornball if you like, but with often enough the milky intimation of a world more delicate than the universe itself. Gossamer tux, bone-marrow wand. Fat man in a loose white suit embroidering his glee with big flourish of the pudgy wrist. Oh yair. The Count of Fin- esse. Pli- able. Dain- ty. What you always wanted but were too crude to say.

SIGMUND FREUD AT 66

When you want a wrong opinion, find a quack. When you cannot stand to know the truth, go to some gross inferior. This is called

331

denial. Then let him carve away at your jaw and palate as if he were making a sandwich in some Viennese delicatessen.

There I was, bleeding to death on a soiled cot in a tiny room, while, stuck in the trench the quack had left in my mouth, a vague retarded dwarf fidgeted and whined. The grotesque bulb of his head wobbled about. And he shouted for a nurse because he was drowning in a tide of my freshly minted blood. Puss in Boots I called him.

After the nurse bustled me out of there, I had to think again, obliged to want an opinion that was right. Rhinologist Number Two said, "*Ach*, Herr Doktor Freud, one dies just as finally from unknown, or unadmitted, truths as from their opposite. Not to wish to die is merely to misinterpret a dream. The death wish is nothing but a state of mind. As for the cigar that graced your mouth, might it not have been safer in your other end, where, although the gasses are flammable, the wind flows outward only?" When I need another opinion, I will ask for it with that very same below-stairs mouth. I will ask the dwarf.

Nominated by M. D. Elevitch, Joyce Carol Oates, Robert Phillips

THE DEAD BODY ITSELF

by SHARON OLDS

from AGNI

I hated it, after he died, the way we left him
alone in the room. For months there had always
been someone with him, if he were asleep or
awake, in coma, we were there, and now we
stood by the door with the minister and
planned the service and there he was
alone—as if all we'd loved was his consciousness,
this man who had so little consciousness, who was
90% his body. So I'd go and
pet him and pet him, I hated the way we were
treating him like garbage, we would burn him, as if
only the soul mattered. Who *was* that
if not he lying there parched and abandoned.
I was ready to fight anybody who
did not treat that body with respect, just
let some medical student make a joke about his liver, I'd
deck him, I so wanted to have someone to deck,
I wanted this man burned whole, don't
let me see that arm on anyone in
Redwood City tomorrow! Don't take that
tongue in transplant or that huge unwilling eye,
So what if his soul were gone, I have known him
soulless, all my childhood seen him
lying on that couch in the unlit end of the
living room on his back with his mouth open
and nothing there but his body,

333

so I stood by him in the hospital and
petted him and petted him, his
arm, his hair, I did not think he was there
but this was the one I had loved anyway,
this raw man of dark rich matter,
this man who was like those early beings who
already lived on this earth before God
took that special clay and made his own set of people.

Nominated by Toi Derricotte, Kenneth Gangemi, Arthur Smith

WHAT THEY WANTED

by STEPHEN DUNN

from THE AMERICAN POETRY REVIEW

They wanted me to tell the truth,
so I said I'd lived among them
for years, a spy,
but all that I wanted was love.
They said they couldn't love a spy.
Couldn't I tell them other truths?
I said I was emotionally bankrupt,
would turn any of them in for a kiss.
I told them how a kiss feels
when it's especially undeserved;
I thought they'd understand.
They wanted me to say I was sorry,
so I told them I was sorry.
They didn't like it that I laughed.
They asked what I'd seen them do,
and what I do with what I know.
I told them: find out who you are
before you die.
Tell us, they insisted, what you saw.
I saw the hawk kill a smaller bird.
I said life is one long leavetaking.
They wanted me to speak
like a journalist. I'll try, I said.
I told them I could depict the end
of the world, and my hand wouldn't tremble.

I said nothing's serious except destruction.
They wanted to help me then.
They wanted me to share with them,
that was the word they used, share.
I said it's bad taste
to want to agree with many people.
I told them I've tried to give
as often as I've betrayed.
They wanted to know my superiors,
to whom did I report?
I told them I accounted to no one,
that each of us is his own punishment.
If I love you, one of them cried out,
what would you give up?
There were others before you,
I wanted to say, and you'd be the one
before someone else. Everything, I said.

Nominated by Henry Carlile, Jane Hirshfield

THE LIMBO DANCER

by JOSEPHINE JACOBSEN

from GRAND STREET

No limbo this week. Or next. Now it turns out
the limbo dancer is dead. Tiles between sea
and bar are clean for the guests' uncertain feet
that search the band's racket for how they should move.
The sea is dark and those rungs of the moon's fire
lead nowhere; but broken and bright the ladder lies.

The limbo dancer had nutmeg-colored feet
with apricot-colored heels, and toes splayed out
inch and half-inch. The guests could barely see
that motion grip the tiles. And how can a man move
inch after half-inch, as his body lies
horizontal on air? In his teeth he carried fire.

When the rod was high (and there was no fire
yet) the limbo dancer addressed it: his feet
shifted in place, his pelvis jumped in, and out,
and the light from the sequins and sweat, that flies
over the ribs, showed how bone and muscle move.
His eyes shone too, at whatever they managed to see.

The pans, sweet and metallic, that sent out
a torrent, hushed; and the dark drum, four feet
high, spoke, as the rod dropped into its last move.
The limbo dancer, tall, taller than drums, Watusi-

337

tall, beaten forward inch by inch, as inch relies
on inch-space, moved, moved: toes, heels, and fire.

Whatever more liquidly indifferent than the sea?
But the guests, diverted from rum and drawn by fire,
stared, as the head came under, and the great feet
shot up, the limbo dancer's flame put out
in his mouth's cavern. For a shocked space, the move
was into that joy where gravity's laws are lies.

The limbo dancer, together with his feet,
has disappeared, and the guests are put out.
In shadows, on sand, by the suddenly noisy sea,
the old foe gravity (plane, bird, poem) lies
in wait. If that stretched body fails to move,
who will kill gravity by inches, spring up, eat fire?

The limbo dancer's fire is certainly out.
The guests say, See, alas, he does not move.
But gravity lies beneath the dust of his feet.

Nominated by Lloyd Van Brunt

PAST, FUTURE, ELSEWHERE

fiction by EILEEN POLLACK

from PLOUGHSHARES

BARBARIANS WERE CHURNING the farms into mud, polluting our wells. I had to escape.

This was 1969. I was thirteen years old, hiding in the basement. The frayed plastic webbing of my father's green lounge chair tickled my legs, which were only half-shaped—curved here, blockish there. A photo from *Life* was taped to the window: the earth from the porthole of Apollo 11. The light from behind made the earth luminescent and nearly 3-D. It stared down upon me, a cloudy blue eye.

The hot-water heater kindled itself in the basement's black heart.

"We have lift-off," I said. "We have separation," and I could feel gravity slipping away.

Then the heater stopped roaring.

"We have engine malfunction"—my voice stony calm—"I repeat, engine failure." I arose from the lounge chair, swimming my arms. With my ear to the tank, which was warm as a chest, I heard: *tickticktick sigh, tickticktick slosh*, like the slosh of a stomach. I rubbed the tank, soothed it. The tank purred. Then: BROOSH.

"Thank God," Houston said, "The experts were stumped. How did you fix it?"

Though I was too old to be playing such games, the lounge chair seemed to beckon as a first love might do. Other girls had crushes on Dylan, Mick Jagger, but these men seemed dangerous. I dreamed of Neil Armstrong in his white padded suit. We'd be bounding through the vacuum of an unexplored planet when a meteor would sizzle through the sky toward his head. I would push him to safety and be crushed in his place. As he carried me tenderly back to the ship I would smile at him weakly, but the pain would win out and . . .

"Judith, are you down there?"

My parents were standing at the top of the stairs; the door to the kitchen was open behind them so a shaft of gold light cut through the murk. This made me feel lonely, as a small fish must feel in the shadowy depths.

"I'm thinking," I said. "Can't a person find anywhere in this whole house to think?"

Ordinarily my parents would have flinched at that word. Because I was smart and obviously destined to travel much farther from Bethel than they had, they made the mistake of treating me as though I were older and braver and needed no help understanding the world. But this time my mother wanted to know: Was anything wrong? Was I feeling . . . unwell? She whispered to my father, and since they were both timid and small they looked then like children daring each other to venture downstairs.

"It isn't that!" I said, and wished for a blanket to cover my body, which stretched out before me with its landscape of breasts, rib cage, belly, pelvis and knees.

All week the paper had been lurid with photos of the naked barbarians who'd overrun our town—sunbathing on car hoods, dancing to music at this "festival" of theirs—but an inky strip covered each interesting part, like a gag on a mouth. I scraped at those boxes, even turned the page over to see from the other side what was masked on the front. I felt the reporters had found out my future and printed it here, but blotted the facts I most wanted to know. At the same time I wished every inch of those bodies had been blackened with ink; the editors were publishing my most shameful secret with only this slight disguise of my features, and the secret was this: that I wasn't destined to leap on the moon but to grovel in mud.

I took out a book from under my chair. "I'm reading," I said.

"You'll ruin your eyes, sweetheart," my father clucked sadly. "If you'd only take that paper off the window . . . "

"That's not just some 'paper.' That's our planet. That's *Earth*. Don't you know anything?"

My father retreated, noiseless as the dust motes that chased around his head. My father was a milkman; he woke up at three and was so schooled in silence that floorboards wouldn't whimper under his feet, doorjambs wouldn't click.

"We're leaving the house." My mother moved down a few steps, as though the stairs were a seesaw and she had to balance her husband's retreat. "Some of us are going to try to get food to those poor hungry children."

Two days before, when the roads were still open, she'd made her weekly shopping trip to Monticello (the only stores in Bethel sold beef jerky, beer and Eskimo pies) and she'd found the streets jumbled with barbarians foraging for something to eat.

"I even saw people I know selling water. From their hoses!" she said. "At a dollar a glass!"

It surprised me that anyone would think to sell water. I still regarded water, air, food and land, even gas for the car, as the barest supplies that God could hand out so all human beings could make do on Earth, the way that a teacher would supply every student with pencils and paper on the first day of class. But my mother's condemnation seemed far too harsh.

"Do you blame them?" I asked. "I wouldn't let those animals drink from our *hose*."

This clearly disturbed her. My mother was plump, with a plump olive face, and her moods were as easy to read as a child's. When she was disturbed, everything drooped—her hair, cheeks and bosom. Even her ankle socks seemed to droop. "I know they look strange . . . but I couldn't help but think they might be my own daughter and wouldn't I want somebody else's mother to feed her?"

I was sick with the insult. "If they were too stupid to bring enough food you should let them go hungry."

"Well, foolish or not," my mother admitted, "I saw this young woman . . . she was seven months pregnant . . . she couldn't find her husband and he had the money . . . "

"Don't tell me you gave this woman our groceries!" I would have been embarrassed to be so naïve, but my mother wore her

341

innocence as proudly as she'd wear a suit of bright armor; if she thought well of everyone, this would deflect all ugly intentions and no one would hurt her.

"Only the bread," she told me. "And cheese. She didn't want the chicken, it was too hard to cook."

And so we had eaten our Friday-night supper without any challah, sucking our chicken bones to amplified shrieks—"Give me an *F*! Give me a *U*!"—as though Satan himself were holding a pep rally just down the road.

After dessert we turned on the news, and we saw on the screen not an invasion of a faraway hamlet, but our own town this night, not a mob of barbarians screaming outside the Pentagon, but outside our house. On the black-and-white set, even the film taken earlier that day was lifeless as ash so it seemed these intruders had stolen the color from the land near our home. Then the newscast went live and the cameras flew over the field near the stage, which looked like a pond writhing with newts in the beam from a flashlight, and the chop of the rotors over our roof was the same *chop-chop-chop* as from the TV. These were our roofs, our fields, the mob down the road, and my insides went cold with the helplessness of watching yourself in a dream while you drop from a cliff.

On Saturday my parents walked to the synagogue, pretending they saw nothing amiss, as Lot and his wife must have tried to look casual as they picked their way through the outskirts of Sodom. And after the service they'd found out how bad the emergency was—not a few hungry kids, but a few hundred thousand. The people in charge of the festival hadn't prepared for such crowds. All the highways were choked. No food could get through. No one had wanted these young people here, but seeing they *were* here . . .

So now, Sunday morning, my father and the other deliverymen at Yasgur's were planning to carry milk to the hordes, while my mother would help the Ladies Hadassah spread tuna on white bread, which nuns from the convent would deliver on foot.

"Great," I said, "fine, go feed the enemy, only leave me alone."

"Well, if you're sure," and I heard the stairs sigh, watched the light disappear.

I was cruel to my parents and I've lived to regret this, but then I felt justified, as though I were the parent, yanking the arms of a daughter and son who insisted on watching a worm on the ground while a yellow-haired comet blazed through the sky. Just four weeks before, while I'd been transfixed by two men in white leaping and landing with infinite grace on the moon—on the *moon*—my mother had wandered in from the kitchen, rubbing a glass. "Judith," she said, "this is historic," but she hadn't stopped rubbing that glass with her cloth, and my father kept saying, "Such brave men these are," shaking his head in a way that implied "not brave but foolish," while I felt the Messiah had announced the new kingdom: we were no longer animals whose feet had to stick in the muck of the earth, we could leap on the moon, anything was possible. But how could I argue with people who preferred a lifetime in orbit around this small town—delivering milk, shopping and cooking and washing the pots—to a flight to the moon?

That night as I lay on my back in our yard, plotting my course by connecting the stars, I whispered: "I'm coming." And the next day I bicycled up and down hills to Monticello and took out some books about space travel, asteroids, gravity, light. I didn't understand a word that I read but I felt their mere presence would help me become an astronaut sooner: I could stack these thick books, climb on top, brush the stars.

Then a boy I knew, Steven, informed me that astronauts had to be men, in perfect condition, with 20/20 eyesight so their glasses wouldn't float from their faces or break at critical times. After that I spent hours chinning myself from the beams in the basement until my arms grew as muscular as any boy's, though I later found out no boy would have felt that fullness and throb as he pulled himself up, thighs pressed, legs crossed. I did twenty push-ups, palms damp on the floor, jumped rope, *slap, slap, slap*. I spun in a circle so I *would not* throw up when tested for the job in that bucket in Houston. And I strengthened my sight by taking off my glasses, lifting a corner of the photo on the window and straining to read the signs on the farm stand in the Dwyers' front yard.

"Sweet corn," I said, though I knew I was reading from common sense—what else would the Dwyers be advertising at this time of year? I was squinting to make out the next line of print—

tomatoes? peas? melons?—when an ambulance pulled up and Steven jumped out. He trotted up our drive like an overwound toy. He was always so scrubbed he appeared to be wearing a doctor's white coat even when dressed in corduroy trousers and a polo shirt for school; now that he actually was wearing a lab coat (it hung past his knees) he was blindingly clean.

Of everyone I knew only Steven had dreams as intense as my own, and this must have been the reason I'd let him lead me one night to the Little League field behind the Jewish cemetery and why I'd confided what others would have mocked, pointing to illustrate at the pulsing full moon. That's when he said that astronauts weren't allowed to wear glasses, and he lifted off mine, leaned down, kissed my cheek where it merged with my nose, and told me his dream of mapping each neuron and cell in the brain so he could determine the tangles and gaps that made people ill, as his mother was ill. Using his thumb, he traced the long nerve from my toes to my thigh, and I knew he was using his dream as a reason to touch me this way, but right then the moon seemed very far-off, a circle of ice, and his fingers were warm.

"You're cold," Steven said. "It's like you're not here."

And even as I lay there I thought this was true. I regarded my body as some sort of spaceship that workmen were building and I wasn't yet sure I could trust their designs, things might go wrong—already I'd witnessed that leaking of blood—so I hadn't decided if I should move in. I saw myself lying on the bleachers near Steven, long, narrow, stiff, with an angular chin, eyes pale as slugs with my glasses removed.

"Even your hair is cold," Steven said as his hand fell away.

Now he bent to my window, and his face gleamed behind the earth like a bulb.

"You've got to come quick. The kids at the concert are really getting hurt. They're all on bad trips. Someone called up my father and asked him to come."

Steven's father was a surgeon, a swaggering man though just five foot two. Dr. Rock ran the hospital as if any question of his authority would be punished by traction, so no one objected when he let his son Steven take blood from patients, give shots and stitch wounds, though Steven had only just turned fifteen.

"I'll be his assistant," Steven said now, "and you can help *me*. But you have to hurry up. It took us all morning just to get this

344

far and we still have the hardest half-mile to go. We can't leave the ambulance, it's full of supplies."

"How could you?" I said. "They're our enemies, remember? These people think you can cure a disease by rubbing a certain part of your foot! They don't like machines, they don't like *computers*. You can't reach the moon without a computer! If they want to louse up their minds with those drugs, why don't you let them?"

His expression was blank, as though he had never heard this before, and I realized he hadn't; I'd been the one who'd done all the talking and he'd only nodded to humor this girl he wanted to kiss.

"It's a great chance to practice. Maybe I'll get to help my dad operate."

The ambulance whined.

"Sure you won't come?"

I shook my head no.

"Well, if you do, he said we'd be working in some kind of tent." And he trotted away.

With Steven's departure the cellar seemed twice as dim as before. I lay on the lounge chair and suddenly felt chilled, though the air was so heavy I felt I was lying smothered beneath a big, musty cow. With my book on my chest I daydreamed I'd left this planet behind—it was charred and defiled, and I was the last civilized being, in a ship so advanced that I would lack nothing, except somewhere to land, someone to greet me when I returned.

"Guess no one's home." A voice from outside, or maybe a dream.

"Hey, trick or treat!" A reedy voice, singsong. "Give us some food or we'll give you a trick."

"Shit, man, I'm hungry." This voice was deep, its edges were rough. "Can't you just smell that food? Bourgeois fuckin' pigs, hiding in the dark and stuffing their faces while the people are eating berries and shit. Let's liberate the food. Food for the people!"

And I charged up the stairs the way that a sleeper will bolt from her bed swinging her arms to ward off a dream before she wakes up and knows where she is, so I found myself standing with nothing but a book and a flimsy screen door protecting me from three starving barbarians.

345

The smallest was scraggly, with a beard like a goat's. He was shirtless, in cut-offs and small muddy sneakers. The second was a black man with a square-cut black beard in a dozen thin braids, each laced with gold. The biggest barbarian was shaggy, unkempt, but even in my fear I could sense something sweet and harmless about him, a circus bear fed on popcorn and nuts. He had on a jump suit; the patch on the chest was embroidered with RUFE. His feet were enormous and hair sprouted from his toe joints.

"Jesus, we scared her," the goat-boy was saying. "We didn't mean to scare you. Jesus, we'd never . . . We were kidding around. Pretending to be these tough guys, you know?"

The black one said, "Shit. We just need a phone. Fitz here, Fitzgibbon"—he pointed to the goat-boy—"was on his way home when we shanghaied him here. His poor momma must be shitless by now so we thought he could call."

"And then we smelled food," the goat-boat said, wistful. "We thought maybe your parents would give us some food."

I kept the door locked, my book poised to strike. Who'd believe a barbarian cared if his mother knew where he was? But they did seem upset, as though the Three Stooges had realized their slapstick had really hurt someone. I hadn't had time to put on my glasses and this made them blurry, less capable of harm.

"Well, then, come on," the bearish one said. "Can't you see that we've frightened her out of her gourd?" His accent was Southern, his tongue thick and slow as a bear's tongue would be. It struck me as right that a bear should be Southern—I suppose that the bears in some Walt Disney movie had spoken like this, and bears were slow-witted and crude in a way I'd grown up thinking Southern men were. But I couldn't figure out . . . Didn't Southern men hate black men? Didn't they hang them from trees?

The bear swiped his friend's arm and I almost expected to see bloody claw marks. "Imagine just can't you if some big ugly fella with braids in his beard showed up at *your* door? You figure your sister should welcome him in?"

"Braids? Hey, I . . . Shit." He touched his beard. "Shit. There was this girl, and she asked if she couldn't put braids in my

346

beard, and I said why not, it would help kill the time. Just a game, man, you know? Don't you ever play games? Don't you ever dress up in your momma's high heels?"

This was too much to tolerate. "I have better things to do."

"Can see that," the bear said. He narrowed his eyes and recited the title of the book I was holding. "*Gravitational Theory.* That's awful heavy reading for someone your age."

"How would *you* know?" I asked.

"Sure he knows," chimed the goat-boy. "At Princeton they call him the Astrophys Whiz."

This didn't take me in. None of the astronauts *I'd* ever seen would walk around barefoot, though I had seen Neil Armstrong wearing a jump suit . . .

"Don't let the hair fool you." The goat-boy was grinning. "I mean, think of Einstein. Now *he* was a mess."

"And you two?" I sneered. "I guess you're both Einsteins?"

"Jesus no," said the goat-boy. "Do you think we'd do anything as practical as that? Leon here"—he pointed—"when Leon grows up he's going to be a pure mathematician."

"Pure as the snow! Pure as the rain!" Leon crossed his white T-shirt. "And Fitz here's a classicist," though I had no idea what a classicist was. "Fitz, do your shit, man. Show her how useless a classicist is."

And the goat-boy threw back his long, skinny neck and recited— no, sang—a poem in a language I didn't understand, though I did feel the poetry, like the gallop of horses, and the goat-boy kept singing until I was hypnotized and let down my book.

"Sorry to have troubled you." The bear turned to leave. "We'll just go next door."

"Oh no," I said quickly, "the Dwyers have Dobermans and old Mr. Dwyer said he'd turn the dogs loose . . . " I stopped there, ashamed to remember that I had once been in favor of old Mr. Dwyer siccing his dogs on any barbarian who came near his farm. "You can use the phone here."

"You're sure of that?" the bear said. "If you'd rather we didn't . . . "

Suddenly I felt my bravery in question: he thought I was scared!

"All right, if you're sure. Fitz can go in, and Leon and me, we'll stay on the porch."

The goat-boy pawed his sneakers to scrape off the mud. If he meant to slice me open and paint the walls red he wouldn't be so careful to clean off his shoes. I lifted the latch.

"It's a big house," he said as we walked through the living room. "I grew up in the city, we just had two rooms."

We got to the kitchen and I watched him dial 0.

"Yes, thank you, ma'am, I'd like to place a call, long-distance, collect, to Mrs. Anne Fitzgibbon from her son Timothy."

When his mother got on I could tell she'd been crazy from fright where he was.

"Yes, Mom, I'm sure, Mom, I really didn't mean to give you such grief but this was my first chance to get to a phone," and he tried to assure her that he was all right, getting plenty to eat, so his words made me feel like a kidnapper who had treated him badly and forced him to lie to his mother at gunpoint.

He hung up the phone. "What a wonderful smell." He sniffed with his mouth. "I'll bet you had chicken. I smell pickles . . . and potatoes . . . I even smell your mother."

"*I* don't smell anything." I was horrified that anyone should say our house smelled; most of our neighbors wore the odor of their barnyards like ratty old coats they couldn't stand to part with, but my family took pride in how often we bathed, how the kitchen floor shone.

The goat-boy said, "A person can't smell her own house. You need an outsider. Someone who's trained. Archaeology, see? When you dig up some ruins you have to be able to sniff out the food the people once ate there, what sort of clothes and perfumes they wore, how they treated their slaves."

I knew he was lying, but believed him enough to feel sad that no one would stand here and sniff and know I had lived. And I nearly believed he could sniff out my future, as he'd sniffed out the past. I wanted to ask: Would I go to the moon? Or would the barbarians destroy the world first?

We'd reached the front door. Leon and the bear stood up and stretched.

"I could make you some sandwiches."

"Oh, we don't want to bother—"

"No, it's okay. You just stay here."

I ran to the kitchen. We didn't have much food but I found a few slices of stale pumpernickel . . . a jar of peanut butter . . . and honey. A bear would like honey, I thought, so I spread that on too.

The barbarians stuffed their mouths with these sandwiches, then they couldn't say a word.

"W-w-w-w," moaned Leon, "w-water," and I thought of the hose, but I ran off and got them glasses of milk.

"Ahh," said the goat-boy. He lifted his glass. "Milk fit for gods." And I had to laugh because he and Leon had milky white rings encircling their mouths—they didn't look like gods but surprised little boys. The two seemed offended, but they glanced at each other and swiped at their mouths with the backs of their hands.

"I don't suppose you'd know a place we could wash at?" The bearish one stood and yanked down his jump suit, where it caught in his crotch. "Some swimming hole nearby?"

"Yeah," Leon said, "I sure as shit could go for a swim."

"There's a pond," I said, happy to have the right answer, though sorry to think they would soon leave my porch.

Leon wrinkled his nose. "Not some little cow pond covered with green shit and pissed in by a half-million hippies like the cow pond back there?"

"No, this one's big, and the water's really clean." I flushed with the arrogance of access to places that strangers couldn't find. Then I realized these strangers wouldn't be able to find the pond without me. "I could show you," I said, then wished that I hadn't.

"That would be awful nice," the bear said, and smiled. "Then you and I can talk about gravity. That is, if you want."

"Just a minute," I said, and ran to the cellar to put on my glasses, so when I came back I saw all three clearly, their pimples and dirt, the pores where the beard hairs poked through their skin, and this made them seem less frightening, and more.

"Follow me," I said. And I led our parade down a trail through the woods—it seemed the cool air had fled the other barbarians and was trembling here beneath this camouflage of leaves. The trail passed a tractor whose tires had been used for archery practice. I felt someone draw the metallic tip of one of those arrows

349

down my neck, down my spine, but I turned and saw no one except for the goat-boy, who was sniffing the air and skipping a little, and the other two behind him.

When we got to the pond I heard Leon whistle.

"Shit, look at that. In Newark, man . . . shit."

I didn't understand. This was only the pond down the road from my house. Then I saw it as a boy from a city might see it, and if I'd accused the barbarians of stealing the color from Bethel, they gave it back doubly, once right-side up and again upside down. Every orange salamander and blue darning needle signaled me like some code from beyond.

The goat-boy and Leon stripped to their undershorts, then dove in long arcs, came up again and started to race, one heavy black arm and one scrawny pale arm rising and falling, the gold-threaded braids of Leon's beard floating out from his chin like some intricate lure.

"Hmm, I'm afraid . . . " The bearish one was fiddling with the zipper on his jump suit.

"Afraid of the water?" I asked.

"No, afraid I don't have any underwear."

"I won't look," I promised, though I found when he started to pull down his zipper I couldn't turn away. As he stepped from the jump suit I expected to see a heavy black rectangle blocking his crotch. Instead, what I saw was my first naked man, layered in fur so he seemed like an animal, a burly brown bear, and poking from the pouch that hung between his legs was a separate little animal—a baby, a pet, like a baby kangaroo peeking out shyly and waving its arm. And what I felt then wasn't love at first sight, but my first sight of love, of what it could mean to love someone else, a stranger, not family, and how risky this was, loving a pitifully weak, naked man.

He clumsily paddled out a few yards, furry bum in the air. "Don't you want to come in? Water's just right."

I shook my head no. "I don't have a suit," though this was ridiculous—neither did he. And the way that he looked at my body just then made me want to disclaim it: "That body's not mine, I haven't moved in." But I knew that I had, though I didn't feel at home yet, its corners still dark, its workings mysterious.

He was standing in the shallows up to his waist, slapping the water as a bear tries to slap a fish onto shore. This made the reflections of the trees and sky shimmer, then shatter to fragments of green, blue and white, which were fragmented further by the drops on my glasses.

The goat-boy and Leon dragged themselves, dripping, onto the rocks to warm in the sun. "Man, don't those lizards have the right idea?" And they both fell asleep.

Grumbling because the stones cut his feet, the bear hobbled through the shallows. He sprawled by my side, draping his jump suit over his thighs.

"I'm lying here naked and you don't know my name." He held out a paw. "Meyer Rabinowitz. Pleased to meet you."

"Not Rufe?"

"Rufe? Oh yeah, this." He plucked at the jump suit. "Guess somewheres outside Atlanta, Georgia, a fella named Rufe is pumping gas naked."

"You're Jewish. And Southern." None of our relatives lived farther south than Paramus, New Jersey.

"If your mind can't stretch over those two categories, you'll never be a physicist. You've got to be able to imagine a thing"—the word came out *thang*—"being two thangs at once."

"A physicist? Who said I'd want to be that? Is that what you are? I thought they said you were some kind of astronaut."

"That's all right," he said. "Even my mother can't keep it straight. The difference is this: an astronaut goes up there, flying in space, but an astrophysicist only *thinks* about going, what the trip would be like."

"You never leave Earth?"

"A fat guy like me? Besides, I got asthma."

I was very disappointed, but glad that I hadn't really believed this was a man who could pass NASA's test. "It doesn't make sense. I don't understand how you think about space. What do you think about?"

"For now I just think about whatever my professors tell me to think about. But later . . . I mean, when I'm out on my own . . ." He leaned forward, excited, and his jump suit slipped a little, exposing his navel; its pattern resembled the continents and oceans dividing the earth. "What I'd really like to think about is what it's like living in higher dimensions."

I'd been fooled after all. "You're not talking science. You're talking the way the barbarians talk."

351

"Barbarians?"

I waved my hand toward the dairy.

He wagged his head, laughing. "That what you call them? How come 'barbarians'?"

"We learned it in school. The barbarians came down and took over Europe and except for the monks there, nobody read. They kept alive science while the vandals outside their caves pillaged and sacked."

"That what you think? You're really afraid of those hippies out there? You're an awful strange kid."

I should have felt strange then. I'd felt strange all my life. I'd had the premonition I would never have allies, except false ones like Steven. But now I could see I was part of a team, and though our team, the monks, might be greatly outnumbered, I wouldn't have to fight the barbarians alone.

"Guess I'd better tell you about higher dimensions, in case it's all up to you." He slid down the rock; his toe stirred the pond. "It's this way," he said. "Suppose you had left a note for your parents: 'I went for a swim, and if you come looking here's where I'll be.' "

The example seemed ominous. Was he trying to say that I had been foolish not to leave such a note?

"Well, you'd need three dimensions to say where you were, three dimensions in *space*. And you'd have to let them know *when* you would be here or they'd miss you entirely. You and your parents would pass through each other in space-time, now wouldn't you?"

I guessed that we would and this made me feel sad, like Dorothy in Oz when she'd seen Auntie Em in the witch's glass ball and called out her name, "Auntie Em, Auntie Em," but hadn't been able to make her aunt hear.

"It's like this," he said, using a stone to draw on the rock the way little girls draw boards for hopscotch. When he finished I saw two ice cream cones with their pointy ends touching.

"See this point here?" Meyer placed his finger where the ice cream cones met. "That's us, here and now. And all this up here"—rubbing his finger on the right-side-up cone—"that's our future, okay? All the places and times we'd be able to reach moving at any speed slower than light. Because no one can ever go faster than light. You must have read that."

Although I had read this, the equations that proved it were a dense drape of lace I could not peer through to the reasons beyond, and so, in my ignorance, I was free to believe that once I got up there I'd show they were wrong, my rocket would tear that paper-thin curtain, that barrier of light.

I nodded. "I read it."

"But you think maybe somehow *you'll* find a way to go faster than light?"

I shrugged. I didn't want him to think I was boasting.

He snorted. "Okay. Everyone thinks that. But you'll find out you're wrong. This is the only future you'll have. And this cone back here, this cone's our past. And all of this other stuff, outside the cones, all this is elsewhere."

"Elsewhere?" I said.

"Sure," Meyer said. "Out here is elsewhere, the places you and I can't ever reach, can't ever have been, because even if we traveled fast as a light beam all our born days, that's far as we'd get."

I still felt defiant. "How do they know?"

"Because there are limits. Who knows, maybe angels can live out in elsewhere, but people can only live in the past, or the future, or now." He seemed to be thinking aloud for my benefit and this eased the frustration of having to travel slower than light. "Animals, I suppose, can just live in now, we're ahead of them there. People at least can imagine what it's like to live out in elsewhere. At least we have that."

I was going to ask him to help me imagine what elsewhere was like, but a cough tore the stillness. The goat-boy and Leon had awakened, I saw, and were passing a cigarette back and forth, back and forth. I was stunned by this intimacy. Then something—the smell, like some bittersweet flower, or the curve of their cheeks as they sucked at the smoke—shocked me the way that seeing a movie star in person can shock.

"But they're smart guys!" I said. "Leon knows math."

He shrugged his big shoulders. "Smart guys do dumb thangs. Leon thinks it helps him visualize thangs like imaginary numbers. And Fitz, well, he likes it, he can't seem to stop."

I suddenly glimpsed the future and it had no Fitz in it. His mother was weeping, haunting this rock and weeping for a son who had killed himself smoking too much marijuana.

"Why are you here?" I asked Meyer brusquely.

"You mean, why are the three of us here at this pond?"

"No, I mean all of you. Why did you come?"

"Me? I don't know. The music, I suppose. I needed a rest before the next term. I like the outdoors. And I figure it's good to pack in as many thangs as you can before you're too old. Some of them, like Fitz, they came for the ride. And a few of them were hoping to find somethang . . . big. I guess they found that. Somethang big, somethang pure. You know what you see when you look at the moon? You think it's all right to spend your whole life trying to get there, it's so big and pure? That's how they feel. They don't even see the mud that they're sitting in. They found somethang pure."

"Does that mean they'll *stay*?"

He laughed. "I don't think so. No matter how stoned you are, you can't ignore the mud and the stink and the hunger for more than a while. Not if you're human. You can't live in elsewhere, you can't live in space, you can't live in squalor much more than a week."

My relief didn't last long; he asked me politely if I'd please turn my head, and when I looked back he was standing and dressed.

"Hey, don't y'all think we should go?" he shouted to the others. "Don't want to miss Hendrix. That's why I came." Then he turned back to me. "You've been very kind." He held out his hands and lifted me up. "Don't look so glum. World's not so big. We could meet again."

I wanted to set a place and a time, all four dimensions, so I'd know he'd be waiting and the years wouldn't feel long. Before I could say this, Leon had bowed and the goat-boy had kissed the back of my hand and all three had left.

I must have found my way back to the house, lain brooding on my lounge chair, but no events marked the passage of time so those hours are lost. I only remember when my parents returned. I heard noise in the kitchen and went up to join them.

"I've a mind to press charges!" My father was rifling the drawer by the sink. "The cowards!" he said. He took out the Band-Aids and slammed the drawer shut. This noise from my father was as shocking as speech from a mute would have been. He handed the box of Band-Aids to my mother, who was slumped on a stool, and that's when I noticed her checked blouse was ripped. A safety pin held the pieces together but a slice of bright pink brassiere still winked through.

"How did you do that?"

"There's no need to tell her," he cautioned my mother. "The son's in her class."

"It was someone I know?" Why would anyone I know rip my mother's checked blouse?

She applied a small Band-Aid to a scratch on her wrist. "Oh it's nothing," she said, though she'd never drooped so badly—her anklets had vanished into her shoes. "We ran into old Mr. Dwyer in town, and he and a few of the neighbors are furious that we'd try to help—"

My *father* was furious. "If they don't want to buy Max's milk anymore, that's their prerogative. But ripping a blouse! Scratching a woman who tries to do good!"

Since my father spent his days delivering milk and was so smooth and pale, I'd always half-thought his essence was *milk*, which I guess meant untroubled, innocent, clean, but his face was so streaked and his features so clouded I couldn't help but think of the milk behind the dairy that was left to be dumped, it was tainted or sour.

My mother was holding her hands to her blouse, hanging her head. "It was partly my fault. When I pushed him away my arm caught his buckle."

I tried to imagine my mother wrestling with old Mr. Dwyer— he was only an inch or two taller than she was, and quite a bit plumper.

"And blaming the Jews! To say Max is a kike who rented his land to Communists because he can't resist money!" He had always assumed that since he was privileged to open the boxes on his neighbors' back stoops and decipher the notes they'd left him inside ("Judd has an ulcer . . . " "Can't pay this week . . . " "Miscarriage . . . " "Transfer . . . "), because they allowed him to see them in curlers and torn robes or long johns he knew who they were.

"If that farmer wants a lesson in manners," he said, "he should look at those kids. Who would expect they would be so polite? Look what they gave, for a few quarts of milk." He pulled a feather from his pocket; in a crate by the door were a string of

purple beads, a collection of hats of all sorts and shapes, a broken
guitar, a bouquet of weeds in a ponytail wrapper, a freshly whit-
tled flute and a cookbook whose recipes were blessed by a man
whose mustache and nose made him resemble my grandfather
Morris. "So maybe they don't act like people like us. The young
men don't mind if their girlfriends show off their bodies in
public—not to say the girls have bodies to shame them. Such
big, healthy girls!" And his face made me think he was seeing
them now, those big, naked girls.

"And the little ones." My mother refastened the pin so it hid
the pink bra. (Why had she bought it? Her others were white.)
"In town they were saying the diseases are dreadful—they can't
get the pumps in to drain out the toilets."

My father joined in. "If a fire breaks out . . . "

"I guess I should open a can of soup for dinner." My mother
didn't move. "But I'd feel guilty eating with those poor hungry
children . . . and sleeping tonight on a bed with clean sheets . . . "

That was it! I'd invite them to sleep in our house, in cots in my
room.

I left my parents sitting on the floor in the kitchen, sifting
through the relics they'd acquired that day, and I almost wish I
hadn't—my father was never so silent again, my mother drooped
much more often, it seemed. And though their confrontation
with old Mr. Dwyer only began a chain of events that made them
feel less and less part of the town, I blame this beginning for
their decision many years later to do what they'd said they never
would do: they moved away from Bethel when my father retired.
And then they kept moving, trying new places—they even
bought a camper, lived in that for a year—as if once they'd been
knocked from their tiny fixed orbits, they wobbled, unrestrained,
all over the country: first Florida, then Phoenix, then Houston
near me (I was glad when they left, afraid they'd find out I wasn't
as smart as they'd once thought, wasn't destined for greatness;
the machines made my job seem more impressive than it actually
was). They still tried to see only the best in the people they met,
even if this meant they had to move on before seeing the worst.
And whenever I got a postcard from someplace like L.A. or
Reno, I feared for their innocence as once I had scorned it, and I
was impatient with their wanderings as I had once been impa-

tient with their unchanging lives. Because even though I didn't
want to go home to Bethel, I felt they should be there in case
that I did; I felt I'd gone swimming and they'd stolen the shore.

It was five when I left them. The day had been clear, but now,
as I walked, two thin black clouds swirled through the sky like a
helicopter's rotors slicing the sun. In the shadows of a corn field I
made out two men, one holding his fly, the patter of his urine
spraying the stalks, the other man squatting with his pants to his
knees. When the wind came I thought it was bringing their
smell, but as I walked on, the air thickened with the odor of
three-day-old garbage and I had to pull the neck of my jersey
over my nose to inhale the fresh breeze captured in the fabric
days before on the line. How could they stand it? But then I remembered what the goat-boy had said about people not being
able to smell their own smell, and what Meyer had told me about
people who wanted so badly to think they'd found something
pure that they *wouldn't* smell its smell, at least for a while.

The sky was gray-black and the winds had picked up so they
swirled bits of litter over my head. I heard human howls and
grunts from the woods, saw flames here and there, and I almost
turned back—the trucks wouldn't get through and we all would
be burned. But then I saw faces bobbing over the flames like
yellow balloons and I realized these people were cooking their
dinners, what little they had, though how could they eat with so
many flies? These rose from the mud with each step I took, settled on my eyelids, trapped themselves in my ears. I could hear
trees and wires snapping like whips, and the throb of the
music—I couldn't hear the words—and thunder, in the distance,
and the helicopters grinding over our heads.

And though I brag now about having grown up there, having
been in that crowd when I was thirteen, the truth is I only remember my terror, my wish to escape. I wandered those fields
I'd known all my life, picking my way among feet, heads and
limbs. I stepped over bodies face-down in the mud, and I knew it
was hopeless, I'd never find Meyer or the goat-boy or Leon.

I saw a big tent. I went in and stood. A woman in a uniform
came up and said: "Honey, are you in there? What did you take?"
snapping her fingers in front of my eyes.

"No time for that, just get her a blanket." Dr. Rock, rushing by,
glanced at my face without recognition. "These fucking asshole
parents ought to be shot, exposing a kid to something like this."

357

The nurse took my arm but I shook her off. I saw Steven kneeling by a female barbarian, swabbing a cut. He was still shining white but the whiteness was stained, which unsettled me as much as seeing a statue spattered with blood. His eyes weren't focused, so it took him a while to see that I'd come.

"You're too late," he said. "This woman had a baby . . . and this other one, she had . . . My father said some butcher must have done a bad job but I'm not really sure. . . . And this kid, he was sleeping, and some jerk on a tractor thought the sleeping bag was empty. . . . And this one diabetic who didn't bring her insulin, she went into shock. What jerks! I mean, coming to someplace like this and you don't bring your medicine? And these guys on bad trips, one had this knife and he came at my father—"

"Goddamn it, Steven, get your ass over here!"

Steven obeyed, leaving me at the edge of the tent. The wind ripped right through, blowing gauze pads from carts rattling bottles. The canvas roof billowed and the center pole shook so I went back outside, out in the rain, which tore at my skin. A dozen barbarians were stomping and sliding and splashing one another but everyone else was huddled together close to the ground, holding garbage bags, sleeping bags, parkas and blankets over their heads; in the half-light it seemed the ground itself shook.

"Hey, come on in."

Slowly I knelt and took shelter under a huge plastic tarp. It was humid and dark, body to body. Someone put an arm over my shoulder and we started to sway; people were chanting "no rain, no rain" as though this were a spell to make the rain stop. We were so many people so close together I had the sensation of losing my boundaries—the wind had stripped off the walls of the house that I had moved into only that day, and I had trouble telling where my own body ended and the others began.

This scared me so much I said half-aloud: "I'm not far from home. I've been here before." And I pictured the field the way I had seen it thousands of times, the green and gold pasture with its intricate shading and texture of weeds, clover, alfalfa, a great green bowl rising to a rim where it met a blue sky with clouds like the blue-and-white china in my mother's glass cabinet, and the land beyond that, with its swells and depressions, so a tractor would sink and disappear a moment, then float back to view.

I tried to imagine the scent of fresh hay warmed by the sun, but the stench of the present brought me back to this place. I was stuck in this time and would never get out. We would die in this place, buried in mud, so that years in the future, archaeologists would stand here and see only dirt, though they might sniff our presence under the earth and know we had lived, know we had once been huddled together under this tarp chanting "no rain, no rain" as if we believed that we could get elsewhere simply by wishing as hard as we could.

Nominated by DeWitt Henry

TWO STORIES

fiction by DIANE WILLIAMS

from TIKKUN and CONJUNCTIONS

PERFECT

"YOU WANT AN INSIGHT? I'll give you an insight," said a perfect stranger at the children's ball game. Then he gave me his insight which proved to be exactly correct.

"People will cheer him when he gets himself up," the man said.

I had thought that the child's ankle was probably shattered—that was *my* insight—that the child would not be able to walk, that he would need to be lifted and carried, that he'd never walk again. I thought, Now he is a cripple for the rest of his life.

"He's fine," the man said. "I know he's fine, because, you see, he's hiding his head. He's hiding his face. He's making such a big deal. I know. Sure, it's very painful."

The man had told me that the hardball had hit the child in the ankle. I didn't know where.

I said, "How do you know? It might be shattered. He's not moving."

"Because he missed the ball—" the man said, "because he wants everyone to forget he missed the ball, that's why he's making such a big deal."

If I could have an insight about this man's insight, I could probably save myself. That's my insight. I could save my children, my marriage, the world, if I could let enough people know—that there's a powerful solution in here somewhere—a breakthrough trying to break through.

The stranger was so angry talking to me. I don't think he believed I was believing him, and I didn't.

Will you please rise and Shame us not, O Father.

* * * *

THE HAG WAS TRANSFORMED BY LOVE

The guys, oh, how you longed for them, round and savory, and
just how they get after a few days in their gravy, in the pot, in the
refrigerator, and then they are heated up, and then they are
eaten up.

I know what Terri Great thought because I remember my
thoughts to a tee exactly about my own little new potatoes I just
ate, and I am calling myself for the hell of it, *Terri*!

She was sticking her fork—Mrs. Alexander Great—into the little new potato, thinking, I may be the only one who likes this!

For the hell of it, Mrs. Great, you should have stayed there
sticking in your fork, tasting and enjoying, and eating up little
new potatoes until you had finished all four of your potatoes, *Terri*!

Say it, Terri, from the two and a half little guys that you did
eat, you got all the stimulation from the spree you thought was
wise, because, if she's going to say, "This is the best it gets from
a potato," then Terri Great has stretched her mind beyond the
wisecrack fully—stop!

Terri left the house then, and her husband Alexander never
saw her again, nor her little guy Raymond, nor her little guy, Guy.

She spent most of her time in the company of people like herself who said they knew what they were thinking. For instance,
she thinks any penis is ugly.

The enormity of what she had done, leaving her family
abruptly, suddenly, and with no warning, gave her lots of other
thoughts, too.

She did not upon arrival, speak well the language of the country she had fled to. When she asked a man, for example, on the
street, her first day in town, "Where is the train station?" the
man told her kindly that there had not been a war in his country
for forty years. (He wore a brown, ankle-length, belted trench
coat, was about sixty years old.) Miraculously, she thought she

361

could comprehend every word that he had said. It was a miracle too, that when he flashed it at her, she thought *his* penis was a beauty. Like magic—the colors of it, were the colors to her of her own baby's shirt, face and hat that she had only just left far behind, and the form of it was like a much much much bigger dewdrop.

At home, this rich man had a thin wife. He supposedly worshipped his old wife until old Terri Great came into the picture. Then just forget it. (Things keep happening so perversely for zealots.)

For Terri, she got her first six orgasms during penetration with this man during the next fifteen weeks of their intercourses together.

In the weeks that followed these events, she renewed her days, and she became intrigued with finance.

Nominated by Lydia Davis and Daniel Hayes

THE DONALD BARTHELME BLUES

by CHARLES BAXTER

from THE GETTYSBURG REVIEW

THE SAME DAY that a friend called with the news that Donald Barthelme had died, a freight train derailed outside Freeland, Michigan. Among the cars that went off the tracks were several chemical tankers, some of which spilled and caught fire. Dow Chemical was (and still is) reluctant to name these chemicals, but one of them was identified as chlorosilene. When chlorosilene catches fire, as it did in this case, it turns into hydrochloric acid. Upon being asked about the physical hazards to neighbors and on-lookers near the fire, a company representative, interviewed on Michigan Public Radio, said, "Well, there's been some physical reactions, yes, certainly. Especially in the area of nausea, vomiting-type thing."

The area of nausea, vomiting-type thing: this area, familiar to us all, where bad taste, hilarity, fake authority, and cliché seem to collide, was Donald Barthelme's special kingdom. "I have a few new marvels here I'd like to discuss with you just briefly," says the chief engineer in "Report." "Consider for instance the area of realtime online computer-controlled wish evaporation." Like his creation Hokie Mokie, the King of Jazz, no one could top Barthelme at deadpan riffs like these—these collages built from castoff verbal junk—and imitation was beside the point, because the work was not a compendium of stylistic tics but grew out of—has anyone bothered to say this?—a spiritual enterprise owned up to in the work, a last stay against the forces of wish evaporation. Comedy is partly the art of collage, of planned incongruity—the Three Stooges as brain surgeons, King Kong as an adjunct professor of art history—and Barthelme was a master tailor of these ill-fitting suits in which our culture likes to dress itself. A yoking of the virtuosic-articulate with the flat banal; an effort to preserve wishes, and certain kinds of longings, in the face of clichés; not innocence, but a watchful clarity, even an effort to preserve the monstrousness of Being itself: all these difficult ambitions seemed to be part of the project. The work was a comfort, in the way the blues are a comfort, in its refusal to buy stock in the official Happiness Project, in its loyalty to "inappropriate longings," a phrase whose ironic positive side he particularly valued.

As an undergraduate I was taught that when a writer starts a story, he or she must begin with *a character*, an active, preferably vivid, ideally sympathetic, character. It takes a bit of time to see that stories don't in fact begin with characters, not from here, at least, not from behind this keyboard. They begin with words, one word after another. It seems doltish to point this out, but in Donald Barthelme's fiction, that's where the project begins: with the stress first on the language, the medium, and then on the problem of who owns it. Who does own language? I can evade the question by saying that no one does; it is just out there, part of the culture. But Barthelme did not practice this evasion. In his stories, all kinds of disreputable people claim to own both language and its means of distribution. They invent instant clichés that they want you to buy and use; they want you to join and submit to their formulas. Invariably, they are selling something that can only be sold if they trash up the language first. They are lively practitioners of a black art, these commodifiers, and Barthelme's stories don't mind saying so.

Barthelme's characters inhabit not the prison-house of language, but the prison-house of official cliché—which is not the same thing as saying "Fine" when someone asks how you are but is more a processing of statements into the professional formulas usually called jargon, like the analyst's transformation of Susan's statement (in "The Sandman") that she wants to buy a piano into, "She wished to terminate the analysis and escape into the piano." The narrator, Susan's boyfriend and a slightly irritable opponent of normative psychotherapy, observes that the analyst is method-ologically horse-blindered: "The one thing you cannot consider, by the nature of your training and of the discipline itself, is that she really might want to terminate the analysis and buy a piano."

What *are* the conditions under which we lose the ability to know what we want? And what are the exact words for longing? Most of the words we have are not the words for what we really want. "What we really want in this world, we can't have" ("The Ed Sullivan Show"). There is a certain stranded quality to the Barthelme protagonist, sitting in an easy chair at twilight with eleven martinis lined up in soldierly array. A fastidiousness, this is, and a humor about the shipwrecked condition, the orphaned longings, and something like an investigation of the possibilities inherent in melancholy. The heroes and heroines in this fiction are the not-joiners, the *non serviam* types, like Cecelia in "A City of Churches," who has come to Prester to open a car-rental office. Mr. Phillips guides her around. It turns out that in Prester everyone lives in a church of one kind or another, "the church of their choice." Mr. Phillips asks Cecelia what denomination she is: "Cecelia was silent. The truth was, she wasn't anything." She tells him, however, that she can will her dreams. What dreams? " 'Mostly sexual things,' she said. She was not afraid of him." Mr. Phillips admits to a certain discontent with Prester, despite the town's perfection. "I'll dream the Secret," Cecelia says. "You'll be sorry."

Notice the capitalization of the word *secret*. Our secrets might be the last places where we have hidden ourselves away, where we are still upper-case. Susan wants her piano; Cecelia wants her dreams; and the Phantom of the Opera resists the operation that would, as we might say now, *renormalize* him. All any of these heroes would have to do to be renormalized is trade in their desires for rooms furnished with comfortable clichés: nice wing chairs, plastic slipcovers. The Phantom's friend waits, patiently, "until the hot meat of romance is cooled by the dull gravy of common sense once more." That's a long time, if you're loyal to your desires.

The price one pays for being loyal to certain kinds of anomalies is typically melancholy or acedia: more of this later. What Bar-thelme's fiction asserts is that one of the first loyalties serious people give up in the theater of adulthood is a claim upon what they actually want. Of course, other desires are available, and can be acquired, but they are curious grafts, what other people want you to want—not desires so much as temptations, desires-of-convenience. Barthelme's stories are obviously and constantly about such temptations, which might itself be called the temptation to become unconscious and let others program your yearnings. The stories exude an almost religious seriousness about this subject; although they are not pious, they do move obsessively around ethical-theological quandaries. A good deal of reading about religion is made visible in them. The Barthelmean character is tempted not by ordinary sins but by the ordinary itself. Does God care about adultery? Sins generally? "You think about this staggering concept, the mind of God, and then you think He's sitting around worrying about this guy and this woman at the Beechnut Travelodge? I think not" (*Paradise*).

It wasn't activities like adultery that caught Barthelme's attention, but the inclination to disown one's wishes and to give in to the omnipresence of the Universal Banal. Barthelme was not a snob in this respect; plain common pleasures—food, sex, Fleetwood Mac, John Ford movies, dull days at home—find themselves celebrated (however mildly) in his pages; ordinary pleasures are all right if that is what you really want. But no, the problem is not the banal as such but banality's hope that you will dumbfoundedly join in its program, spend yourself in it: that's the problem. In Barthelme a saint is tempted not by sin but by life in the suburbs: "St. Anthony's major temptation, in terms of his living here, was maybe this: ordinary life" ("The Temptation of St. Anthony"). People want to see his apartment; they want to look at the carpet from Kaufman's, and the bedroom. How might a saint resist the ordinary?

A simple question, calling forth slyly complicated answers. One begins by talking about deserts (where the Saint goes), grottos, the stony home of the grotesque. In a catalogue commentary on a Sherrie Levine exhibit, Barthelme put it this way:

> Where does desire go? Always a traveling salesperson, desire goes hounding off into the trees, frequently, without direction from its putative master or mistress. This is tragic and comic at the same time. I should, in a

well-ordered world, marry the intellectual hero my
wicked uncle has selected for me. Instead I run off
with William of Ockham or Daffy Duck.

William of Ockham or Daffy Duck: yes, the true object of your
desire quite often looks and sounds a bit, well, bizarre, and hard
to introduce to your wicked uncle. The more bizarre the object,
the more Barthelme seems to like it. There is a pleasant sideshow quality, a circus element, to the spectacle of desire. It generates dwarves and witches (*Snow White*), a son manqué (eight
feet tall and wearing "a serape woven out of two hundred transis-
tor radios" in "The Dolt"), monsters, and impossibly beautiful
women. It's as if longing generates out of itself, as Susan Stewart
has argued in her book on the subject, narratives of the gigantic
and tiny, narratives of altered proportion: there is the dead father, that huge living corpse of origination, being dragged around
by the bickering sons; there are the zombies, spouting their
death-in-life clichés; there is King Kong, already alluded to, the
adjunct professor of art history at Rutgers. Big and little: figures
of all sizes and shapes have their moment in the most highly invented sentences grammar and sense permit. This sideshow resides very comfortably, too, in the short story form, a haven, as
Frank O'Connor has claimed, for the otherwise disappeared, all
the everyone-elses who fall between the cracks of the more official forms, such as the novel and the sonnet.

Sometimes behind this cultivation of the beautiful grotesque,
this show-and-tell of the alien wish, a certain weariness is sometimes apparent. One is after all confronted by the banal in the
midst of the weird; there is also that terrible moment familiar to
all members of the avant-garde when the weird *becomes* the banal. "Some things appear to be wonders in the beginning, but
when you become familiar with them, are not wonderful at
all. Sometimes a seventy-five-foot highly paid cacodemon will
raise only the tiniest *frisson*. Some of us have even thought of
folding the show—closing it down" ("The Flight of Pigeons from
the Palace").

What is the secret name of this weariness? At first it is called
irony, and then acedia.

Under the powerful microscope of post-structuralist Neo-Marxist
semiotically-based hyphen-using critical theory, Barthelme's fiction

at first seems to be all about cultural junk, verbal junk, "the leading edge of the trash phenomenon," and about the way structures of meaning, let loose from the objects they're supposed to represent, are pasted onto something else (the Campbell's Pork-and-Beans labels on my necktie; Elvis's *Jailhouse Rock* on dinner plates from the Franklin Mint; the Batman label on sandwiches). Words go wild. They are set free from the house of correction and have a party ("Bone Bubbles") or, freed up like a chatty aunt off her medication, go on and on ("Sentence"). For a time in the early seventies, Barthelme and John Ashbery seemed to be operating similar circuses in different parts of town. This period included the moment of greatest academic interest in Barthelme's work; critics had much to say about the mechanisms of meaning in the fiction, about the arbitrariness of the sign and the problems of language. The defamiliarization in the work matched the defamiliarization of American social life. But semiotics and fragments are not the essential subjects of these stories. I'm not sure how often it has been noticed that Barthelme's imagery, cast of characters, and preoccupations are drawn from religious sources. Who is the dead father in *The Dead Father*? The father and The Father. In "City Life," Ramona gives birth to Sam; it's a virgin birth. Angels, in their current earthly diminished lives, have their say in "On Angels." Kierkegaard is invoked several times. Such maneuvering has an element of travesty in it, a playing-around with the broken relics of religious iconography and meaning-creation; but religion appears so often and with such odd sideways intensity that it signals a persistent curiosity about the Absolute and such of its elements as authenticity (in post-structuralist thinking, a completely discredited category).

In Barthelme's early stories, modern culture is gleefully and relentlessly unmasked: engineers, doctors, politicians, newspapers, television quiz shows, and the plastic assembled-with-glue language they use. There is a certain violence in the ripping off of the masks here, a ferocity that produces a prose poetry (Barthelme probably would have hated the term) of rage and clarity. Lines often-quoted from the first paragraph of "The Indian Uprising" hit this note and sustain it: "People were trying to understand. I spoke to Sylvia. 'Do you think this is a good life?' The table held apples, books, long-playing records. She looked up. 'No.'"

These early stories sometimes seem to demonstrate that the serious world is about as well-constructed as a puppet show; it is certainly no more real. All experience gives way to representation. You pull back the pretense: another pretense. Pictures give way to pictures, acts to acts. It's unhinging, the metaphysics of the onion-skin giving way to nothing: the wisps and whiffs of frenzy I hear in *Come Back, Dr. Caligari, Unspeakable Practices, Unnatural Acts,* and *City Life* strike me as sounds made by someone reaching for the irreducibly real but coming up with fistfuls of sand—or an empire of signs, themselves nauseating and revealing of nothing. Knowing—as the Barthelmean narrative knows so well—that this reaching, this frenzy, and this sand are commonplaces in the history of twentieth century spiritual-critical life is no solace. What good is it to know that your metaphysical nausea, which you suffer from daily, has been experienced before and expressed very well by Mallarmé, Sartre, and the others? As the stories themselves say, "No good at all!"

Starting with "Kierkegaard Unfair to Schlegel," in *City Life* and then intermittently throughout the other books, Barthelme seemed to be setting himself a challenge to go beyond this un-masking process—a process that would, if continued indefinitely, have yielded up wacky but tedious self-repeating satires, or exercises in dry malice. The nature of this challenge is not easy to state discursively, but it may be at the center of any life which is simultaneously mindful and bourgeois (if in fact those two categories can be placed next to each other). We can call it, in honor of one of its first diagnosticians, the Chekhov problem, which goes something like this: what does one do, do actively, with one's honest revulsion and disgust with the cruelties, lies, and deceptions of middle-class life? Chekhov's response to this challenge—this is a gross oversimplification—is to show that, hidden under the outward mimes of character there lies the substance of real character, a kind of essence. Something genuine sooner or later will show itself; all we need do is wait, observe, and hold onto those moments when they arrive. In this way, weariness and cynicism are kept at arm's length. Because no character can be wholly co-opted by any system, some particle of the genuine will emerge at some point.

This solution, if one can call it that, was closed to Barthelme almost from the beginning. Either he did not believe in character in this sense (one cannot imagine him using so square a phrase as "real character underneath"), or he had no feel for it as a writer. As a result his characters tend toward allegory and stylization. Exceptions exist, notably in the Bishop stories, but they are few. It is not so much that the characters in Barthelme's fiction are unreal but that they seem to have been constructed more out of pre-existing emotions than out of motivations, a more common writerly starting-point. In any case, without the solution of character, we are back at the original problem of what to do after all the lies have been exposed. And of course we are still enjoying the unreflecting privileges of middle-class life.

This far from trivial problem exists only if you assume that middle-class American life does carry with it a gnawing burden of guilt. I think I could argue that a significant number of the strategies of contemporary American "serious" fiction are maneuvers for dealing with the issue of middle-class guilt. One possibility is to handle it more or less as Chekhov did. Another, also very common, is the strategy of cynicism, enjoying the benefits of middle-class life while holding oneself slightly above it. A third response, almost always characterized as "toughness," has been a part of American culture for at least a century. Toughness is the obverse side of sentimentality, fighting against and reflecting it all at the same time. It is the poetry of denial. What it refuses to give to character it lavishes on its prose, which typically is highly stylized and self-regarding. The idea is to withhold expressions of human sympathy—because they seem "weak" and because they capitulate to a false order of experience. Hemingway is the great bard of this mode, saying in effect I-may-be-here-but-I'm-not-really-part-of-this-scene. Obviously, cynicism and toughness may be easily combined as strategies. They carry with them a certain feeling for hermit life, for withholding, and for clipped sentences, oracular statements, and derailed ordinary language. However, the toughness mode is crabbed and repetitious, qualities that Barthelme never sought. He invented situations and sentences: I'd like to quote page after page of them, hair-raising for their sheer sound, their surprises and elaborations. Their shine. No: toughness, the metaphysics of the hermit crab, was not enough.

Which returns us to the problem of cynicism, which does not seem an adequate response to the problem of being located inside conflicting desires, of being the very person one does not want to be. Cynicism and its spiritual second-cousin, irony, are regular combatants in Barthelme's stories, but there is something wrong with both of them; the stories work hard to disclose what it is. For one thing, cynicism is hypocritical: it enjoys what it claims to despise. It is happy in its unhappy consciousness. It understands the destructiveness of its own pleasures but does nothing to stop it. It is enlightened about its own moral condition. It will agree to any accusation made against it. World-weariness is its poetry. Growing out of snobbery, its only pleasure is manipulation. Cynicism is irony that has moved into a condition of institutional power; cynicism and power have a tendency to breed each other. But Barthelme's stories—especially the early ones and the novel *Snow White*—typically struggle against institutional cynicism and the language employed in its cause. To use a phrase by the German philosopher Peter Sloterdijk, employed in another context, these are "études in the higher banalities." Far from being an exercise in cynicism, the narrative voice in Barthelme consistently attacks cynicism—the cynicism of official institutional spokespersons. But the weapon that comes most readily to hand is irony, which creates the (as Barthelme might say) *interesting* struggle and tension in his writing.

The nature of the problem, if you simultaneously feel guilty and disgusted by the progress of modern culture, is the temptation to become a snob, to join a like-minded coterie of people with good taste who define themselves by an awareness of all the vulgarities they do not perform. Or you can become a hermit like Saint Anthony, benefiting from the culture while pretending not to live in it. Viewed unsympathetically, this is a central impulse in Modernism, one of its worst errors. Barthelme's fiction never makes this error: it challenges readers but never insults them or pretends to instruct them from an angle higher than their own. It disclaims righteousness. "The Party" concludes by asking: "Is it really important to know that this movie is fine, and that one terrible, and to talk intelligently about the difference? Wonderful elegance! No good at all!"

At this point, the really astonishing difficulties of Barthelme's project start to become apparent: exiled from character-drawing, and in the midst of (one might almost say "drowning in") cultural sign-systems, most of which are duplicitous, the Barthelmean narrator must struggle simply in order to find a location, a place to stand and speak that is not so far inside the culture that it replicates its falseness and lies, and not so far outside that it becomes cold, snobby, or self-righteous. This is a problem not just for writers but for anyone who lives in a powerful and culturally dominant country. And it is not an issue that anyone finally "solves." Writers must devise strategies for dealing with it, some of which are more effective than others. Some are distracting—and Barthelme's work is very high, one might almost say intoxicated, with distractions—while also presenting roads and avenues, certain kinds of metaphorical paths for action. And they do so, it has always seemed to me, with a good deal of warmth—as in the ending of "Daumier," where Celeste is in the kitchen, making a *daube*, and the narrator says he will go in to watch her. The story ends with two sentences that, in their quietness, modesty, and precision, have always moved me. "The self cannot be escaped, but it can be, with ingenuity and hard work, distracted. There are always openings, if you can find them, there is always something to do."

One word for this technique is *forbearance*. Starting with the stories in *City Life*, we move onto a thematic ground governed by a feeling where piano music instead of analysis might be possible, where "little dances of suggestion and fear" might be staged: "These dances constitute an invitation of unmistakable import—an invitation which, if accepted, leads down many muddy roads. I accepted. What was the alternative?" ("City Life"). Odd, the fastidious articulation of these feelings, their insistence on the possibility of continued action. And beautiful, the playing with children, the turning to childhood, in two late stories, "Chablis" and "The Baby."

As for religion: can one discard its content and still admire its interest in, perhaps its necessary commitment to, the issue of where one places oneself in relation to one's own experiences? This is exactly the question that arises in two of Barthelme's most interesting stories, "Kierkegaard Unfair to Schlegel" and "January" (the last story in *Forty Stories* and therefore something of a curtain-speech). In both stories we are in the presence of a ghostly sort of interview, considerably more ghostly in the Kierkegaard story, that gives the sense of an internal quarrel or an interview between two spirit entities.

Characters named Q. and A., question and answer, argue in "Kierkegaard Unfair to Schlegel," with Q. being particularly annoyed by A.'s inability to get enthusiastic about "our machines": "You've withheld your enthusiasm, that's damaging . . . " Something like the problem of cynicism arises here, the question of spiritual snobbery. A. answers by discussing irony, which he uses in conjunction with political activism:

> I participate. I make demands, sign newspaper advertisements, vote. I make small campaign contributions to the candidate of my choice and turn my irony against the others. But I accomplish nothing. I march, it's ludicrous.

This sense of self-irony leads into a discussion of Kierkegaard and his analysis of irony as a magical power that confers upon its user a "negative freedom." When irony is directed against the whole of existence, the result, says Kierkegaard, is "estrangement and poetry"—a poetry that "opens up a higher actuality, expands and transfigures the imperfect into the perfect, and thereby softens and mitigates the deep pain which would darken and obscure all things." Thus Kierkegaard. Unfortunately, this variety of poetry does not reconcile one to the world but produces an animosity to the world:

> A. But I love my irony.
> Q. Does it give you pleasure?
> A. A poor . . . a rather unsatisfactory. . . .
> Q. The unavoidable tendency of everything particular to emphasize its own particularity.
> A. Yes.

If Barthelme were the kind of ironist described by Kierkegaard, the sort who turns his irony upon the "whole of existence," then he would be tracking Beckett in pursuit of an absolute negativity, thinking directed against being itself. Or he would be following William Gass into a principality built out of the toothpicks and straw of words. But though this irony has the virtue of purity, it can in no way account for the pleasures we consciously enjoy in Barthelme's fiction. What is their ultimate source?

Answering this question seems to me the task Barthelme set himself in his novel *Paradise*, published in 1986. If it is about anything, this book is about pleasures, even beatitude: the pleasure of sex and the friendship it can produce; the pleasure of making and building (its protagonist, Simon, is an architect); the pleasure—unbelievable to imagine this in the early books—of improving the world. The tone of this book, in its mixture of fantasy, high comedy, and caring, is close to *blessedness*. Barthelme of course gives his usual warnings about stupid optimism:

> Simon wanted very much to be a hearty, optimistic American, like the President, but on the other hand did not trust hearty, optimistic Americans, like the President. He had considered the possibility that the President . . . was not really hearty and optimistic but rather a gloomy, obsessed man.

Because the fantasy in this story—a single man living with three beautiful women—is so stylized, the imaginative force seems to move from the specific situation to the nature of the lineaments of gratified desire. The book is therefore about happiness. It is as if Barthelme were saying that we must try to imagine happiness. This book is one version of it. Happiness, in these times, may be the last frontier of the imagination, the most difficult challenge of all. But if happiness cannot be imagined, if alienation cannot be balmed at the source, then truly one might as well do nothing, or simply drift toward death. Near the end of *Paradise*, Barthelme argues that our desires inhabit and inspirit us:

> Simon flew to North Carolina to inspect a job he'd done in Winston-Salem, a hospital. The construction was quite good and he found little to complain of. He admired the fenestration, done by his own hand. He spent an agreeable night in a Ramada Inn and flew back the next day. His seatmate was a young German woman on her way to Frankfurt. She was six months pregnant, she said, and her husband, an Army sergeant in Chemical Warfare, had found a new girl friend, was

divorcing her. She had spent two years at Benning, loved America, spoke with what seemed to Simon a Texas accent. Her father was dead and her mother operated a candy store in Frankfurt. They talked about pregnancy and delivery, about how much wine she allowed herself, whether aspirin was in fact a danger to the baby, and how both of her brothers-in-law had been born in taxis. She was amazingly cheerful given the circumstances and told him that the Russians were going to attempt to take over Mexico next. We had neglected Mexico, she said.

Over the Atlantic on the long approach to Kennedy Simon saw a hundred miles of garbage in the water, from the air white floating scruff. The water became agitated at points as fish attacked the garbage and Simon turned his mind to compaction. When they landed he kissed the German woman goodbye and told her that although she probably didn't feel very lucky at the moment, she was very lucky.

That's beautiful. The balance is miraculous: everything that is—including abandonment, garbage, ecological decay—is held in equilibrium with what is possible: delivery, compaction. There is always something to do. The style is also beautiful, because of all the hurricanes Barthelme has traveled through in order to formulate this difficult calm. The book ends up radiating not a sense of peacefulness but a sense of high intellectual and spiritual comedy, a form of art characteristic of late middle and old age.

"January" concludes Barthelme's final collection, *Forty Stories*. The first month. This piece (*is* it a story? of what sort?) presents an interview with theologian Thomas Brecker, whose dissertation was written in the forties on the subject of acedia:

The thesis was that acedia is a turning toward something rather than, as it's commonly conceived of, a turning away from something. I argued that acedia is a positive reaction to extraordinary demand, for example, the demand that one embrace the *good news* and

375

become one with the mystical body of Christ. . . . Acedia is often conceived of as a kind of sullenness in the face of existence; I tried to locate its positive features. For example, it precludes certain kinds of madness, crowd mania, it precludes a certain kind of error. You're not an enthusiast and therefore you don't go out and join a lynch mob—rather you languish on a couch with your head in your hands.

Brecker goes on to talk about the healing power of absolution, its ability to create new directions. He thinks about his own death, "I hate to abandon my children," and concludes the story this way:

The point of my career is perhaps how little I achieved. We speak of someone as having had "a long career" and that's usually taken to be admiring, but what if it's thirty-five years of persistence in error? I don't know what value to place on what I've done, perhaps none at all is right. If I'd done something with soybeans, been able to increase the yield of an acre of soybeans, then I'd know I'd done something. I can't say that.

Barthelme's last collection of stories ends here, in a perfectly serious tone of modesty, not to say humility. "I was trying," Brecker says, "to stake out a position for the uncommitted which still, at the same time, had something to do with religion." It would be incorrect to say that Barthelme, the chronicler of word-nausea, had mellowed into the drabness of total sincerity. What actually seems to have emerged toward the end is both more interesting and more complicated: a kind of tenderness toward existence, isolated from the junk of culture through which it is commonly viewed. Though still surrounded by intellectual defenses, and therefore still enveloped and distracted, these later stories are generous; almost miraculously they transform metaphysical irony into caring watchfulness. Giving up finally *does* turn into giving over. Though it is not typically American to have a second act in one's career, and then a third, and even a fourth, Barthelme had them. And despite what was sometimes said against him, he did not repeat himself, did not endlessly replay the old tricks. He found new tricks, and then, toward the end, discarded most of them. How rare, also, in America, to see writing develop into such variety and generosity! Almost unheard-of. Almost unseen.

Nominated by Marianne Boruch, Edward Hirsch, Francine Prose, and Lee Upton

MEDIA

by HOWARD NEMEROV

from MISSISSIPPI VALLEY REVIEW

The tv has been showing movies of dead poets
lately, they come on once a week or so,
movies mostly of stills of the dead poets,
the passport photographs, the family groups
with the child poet circled in sepia ink.

The black and white poets are read and discussed
by poets in living color, though some have died since.
The camera doesn't always know what to do
while the poems are being read, but drifts
across a crowd of faces or a rural scene
or waves breaking in splash and spray
against black rocks and leaving a shampoo of foam;
sometimes referring to the words that are being said,
oftener not, but always in images poetical
suggestive of the well-loved themes of poetry,
nature and innocence and cruel indifference,
sorrow, and memories cemetery-still,

while the living poets read and interrupt
the reading with reminiscences of praise
and remarks interpretive about the dead poets
whose transitive poems are being printed out
across the screen, across the crowd of faces,
and all is again as though it had never been.

Nominated by Maxine Kumin

LAVA

by ADAM ZAGAJEWSKI

from PARTISAN REVIEW

And what if Heraclitus and Parmenides
are both correct
and side by side, two worlds exist,
one calm, the other frantic; one arrow
rushes heedlessly; another watches it
with indulgence, the same wave moves and stands still.
Animals are born and die at once,
birch leaves play in the wind, and at that very moment
disintegrate in the rusty cruel flame.
Lava kills and preserves, the heart beats
and is beaten; there was a war and there wasn't,
Jews died, Jews live, cities burned down,
cities stand, love fades, the perpetual kiss,
the wings of hawks have to be brown,
you are still with me though we are no more,
ships sink, sand sings, clouds wander
like wedding veils in decay.
All is lost. So much dazzlement. The hills
descend tenderly, bearing long banners of trees.
Moss inches up a stone churchtower
and its small mouth shyly praises the North.
At dusk, jasmine glows like savage lamps
possessed by their own luminescence.
In a museum, before a somber canvas,
someone's catlike eyes narrow. All is over.
Riders gallop upon black horses, a tyrant composes

a death sentence full of grammatical errors.
Youth turns to nothing in
one day, the faces of girls freeze
into medallions, despair becomes rapture,
and the hard fruits of stars are growing in the sky
like grapes, and beauty endures shaken, still,
and God is and dies; night returns to us
every evening, and dawn is gray-haired from dew.

Translated from the Polish by Renata Gorczynski and Benjamin Ivry

Nominated by Laurie Sheck, Robert Pinsky

WAITING FOR MR. KIM

fiction by CAROL ROH-SPAULDING

from PLOUGHSHARES

W HEN GRACIE KANG'S elder twin sisters reached the age of eighteen, they went down to the Alameda County Shipyards and got jobs piecing battleships together for the U.S. Navy. This was the place to find a husband in 1945, if a girl was doing her own looking. They were Americans, after all, and they were of age. Her sisters caught the bus down to the waterfront every day and brought home their paychecks every two weeks. At night, they went out with their girlfriends, meeting boys at the cinema or the drugstore, as long as it was outside of Chinatown.

Gracie's parents would never have thought it was husbands they were after. Girls didn't choose what they were given. But the end of the war distracted everybody. While Mr. Kang tried to keep up with the papers and Mrs. Kang tried to keep up with the laundry, Sung-Sook slipped away one day with a black welder enrolled in the police academy and Sung-Ohk took off with a Chinatown nightclub singer from L.A. with a sister in the movies.

Escaped. Gracie had watched from the doorway that morning as Sung-Sook pulled on her good slip in front of the vanity, lifted her hair, breathed in long and slow. Her eyes came open, she saw Gracie's reflection. "Comeer," she said. "You never say goodbye." She kissed Gracie between the eyes. Gracie had only shrugged: "See you." Then Sung-Ohk from the bathroom: "This family runs a laundry, so where's all the goddamn towels?"

When the girls didn't come home, the lipstick and rouge wiped off their faces, to fold the four o'clock sheets, she understood

what was what. On the vanity in the girls' room she found a
white paper bell with sugar sprinkles. In silver letters, it read:

CALL TODAY!
Marry Today!
Your Wedding! Your Way!
Eighteen or Over?
We Won't Say Nay!
(May Borrow Veil and Bouquet)

As simple as having your hair done. Gracie sat at the vanity,
thinking of the thousand spirits of the household her mother was
always ticking off like a grocery list—spirit of the lamp, the
clock, the ashtray. Spirit in the seat of your chair. Spirit of the
stove, the closet, the broom, the shoes. Spirit of the breeze in
the room, the Frigidaire. Gracie had always been willing to believe in them; she only needed something substantial to go on.
Now, in her sisters' room, she felt that the spirits had been there,
had moved on, to other inhabited rooms.

Those girls had escaped Thursday evenings with the old *chong-
gaks,* who waited effortlessly for her father to give the girls away.
No more sitting, knees together, in white blouses and circle
skirts, with gritted smiles. Now Gracie would sit, the only girl,
while her father made chitchat with Mr. Han and Mr. Kim. Number three daughter, much younger, the dutiful one, wouldn't run
away. If her mother had had the say, the girls would have given
their parents grandchildren by now. But she didn't have the say,
and her father smiled his pleasant, slightly anxious smile at the
chong-gaks and never ever brought up payment.

He was the one paying now. No one got dinner that night. Pots
flew, plates rattled in the cabinets, the stove rumbled in the corner, pictures slid, clanked, tinkled. "Now we'll have a nigger for a
grandson and a chink for a son-in-law, Mr. Kang!" her mother
shouted. She cursed Korean, but had a gift for American slurs,
translating the letter found taped to the laundry boiler into the
horrors of marrying for love.

Gracie and Little Gene pressed themselves against the wall,
squeezed around the Frigidaire, sidled to the staircase. They sat
and backed up one step at a time, away from the stabs and
swishes of the broom. "Or didn't you want Korean grandchildren,

Mr. Kang? You're the one who let them fall into American love. Could I help it there aren't any good *chong-gaks* around? Thought we'd pack the girls off to Hawaii where the young ones are? Ha. I'd like to see the missionaries pay for that!"

Their father came into view below. Hurried, but with his usual dignity, he ducked and swerved as necessary. Silently, solemnly, he made for the closet, opened the door, and stepped in among the coats. The blows from first the bristled then the butted end of the broom came down upon the door.

Little Gene whispered, "I'm going outside."

"Fine," Gracie told him. "If you can make it to the door."

"Think I can't manage the window? I land in the trash bin, pretty soft!"

Gracie told him, "Bring me back a cigarette, then," and he left her there. A year younger than she and not very big for thirteen, he was still number one son. Gracie stuck her fingers in her mouth all the way to the knuckle, clamped down hard.

She chopped cabbage, scrubbed the bathhouses, washed and pressed and folded linen and laundry, dreaming up lives for her sisters. From their talk and their magazines, she knew how it should go. Sung-Sook stretched out by the pool in a leopard-print bathing suit with pointy bra cups and sipped colored drinks from thin glasses, leaving a pink surprise of lips at the rim. Somebody else served them, fetched them, cleaned them. Her husband shot cardboard men through the heart and came home to barbecue T-bones. Every night they held hands at the double feature. Sung-Ohk slipped into a tight Chinese-doll dress and jeweled cat-eyes, sang to smoky crowds of white people from out of town. Her lips grazed the mike as she whispered, "Thank you, kind people, thank you." In the second act, her husband, in a tux, dipped her, spun her, with slant-eyed-Gene-Kelly-opium flair. All the white people craned their necks and saw that Oriental women could have good legs.

They left Gracie and her mother with all the work. At first, her father tried to help out. He locked up the barbershop at lunch, crossed the street, passed through the kitchen, and stepped into Hell, as they called it. But her mother snapped down the pants press when she saw him and from a blur of steam shouted, "Fool for love! I'm warning you to get out of here, Mr. Kang!"

She bowed her head at the market now. She had stopped going to church. Lost face, it was called. And there was the worry of it. No one knew these men who took the girls away. Maybe one was an opium dealer and the other was a pimp. Maybe those girls were in for big disappointment, even danger. Her father twisted his hands, helpless and silent in the evenings. Her mother clanked the dishes into the sink, banged the washers shut, punched the buttons with her fists, helpless, too.

It was true he was a fool for love, as far as Gracie could tell. Her mother slapped at his hands when he came up behind her at the chopping board to kiss her hair—pretty brave, considering that knife. When her mother tried to walk behind him in the street, he stopped and tried to take her hand. Gracie and her mother were always nearly missing buses because she'd say, "Go on, Mr. Kang. We're coming," and they'd stay behind as she cleaned out her purse or took forever with her coat, just to have it the way she had learned it, her husband a few paces ahead, women behind. Maybe the girls would never have gotten away if he'd been firm about marriage, strict about love.

Where her parents were from, shamans could chase out the demon spirits from dogs, cows, rooms, people. Maybe her father had had the fool chased out of him, because when Thursday came around, he sat in the good chair with the Bible open on his knees, and Gracie sat beside him, waiting. Life was going to go on without her sisters. Her life. Gracie watched her father for lingering signs of foolishness. Above the donated piano, the cuckoo in the clock popped out seven times. As always, her father looked up with a satisfied air. He loved that bird. Her mother believed there was a spirit in the wooden box. The spirit was saying it was time.

Little Gene was free in the streets with that gang of Chinese boys. She waited for her cigarette and his stories—right now, he might be breaking into the high school, popping open the Coca-Cola machine, busting up some lockers. There weren't any Jap boys left to beat up on, and they stayed away from the mostly black neighborhoods or they'd get beat up themselves. Gracie sat with her hands clasped at her knees, worrying about him, admiring him a little.

First came the tap-tap of the missionary ladies from the United Methodist Church. Their hats looked like squat birds' nests through the crushed ice window. Every Thursday, they seemed to have taken such pains with their dresses and hats and shoes, Gracie couldn't think how they had lasted in the mountain villages of Pyongyang province. She had never been there herself, or been to mountains at all, but she knew there were tigers in Pyongyang.

Her father rose and assumed his visitors smile. "Everyone will be too polite to mention the girls, Gracie," he told her. That was the only thing at all he said about them to her.

The ladies stepped in, chins pecking. One bore a frosted cake, the other thrust forward a box of canned goods. American apologies. As though the girls had died, Gracie thought. Her father stiffened, but kept his smile.

"We think it's wonderful about the war," the cake lady began.

"Praise be to God that we've stopped the Japanese," the Spam lady went on. They looked at one another.

"The *Japanese* Japanese," said the second. She paused. "And we are so sorry about your country, Mr. Kang."

"But this is your country now," said the first.

Her father eased them onto more conversational subjects. They smiled, heads tilted, as Gracie pressed out "Greensleeves," "Colonial Days," "Jesus, We Greet Thee," on the piano. And at half past the hour, they were up and on their way out, accepting jars of *kimch'i* from her mother with wrinkle-nosed smiles.

The barbershop customers did not come by. Mr. Woo from the bakery and Mr. and Mrs. Lim from the Hunan restaurant stayed away. All the Chinese and Koreans knew about saving face. Except the *chong-gaks*, who knew better, surely, but arrived like clockwork anyway, a black blur and a white blur at the window. They always shuffled their feet elaborately on the doorstep before knocking, and her father used to say, "That's very Korean," to Sung-Sook and Sung-Ohk, who didn't bother to fluff their hair or straighten their blouses for the visitors. They used to moan, "Here come the old goats. Failure One and Failure Two." Her father only shushed them, saying, "Respect, daughters, respect." Gracie saw that he could have done better than that if he really expected the girls to marry these men, but after all, the girls were right. Probably her father could see that. They were failures. No families, even at their age. Little money, odd jobs, wasted lives. A week before, they had been only a couple of

385

nuisances who brought her sticks of Beechnut gum and seemed never to fathom her sisters' hostility. They were that stupid, and now they were back. One Korean girl was as good as any other.

Gracie could actually tolerate Mr. Han. He had been clean and trim in his black suit, pressed shirt, and straight tie every Thursday evening since her sisters had turned sixteen. He was a tall, hesitant man with most of his hair, surprisingly good teeth, and little wire glasses so tight over his nose that the lenses steamed up when he was nervous. Everyone knew he had preferred Sung-Ohk, whose kindest remark to him ever was that he looked exactly like the Chinese servant in a Hollywood movie. He always perched on the piano bench as though he didn't mean to stay long, and he mopped his brow when Sung-Ohk glared at him. But he never pulled Gracie onto his lap to kiss her and pat her, and he never, as the girls called it, licked with his eyes.

He left that to Mr. Kim. Mr. Kim in the same white suit, white shirt, white tie, and white shoes which had never really been white, but always the color of pale urine. His teeth were brown from too much tea and sugar and opium. This wasn't her hateful imagination. She had washed his shirts ever since she'd started working. She knew the armpit stains that spread like an infection when she tried to soak them. The hairs and smudges of ash and something like pus in his sheets. She could smell his laundry even before she saw the ticket. His breath stank, too, like herring.

Mr. Kim found everything amusing. "It's been too warm, hasn't it, Mr. Kang?" he said by way of greeting. Then he chuckled, "I'm afraid our friend Mr. Han is almost done in by it."

"Yes, let me get you some iced tea," her father announced. "Mrs. Kang!"

Mr. Kim chuckled again at his companion. "Maybe his heart is suffering. Nearly sixty, you know. Poor soul. He's got a few years on me, anyway, haven't you, old man?"

Mr. Han lowered himself on the piano bench. "Yes, it's been too warm, too much for me."

His companion laughed like one above that kind of weakness. Then he said, "And how is Miss Kang? She's looking very well. She seems to be growing."

Gracie hunched her shoulders, looked anywhere but at him.

"Yes, she's growing," her father answered carefully. "She's still a child." The men smiled at each other with a lot of teeth showing, but their eyes were watchful. "Of course, she's a little lonesome nowadays," her father continued. Mr. Kim eyed him, then he seemed to catch on and slapped his knee—good joke. Mr. Han squinted in some sort of pain.

If Mr. Kim hadn't been in America even longer than her father had, with nothing to show for it but a rented room above the barbershop, then he might have been able to say, "What about this one, Mr. Kang? Are you planning to let her get away, too?" But if he'd had something to show for his twenty or so years in America, he wouldn't be sitting in her father's house and she wouldn't be waiting to be his bride.

Then from the piano bench: "Lonesome, Miss Kang?" Everybody looked. Mr. Han blinked, startled at the attention. He quietly repeated, "Have you, too, been lonesome?" Gracie looked down at her hands. Her father was supposed to answer, let him answer. At that moment, her mother entered, head bowed over the tea tray. Gracie could hear the spirit working in the cuckoo clock.

Her father had told her once that he'd picked cotton and grapes with the Mexicans in the Salinas Valley, and it got so hot you could fry meat on the railroad ties. But that was nothing compared to the sticky summers in Pyongyang, where the stench of human manure brought the bile to your throat. That was why he loved Oakland, he said, where the ocean breeze cleaned you out. It reminded him of his childhood visits to Pusan Harbor, when he'd traveled to visit his father who had been forced into the service of the Japanese. And it reminded him of the day he sailed back from America for his bride.

Bright days, fresh wind. Gracie imagined the women who had waited for the husbands who had never returned. Those women lived in fear, her mother had said. They were no good to marry if the men didn't come back, or if they did return but had no property, they had no legal status in America and no prospects in Korea. Plenty of the women did away with themselves, or their families sold them as concubines. "You think I'm lying?" she told Gracie. "I waited ten years for him. People didn't believe the letters he sent after a while. My family started talking about what to do with me, because I had other sisters waiting to marry, only I was the oldest and they had to get rid of me first!"

Gracie imagined those women, their hands tucked neatly in their bright sleeves, their smooth hair and ancient faces looking out over the water from high rooms. And she thought of Mr. Han gazing from his window out over the alley and between skyscrapers and telephone poles to his glimpse of the San Francisco Bay. Where he was, the sky was black, starless in the city. Where she was, the sun rose, a brisk, hopeful morning.

On a morning like that, Gracie took the sheets and laundry across the street and up to the rented rooms. Usually the *chonggaks* had coffee and a bun at the bakery and then strolled around the lake, but Gracie always knocked and set the boxes down.

Mr. Han's door inched open under her knuckles. The breeze in the bright room, the sterile light of morning in there, the cord rattling at the blinds. Something invisible crept out from the slit in the door and was with her in the hall.

"Mr. Han? Just your laundry, Mr. Han." Spirits of memory—she and Little Gene climbing onto his knees, reaching into his pockets for malted milk balls or sticks of gum. "Where are *your* children?" they'd ask. "Where is your stove? Where is your sink? Where is your mirror?" Mr. Han had always smiled, as though he were only hiding the things they named, could make them appear whenever he wanted.

She pushed the door open, and the spirits of memory mingled with the spirits of longing and desire. The bulb of the bare night light buzzed, like a recollection in a head full of ideas. Mr. Han lay half-on, half-off the bed. One shoe pressed firmly on the floor, as though half of him had had somewhere to go. The glasses dangled from the metal bed frame. That was where his head was, pressed against the bars. His eyes were rolled back, huge and amazed, toward the window. And at his throat, a stripe of beaded red, the thin lips of flesh puckering slightly, like the edges of a rose.

Spirits scuttered along the walls, swirled upwards, twisting in their airy, familiar paths. They pressed against the ceiling. They watched her in the corner. His spirit was near, she felt, in the white field of his pillow. Or in the curtains that puffed and lifted at the sill like a girl's skirt in the wind.

Gracie squatted and peered under the bed. The gleam there was a thing she had known all of her life, a razor from the barbershop. Clean, almost no blood, like his throat. She knew it was loss of air, not loss of blood, that did it. She knew because she'd heard about it before. Two or three of the neighborhood Japs had done the same, when they found that everything they thought

388

they owned they no longer had a right to. They'd had three days to sell what they could and go. She didn't know where. She only knew that her father had been able to buy the barbershop and the bathhouse because of it.

Wind swelled in the hall, with the spirits of car horns, telephone wires, shop signs, traffic lights, and a siren, not for him. They were present at the new death—curious, laughing, implacable. They sucked the door shut. Gracie started. "Leaving now," she announced. "Mr. Han," she whispered to the *chong-gak*. Then she remembered he'd become part of something else, something weightless, invisible, near. She said it louder. "Mr. Han. I'm sorry for you, Mr. Han."

Mr. Kim ate with the Kangs that afternoon, after the ambulances had gone, and again in the evening. His fingers trembled. He lowered his head to the rice, unable to lift it to his mouth, scraping feebly with his chopsticks. Of the death he had one thing to say, which he couldn't stop saying: "I walked alone this morning. Why did I decide to walk alone, of all mornings?"

Mrs. Kang muttered guesses about what to do next, not about the body itself or the police inquiry or who was responsible for his room and his things, but about how best to give peace to the spirit of the *chong-gak,* who might otherwise torment the rest of their days. He didn't have a family of his own to torment. She'd prepared a plate of meat and rice and *kimch'i,* saying, "Where do I *put* this?"

Little Gene, jealous that Gracie had found the body and he hadn't, offered, "How 'bout on the sill? Then he can float by whenever. Or in his room? I'll stay in there all night and watch for him." Then he patted his stomach. "Or how 'bout right here?"

"Damn," her mother went on. "I wish now I'd paid more attention to the shamans. But we stayed away from those women unless we needed them. My family was afraid I'd get the callbecause I was sickly and talked in my sleep, and we have particularly restless ancestors. But I didn't have it in me. Was it food every day for a month or every month for a year? What a mystery. Now we'll have spirits till we all die."

"Girls shouldn't be shamans, anyway," Little Gene announced. "Imagine Gracie chasing spirits away."

Asshole, Gracie mouthed. Little Gene flipped her off. None of the adults understood the sign.

"You don't chase them, honey," Gracie's mother said to her. "You feed them and pay them and talk to them."

"Tell *him,*" Gracie answered. "He's the one who brought it up."

"Feed everyone who's here first," Little Gene suggested. Gracie flipped him off in return.

"What's that you're doing with your fingers, Gracie?" he shot back. She put her finger to her lips and pointed at her father. His eyes were closed. He kept them that way, head bowed, lips moving.

"Fine," her mother announced. "Let's do Christian, Mr. Kang. It's simpler, as far as I'm concerned."

Mr. Kim lifted his head from his rice bowl, looking very old.

Her mother eyed him sternly. "Cheaper, too."

That night Gracie lay in her bed by the open window. Where was his spirit now? In heaven, at God's side? Or restlessly feeding on *bulgogi* and turnips in his room? Or somewhere else entirely, or nowhere at all? Please God or Thousand Spirits, she prayed. Let me marry for love. Please say I'm not waiting for Mr. Kim. It's fine with me if I'm a *chun-yo* forever.

They held a small service at the Korean United Methodist Church. Her father stood up and said a little about the hard life of a *chong-gak* in America, the loneliness of these men, the difficulties for Oriental immigrants. Gracie felt proud of him, though he was less convincing about heaven. No one even knew for certain if Mr. Han had converted.

Mr. Kim sat in white beside Gracie. "Thy kingdom come," he murmured, "thy will be done." And he reached out and took her hand, looking straight ahead to her father. His hand was moist. She could smell him.

"And forgive us our trespasses," she prayed.

"As we forgive those who trespass against us," he continued, and he squeezed her hand with the surety of possession, though her fingers slipped in his palm.

Gracie never got to the "amen." Instead, she leaned into his side, tilted her face to his cheek, and brought her lips to his ear. "You dirty old bastard," she whispered. Then she snatched her hand back and kept her head bowed, trembling. She wished she could pray that he would die, too, if it was the only way. From

390

the corner of her eye, she could see Mr. Kim's offended hand held open on his knee. Sweat glistened in the creases of his palm. She would never be able to look into his eyes again. For a moment, pity and disgust swept through her. Then, as the congregation stood, she said her own prayer. It went, Please oh please oh please.

Little Gene stuck his head in the laundry room. "Hey, you! Mrs. Kim!"

Gracie flung a folded pillowcase at him.

"Whew. Step out of that hellhole for a minute. I've got something to show you."

He slid a cigarette from behind his ear and they went out the alley-side steps and shared it by the trash bin. "The day they give you away, I'll have this right under your window, see? I'll even stuff it with newspapers so you'll land easy."

"Nowhere to run," Gracie told him. It was the name of a movie they'd seen.

"Isn't Hollywood someplace? Isn't Mexico someplace?"

Gracie laughed out loud. "You coming?"

"'Course I am. Mama's spirit crap is getting on my nerves."

Gracie shrugged. "You're too little to run away. Why should I need help from someone as little as you?"

Little Gene stood on tiptoe and sneered into her face. "Because I'm a boy." Then he grinned and exhaled smoke through his nose and the sides of his mouth.

"Dragon-breath," she called him.

"Come on, Mrs. Kim. This way." They scrambled up the steps, took the staircase to the hall, then stepped through the door that led down again to the ground floor through an unlit passage to the old opium den. It was nothing but a storage room for old washers now, a hot box with a ceiling two stories above them. It baked, winter or summer, because it shared a wall with the boiler.

They'd hid there when they were little, playing hide-and-seek or creating stories about the opium dealers and the man who was supposed to have hung himself in there. They could never figure out where he might have hung himself from since the ceiling was so high and the walls so bare. They looked up in awe. Once, Little Gene thought he'd be clever, and he shut himself in the dryer. Gracie couldn't find him for the longest time, but when she came back for a second look, the round window was steamed up and he wasn't making any noise. She pulled him out. He was grinning, eyes vacant. "You stupid dumb stupid stupid kid."

Little Gene felt for the bulb on the wall, pulled the chain. Now the old dryer was somehow on its side. There were two busted washers and a cane chair. The air was secret, heavy with dust and heat. Gracie felt along the walls for loose bricks, pulled one out, felt around inside like they used to do, looking for stray nuggets or anything else that might have been hidden and forgotten by the Chinese who had lived there before.

Little Gene got on his hands and knees. "Lookit." He eased out a brick flush with the floor. "Lookit," he said again.

Gracie crouched. He crawled back to make way for her, then pushed her head down. "Down there, in the basement."

She saw dim, natural light, blackened redwood, steam-stained. The bathhouse. "So what? I clean'em every day of my life."

"Just wait," he said.

Then the white blade of a man's back rose into view. Little Gene's hand was a spider up and down her side. "See him, Mrs. Kim? Bet you can't wait."

The back lowered, rose, lowered again, unevenly, painfully. She saw hair slicked back in seaweed streaks, tea-colored splotches on his back, the skin damp and speckled like the belly of a fish. Little Gene's hand was a spider again at her neck. Gracie slapped at him, crouched, looked again. "What the hell's he doing? Rocking himself?"

Little Gene only giggled nervously.

The eyes of Mr. Kim stared toward the thousand spirits, his mouth hung open. Then those eyes rolled back in his head, pupil-less, white, and still. "God, is he dying?" Gracie asked. If she moved a muscle, she would burst. "Is he dying?" she asked again. "Don't touch me," she told her brother, who was impatient with spidery hands.

Little Gene rolled his eyes. "That's all we need. He's not dying stupid. Unless he dies every day." Life in a dim bathhouse, Gracie thought. Deaths in bright rooms.

A door slammed hard on the other side of the wall. Her mother cursed, called her name. Little Gene giggled and did the stroking motion at his crotch, then Gracie scrambled to her knees and pulled him up with her. He grabbed for the chain on the bulb. Dark. "Don't scream," he giggled.

"Gracie! Damn you!" her mother called.

Then his hands flew to her, one at her shoulder, the other, oily and sweet, cupping her open mouth.

A letter arrived the next Thursday. Sung-Sook had used her head and addressed it to the barbershop. Her father brought it up to her in the evening. Gracie was at her window, leaning out, watching the sky begin to gather color. "For 'Miss Gracie Kang,' " he read. " 'Care of Mr. Park A. Kang.' " There was no return address. The paper smelled faintly like roses.

With his eyes, her father pleaded for news of them. He said, "You look like you're waiting for someone."

She shrugged. "It's Thursday." She wanted him to leave her alone until it was time to go downstairs and sit with Mr. Kim. Instead, he came to the window and looked out with her. "Where's your brother?"

"Wherever he feels like being."

He only smiled. Then he told her, "Mr. Kim has given me money. A lot of money."

She drew herself up. She couldn't look at him. "What money?"

"It's for a ticket, Gracie. He wants me to purchase him a ticket to Pusan and arrange some papers for him."

"Alone?" she asked.

"Alone."

She smiled out at the street, but asked again, "What money?"

Her father answered, "He will be happy to have a chance to tell you goodbye." And he left her at the window.

His money, she knew. Her father's. She kept still at the window. With her eyes closed, she saw farther than she had ever seen. "Did you hear that?" she said out loud, in case any spirits, celestial or domestic, were listening.

Then she carefully opened her letter. There was a piece of pale, gauzy paper, and a couple of photographs—a good thing, since the girls had stolen a bunch of family snapshots when they left.

Dear Gracie,

I hope they let you see this. You're going to be an auntie now. Sung-Ohk's the lucky one, but me and El

393

are really trying. For a baby, you know. That's El in his rookie uniform and I'm in my wedding dress. We're at the Forbidden City, the club in San Francisco. Louie, that's Sung-Ohk's husband, got us in free on our wedding night. The other picture is of Louie and Sung-Ohk at Newport Beach. Isn't he handsome? Like El. We all live near the beach, ten minutes by freeway.

You'd love it here, but I guess you'd love it anywhere but Oakland. How are the old creeps, anyway? Maybe they'll die before Mom and Dad give you away, ha-ha.

Be good. Don't worry. We're going to figure something out. El says you can stay with us. Sung-Ohk sends her love. I do, too.

The letter fluttered in her hand in the window. She pulled open the drawer at her bedside table, folded the paper neatly back in its creases, and set it inside. Then she took out the only thing her sisters had left behind, the sugar-sprinkled, silver-lettered, instant-ceremony marriage advertisement. Gracie breathed in deeply, as her sister had done with the hope of her new life—as, perhaps, Mr. Han had done, with the hope of his release. Somewhere near, Little Gene laughed out loud in the street. Her mother banged dinner into the oven. Her father waited below, his Bible open on his knees, to greet the missionary ladies, to say goodbye to Mr. Kim. Below, a white, slow figure stepped from a door and headed across the street. Again, she breathed in. And what she took in was her own. Not everything had a name.

Nominated by Ploughshares

THE FACTS BEHIND THE
HELSINKI ROCCAMATIOS

fiction by YANN MARTEL

from THE MALAHAT REVIEW

pour J. G.

I HADN'T known Paul for that long. We'd met at Trent University in Peterborough in the fall of '87. Having worked and traveled around a bit, I was older than him, twenty-four and in fourth year. He had just turned nineteen and was entering first year. They have this system at Trent where at the beginning of the year some upper year students introduce the new students to the university. There are no pranks or anything like that; the upper years are there to be helpful. They're called "amigas" and the first years "amigees," which shows you how much Spanish they speak in Peterborough. I was an amiga and most of my amigees struck me as good-humoured and eager children. But Paul had a laid-back intelligent curiosity and a sceptical turn of mind that I liked. And it happened that because of our parents' jobs we'd both lived in Mexico City for a few years when we were kids. The two of us clicked and we became good friends. We did things together and talked all the time. Because I was older and I'd seen more things, I'd usually fall into the role of the wise old guru and

Paul of the young disciple. But then he'd say something that would throw my pompousness right to my face and we'd laugh and break from these roles.

Then, hardly into second term, Paul fell ill. Already at Christmas he'd had a fever. And since then he'd been carrying this cough around. If he moved suddenly, if he sat down or got up too quickly for example, he would erupt into a dry, hacking cough. Initially, he, we, thought nothing of it. The cold, the dryness of the air—it was something to do with that. But slowly things got worse. Now I remember signs that I didn't think twice about at the time. He complained once of diarrhea. He seemed less energetic. One day we were climbing the stairs to the library, hardly forty steps, and when we reached the top, we stopped. I remember realizing that the only reason we had stopped was because Paul wanted to rest. He was out of breath. He was never finishing his meals, either, and seemed to be losing weight. It was hard to tell what with the heavy winter sweaters and all, but I did seem to remember that his frame was stockier. Finally, when he was getting out of breath at the smallest effort, it became clear that something was wrong. We talked about it—nearly casually you must understand—and I played doctor and said "Hum. Out of breath, cough, weightloss, tiredness. Paul, you have pneumonia." I was joking of course. Ironically, that's in fact what he had. It's called Pneumocystis carinii pneumonia. Late in February, Paul left for Toronto to see his family doctor.

Eight months later he was dead.

AIDS. He said it to me over the phone in this strange, removed voice. He'd been gone for two weeks. He'd just gotten back from the hospital, he told me. I reeled. AIDS! My first thoughts were for myself. Had I ever borrowed his toothbrush? Or drunk out of his glass? Then I thought of him. At first I thought of sex, of homosexuality. But Paul wasn't gay. I mean he'd never told me so outright, but I knew him well enough and I had never detected the least ambivalence. But that wasn't it. Four years ago, when he was fifteen, he had gone to Jamaica on holiday with his parents. They'd had a car accident and Paul had been gashed in the left thigh. He'd lost a quantity of blood and had received a transfusion at the local hospital. Six witnesses of the accident had come along to volunteer blood. Three were of the right blood group. Several phone calls and a little research turned up the fact that one of the three had died two years later of toxoplasmic cerebral lesions while being treated for pneumonia, a suspicious combination.

I went to visit Paul that weekend at his home in Rosedale. I asked him if he was sure his parents wanted a visitor, but he insisted I come. I was right because what hurt most that first weekend was not Paul, but Paul's family. After learning how he had probably caught the virus, Paul's father didn't utter a syllable for three days. Then, early one morning, he fetched the tool kit in the basement and went out and destroyed the family car. Because he had been the driver when they had had the accident; even though it hadn't been his fault and it had been in another car, a rented car. He took a hammer and shattered all the windows and lights and then he scrapped and trashed the body and then he banged nails into the tires. Then he siphoned the gasoline from the tank, poured it over and inside the car and set it on fire. The neighbours called the police and the fire department and they rushed to the scene, but when he blurted out why he was doing it, they were very understanding and put the fire out and left without charging him or anything, only asking him if he wanted to go to the hospital, which he didn't. So that was the first thing I saw when I walked up to Paul's house—a burnt wreck of a Mercedes covered in dried-out foam.

Paul's father didn't shake my hand when Paul introduced me. He was walking about the living room, trembling like a leaf in a storm and constantly rubbing his face with his hands. Paul's mother was in their bedroom. As a young woman she had been a linguistics student with a promising academic future and a highly ranked amateur tennis player. Paul was very proud of her, and that childrearing and spouseplaying had turned her talents into hobbies nourished in him (though not in her) the faintest residual of resentment against his father, who was a hardworking nonathlete who practiced the non-sexy profession of lawyer, corporate at that. Paul's mother was a very good-looking, nimble-minded, energetic woman. He had shown me pictures. But here she was, sitting on the edge of the bed, looking like a balloon that has become deflated and wrinkled. Like all the vitality had been yanked out of her. She was staring in mid-air, slowly and methodically chewing her fingernails to the quick till they bled. When I brought out my hand, she just looked at it, baffled, and I quickly pulled it back. Paul's sister, Jennifer, who was twenty-one and an architecture student at the University of Toronto, was the most normally hysterical. Her eyes were red, her face was puffy—she looked terrible. I don't mean to be grimly funny, but even George H., the family Labrador, was grief-stricken. He had squeezed himself under the living room sofa, wouldn't budge and was whining all the time. Confirmation of the verdict had come on Monday and since then (it was Friday), none of them, George H. included, had eaten a particle of food. The whole family structure had fallen apart. Paul's father, who had worked with the International Monetary Fund for several years and who was now a partner in a Toronto law firm, and his mother, who was a part-time librarian and a full-time NDP militant, hadn't gone to work and Jennifer hadn't gone to school, had hardly even left her room. They slept, when they slept, fully dressed and wherever they happened to be. One morning I found Paul's father slouched on the living room floor.

In the middle of it all was Paul, who wasn't reacting. He introduced me to his family like an asylum director who would showcase his most deranged inmates. He was frightened dumb. Only on the fourth day of my stay did he start to reach. He couldn't understand what was happening to him. He knew it was awful, but he couldn't grasp it. He spoke of his condition as if it were a theoretical abstraction, a moot point of philosophy. He would say "I'm going to die," as he might "The game was a tie." Death was just a word.

I had meant to stay for the weekend only—there was school—but I ended up staying for two weeks. I did a lot of housecleaning and cooking during that time. The family didn't seem to notice or care, but that was all right. Paul helped me and he liked that because it gave him something to think about. We had the car towed away, replaced the phones that Paul's father had pulverized, cleaned the house spotlessly from top to bottom, walked George H. and gave him a good bath (George H. because Paul really liked the Beatles and it was Paul who brought George into the band and when Paul was a kid he liked to say to himself when he was walking the dog or, rather, when the dog was walking him, since George H. was an affectionate but generally ill-mannered beast, he liked to say to himself "At this very moment,

398

unbeknown to anyone, absolutely incognito, Beatle Paul and Beatle George are walking the streets of Rosedale," and he would dream about what it would be like to sing "HELP" in Shea Stadium or something like that) and nudged the family into eating. I say "we" and "Paul helped"—what I mean is I did everything in his presence. Drugs called dapsone and trimethoprim were overcoming Paul's pneumonia, but he was still weak and out of breath. He moved about like an old man, slowly and conscious of every exertion. I spent myself without respite.

It took the family a while to break out of its daze. In the months of Paul's illness, I noticed three states they would go thru. One, common in the beginning, at home, when the pain was too close, they would isolate themselves from each other and do their thing: Paul's father would destroy something sturdy, like a table or a major appliance; Paul's mother would sit on the edge of her bed and make her fingernails bleed; Jennifer would cry in her bedroom; and George H. would hide under the sofa and whine. Two, later on, at the hospital mostly, they would come together and hold hands and sit on the bed beside Paul and they would talk and sob and encourage each other and whisper. And finally, three, I suppose what you could call normality, a deadened calmness, an ability to go thru life as if death didn't exist, an ability most people are lucky to be able to display every day of their lives except on the day they die.

I'm not going to talk about what AIDS does to a human body. Imagine it very bad—and then make it worse. Go look at the pictures of the people who were rescued from Auchwitz-Birkenau. Look up in the dictionary the word "flesh"—it's a healthy, pink word—and then look up the word "melt."

Anyway, that's not the worst of it. The worst of it is the resistance put up, the I'm-not-going-to-die virus. It's the one that kills the most people because it kills the living, the ones who surround and love the dying. That virus infected me early on. I remember the day precisely. Paul was in the hospital. He was eating his supper, eating his whole supper, eating every morsel though he wasn't at all hungry. I watched him as he carefully pricked every carrot and every pea with his fork and as he consciously masticated every mouthful before swallowing. "It will help my body fight. Every little bit counts." I could see this was what he was thinking. It was written all over his face, all over his body, all over the walls. I wanted to scream, scream "You're going to die, Paul, DIE! Like people in cemeteries, you know." Except that "death" was now a tacitly forbidden word. So I just sat there, my face emptied of any expression, this painful anger roiling me up inside. My condition got much worse every time I saw Paul shave. You see, though Paul was nineteen, all he had were a few downy whiskers on his chin. Still, from the very first day of his illness on, he started to shave as if he were Sean Connery. Every single day he would lather up his face with a ton of shaving cream and would scrape it off with a Bic razor. That's the image that rips thru me: a vacillatingly healthy Paul standing in front of a mirror turning his head this way and that, pulling his skin here and there, meticulously doing something that was utterly, utterly useless.

I completely botched my academic year. I was missing classes at the drop of a hat. I was incoherently angry at everything and everybody and I didn't, couldn't, write any essays. I developed a loathing for Canada, Canadians and things Canadian, a loathing which still hasn't left me entirely. This country reeked of insipidity, comfort and insularity. Canadians were up to their necks in materialism and from the neck above it was all American television. Nowhere could I see idealism or transcendentalism, a concern for something come what may. No, I always hit upon, hit upon, hit upon a deadening, flavourless realism. My instinct was to despise Canadian politicians, starting with the Prime Minister. Bill Domm, the Member of Parliament for Peterborough, the opaque dimwit who led the fight to reestablish the death penalty and to stop the adoption of the metric system, struck me as typical excrement of the Canadian mediocratic system. Canada's policy on Central America, on Native issues, on Reagan, on everything, made my stomach turn. Really, there was nothing about this country that I liked.

Yes, I know—as if political activism or Gandhi-like asceticism could do anything about AIDS.

One day in a philosophy class—that was my major—I was doing a presentation on Hegel's philosophy of history. The professor, a highly intelligent and considerate man, interrupted me and asked me to elucidate a point he hadn't understood. I was silent

400

for a second—I was confused; I couldn't make sense of anything; I looked about the cosy, book-filled office where we were having our class—and then I exploded. I screamed, took the Hegel book, a hefty hard-covered brick, and projected it thru the window. Then I stormed out of the office and slammed the door as hard as I could, kicking in two of its nicely sculptured panels for good measure.

I tried to withdraw from Trent, but I missed the deadline. I appealed and appeared in front of a committee, the Committee on Undergraduate Standings and Petitions, CUSP they call it. My grounds for withdrawing were Paul, but when the chairman of CUSP prodded me and asked me in a glib little voice what exactly I meant by "emotional distress," I looked at him and decided that I wasn't going to decorticate Paul's agony for him. But I didn't make a scene. I just stood up, walked out without saying a word and quietly shut the door behind me.

So I failed my year. But I didn't care and I don't care. I hung around Peterborough.

But what I really want to tell you about, the purpose of this story, is the Roccamatio family of Helsinki. That's not Paul's family of course. His last name was Atsea. Nor is it mine.

You see, Paul spent months in the hospital. When his condition was stable he came home, but mostly I remember him at the hospital. The structure of his illness and treatments became the structure of his life. Against my will, I became familiar with words like azidothymidine, dapsone, trimethoprim, alpha interferon, domipramine, nitrazepam. When you're with people who are really sick—AIDS or cancer or whatever—you discover what a chimera science can be.

I'd visit Paul. I didn't manage to get a job in Toronto—I'm not from there; I hardly know the city—but in the spring I got one in nearby Oshawa. I was coming into Toronto to see Paul once, twice a week, often on weekends too, and I was calling him all the time. When I visited, if he was strong enough, we'd go to a movie or a play or for a walk, but generally we just sat about. But when you're between four walls and neither of you want to watch television or a video and the papers have been read out loud and you're sick of playing cards and chess and Trivial Pursuit and you can't always be talking about *it* and *its* progress, you run out of things to do. Which in a way was fine. Neither Paul nor I minded just sitting there lost in our thoughts, listening to quiet music.

But I started feeling that time was running out and we had to do something. I don't mean put on togas and ruminate philosophically about life, death, reality and God. We'd done all that in first term before we even knew he was sick. That's the basic staple of undergraduate life. What else is there to talk about when you've decided one night not to go to bed until seven in the morning? Or when you sit in a quiet corner of the library and read Descartes or Berkeley for the first time? And anyway, Paul was nineteen. What are you at nineteen? You're a blank page. You're all hopes and dreams and uncertainties, you're all future and little philosophy. No, what I meant was that between the two of us we had to do something that would go beyond life and death and dying of AIDS, something that would make sense of nonsense.

So what I thought Paul and I would do—the idea came to me on a Go transit bus back to Oshawa; what an excellent way of destroying void, I thought—was create something with our imaginations, a story that we'd tell each other each time we were together.

I gave it a good thinking. I had plenty of time to think on my job. I was a gardener for the municipality of Oshawa. I spent my time mowing lawns, tending flower beds and grooming my tan. It would be like *The Decameron;* except that instead of being ten people, we would be two; and it wouldn't last ten days, but indefinitely. Nor would it be discrete, unrelated short stories. I wanted continuity, something that would develop and meander. And come to think of it, *The Decameron* is about ten healthy people fleeing a world dying of the Black Death who tell each other raunchy little stories only to pass the time. The symbolism never struck me as quite right. Our situation would be very different. We the storytellers would be the sick this time; and we would be fleeing a healthy world and telling each other a story not to pass the time, since time was limited, but to recreate ourselves. The more I thought about the idea, the more I liked it. It was important that I convince Paul that he had no choice, that it wasn't a game or something on the same level as watching a video or listening to music or talking about politics. He had to see that everything else was useless, even his desperate existential thoughts that did nothing but frighten him. I would have to be well prepared, so well prepared that I could carry the story all by myself when he was too weak or depressed. And when he was up to it, I would have to be a firm guide and not let it slide into autobiography.

But fiction doesn't spring from nothing. If our story was to have any stamina, any breadth and depth, if it was to avoid both true life and irrelevant fantasy, it would need a structure, a guideline of sorts, some curb along which we could tap our white cane. As I mowed Oshawa lawns, I racked my brains trying to think of just such a structure. The story would be about a family; a large family, to allow diverse yet related stories; it would be contemporary and Western so that cultural references would be easy. But I needed something more firm, something that would both restrict and inspire us. Finally, while clipping a hedgerow, I hit upon it: we would use the history of the twentieth century! Not that the story would start in 1901 and progress up to 1987— that wouldn't be much of a guideline; rather, we'd use one event of each year as a metaphorical guideline. Yes, the twentieth century would be our mold. It would be a story in eighty-seven episodes, each episode echoing an event of a year of the twentieth century.

To have figured out what to make of my time with Paul electrified me. I was bursting with ideas. Nothing struck me as more worthwhile than making the trip Oshawa-Toronto—commuting, imagine—to invent stories with Paul.

I explained it carefully to him. It was at the hospital. He was undergoing tests.

"I don't get it," he replied. "What do you mean by 'metaphorical guideline'? Will the story start in 1901?"

"No, it'll start nowadays. It doesn't really matter. The historical events we choose will just be a parallel, something to guide us in making up our stories. Like a builder uses an architect's plans. Even better: like Homer's *Odyssey* for Joyce's *Ulysses*."

"I've never read the book."

"Nor have I. The point is the novel takes place in Dublin in 1906 but it's named after an ancient Greek story. Joyce uses the ten years' wandering of Ulysses after the Trojan War as a parallel for his story in Dublin. His story is a metaphorical transformation of it."

"Why don't we just read the book out loud, since we've never read it?"

"Because we don't want to be spectators."

"Oh."

He seemed sceptical—he was tired—but I insisted. I even got a touch annoyed—I didn't use the D word but it was in the air—and he started to cry. I apologized immediately and felt like an insensitive brute. Yes, we would read *Ulysses* out loud, what a good idea, and then, why not, *War and Peace*.

But I was about to step into the elevator when a yell suddenly exploded in the corridor, freezing everyone.

"HELLLLLSINNNNKIIII!"

You see, Paul and I were on the same wavelength. We were young and the young can be radical. We're not encrusted with habits and traditions. If we catch ourselves in time, we can start again.

So the story would take place in Helsinki. It was a good choice. Neither of us had been there and we knew next to nothing about it. I returned to Paul's room.

"The video machine will have to go," he said. Hip, hip, hurray! What about the name of the family? He pouted his lips and narrowed his eyes. Then he expelled the word "Roccamatio." Roccamatio? I wasn't very keen about that one. Not very realistic. I would have chosen a more Scandinavian-sounding name, like Karlson or Harviki. But Paul insisted: the Roccamatios were a Finnish family of Italian extraction. So be it. The Helsinki Roccamatios were located and baptized. We agreed on the rules: I would be the judge of what was fictionally acceptable; transparent biography was forbidden; the story would take place, or at least start, nowadays, the 1980s; each episode would resemble an event of our choosing of each consecutive year of the twentieth century; each episode would take into account what had taken place in previous ones and would be related in one sitting; we would alternate in narrating the story. We agreed that the basic facts about Helsinki were: one, it was an important port; two, it had a population of one million inhabitants; three, it was in all ways the capital of Finland —political, commercial, industrial, cultural, etc.; and four, it had a small but significant Swedish-speaking minority. Finally, we agreed that the Roccamatios would be a secret between the two of us.

404

We decided that after a period of thinking about it and doing research, I would start with the first episode. I brought Paul some paper, a pen and a thick, three-volume work called *A History of the 20th Century*. His father took the video machine away, set a small bookcase with wheels beside his bed and filled it with all thirty volumes of Encyclopedia Britannica.

Now understand that you're not going to hear the story of the Helsinki Roccamatios. Certain intimacies shouldn't be aired. At most they should be known to exist. The telling of the story of the Roccamatios was difficult, especially as the years went by. We started brave and strong, arguing about facts and events, interrupting each other, surprising ourselves with our inventiveness— but it's so tiring recreating the world when you're not in the peak of health. As I feared, in time, I often had to bear the weight of the Roccamatios alone. Paul was not so much unwilling—he would still redirect me or correct me with a word or a scowl—as unable. Even listening became tiring.

The story of the Helsinki Roccamatios was most often whispered. And it wasn't whispered to you!

All I've kept—outside my head—is a record of sorts:

The AIDS Years

1901—After a reign of sixty-four years, Queen Victoria dies. Her reign had witnessed a period of incredible industrial expansion and increasing material prosperity. In its own blinkered and delusional way, the Victorian age was the happiest of all. It was an age of stability, order, wealth, enlightenment and hope. Science and technology were new and triumphant and Utopia seemed at hand.

I begin with an ending, with the death of Sandro Roccamatio, the patriarch of the family. It's dramatic and it allows me to introduce the family members.

1902—Under the forceful leadership of Clifford Sifton, the settlement of Canada's West is in full swing. Sifton sends out millions of pamphlets in dozens of languages and strings a net of agents across northern and central Europe. The shipping lines, having just dumped their Canadian wheat on the Old Continent,

405

bring home the catch. In less than a decade, the population of the Prairies increases by close to a million inhabitants and wheat production jumps fivefold. The origins of the new settlers are myriad: Ukrainian, German, Mennonite, Scandinavian, Hutterite, British, Austrian, American, Polish. It's called "the Canadian miracle."

1903—Orville and Wilbur Wright fly at Kill Devil Hills, North Carolina. Their powered machine, "Flyer I" (now popularly called "Kitty Hawk"), stays in the air for twelve seconds on its first flight, fifty-nine seconds on its fourth and last.

1904—As a direct result of the Dreyfus affair, Prime Minister Emile Combes of France introduces a bill for the complete separation of Church and State. The bill guarantees complete liberty of conscience, removes the State from having any say in the appointment of ecclesiastics or with the payment of their salaries, and severs all other connections between Church and State.

A routine to our storytelling has already developed. It's nearly a ceremony. First, and always first, we shake hands every time we meet, like the Europeans. Paul takes pleasure in this, I can tell. Then we small talk, usually about politics since we're both diligent newspaper readers. Then, if there's a need, we deal with health and therapy. Finally, after a short pause to collect ourselves, we get on with the Roccamatios.

1905—The German monthly Annalen der Physik *publishes papers by Albert Einstein, a twenty-six-year-old German Jew working as an examiner in a Swiss patent office in Bern. The Special Theory of Relativity is born. There is energy everywhere. $E = mc^2$, as Einstein puts it.*

1906—Tommy Burns becomes the first (and only) Canadian to win the world heavyweight boxing championship when he beats Marvin Hart. A tenacious and hard-hitting fighter, Burns defends his title ten times in thirty-three months, notably knocking out the Irish champion Jem Roche in one minute twenty-eight seconds, the shortest heavyweight title defense ever.

Paul is nearly well. He's plagued by minor ills—fever here, diarrhea there—and a lack of energy, but it's nothing so dramatic. He's at home, and never having been sick before a day in his life the routine of illness has an exotic appeal. He is started on a program of azidothymidine (AZT) plus multivitamins and is going to the hospital several times a week, sometimes staying overnight. He likes the hospital. The knowledgeable-looking men and women in white, the innumerable tests, the whiteness and cleanness of the place—they exhaust and reassure him.

We speak of the future, make plans. We speak of travel. I've traveled some, Paul less, mostly with his family, and we both perceive travel as essential to growth, as a state of being, as a metaphor. We hardly speak of Europe—we've touched on the south of France and Iceland, but that's it. We are going to be travelers, not tourists. The travelers will go to North Yemen, will wander the streets of Sa'na and Hodeida and perhaps chew qat. The travelers will go to India, will get to know the Punjab and Bengal and Uttar Pradesh as they know the backs of their hands, as they will know Mexico again and Bolivia and Peru, as they will know South Africa and the Philippines and Indonesia. The travelers will travel.

1907—A new strain of wheat, Marquis, is sent out to Indian Head, Saskatchewan, for testing. The result of an exhaustive, scientific selection process, the credit for its development goes to Charles Edwards Saunders, cerealist at the Ottawa Experimental Farm. The new strain's response to Saskatchewan conditions is phenomenal. It is resistant to heavy winds and to disease and it produces high yields that make excellent flour. Most importantly, it matures early, thus avoiding the damage of frost and greatly extending the areas of Alberta and Saskatchewan where wheat can be grown. By 1920 Marquis will make up ninety percent of prairie spring wheat, helping make Canada, already known as a wheat-growing area, one of the great breadbaskets of the world.

If I'm not distracted by other people and their words or by thoughts of food, transportation and the like, I think of the Roccamatios. They are my mind's natural subject. I have to find historical events. Then I have to think of plot and parallel, of the way in which the story will resemble the historical event, whether in an obvious way or a subtle way, whether for one symbolic moment (at the beginning or the end?) or all along. These thoughts pester me, challenge me, make me go on. I am hardly aware of Oshawa.

1908—Ernest Thompson Seton, famous author, naturalist and artist, organizes the Boy Scouts of Canada. The aim of the organization, like that of the Girl Scouts founded two years later, is to foster good citizenship, decent behaviour, love of nature, and skill in various outdoor activities. The Scouts follow a moral code

407

and are encouraged to perform a daily good deed. They go camping, swimming, sailing and hiking. They undertake community service projects. Their motto is "Be Prepared" and they shake hands with the left hand.

I had not envisioned the Roccamatios so ambitiously. The death of the patriarch, marriages, the runaway daughter, the bitter but liberating divorce, childbirths, entrepreneurial success, romance, community leadership—they are an energetic family. Paul and I go about them briskly. I meant it that we should alternate years, but so far they've been a cooperative endeavor.

But there are clouds on the horizon. 1909 is my year. I see adventure and mistake in my story; Paul, adventure and fraud. It's the first time we quibble. And I'm troubled by his story for 1910.

1909—Commander Robert E. Peary claims to reach the North Pole. Though generally accepted, the claim is questioned by some because of the inadequacy of observations and the incredible timetable of distances submitted. Possibly Peary never reached the Pole.

1910—Japan, increasingly militaristic and expansionist, annexes Korea and begins a program of development and attempted assimilation.

I launch the Roccamatios into municipal politics.

1911—A federal election is called in Canada. The dominant issue of the campaign is reciprocity, an arrangement to lower tariffs between Canada and the United States, which will allow Canadian primary products to flow south at the price of giving Americans a better chance to sell their manufactured goods in Canada. Liberal Prime Minister Wilfred Laurier favours reciprocity; Conservative Opposition leader Robert Borden doesn't. Eastern Canadian manufacturers suggest that such an economic accord would be the first step in a political takeover. Certain statements by influential Americans—"I hope to see the day when the American flag will float over every square foot of the British North American possessions, clear to the North Pole": Champ Clark, Speaker of the House of Representatives—do nothing to appease these fears. Laurier and his Liberals go down to a resounding defeat. Eight cabinet ministers lose their seats and the two parties practically switch places: the Liberals go from 135 seats to 87, the Conservatives from 85 to 134. Robert Borden becomes Prime Minister.

408

Paul's moods are changing. I think he's starting to realize that he's in for a long haul. Initially his pills and injections were a source of delight. "Here comes health," he probably said to himself. But health seems to elude him and he's angry about it. He still takes all his medicines religiously, but they are bitter now, not sweet. Nineteen twelve was the year the Minimum Wage Law was passed in England, was the year Roald Amundsen reached the South Pole, was the year Queen Nefertiti was discovered in Egypt by Ludwig Borchardt. But Paul would have none of these. His story is nasty.

1912—After a siege of five hours in Choisy-le-Roy, a suburb of Paris, a group of anarchists known as the "bande à Bonnot," after their leader Jules Joseph Bonnot, is exterminated. Practicing nihilists, they had committed numerous bare-faced bank robberies during several of which they had killed tellers, guards, customers, passers-by. In the final attack on their hold out, the police used guns, machine guns and cannons. Bonnot was found wrapped in a mattress.

Durable optimism can be the product of only one thing: reason. Any optimism that is unreasonable is bound to be dashed by reality and result in even more unhappiness. Optimism, therefore, must be girded by reason, must be unshakeably grounded in it, so that pessimism becomes a foolish, short-sighted attitude. What this means—reasonableness being the inglorious, tepid thing it is—is that optimism can arise only from small, nearly ridiculous, but undeniable achievements. In 1913 I put my best foot forward.

1913—G. Sundbank patents the zipper.

Paul is hospitalized; he has a relapse of Pneumocystis carinii. He's put on dapsone and trimethoprim again, but this time he suffers side effects: a fever, a rash all over his chest and neck. And he is amazingly thin; he hardly eats and has intractable diarrhea. He has a tube up his nose. He has Marco Roccamatio have a serious fall out with his brother Orlando.

1914—Austria declares war on Serbia,
  Germany on Russia,
  Germany on France,
  Germany on Belgium,
  Great Britain (and therefore, nearly automatically,
  Canada,

India, Australia, New Zealand, South Africa and
*   Newfoundland) on Germany,*
Montenegro on Austria,
Austria on Russia,
Serbia on Germany,
Montenegro on Germany,
France on Austria,
Great Britain on Austria,
Japan on Germany,
Japan on Austria,
Austria on Belgium,
Russia on Turkey,
Serbia on Turkey,
Great Britain on Turkey,
France on Turkey,
Egypt on Turkey.

I tell Paul 1914 was the year aspirin was commercialized and wouldn't it make a more pleasant story.

"Your history is a bias," he replies.

"So is yours," I answer back.

"But mine is the correct bias."

"How do you know?"

"Because mine accounts for the future."

I can't understand it. I've read of people who have AIDS who live for years. Yet week by week Paul is getting thinner and weaker. He's receiving treatments, yes, but they don't seem to be doing much, except for his pneumonia. Anyway, he doesn't seem to have any particular illness, just a wasting away. I ask Science about it, nearly complain about it: I ask a doctor who is standing in a doorway. He has his eyes closed and is rubbing his eyebrows. He listens to my litany without saying a word—he's a big man and his eyes are a bit red—and then he doesn't say anything and finally after several seconds he says in a low, gentle, measured voice "We're—doing—our—best."

It is my turn. But I must be careful. I must neither give in to Paul nor ignore him. I must steer between abstraction and reality, between removal and reflection. I would like Einstein's announcement of his General Theory of Relativity, but a reminder that the Universe is created anew would not please Paul.

410

But I, on the other hand, refuse to invoke further declarations of war. I tread carefully. I go for the ambiguous.

1915—Alfred Wegener, in Die Entstehung der Kontinente und Ozeane, *gives the classic expression of the controversial theory of continental drift.*

"Continental drift? Drift?" Paul smiles. He likes my story too.

1916—Germany declares war on Portugal,
> *Austria on Portugal,*
> *Roumania on Austria,*
> *Italy on Germany,*
> *Germany on Roumania,*
> *Turkey on Roumania,*
> *Bulgaria on Roumania.*

More tests. Paul has a thing called Cytomegaloviruses, which may account for his diarrhea and his general weakness. It's a highly disseminating infection, could affect his eyes, liver, lungs, gastrointestinal tract, spinal cord, brain, anywhere. There's nothing to be done; no effective therapy exists. Paul is speechlessly depressed. I give in to him.

1917—The United States declares war on Germany,
> *Panama on Germany,*
> *Cuba on Germany,*
> *Bolivia severs relations with Germany,*
> *Turkey with the United States,*
> *Greece declares war on Austria, Bulgaria, Germany and Turkey,*
> *Siam on Germany and Austria,*
> *Liberia on Germany,*
> *China on Germany and Austria,*
> *Peru severs relations with Germany,*
> *Uruguay with Germany,*
> *Brazil declares war on Germany, the United States on Austria,*
> *Ecuador severs relations with Germany,*
> *Panama declares war on Austria,*
> *Cuba on Austria.*

In 1918 Paul wants to invoke further declaration of war— Guatemala declared war on Germany, Nicaragua on Germany and Austria, Costa Rica on Germany, Haiti on Germany and Honduras on Germany if you must know—but for the first time I use

411

my power of veto and declare these fictionally unacceptable. Nor do I accept the publication of Oswald Spengler's *The Decline of the West,* in which Spengler gives a cyclical interpretation of history and forecasts as inevitable the eclipse of Western civilization. Enough is enough, I tell Paul. There is hope. The sun still shines. Paul is angry at me but he is tired and submits. I think he was expecting my censure for he surprises me with a curious event and a fully prepared Roccamatio story.

1918—Harlow Shapley, after an extensive study of the distribution of globular clusters and of Cepheid and RR Lyrae variable stars, increases the estimated size of our Galaxy about ten times. He envisions it as a flattened, lens-shaped system of stars in which our solar system occupies a position far away—some thirty thousand light years—from the centre.

"Isn't it grand," I say.

"Aren't we lonely," he replies.

His story is sordid.

1919—John Alcock and Arthur Brown, make the first nonstop airplane crossing of the Atlantic. Taking off from St John's, Newfoundland, they land in a bog near Clifden, County Galway, Ireland, sixteen hours and twelve minutes later.

"This AZT is exhausting," says Paul. He is anemic because of it and receives transfusions regularly.

In 1920 I forbid the publication of Freud's *Beyond the Pleasure Principle,* in which Freud concludes that the fundamental aim of all instincts is to revert to an earlier state, a notion that is soon popularized as the "death wish." Paul changes historical events while keeping the same Roccamatio story.

1920—With Tristan Tzara at the helm, Dada triumphs.

Over the phone, Paul tells me he is developing Kaposi's sarcoma. He has purple, blue lesions on his feet and ankles. Not many, but they are there. The doctors zero in on them. Tests. He is put on alpha interferon. He will have radiation therapy. Paul's voice is shaky. But we agree, we strongly agree, that radiation therapy has been found to be successful against localized Kaposi's and he's only got it on his skin, in fact, only on his feet, and it doesn't hurt and at least his lungs are fine. I promise to come that day.

Paul is quiet. He is in his usual, favourite position: lying on his back at a particular angle against a carefully arranged pyramid of three pillows. It is my turn so he lies waiting.

1921—Frederick Banting, Charles Best, Bert Collip and John MacLeod discover the long-sought internal secretion of the pancreas. They call it insulin. It is immediately and spectacularly effective as a therapy for diabetes. Banting, the most famous of the discoverers though actually the least skilled as a scientist, is an accomplished amateur painter. In his style he is clearly influenced by his good friend the painter A. Y. Jackson.

I am halfway thru my story when Paul interrupts me.

"In 1921 Albert Camus died in a car crash."

He doesn't say anything more. I continue. Until he interrupts me once again.

"In 1921 Albert Camus died in a car crash."

"Paul. He didn't. Albert Camus died in 1960."

"In 1921 Albert Camus died in a car crash. He was in the car, a Facel-Vega—never heard of it, have you?; it was a small series French copy of a Chrysler, not very road-tested—he was in the car with Michel and Janine Gallimard and their daughter Anne. Camus was—"

"Paul, Albert Camus died in 1960."

"In 1921 Camus was beside Michel Gallimard, who was driving. The others were at the back. They were returning to Paris from Loumarin, in the Luberon in the south of France, where Camus had bought a beautiful white house with his Nobel money. Near a village called Villeblevin, the road was s—"

"Paul, stop it. It's my turn."

"—the road was straight and dry and empty. Michel Gallimard was a good driver and near Villeblevin he was driving well. Along the road were trees, plane trees; the French like plane trees. Suddenly—"

"Paul, I said it was in 1960. 1960!"

"In 1921, suddenly—an axel that broke? a wheel that blocked? —for no reason, the car—"

"Paul, you're not following the rules, you're chea—"

"—THE CAR SLID AND HIT ONE TREE and then another fifty metres further along. Albert Camus was crushed, quite crushed, against a tree trunk. Body all mangled, organs squeezed out. As for Michel Gallimard, the steering shaft went thru his fucking chest and pinned him like a but—"

"STOP IT."

"—terfly. Janine and Anne Gallimard survived. To tell the tale. In fact, they were hardly injured."

"In 1921 Banting, Best, Collip and MacLeod discovered the long-sought internal secretion of the pancreas and called—"

"IN 1921 THE ATOMIC BOMB WAS DROPPED ON HIROSHIMA."

"IN 1921 BANTING, BEST, COLLIP AND MACLEOD DISCOVERED THE LONG-SOUGHT INTERNAL SECRETION OF THE PANCREAS AND C—"

"IN 1921 THE ATOMIC BOMB WAS DROPPED ON HIROSHIMA—"

"NO IT WASN'T, PAUL!"

"—AND IT WENT THRU ALBERT CAMUS'S FUCKING CHEST!"

Paul lunges for me. I am startled and pull back but he's going to fall to the ground so I catch him. I am kneeling on the floor with him over me, his legs still on the bed. I'm amazed at how light he feels. His hands go to my throat and he starts to strangle me. Or as best he can, which isn't much. He begins to sob in a most pathetic way.

"It's all right, Paul, I'm sorry," I whisper. "It's all right, it's all right. I'm sorry. In 1921 Banting, Best, Collip and MacLeod didn't discover insulin. In 1921 Sacco and Vanzetti were sentenced to death. Sacco and Vanzetti, Paul, Sacco and Vanzetti, Sacco and Vanzetti."

He relaxes his grip but continues sobbing. His heavy tears are dripping on my face. I lift and push him back onto his bed.

"Sacco and Vanzetti, Paul, Sacco and Vanzetti. It's all right. I'm sorry. Sacco and Vanzetti, Sacco and Vanzetti, Sacco and Vanzetti."

He lets go of my throat. I wipe my face carefully with a Kleenex and then I take a wet hand cloth and gently wipe his face and comb his hair with my fingers.

"It's all right, Paul. Sacco and Vanzetti, Sacco and Vanzetti, Sacco and Vanzetti, Sacco and Vanzetti."

I improvise a grim story. As a consequence of a minor but overblown problem at Helsinki University—a ridiculous case of plagiarism—Loreta Roccamatio drowns herself.

1921—Nicola Sacco and Bartolomeo Vanzetti, both poor Italian immigrants and anarchists, are found guilty and sentenced to death for the murders of a factory paymaster and a guard during a robbery in South Braintree, Massachusetts. In spite of flaws in the evidence, irregularities at their trial, accusations that the judge and jury were prejudiced against their political beliefs and social status, evidence that pointed to a group known as the Morelli gang, in spite of worldwide protests and appeals for clemency, Sacco and Vanzetti will be executed in 1927.

Paul is put on anti-depressants—amitriptyline at first, then domipramine. It will take about two weeks before they become effective. In the meantime he is kept under close surveillance, especially at night, when he sleeps only in fits. Just in case, just in case. The clinical psychologist comes by nearly every day. I call Paul about five times a day.

1922—Benito Mussolini, whose fascist squadristi have been provoking and intensifying an anarchic situation in Italy, receives a telegram from King Victor Emmanuel III. He is in power.

"Sometimes I can feel them in my blood. I can feel every virus as it courses thru me, as it goes up my arms, across my chest, into my heart and then shoots out to my legs. And I can't do anything. I just lie here, waiting, waiting, knowing it's going to get worse."

He is fragile, so fragile. I give in to him.

1923—Germany is incapable of paying on schedule the war reparations imposed on her by the Allies (set at 132 billion gold marks, roughly 33 billion dollars). France and Belgium, using a technical default of coal and timber deliveries, occupy the Ruhr district to force compliance or, if necessary, to collect reparations by direct seizure. The German government orders a ban on all reparation deliveries and encourages passive resistance to the occupation forces' attempts to get the mines and factories working. The French and Belgians respond with mass arrests and an economic blockade that cuts off not only the Ruhr but the greater part of the occupied Rhineland from the rest of Germany. The German economy is devastated. By the end of the year 1923 a loaf of bread in Berlin costs 140 billion marks. The Weimar republic is foundering. The ground is fertile for extremists.

1924—Lenin dies of sclerosis at the age of fifty-four. Stalin, whom Lenin had unsuccessfully tried to have removed as Secretary-General of the Communist Party, starts the edification of the Lenin myth, thus portraying himself as his great defender and partisan.

I bump into Paul's parents as I'm leaving the hospital. I've gotten to know the Atseas quite well. They've taken to me, as I have to them. I used to call ahead and ring at the door when I came to visit Paul at home, but quickly I was given a key and told that I was welcome any hour of the day or night, seven days a week, three hundred and sixty four days a year. It's like I have three parents now instead of one: Jack pats me on the back and Mary smiles at me and touches my forearm lightly and informs me that there are sugar-cane yogurts in the fridge now, my favourite, for when I come to their house next.

1925—Hitler publishes Mein Kampf.

Paul seems to be improving. His Kaposi is uncertain but his diarrhea is nearly gone.

1926—Rudolf Valentino, thru the intercession of appendicitis, enters immortality at the age of thirty-one in New York City. Valentino came to the United States from Italy in 1913 and worked for a time as a gardener, as a dishwasher, as a dancer in vaudeville. In 1918 he went to Hollywood, where he played small parts in films until he was given the role of Julio in The Four Horsemen of the Apocalypse *(1921). He immediately became one of the greatest stars of the silent movie era. His death causes worldwide hysteria, several suicides, and riots at his lying-in-state, which attracts an eleven-block-long crowd.*

Paul *is* feeling better. He has an appetite and hardly any diarrhea. And his Kaposi is looking great. He shows me his left foot. The lighter lesions are gone and the bigger ones are smaller and paler in colour. And, most importantly, his mood is good. On a Saturday morning I am at the hospital with his family. They are in an expansive mood. Paul is coming home. He's just had a transfusion and he feels fine. He puts on his street clothes, which he hasn't worn in several weeks. They fit him loosely. His pants looks like they're empty and his shirt hangs flat, hardly betraying a body behind it. I notice it, we all notice it, but we all ignore it. Paul walks a bit unsteadily but there are plenty of arms willing to support him.

1927—The near-bankrupt picture company of Warner Brothers releases The Jazz Singer. *In an otherwise silent feature film, they add a recorded musical accompaniment, four singing sequences and a little dialogue that replaces the title cards and helps move the plot along. For the first time, sound is integrated with plot and narration becomes more fluid and gripping. The movie is an enormous success. The talking pictures era has begun.*

To do something, to pass the time, to assert control over something, Paul and I rearrange his room. He gives orders: I execute. We make a circus of it. I huff and puff while lifting a book, then move the bed pretending it is nothing. Paul laughs, which is the aim of it all.

1928 is Paul's year and a very good year it was. Suffrage is extended to women in Great Britain; the Kellogg-Briand Pact, which outlaws aggressive war as an instrument of national policy, is signed in Paris by sixty-three countries; Amelia Earhart flies across the Atlantic, the first woman to do so; the Hungarian biochemist Albert Szent-Gyorgyi discovers Vitamin C; Canada's Percy Williams is the sensation of the Amsterdam Olympics, winning gold medals in the one hundred metre and two hundred metre sprints against the fastest field ever assembled; Ravel's *Bolero* is a world-wide hit—yes, it could only be a good year for the Roccamatios.

1928—The world meets Mickey Mouse in the first animated sound cartoon, Steamboat Willie, *by Walt Disney and Ub Iwerks. Disney and Iwerks had actually already made two silent cartoons with a cheerful, energetic mouse—*Plane Crazy, *in which the mouse was called Mortimer Mouse, and* Galloping Gaucho—*but when they saw* The Jazz Singer, *they recognized the limitless possibilities for sound in animated cartoons, put these two silent shorts aside and quickly produced* Steamboat. *It is a hit.*

Paul shows me some photos. The second one is of two boys, fifteenish, sitting in a pile of orange and brown leaves, dressed in jeans and heavy sweaters. They both have wide, slightly demented grins.

"That's James, my best friend in high school, on the left and that's me on the right."

I manage to check my gasp. But I stare. I try to find one point of resemblance—the hair, the chin, the nose, the glint of the eyes, anything—but there's nothing, nothing at all. Paul Photo and Paul Beside Me are two different people. Paul Beside Me doesn't notice my horror. Nothing sharpens the memory, evokes the past, rejuvenates the sick and the ageing, raises the dead,

417

like a collection of family photographs. These flashbacks to a healthy past, to a time of energy, pleasure and clear skin, cheer up Paul. I stare at the other pictures of this stranger without saying a word.

We go for walks, slow walks. Paul moves carefully, dragging his feet lightly, as if feeling the terrain so as to avoid the tiring jerks of normal walking. Fortunately the spring weather is fantastic. Paul is bowled over by the beauty of green grass. His optimism is radiant and fragile. I manage to make 1929 a fun story.

1929—The Belgian Georges Remi, better known as Hergé, creates Tintin. It's a wonderful creation. In twenty-three albums, from Tintin au Pays des Soviets *in 1929 to* Tintin et les Picaros *in 1976, the rich, detailed, beautifully coloured Tintin cosmology unfolds and enraptures. General de Gaulle will confess one day to André Malraux that Tintin "est mon seul rival international."*

Paul has been home for over two weeks. The house is like a planetary system with Paul's bedroom or, more precisely, Paul as the sun, the centre of it all. In every important room there's an interphone that is linked to his room. The system is on all the time so there's a quiet static in the air. This static fills the house. The kitchen is littered with Paul's culinary whims, quantities of wasted delicious food. Articles and books on AIDS, which his parents secretly loathe but which Paul reads assiduously, are in bookshelves, on tables, on the floor. Paul's things—a sweater, a half-drunk glass of orange juice, an open book, slippers, an unfinished crossword puzzle, a portable electronic game—are everywhere, left not because he's spoilt but because he's tired and forgetful. The routine of the household, as regards his parents and Jennifer, is medico-military: everything is on time, structured, well-done. The general's staff relays itself in gently waking the general at midnight so that he can take his AZT. This isn't a sharing of a burden: it's that they all want their turn.

Paul talks of starting his studies again. By correspondence or, better, part-time at York University. We're enthusiastic. He wants to major in philosophy and film.

1930—The American Clyde Tombaugh discovers the ninth planet of our solar system, Pluto.

The Roccamatios are interrupted for eight days. Paul and his parents are up north at their Georgian Bay cottage.

418

"It's for my white globules," he tells me. "They don't want to go up. Big spaces, fresh air—it'll be good for them."

His optimism seems tired.

1931 is my year but Paul asks to do it. My story is trite and strikes me as inappropriate—the American J. Schick invents the electric razor—and I feel sad that day so I let him have it. Just before he leaves, he tells me a brief, puzzling story and afterwards, when he's gone, I feel even sadder.

1931—Kurt Godel publishes Uber Formal unentscheidbare Satze der Principia Mathematica und verwandter Systeme, *showing that in any formal mathematical system in which elementary arithmetic can be done there are propositions whose truth or falsity cannot be proved on the basis of the axioms within that system and therefore that it is uncertain whether the basic axioms of arithmetic will not give rise to contradictions.*

Paul returns to Toronto in catastrophe. He has abdominal pains that keep him bent in two. He goes straight to the hospital. His mood is black, black.

Five hundred white globules. Christ. Next to no immunity protection left. He's wide open. He receives a transfusion.

1932—Paul Doumer, President of France, is shot twice by a Russian immigrant, Pavel Gorgulov, and dies of his injuries.

It's a ridiculous thing to put in a balance, but in the balance of things it's better to be losing a brother than to be losing a son. There's something profoundly debilitating, disturbing, about a child dying before a parent, about the future dying before the present. It means worse than death: it means extinction. It is the ultimate hopelessness: it denies vicarious immortality. No one adapts well to morbidity, but Jennifer is doing it the least badly. As it has done for me, Paul's illness has sobered up her "folly of youth." She is more deliberate, less distracted. But she tells me that often at night she thinks of death—not Paul's, but her own. She worries about the small, fatal risks of ordinary life and can't fall asleep for them. They terrify her not for her own sake—as you might think—but for her parents'. With Paul going, she feels a silent pressure from Jack and Mary: love. She feels that she mustn't at any cost let them down and die. She doesn't ride her bicycle anymore for fear of sewer grates and opening car doors.

I don't want to deal with 1933. It's easy to relax so why don't we relax? I bring an oriental game that a friend has recently

419

taught me called Go. The rules are very simple—you play with black and white beads on a criss-cross board; the aim is to surround your enemy—but the game is as complex as chess. Still, it's more accessible to beginners than chess is and I think Paul might get into it. But he just interrupts me.

"You've forgotten something, haven't you?"

"I don't feel like it."

"Oh no you don't. We're in 1933. Do you know what happened in 1933?"

"You mean the beginning of the New Deal legislation?"

"Try again."

"Edwin Armstrong invents FM radio?"

"One more time."

"The rumba is the craze?"

"Again."

"Welcome King Kong and false eyelashes?"

Paul kidnaps my year. Marco achieves an unfriendly buyout of Orlando's group of small shareholders and forces him off the Board of Directors.

1933—Hitler becomes chancellor. The Third Reich is proclaimed from Potsdam. The first concentration camp is opened on the site of a former ammunitions factory in Dachau. Between 1933 and 1945 it will hold more than 206,000 registered prisoners. Besides the thousands killed before registration or sent for extermination elsewhere, thirty-two thousand men, women and children will die at Dachau.

Since Paul took 1933, I take 1934, his year, and keep 1935. I impose myself. There's no greater, more beautiful surprise than the strength of love one discovers one has for a newborn baby. I announce the birth of Lars Roccamatio!

1934—In Callander, Ontario, in a poor French-Canadian farmhouse, the Dionne Quintuplets—Annette, Cecile, Emilie, Yvonne and Marie—are born. And live. No identical quints in the history of the world (all two of them) had ever survived for more than a few hours. The news amazes and delights a world in need of good news. Gifts of money, clothes, food, breast milk, equipment and advice begin to pour in from all sides. The Red Cross decides to build a special, ultramodern hospital for them across from their farmhouse. But people want to see, see for themselves, these miraculous mites. The world begins to move in on the Dionnes. They become the biggest tourist attraction in Canada, bigger than Niagara Falls. The Ontario government of Mitch Hepburn, concerned with protecting the children from exploitation (or is it "concerned with protecting the exploitation of the children"?), passes the Dionne Quintuplet Act, which makes them wards of the province, and appoints a board of guardians. A good road is built from Highway 11 to the hospital, which is expanded and becomes the centre of a complex called "Quintland." A solid fence is built around the whole place. Police keep guard round-the-clock. Tourists come and come and come, as many as six thousand a day, three million in all, to see thru a one-way glass the cutesome five as they gambol about their special playground. They spend fifty-one million dollars in 1934, double that two years later, a total in 1944 estimated at half a billion dollars. Real estate values soar in Callander. Hotels, motels, restaurants and souvenir shops proliferate. Newspapers and magazines chronicle the Quints' lives on a nearly daily basis. Those who can't make the trip to see them live can see them in their three Hollywood movies or in the Fox-Movietone newsreels or on the covers of countless magazines or in the advertisements of the various products they endorse—canned milk, syrup, dolls, baby clothes, soap, breakfast foods, baby foods, etc. From India to Germany to Nigeria, Callander becomes the best known—if not the only known—Canadian city. Forget Hitler and Mussolini, the world wants to know how their sweet Quints are today. Yes, there will be troubles later on—the price of too many people, too much money, too little love—but still, the Dionne Quints are the nicest thing to happen to Canada during the thirties.

Then I go for the excitement of a high-powered crisis in the Helsinki municipal council.

1935—Conservative Prime Minister R. B. Bennett calls a federal election. Since Confederation his administration has come the closest to being a one-man, quasi-dictatorial show. A millionaire many times over, he had used his own resources to get his party elected in the 1930 election. He had also flatly guaranteed that he would solve the problems of the Depression. He would "blast a way through all our difficulties," he said; he would "use tariffs to blast a way into the markets that have been closed to you." In 1935 people who can no longer afford gasoline remove the engines from their cars and hitch them to horses; they're

421

called "Bennett buggies." In 1935 the Canadian people blast away Bennett. The Conservatives go down to their worst defeat ever: 40 seats, a loss of 97 in a house of 245 seats. William Lyon Mackenzie King is prime minister again.

Paul hardly listens to me. Then I hear a swallowing and I look up from the little notes I have prepared for my story and I see his eyes are red and his lips are trembling.

"Oh!" he whispers with difficulty, "I just want to live. I'll give up my ambitions." He starts to cry. I stop. "I don't c . . . care if I make nothing of my life, I'll do any l . . . lousy job, anything."

I've seen it before, it's happened before, but for some reason, at that moment, I'm not prepared for it. I panic. I get up, I move towards the door (to get someone?), I sit down again, I get up, I sit on the bed.

"I just want time."

I want to speak but the words (what words?) are stuck in my throat, I want to cry too but I feel I mustn't so I don't, I stand up, I take hold of the glass of water on his bedside table.

"Oh, I sh . . . sh . . . should have married."

I sit down, I put the glass back on the table, I put my hand on his hand, I get up, I sit down.

"I can't take it anymore, I can't take it anymore."

I stand up, I look at the curtains of the room (maybe I should close them?), I sit down.

"Paul,"—I can finally manage some words—"Paul, you have to hang on till they find a cure. You just have to hang on. Do you know how many dozens of millions of dollars are going into research all over the world? I mean in the U.S., in France, in Germany, in Holland, here in Canada, everywhere. Scientists are on to it like never before for anything else. It's like a Manhattan Project thing. The biggest brains around. They're making new discoveries everyday. You know that. Time is on your side, Paul. Hang in there!"

1935—The Depression is still on, hard.

I look out the window of the bus as I'm heading home. "Time is on your side." Fuck.

1936—The Spanish Civil War begins.

Jack never managed the trick, if trick there is. He's a member of that square, hard-working war generation who command salaries nowadays of over a hundred thousand dollars and thanks to

422

whose wealth-producing toil my generation has had it good and easy. Jack is a kind, intelligent man whose happiness operated within a structure. When a bomb shattered that structure to small pieces, he and his happiness fell apart. He is the one who has adapted the least well to Paul's illness. Quite simply, he can't accommodate the pain. It destabilizes him continually. He struggles, and I mean struggles, to cope. He's a fragile man, with a hollow look in his eyes and his hair whiter than before. And he's on anti-depressants, just like his son.

1937—Japan invades China.

Paul has received yet another transfusion. He experiences a moment of strength and—directly related—of euphoria. For 1938 I'm expecting a Kristallnacht story but he surprises me.

"You'll like my story," he tells me. And I do.

1938—Ladislao and George Biro patent the ball-point pen.

Tests, tests, tests. Bad result: lack of oxygen in the blood. Possibly a relapse of PCP. We don't say anything. He's scared; his eyes are wide open. So are mine.

1939—Professor Antanas Smetona, the president of independent Lithuania, broadcasts a last speech over the radio, protesting his country's annexation by the Soviet Union, which will be a brutal affair; one quarter of the Gulag will be composed of Lithuanians by the end of the 1940s. Smetona does not want to make his speech in Lithuanian, which no one outside his small country will understand. But he also refuses to speak the tongues of the oppressors, Russian, Polish or German. Smetona makes his last speech in Latin.

I walk around the hospital. To prepare myself. I breathe deeply. I see people lying in beds. Many of them watch me as I walk by, their heads turned, their eyes wide open. What do they have? Do they have *it?* I don't want to know. I go down a staircase, am approaching Paul's area. At the end of a corridor I see an old man. He is waiting. He is rocking gently from side to side. He looks about meekly. He is holding a bag which I think contains food. He waits and looks about. I smile at him. He is not very well dressed. He waits with infinite patience. I think he is poor; he has the patience of the poor. Is he the father of someone here? Where's your son or daughter? Being examined? Scanner perhaps? Was it sex? Sharing needles? Looking at the man I am overwhelmed by the feeling that he is utterly unimportant. He could die, his son or daughter could die, and it wouldn't matter in the least to anyone. Here is an unimportant man suffering all the suffering that is possible. The solitude of pain is a terrible thing. I feel a sinking in me. I can't face Paul yet. I walk a bit more.

1940—Doctor Karl Brandt receives a single-paragraph letter from high up. "[N]amentlich zu bestimmende Ärzte" (Doctors to be designated) are to be authorized so that "unheilbar Kranken bei kritischster Beurteilung ihres Krankheitszustandes der Gnadentod gewärht werdenkann" (mercy killing can be administered to patients who are terminally ill—as far as can be determined— after a thorough and rigorous examination of their state of health). Operation T4—[Paul interrupts his narrative. "Isn't that an extraordinary coincidence?" he says. "T4. Exactly like the cells in the immune system that are attacked by the HIV. Isn't that extraordinary! I say, I say."]*—operation T4 is set in motion. A home for the physically handicapped run by the Samaritans is taken over and transformed. Early in the year, Graffeneck opens. It is the first of six euthanasia centres (Hadamar, Brandenburg, Hartheim, Sonnenstein, Bernburg). Nine thousand eight hundred thirty-nine "terminally ill" patients will die at Graffeneck, at least ninety thousand in the whole operation, mostly mentally retarded men, mentally retarded women and mentally retarded children. This euthanasia pogrom will end, officially, in August of next year after protests from church groups. But almost immediately the technology, experience and personnel will be transferred outside the country, to Poland for example.*

1941—Marshall Petain institutes Mother's Day.

Mary has developed a limited resilience. She has faith in hope. When her hope is troubled, when the unthinkable forces itself upon her, she seems to find some inner something and— diminished, permanently saddened—she manages to go on. Certainly more than Jack anyway. Maybe she's religious, I don't know. I am careful never to talk about religion. Who am I to kick at people's crutches?

Paul has stopped shaving. He's been losing his hair and it hasn't been growing back well. The doctors offer, want, to shave him bald—"We always recommend it. It will depress him less than going bald hair by hair."—but he bursts into tears and refuses.

1941—Blacks are accepted for the first time in the American army: the American army enters World War II.

A lumbar puncture isn't supposed to hurt—it didn't the last time—but Paul screams. They have to go at it twice before they can get the needle in. I think I'm cool—I look at Jack and Mary in the eyes and tell them it doesn't really hurt, he's just being oversensitive; that it's for a good purpose: that it'll help in establishing a diagnostic and it's harmless and it doesn't take long and everything will be all right—I think I'm cool but when I go to drink I can't hold any water in my paper cup my hand is trembling so much. Finally I bend over and drink from the tap. It turns out Paul has a fungus called Crytococcus neoformans in his spinal fluid. There's a risk of meningoencephalitis. The thing could go to his head. They're going to keep a close watch. At the smallest sign he'll be put on amphotericin B and flucytosine.

I start my story—Monika Roccamatio is on a train, alone in her compartment, when a dignified, disfigured man, with a face like a skull and a right hand that is gloved in spite of the warm weather, steps in and sits down; and eventually they begin a conversation—I start my story, but for the first time I can't complete it. Every time I am about to speak I feel a heat in my eyes and a tightness in my throat. I abandon the story—Monika simply vanishes from the family—but thankfully Paul is exhausted and drops to sleep. He is very pale.

1943—The Final Solution.

My good health, what an insolence.

1944—Saint-Exupéry disappears with his plane somewhere between Corsica and Savoy while on a reconnaissance mission.

The side effects are too serious: Paul stops taking AZT. In a way he's happy about it since he feels better. The announcement stuns me. There's not even the fiction of a cure now. I sit beside his bed trying to contain myself. I do NOT want to talk about it. I am so afraid he's going to interrupt me I have difficulty getting my story out. I can hear my voice trembling. It is the shortest of all the Roccamatio stories.

1945—Hiroshima.

After the hospital, I tramp about the streets of Toronto, salivating with nihilism. I catch the headlines at a newstand—blood in Sri Lanka, the West Bank, Haiti, Iran, Irak; the KKK wins an election in Louisiana; bored youths riot in Switzerland; there's a picture of a Japanese lumber processing ship on the Amazon River—and I'm delighted. It starts me off. The world is metastasizing! We are not a viable species! I exult at the shrinking of the Amazon and the expansion of the Sahara and the emptying of the seas. Long live the greenhouse effect and acid rain and crack and religion. Hail Mister Ochoa! Hail Mister Wojtyla! Boo the white rhinoceros and boo Amnesty International. In Pol Pot and Shining Path we trust. THREE CHEERS FOR APATHY! And what's wrong with apartheid, I mean the South African apartheid? It's just another credit card, no worse than American Express. And Mister Gorbachev, when would you like the West Edmonton Mall? You'll find it solves most human problems. As for the depletion of nonrenewable natural resources, I love it. Petroleum, natural gas, coal, literacy, peat moss, fish, ozone, minerals, arable land, uranium, timber, oxygen—let's get rid of them! Me and my ten billion brothers and sisters will wing it on Hail Marys, Cheez Whiz and television. And if we fail, well then, thank God for the exit of death. Yes, thank God for death. Welcome death, oh welcome!

This attack starts to wear off. Where am I? I'm on Spadina, not far from Brunswick. A shaft of sunlight breaks thru the clouds of this warm, summer afternoon and irradiates the facade of some Lebanese greasy spoon. I'm surprised. I feel something in me unwinding. Nearly against my will, I like what I'm looking at. I look at the slightly rundown but clean place, at the window where a few ads—yoga lessons, rock bands, used books—are taped, where grease spots and grit are made visible by the sunlight. Inside, a slim Middle-Eastern type man with a beautifully thick mustache is preparing a felafel for a tad overweight, red-haired girl dressed in black with black-rimmed glasses. I like this banal, wonderful scene, want a falafel, want to chat up the girl. A bum with a twenty-foot-radius sphere of malodour assaults my nose and asks me for some spare change. I smile, say "Sure" and give him a dollar, telling him not to spend it on a drink, to which he replies "Sure" and staggers off. Yes, I smile. Then I walk up the street, looking at the people and at the stores. I'm dazzled at the multifarious variety of the human thing. There's a smell of curry. A perfume wafts by. I stop and I enjoy the smell of my sweat, the solidity of my body, the flexibility of my fingers and arms, I have a slight erection, I crack my toes, I stretch, I lick my lips—I stop and I exult in the stupid brute fact of my existence.

But don't get me wrong: it's that I've developed a capacity to enjoy catastrophe.

1946—War is declared in Indochina.

1947—As a prelude to the termination of British rule, India is partitioned to accommodate the fears and aspirations of the sub-continent's Hindus and Moslems. And so India achieves independence and Pakistan (Land of the Pure) is created. But Pakistan is geographically absurd: East Pakistan (formerly East Bengal, now Bangladesh) is more than a thousand miles from West Pakistan. Worse still, the delineation of the new borders thru the inter-meshed and irreconcilable communities of Bengal and Punjab envenoms an already violent conflict between the Moslems and Hindus. At the level of the men with power—Gandhi, Nehru, Patel, Jinnah, Mountbatten and others—the creation of the two nations is a dignified affair, perhaps even noble. But at the level of the man and woman on the street of those areas partitioned, it is mostly suffering, loss and bitterness. There is a massive flow of refugees—seven to eight million Moslems leave India for Pakistan; about the same number of Hindus make the journey in reverse—and terrible acts of violence take place. Over 200,000 people are killed.

Paul's horizons are shrinking. There can be no question anymore of foreign travel. Going home is travel. Leaving his hospital room is travel. He hardly has the strength to walk. Only to the bathroom to relieve himself; and even that. . . . The space beside his bed is becoming a horizon.

1948—Gandhi is assassinated.

He's always been a local history buff, but since Paul's illness it's become his passion. The Family Compact, the real Laura Secord, the inflexible Sir Francis Bond Head, the great Sir Isaac Brock ("Did you know he came from the Channel Islands?")—of these and more Jack is endlessly fascinated and he shares it with me and I encourage him and listen attentively and ask thoughtful questions, although nothing interests me less than the Family Compact, the real Laura Secord, the inflexible Sir Francis Bond Head or the great Sir Isaac Brock ("Jersey?" "No, Guernsey.") I love the man because of his pain. When we talk about the Battle of Queenston Heights or the tragic Tecumseh or the eccentric Thomas Talbot, I come away with the impression that we've been talking about Paul.

427

1949—Stalin turns seventy, the occasion for worldwide Communist celebrations. The Stalin Peace Prizes are set up.

1950—China invades Tibet under the indifferent eyes of the world.

Paul is afflicted with hiccups. These involuntary spasmodic jerks drain him completely. He has neither the strength to stay awake nor the peace to fall asleep. He floats in some horrible limbo. The doctors try drugs. Then hypnosis. They are very worried. I am very worried.

The Roccamatios are interrupted for two weeks.

When things are at their worst, they suddenly get better. Paul seems to have entered a period of exhausted stability. Like a miracle his hiccuping has stopped. And his diarrhea too, nearly; I suppose he has no more liquids to lose. His lungs—always a worry; one man in the hospital has had seven bouts of PCP—are all right. He's been off alpha interferon since long ago and his Kaposi has spread, but the nearest mirror is far, far away and, anyway, he's too tired to care—it's the least painful of his problems. He is under perfusion—vitamins, minerals, etc.—sleeps a lot and rarely gets out of bed. Like a pregnant woman he has sudden whims for particular foods, but he can hardly hold them down, vomits often.

1950 is the last year that Paul takes full responsibility for a Roccamatio story. He can simply no longer sustain the effort of concentration. He stops reading, he stops creating. He becomes the critical, obtrusive spectator of my imagination. My only respite is that he tires easily, unbelievably easily. He falls asleep at any moment, even in mid-sentence. He doesn't particularly want to sleep; it's more that it's the favourite state of his exhausted body. Sometimes I wait ten minutes or so—time for him to rest a little and forget what he's been saying—and then I wake him and continue my story; other times—and more frequently as the years go by—I whisper my story knowing he's sleeping.

1951—The Arab League's political committee appeals to its member states to tighten their economic blockade of Israel and, especially, to shut off oil supplies.

Paul finds urinating painful. They check his catheter. Nothing wrong. Some urinary tract infection. Even that simple pleasure will be denied him.

428

1952—The Supreme Court of South Africa invalidates the race legislation of Doctor (in divinity) Daniel F. Malan, Prime Minister since 1948. This legislation institutionalizes the system of "apartness" that has been governing in practice the relations between the races since well before the creation of the Union of South Africa in 1910. Shortly after the Court's move, Parliament approves a government-sponsored bill to restrict the powers of the Supreme Court. Malan, and his successor Strydom, will thereafter pursue the construction of apartheid, but it will be perfectly finished by Professor (of applied psychology and socioliogy; the brilliant scholar) Hendrik Verwoerd, Prime Minister from 1958 to 1966.

Paul doesn't eat anymore, or hardly. Sometimes he sucks on an ice cube. I arrive eating a chocolate bar, a Mars, not thinking about it. Paul stares at me, at my fingers, at my mouth. He doesn't seem to understand, as if eating has become an incomprehensible activity to him. I don't know what to do. I know that if he takes any, he'll vomit. Yet the look in his eyes! Finally, I take the smallest flake of chocolate, a mere ripple off the top, and I carefully place it on the tip of his tongue. I do this with trepidation, as if Paul were a bomb and I were about to trip him. The flake sticks to Paul's pasty tongue. He pulls—I can sense the effort needed in everything that he does—he pulls his tongue in. A few seconds go by. The flake is melting; saliva is wetting Paul's mouth. Suddenly Paul breathes out and opens his mouth and closes his eyes. Nausea! I quickly run my finger on his tongue and remove the half-melted flake. I put another finger in the glass beside his bed and wet Paul's tongue with a few drops of lemon-juice-flavoured water. He remains with his eyes closed. He is on an edge, an edge between nausea and pain on one side and tired numbness on the other. I wait. He opens his eyes. He is in no pain. I smile. "It's bad for you anyway. Cavities." "Pimples too," he replies. He manages a smile. He's in a good mood! At the National High School Debating Competition, held in Turku, Georgio Roccamatio triumphs in the debate "Is television an anti-democratic medium?" and receives the President Kekkonen Award from President Koivisto himself, who tells him he is expecting a call from him the day he turns eighteen.

1953—Dag Hammarskjold is elected Secretary-General of the United Nations.

Paul vomits, vomits blood.

"Internal hemorrhage," drops the nurse.

I can't close my eyes. I can feel them like huge spheres staring out. I can't close them or turn them. There's blood and liquid on the bed sheet, on Paul's hand. The nurse puts on plastic gloves. They're a horrible transparent white. Suddenly I'm afraid—of Paul's blood, of Paul himself. I get to my feet, mutter that I'll be back and leave the room. I head for the bathroom. I lock myself in. I start to roll up my sleeves but then I simply take my shirt off. With hot water and plenty of soap I meticulously begin to wash my hands, my arms, my face. I bring my hands right up to my face and inspect every square millimeter, searching for the least cut, nick, abrasion or blemish.

"There's this"—pause—"burning inside me," he whispers when I get back.

When I make to leave, I place my hand on Paul's sheet over his chest and very gently tap, as if in sympathy for this burning inside him. In fact, I don't want to touch his hand. Then, at home, for the hundredth time, for the thousandth time, I read that there is no empirical evidence, none, none at all, that it can be passed on thru casual contact. I sit down and I consciously go about quelling my panic.

1954—The first hydrogen bomb is exploded by the Americans in the Marshall Islands.

I've thought about it. Not in bed, that's for sure. Better a bang than a whimper: better to be shot in the street in broad daylight by my enemies, just like that, suddenly, as I'm turning a street-corner, seven bullets in the chest.

1955—James Dean dies in a car crash.

Suddenly, just like that, Paul is in pain. It comes from nowhere this pain. He's fine one moment and then he's in pain. I feel like shouting "GET AWAY!" and waving my arms and putting on a menacing expression, as if the pain were a mugger. But I can do nothing except wait and watch.

"It h . . . hurts," he moans (what? where?), fixing me with his eyes. He stares at me like he would hold on to me. If I should break eye contact I think Paul would fall, would fall into death. I don't break eye contact.

1956—The U.S.S.R. invades Hungary.

The transfusion is slow, takes time, but Paul's system takes the shock. He feels stronger, better.

Paul is going to die. All evidence points to this conclusion. I know it. I've known it for a long time. Every time I see him I am reinforced in my knowledge that he is going to die. It is not a surprise. I have been preparing myself for this biological terminus since the first day. I should be able to flick away the pain like I flick away sweat from my forehead with my fingers. "Get away, pain," I should be able to say, should.

Paul has chosen this day to talk about God.

"Do you believe in God?" he asks me in a whisper.

I take note of his tone of voice. I am a perfect turncoat and I lie with perfect conviction.

"Yes, I do."

There is a pause.

"I think me too," comes a clipped response. He seems relieved. Tiny little beads of sweat cover his forehead. Every time he swallows, he closes his eyes. He's forgotten all our arguments at university.

"I believe God is everywhere. In every manifestation of life," I add, seamlessly.

"Me too."

"God flows thru time. There is neither Before nor After. Spirit is timeless."

"Yes."

"He cares for us all.' "

He swallows and falls asleep.

1957—After enduring six years of smears and baseless attacks, the Canadian diplomat Herbert Norman commits suicide by jumping off the roof of an apartment building in Cairo. McCarthyism adds a Canadian to its list of victims.

I drop by the office of the hospital chaplain. There's a nice, bland woman at a desk. I inform her that Patient Paul, Room So-and-so, Wing So-and-so, would probably appreciate the mock fortuitous easygoing visit of Charlie Chaplain. "Easy does it, baby," I feel like adding. "We don't want him reading The Watch Tower, eh?" But I just shut up. I only ask what his visiting hours are. To make damn sure that I never bump into him.

"I don't understand," says Paul. "I haven't had vitamins in over two weeks. Why not? They would be good for me. And why don't

431

I eat anymore? They should give me a drug that makes me hungry. It must exist. They should feed me, don't you think?"

Before I can answer, he falls asleep. Beside his bed is the latest meal he hasn't touched.

1958—Pasternak "voluntarily" declines his Nobel Prize. And is abused and harrassed by the Soviet government until his death two years later.

This disease that leaves you no respite, that eats, eats, eats away, that attacks your breathing and digestion and spinal cord and sullies your skin, that attacks you everywhere—but slowly, slowly, nothing quick, no sudden push into eternity—this slow, inhumane attrition—he's at the bottom of his bed, he can't control his pissing and shitting, he labours to breathe, he weighs seventy-one pounds and dropping, when you look at him you think of garbage spilt on the street—over-ripe fruit, smeared cheese, soiled paper, rotten meat—yet from amidst this putrefaction a quavering voice weakly clamours its humanity by calling out your name—this disease, it's enough, in the absence of anything holier, to make me want to piss on a crucifix.

"What's to be done? Another transfusion? He isn't strong enough. A perfusion to feed him? Why? What for? A few days, a few hours more? He can't even tolerate the least medicine anymore." So say the doctors.

Paul's arms are covered in band-aids, blue spots, black scabs, the legacies of tests, transfusions, perfusions. His skin is like a livid, translucent rainbow. Every shade of black, brown, blue, green, yellow. The rings around his eyes are enormous concentric circles. "Tell me, doctor," I feel like asking, "how does skin get green?"

1959—Swiss male voters defeat a constitutional amendment to allow women to vote in national elections and to run for national office.

I hope to start the new decade with a brighter story, but Paul is having troubles with his eyes. Cytomegaloviruses. Nothing to be done. He's overwhelmed by fear. He asks a nurse to strangle him. He's given nitrazepam; it's supposed to help against "acute anxiety."

"I want to get out of here, I hate it, I'm sick of being their guinea pig, I want to get out, I want to get out, I want to get out,

432

I want to get out, I want to get out, I want to get out, I want to get out, I want to get out—"

He repeats it twenty, thirty times.

I decide to scuttle the Roccamatios.

I am so stressed I think I'm going to explode. "You mean the boy has fever, diarrhea, pneumonia, Kaposi's Sarcoma, cytmegaloviruses, cryptococusses, looks like a carnival-coloured skeleton, has lost his hair and half his weight, is going blind AND YOU CAN'T DO SHIT!" I am having this imaginary conversation in my head with the doctors. "What the hell is all your science for? Do you know how much money we give you?" I leave the hospital trembling. "You're FRAUDS!" Outside I'm walking on a gravel path. The crunching sound annoys me so much I start pounding it with my feet and screaming at it. My legs begin to hurt. I run beside a red brick wall. My hands and fingers feel like hooks. I feel like doing something with them, tearing something, strangling something, I wave them in front of my face. I am aware of the sound of my shirt cuffs flapping against my wrists. My mouth is wide open, like for a scream but with no scream. I shake my head like I'm an ape. I scratch the ground, driving the hard black earth under my fingernails. I am trembling, I am on my knees, I am in a fetal position, I can feel the grit of the soil against my forehead and line of hair. I calm down. "Oh doctors, please do your best."

I head home crossing the suburbs of Toronto, of southern Ontario, those nightmare suburbs of comfort. In Paul's presence, close to death, I feel close to the jugular vein of life. So while I feel relieved when I leave him—it's like an escape from claustrophobia; a vital stretching; a dazed relaxing—I also feel depressed: I'm getting away from the edge of life, from the edge that makes life. Instead I penetrate an environment cluttered with objects, cluttered with hollow niceness, a stifling environment that fills me, like a nausea, with only one powerful feeling: a twenty-first century boredom. I head home, crossing the suburbs of Toronto, of southern Ontario. I think only of Paul and of the Roccamatios. I disrespect everything else.

I can't believe my eyes. There's a sign posted beside the door to Paul's room. "Mr Atsea's visitors are informed that Mr Atsea has gone blind. Could they please identify themselves as they

433

enter." It's even in bilingual. I can't believe my eyes. I go to the bathroom and lock myself in for twenty minutes.

When I go in, Paul is lying there, quietly, waiting for me. His eyes are open. They turn my way. I am terribly nervous. I can't get any words out. Finally I can and I can't help myself.

"F . . . f . . . f . . . fuck, Paul, you're going blind."

And for the first time ever, I cry right in front of him. Great, cracking, uncontrollable sobs.

Who am I to need comfort, but he comforts me.

"Shhh, shhhh, it's all"—pause—"right." I can hardly hear him. "Whose turn"—pause—"is it? What year are we?" Pause. "Is it my turn?"

Oh, fuck everything. I launch forth—it's like a flood. I hadn't even prepared anything—on a despairing story.

1961—Dag Hammarskjold is killed in an airplane crash over the Congo while on a U.N. mission. He was a solitary, remote man, perhaps lonely. He never married and had few intimates.

"Yes," is all Paul says. He's been receiving morphine shots every twelve hours.

Paul is in a wheelchair. It's his birthday today. He's going home, getting out of here. Bundled up in a sweater, scarf, gloves, blanket, toque and black sunglasses, only his nose and upper lip are visible. It's mid-September and the weather is very pleasant; I'm wearing a light jacket. With every jerk of the wheelchair he bounces like bones in a bag of skin.

Last thing I remember from the hospital: I'm walking down the corridor for the last time. In one room I glimpse a trinket on a beside table. A shiny pink porcelain hand holding a bright red heart. Why is so much about death in bad taste?

Paul is lucid. He is lying sideways in his bed at home. He's happy there, never wants to go back to the hospital. The room next door has been fixed up for the nurse who is there twenty-four hours a day.

"I'll do"—pause—"one more year," he whispers.

"We're in 1962."

"No." Pause. "You do that, I'll do"—pause—"another year."

"Which one? Do you want me to help you with the research?"

"No." Pause. "I'll do the year"—pause—"2001." Pause. "I liked"—pause—"the movie."

"So did I. Great movie. Stanley Kubrick."

"Yes." Pause. "Who's left?"

By which I gather that he means which of the Roccamatios are left.

"Ingrid."

"The grand"—pause—"mother?"

"Yes. And Susanna, her grandniece, the actress."

"Oh."

"And Lars, her five-year-old son."

But Paul has fallen asleep, or unconscious, I don't know which, and he doesn't hear about Lars. He slips in and out now.

1962—Marilyn Monroe commits suicide.

I enter his room to the strain of "With a Little Help from My Friends." Beatle Paul is curled up on his side. Beatle George, faithful to the last, is lying on the floor beside him.

"The year 2001?" I asked.

"Not yet."

What can I say? He falls asleep to "All You Need is Love."

I put a pad of paper and a pen beside his hand on the bed.

Today it's "A Day in the Life." But he's asleep.

Death has a smell. It permeates the house.

"Paul?"

"I'm still thinking."

Jack has just bought me a Ralph Lauren suit complete with shirts, ties, socks and shoes. He thinks I always dress like a beggar. His attitudes have changed a lot since the beginning of Paul's illness—he's taken a leave from his job; he mocks his more staid colleagues; he's working on a lengthy essay called "The Dynamics of the Battles of the War of 1812"—but he's still not exactly artsy fartsy granola bar. A few days ago I bought him a casual gift, Mishima's *Sea of Fertility* novels, secondhand, and he jumped at the opportunity of returning my kindness. He puts his arm around my shoulders and finds comfort in giving me some cornball father-son advice. Mercifully, he doesn't ask me what I intend to do with my future. I ask him a question about Egerton Ryerson.

"Paul?"

"Not"—pause—"yet."

I walk George H. I like walking dogs. It gives purpose to aimlessness. I can't stand it when people treat animals like human beings yet I irresistibly find myself conversing with this creature, brain the size of a lemon. He doesn't seem as bouncy as usual.

435

His tail is low and there's no enthusiasm to his sniffing. I think he may be losing weight. I take a stick, wave it in front of his face and throw it. He bounds after it and like any self-respecting ill-mannered dog he proceeds to chew the stick to pieces. He comes back with flakes of slobbered black bark hanging from his mouth. When we've returned home, I ask Mary if she doesn't think he's losing weight. We're in the kitchen, she has her back to me. She doesn't say anything. Then she turns around and fixes George H., who knows something is coming. She walks to a chair, sits down, grabs him by the ears and brings his head up to hers. She presses her dry, white nose against his wet, black one and stares into his bright, dumb eyes. "One sick person in this house is enough, George H." She points to his dish, which is brimming with canine-succulent food. "EAT!" she imperates. And George H. eats, half-heartedly it seems. I smile. I go down to the basement and cry.

"Please, Paul."

"I've"—pause—"got it." Pause. "But later." Sleep.

I've been wondering lately if I shouldn't write down all the Roccamatio stories. As they progress they tend towards the grim, but in high school I was taught that tragedy is cathartic.

"Being for the Benefit of Mr Kite." I just sit there, listening intently. The album starts over. Pulse: 200. Tension: 6–3. He's dying. He's sleeping.

George H. has taken to lying on the bed, right near him but carefully out of his way. He whines quietly. I notice Paul's lips and nostrils are slightly blue. I ask the nurse about it.

"Cyanosis. Which means a lack of oxygen in the blood."

"Which means PCP."

She looks at me. And nods.

Oh man. All this to end with the beginning. A cycle for nothing, for nothing except protracted agony.

I find something scribbled on the pad but I can't make anything of it.

He's too weak to move or speak. He just lies there, his eyes blinking once in a while. He's had his morphine three hours before.

"Paul?"

I kneel right beside him.

"Paul, it's me."

His eyes blink and his mouth trembles.

I don't know what to say. Since my eyes are level with it, I gently start to play with his ear. I rub the lobe between my thumb and forefinger. Then, I gently run my finger inside his ear. The tip of my finger is shiny.

"I'll be back in a second."

I come back with several Q-tips. I gently clean Paul's ear, first the outside, then inside where the wax is yellow and deep brown. Paul's mouth trembles into an approximation of a smile.

"Don't worry, Paul," I whisper deep into his ear. "Soon, soon."

His lips move to make a word. There is no breath to create it. He struggles.

"Two." It barely comes out.

Two. For 2001.

It will be in a few days, hours. Not long at any rate.

I'm never going to write down the Roccamatio stories, never.

For eight days I visit Paul every day. Sometimes he comes to—once Mary even found him sitting up—and he manages to speak, but never when I'm there. I ask in vague terms if he's said anything that was meant for me, but there's nothing.

It would have been 1963 for the Roccamatios. The year JFK was shot and people cried in the streets. The year I was born. Shortly before three in the morning George H. shattered the silence with a barking that was furious and incessant. Mary, who had fallen asleep in the sofa beside the bed, awoke instantly. The nurse, who had checked on him an hour before, and Jack and Jennifer were in the room not three seconds later. George H. was straddling Paul, his tail erect, every hair on his back standing up, his teeth bared and his mouth salivating, looking for the first time ever—and even more so in the profile of the night light—looking evil.

The news comes to me over the phone. Each word is banal in itself, but together they shock me breathless.

Someone touches my shoulder. I look up slowly. A nurse. The nurse. In her mid-fifties. She sits down beside me. A gentle voice.

"I'm sorry about your boyfriend."

I don't react.

"He came to around ten in the evening. We talked for a minute or two. He was thirsty. He asked me to write something down for him and give it to you. It wasn't very clear, you understand, but I think I got it right."

She hands me a folded piece of paper.

For some reason I'm amazed at her handwriting. Incredibly legible. Nice round clear letters. With the i's precisely dotted and the t's precisely crossed. I'm awed. Christ, if you compare it with my handwriting, so jagged and half-hysterical.

"Could you keep this a secret, please?" I ask her.

"Sure."

She stands up. She is looking down at me. There is a pause. Then, just like that, she runs her hand thru my hair.

"You poor boy," she says.

2001—After a reign of forty-nine years, Queen Elizabeth II dies. Her reign had witnessed a period of incredible industrial expansion and increasing material prosperity. In its own blinkered and delusional way, the Elizabethan age was the happiest of all.

Sorry, it's the best I can do. The story is yours.

                                                              Paul

Nominated by The Malahat Review

THERE ARE NO TIES AT FIRST BASE

by TED COHEN

from THE YALE REVIEW

Even if it is now an obsession with me, it did not begin as one. That was many years ago, early in June, the beginning of the summer, during a family picnic held to mark the end of the year's Sunday school. A softball game was under way, one with too many players even though sixteen-inch softball accommodates ten players on each team. We had more: there were a handful of adults and a dozen children on each team. My team was at bat; a small child was at the plate. I can't remember who the child was, not even whether it was a girl or a boy, but someone hit a slow roller toward the left side of the infield. The batter first hesitated, as children do at the plate, and then tackled the infinite distance to first base, running with a child's desperate, furious slowness, while an infielder triangulated carefully and came together with the ball. It was probably the third baseman, although I am not sure of that, and he heaved the ball to first, where it was caught on the bounce. The ball and the runner arrived together, and immediately every child on my team yelled "Safe" while every child on the fielding team yelled "Out." There arose that wonderful American polyphony: "Safe," "Out," "Safe," "Out," overlaid with "He didn't have control of the ball," "He turned the wrong way," "He never touched the base" (said by both teams), and the other initiatory chants of serious ball. Then an adult loped in from the outfield and with calm, good sense, and an

439

intention to soothe, spoke softly but firmly, commanding immediate quiet and attention. "It was a tie. Let's let him be safe."

It was a perfect remark. It was generous and also fair. It was paternal but not patronizing. It satisfied all the children: the batting team was given a runner at first, the fielding team was given respect.

But it was wrong. I alone knew it was wrong, and had anyone else known it, I would have been alone in feeling the necessity of saying so. "If it was a tie," I said, "then you don't have to *let* him be safe; he *was* safe."

The other adult turned his calm on me: "I know it's a convention in baseball that ties go to the runner." With that remark he put me with the children, I suppose, as if I were a perverse child and perhaps a bright one, but a child still. I had a brief thought of letting it go at that, but that thought faded like a weak throw from the outfield, and I became the kind of child/adult who is too much for a sensible man to handle. "It's not a *convention*," I said. "The rule says that the runner is safe unless the ball arrives before him. If the ball arrives at the same time, then it doesn't arrive before him, and so he is safe."

The other adult was silenced. The older children were in awe. I was trembling with a sense of moral triumph. I can remember nothing else from that game.

A few weeks later some men asked if I would help to organize a weekly softball game during the summer months for children and their parents. I have superintended that game ever since. The children are mostly boys and almost all the adults are men— fathers. I show up every Sunday morning from June through August or early September with my son. We bring a plate and bases and a one-hundred-foot measuring tape for laying out the infield. Everyone is grateful to me for maintaining this institution, but the children regard me with a steady ambivalence. On the one hand, I see that the game is played properly and I give good instruction to very young children who have yet to learn how to bat or field or throw the ball. On the other hand, I am insufferable. I control the tempo of the game, refusing to allow the children to dally on their way to the plate; I insist on sensible, attentive play in the field; and I compel a dedicated attention to the rules. On one occasion, a girl hit a ground ball that got through the infield. When the ball was retrieved, she was at second base and the second baseman was her father. He was play-fully tagging her with the ball and pretending to push her off the base while a runner at third sneaked home with an important run. I delivered a quick lecture on the need to bring the ball all the way into the infield, to be aware of all the base runners, and to attend to everything, and finally the second baseman-father said to me, "You're being obnoxious." All the children who play regularly know this about me, and especially my son knows it. But they sense that this goes with the order I give to the game. We play in a large athletic park that holds four ball fields along with other facilities, and many people wander by on Sunday mornings. Some children who live in the neighborhood often come by, and those who have played in our game once usually come back, choosing it over the more informal pickup games elsewhere in the park. They seem to like the structure I supply, the umpiring and the authoritative commentary on the rules, and I think they are entranced by my obtuse scholasticism.

After that initial overture, in which I assessed the value of a tie at first base, I was immediately aware that I must consult the rules. I had spoken with confidence but I was not really sure. I thought I must be right because, like everyone, I have absorbed an encyclopedia of sandlot lore, but unlike almost everyone, I have turned it over in my mind thoroughly enough to force it to make sense. For instance, I never believed that runners were to be called out for leaving the base paths. That doesn't make sense. They transgress only if they leave the path in order to avoid being tagged, or if they are being obstructive—which is altogether a different matter. If a runner is casually, whimsically running out-side the path, he is increasing the distance he must run. Why penalize him for that? So if a runner is to be called safe if he ties the ball, this cannot be a convention: it must be the rule. But I was not sure, and so I checked. There it was, and is: Rule 6.05(j):

> A batter is out when after a third strike or after he hits
> a fair ball, he or first base is tagged before he touches
> first base.

This rule does not say that the runner is safe unless the base is tagged first, but that is its import because the other rules do not

441

give any other reason for calling him out. So I was right. The tie goes to the runner because he has not been put out.

For months after I'd found Rule 6.05(j) I delighted in exhibiting my verbatim acquaintance with it. My delight increased as I discovered that no one but me actually knew the rule, really knew it. People began to solicit opinions and information from me. I would receive calls asking what happens if the pitcher falls dead during his windup or if the ball becomes stuck in the umpire's mask. I had to make clear that I was no authority on the history of baseball and knew little of its infinite tables of figures, and that I had no particular knowledge of the rules of other games; but I cultivated my position as authority on baseball's rules. In fact, I continued to peruse the rule book and became a genuine authority. And then I found Rule 7.08(e):

> Any runner is out when he fails to reach the next base
> before a fielder tags him or the base, after he has been
> forced to advance by reason of the batter becoming
> a runner.

This was stupefying. The anomaly seemed marvelous. For some time my son and I pondered this odd reversal. This rule says, for instance, that when a runner is at first base and the batter hits a grounder, the runner advancing to second will be out if he doesn't beat the ball to second base. And that means that if he ties the ball, he will be out. Why, we wondered, was this tie at second base being called against the runner, while the tie at first base was being called for him? My son produced a brilliant exegesis, speculating that the authors of the rules had attempted to compensate for the greater difficulty in calling force plays at second base. I was wondering whom to consult to learn whether my son was right, when I was struck by the hitherto seemingly trivial 6.09(a):

> The batter becomes a runner when he hits a fair ball.

My God. I saw at once that with 6.09(a) in the works, it was not merely an anomaly that had been uncovered but that 6.05(j) and 7.08(e) are inconsistent with one another. I cannot help putting it this way; I am a philosopher. These two rules together are contradictory. You see it, don't you? The rules in Section 6 concern the Batter. Section 7 is about the Runner. This had led me to believe that they could not ever be in conflict. But 6.09 tells us that under certain circumstances the batter *is* a runner, or has become one. This will happen if a batter hits an infield grounder, and if he then arrives at first base simultaneously with the throw, 6.05(j) says that he's safe, while 7.08(e) says that he's out.

My feelings were very strong, but they were ambivalent. I was deeply troubled by this logical rot in the Official Baseball Rules. I had become extremely fond of the rules. They have charm and, so I had thought, precision. They do not have logical elegance, but that is part of their charm. They have the appearance of having been written by journeymen lawyers. This is the kind of lawyer who has enough experience to be able to imagine most of the cases that his contract or statute will have to comprehend, but who does not have the analytical power necessary to divine a few simple principles that will do the trick, and so he enumerates the cases, one by one, seemingly as he thinks them up. There is a charm in that. The rules have the further charm of their turn-of-the-century idiom. For instance, Rule 5.03:

> The pitcher shall deliver the pitch to the batter who
> may elect to strike the ball, or who may not offer at it,
> as he chooses.

With all that charm, and with their natural appeal for my philosophical sensibility, the rules had won me over. Now I found them wanting at their core.

On the other hand, I anticipated the statutory immortality that would be due me. I would effect a change in the rules. It was unlikely that I would be given a footnote in the rule book itself, but I might well find myself in a Roger Angell essay, and I would certainly let my ball-playing friends know. I imagined myself apologizing to all those I had persuaded of the correct ruling when ties occur at first base, and then going on to inform them that I had seen to it that the rules were rectified.

As I planned how to proceed, I became bolder in announcing my discovery and even in predicting the change it was sure to bring. I told my friends, ballplayers I knew, and even students in my classes—especially students, who found me wonderfully eccentric, except for the few, always a few, who find me tedious and irrelevant.

I did not know what to do next until I thought to call a sportswriter at the city newspaper. It is from my wife, whose father was a newspaperman, that I learned this device. It is amazing what one can learn by calling people who work on newspapers. They know an immense amount, and they know how to find out an even greater immensity, and they genuinely enjoy imparting this knowledge. They are true professors, practical professors. The senior sportswriter whom I called seemed moderately interested in my claim, although I sensed that he did not find it easy to believe that the rules could be axiomatically defective, but he did tell me what I needed to know. He didn't have the address of the rules committee, but he did have the name and address of an executive in the office of the president of the National League. This man had formerly worked for a Chicago baseball team and was known personally to the sportswriter.

Now I knew whom to write, but I was not sure just how to compose my letter. I was on the verge of writing on my own stationery, when my wife made the first of two excellent suggestions. Guessing that the baseball people must receive reams of frivolous mail, she advised me to write on my university letterhead. That would add weight and, perhaps, command the brief attention necessary for my profound purpose to become evident. I worried about compromising my university and my philosophy department, but my wife saw the truth, that my case was proper and urgent, and indeed the university should be proud that another of its faculty was entering history.

Her second suggestion was that I write with no attempt at humor or irony, but that I just do the job.

I took both suggestions, and thus began my correspondence with baseball by way of the Administrator of The National League of Professional Baseball Clubs. As a matter of fact, I am an American League fan primarily, and it was the accident of my sportswriter's acquaintance that led me to the National League. No matter. Both leagues use the same rule book, and that book is seen to annually by the Official Playing Rules Committee. I was certain that I could persuade that committee of the need for re-

444

vision, and I even entertained lavish hopes of being invited to attend one of its meetings.

I wrote seriously and carefully, and with all the lucidity I could manage. Despite that, and despite the acuity of my point and the gravity of my letterhead, I feared that my letter would be consigned to the buckets of crank mail. But no: within a week I had a wonderful reply from the Administrator (from whose letterhead I have learned to call it "The National League of Professional Baseball Clubs"), thanking me for my letter and my interest in baseball, and telling me that I was the first to find this interpretation of the rules, and also informing me that both rules were meant to say that the runner is safe unless the ball beats him, but that because of my interpretation the rules committee would look into the matter at its winter meeting.

Now I was energized and, above all, truly hopeful. Before it had been a lark; now it was serious: a serious lark. In my excitement, I nearly reverted to professorial pedantry—which may be the best part of me anyway—and thought of writing back that it was not a matter of "interpretation," because the only significant term was the word *before* and its meaning was clear and unambiguous. But I restrained myself, realizing that it had been my wife's fine advice which had gotten me this far, and I drafted another sincere, unargumentative letter. I thanked the Administrator for taking me seriously, and added only that it might be of help to the rules committee to note that the current rules had been written as if either the runner beats the ball or the ball beats the runner. That is—although of course I did not write this in the letter—as though the runner beats the ball if and only if the ball does not beat the runner. (That might be put 'rBb iff— bBr', but that kind of flourish would be of scarcely more use to baseball than it is to philosophy.)

All those letters went through in the autumn of 1982. The following December, the time of the winter meeting of the rules committee, came and went and I heard nothing. Six months later, in June, well into the next baseball season, I finally wrote again, asking what had happened. The reply has left me dispirited and confused—permanently, I fear—for I can't think what to do next.

The umpires present at the rules committee meeting told the committee that in their opinion there never are any ties. Therefore, said the Administrator,

445

To set up a special rule, which in effect would allow for ties, we felt would be extremely confusing.

What am I to say to that? I have thought of many things, but none of them will do. I have thought of asking why such a rule would be confusing. Why not humor me and put in a rule which would cover these cases that never arise? If some biologist produced a scientific classification for unicorns, would that be confusing just because no one ever found a beast to apply it to?

Is it that a rule to cover ties would induce unwary umpires to look for ties when in fact there are none to find, and that would be a waste and a shame?

The heart of the matter, of course, is the business about there not being any ties. Why do umpires opine that there are no ties? When they seem to see one, what makes them sure that things are not as they seem? I have heard television and radio baseball announcers also declare that in truth there are no ties, saying this as if it were an arcane scientific fact known only to those who really know baseball, and these announcers are former players. But I really know baseball, and I don't know this fact.

I have toyed with the idea that we are dealing here with difficult matters of modern physics, but I have consulted a good friend who is a philosopher of relativity physics. He has explained that once we restrict attention to the context of special relativity, and take as a background standard the uniform motion of the playing field (and if we don't do that, imagine the problem of umpiring), it is perfectly possible for a foot to touch a base at the same time as a ball touches a glove. At about the same time, I learned a miracle of umpiring from another friend, a philosopher of cognitive psychology. When the umpire is making a close call, particularly at first base, he sometimes looks for the runner's foot to touch the base while he listens for the ball to arrive in the baseman's glove. This has always bothered some of us, because, after all, light travels much faster than sound, and this means, for instance, that in the case of a genuine tie, the umpire will see the runner arrive before he hears the ball. But my friend tells me that recent research has shown that the human brain processes its auditory stimuli much more rapidly than its visual stimuli, just enough so that the look-and-listen method gives very accurate results, and it does that because the distances are right. In football the distances are wrong if, for instance, you're trying to tell whether members of the punting team cross the line of scrimmage too soon while watching from fifty yards away and listening for the punt. It is no surprise that even nature contributes to the perfection of baseball.

I cannot write any of this to the Administrator or to the rules committee. They would take me for a crank. But I cannot rest. If anything in this world could be right, it is baseball; but baseball isn't right with its current rules. I cannot stand it.

I have been reminded, with pain, melancholy, and sweetness, of my personal discovery that I could never play baseball at a high level. This news came to me, as it does to many boys and young men, when I was a high school player. My daughter has complained bitterly that baseball cannot have this place in the lives of girls and young women: because women do not play professional baseball, although girls can learn the game, become significant fans, and even play, they cannot connect these themes with an ambition to play forever better. This saves them some pain, but it costs them the humanity it brings.

Had my daughter had the chance, perhaps the realization would have come to her as a high school player. It comes to some at an earlier age, and to others it doesn't come until later, in college or the minor leagues; but to many it comes, as it did to me, when one must try to bat against an impossible pitcher. Mine was a fastball pitcher, faster by far than any I had seen or imagined. And he was wild. The first pitch came right across the plate and was gone before I even thought to swing. I attempted to adjust, to accelerate my mind, my eyes, my arms—everything—and I did swing at the second pitch, but only when it was already in the hands of the catcher. Strike two. Now I wanted desperately just to be able to touch the ball with my bat, and I stood tense and rigid in the box. The third pitch was wild, coming right at my head, at least as I saw it, and I leaped backward in terror. That terror is still with me. It is permanent. And it was with me then, when I stepped up with the count one-and-two. It made no difference whatever where the pitcher might have thrown the next ball. I was backing away from the instant his arm came forward, and although I swung, I could not have reached the ball.

So I struck out, and I knew I would always strike out against that pitcher. And that was painful, but it was not the occasion for the metaphysical pain I recalled when I struck out with the rules committee. That pain came the second time I batted against the same pitcher, two or three innings later. That at-bat began with two quick strikes, both swinging, and with me flailing as I bailed backward out of the box. The third pitch, which I foresaw as the inevitable third strike, was another wild one. This time the ball sailed at least five feet over my head, and I swung. I did not swing involuntarily, nor was I enfeebled by fear. I did it on purpose, with calculation, and I immediately dashed for first base. I was safe by a mile. The ball had gone by well above the reach of the catcher and it nearly cleared the backstop. Had it done so, and gone on into the cornfield behind the diamond, I was ready to go on to second base. You know that if the catcher does not catch the third strike, and there is no one on base, and so on, the batter may run to first, and he will be safe there if he beats the catcher's throw (or, to put it properly, if the catcher's throw does not beat him). This catcher did not even make a throw.

I had never been as proud of myself athletically as I was in that moment, in which I had overcome the finest pitcher I knew. I could not do it by hitting, but I had done it by knowing the rules and thinking fast despite a nearly paralyzing fear. And then my soul was squeezed. By my teammates. They did not care for what I had done. I did not receive even grudging admiration. I barely got grudging acceptance. It was not that they found me unmanly, although perhaps they did do that. They regarded me as someone who did not really grasp the nature of the game. I thought that in knowing the rules I knew the game; they knew the game in some other way. It was this ache that reappeared when I heard the last word from The National League of Professional Baseball Clubs.

There have been two sequels, one cosmic and one personal. The cosmic one has to do with Chicago baseball. In an effort to add a slight light touch, I ended my first letter to baseball with this jest: "I am very fond of the rules of baseball (perhaps partly because we in Chicago have been driven to a somewhat academic interest in the game)," and that was during the 1982 season. In 1983 the White Sox won the Western Divison championship of the American League. The Cubs won the National League's Eastern Division championship in 1984, and did it again in 1989. The 1989 win was sweetly unexpected, humble and inspiring, truly cosmic in the way in which only gentle things can be cosmic, without the irrelevant distractions of sound, fury, and apocalypse. In the interim the Bears had one magnificent, terrorizing season, during which they won every game but one, an insignificant one, usually not only winning but winning easily, often giving up no points, and almost always hurting their opponents. Football does not engage me much, nor do its rules. It has some interest as a struggle to determine whether it will be a game of players or a game of rules, much like the epic struggle in modern states to decide whether they will be societies of men or societies of laws. And its racial features may be interesting. But I have found nothing in football approaching the metaphysics of baseball.

In all, Chicago sports swung up during the 1980s. My logic was offended, but my world improved.

The personal note is sad. My confidence in the order of our summer softball games has been shattered. My heart is no longer in it when I articulate and administer the rules, and that leaves me with nothing to dwell on but the rate at which the children in the game have overcome the strength and speed of us adults.

What good are the rules if no one knows them? What good is it to know the rules if no one believes you? And what if they believe you but just don't care?

Nominated by The Yale Review

A CALL FROM KOTZEBUE

fiction by BEN GROFF

from ALASKA QUARTERLY REVIEW

S HE WANTED TO know how it felt, the poor dead child. Now she knows.

She wanted to know what I thought about it, what my "reaction" was. There's no accounting for white people, they have the minds of children. You can't tell them the truth, but in an equally annoying sense, they won't let you lie to them, either. All you can do, I've decided, is tell them stories.

I told Mary this story, and she spoiled the ending by believing it. When it was finished, she still wasn't satisfied, but asked me again how it felt—to have cancer, and know you'll be dead sometime soon, how it feels to be dying. What could I say? I lost my temper. Who feels anything about the loss of the soul? Isn't that the one single thing that no one can feel? The hell with her questions, her and Raigili both. All I could think and all I could feel was that Aargun would have flensed her like a whale. He would have taken out his long, sharp knife, and made a few short answers—

No, he would not. He would have known she was a child. Even though she was a nurse and wore a nurse's pure white uniform, she was a nurse-child, as this doctor of mine is a doctor-child, and Aargun would have accepted that and have smothered his rage beneath an unhumiliated smile, and shaken his head wordlessly. That's the difference, unfortunately, between him and me. They'd have thought he was stupid, just like they think I'm crazy. Now she's dead, and it could be I killed her, which I have to admit

450

would throw a whole new light on everything. Killed her at a distance, even without the stones, like the shamans used to. Killed her with my thoughts, God forgive me, though I don't believe one syllable of all that crap—shamans, or God, or forgiveness, none of it. It's just words. But a ripped-out jugular isn't, and that's how she died—thrown eighty feet down the hill by a runaway car at the crosswalk right down here in front of the hospital, and all they could find were five raking gashes in a line from her right ear down to her collarbone. The Old Man always strikes with his left hand, the Inupiat tell you. Never say you never feared the grizzly, Mary child, it's bad luck. It's worth your life. And maybe it's not too late to start believing my own stories.

My name is Margaret Leithorn. I come from Fairbanks, Alaska, and to set the record straight right at the start, I am a white woman just like Mary. I was born in Portland seventy-six years ago, married a younger man who was a carpenter, and went cheechako with him in '38. Alaskan ever since, which is close to forty years. They don't come much more seasoned, and the seasoning is salt, not cilantro. I have been a housewife, a journalist, a free-lance writer, an explorer by God and a self-taught authority on the Eskimos of the Brooks Range. I am sitting now, not smoking, for the bastards don't allow it, on a bed in a room in a hospital in Seattle, in December, which is Aageluuleraavik, the Month of the Shining of the Morning and the Evening Star, with rain streaming down the windows in long gray sheets, and the only star visible this neon job on the roof of the main department store downtown. Now they tell me that I'm dying, and I'm going to tell you a little secret: I don't believe it.

I don't believe, I fear.

The Eskimos had that saying, in the old days, before they were all Quakers or Anglicans. It's a good saying. There is plenty to fear and not much to believe for anyone who knows how close the heart lies to the edge of life. There is darkness, and leaping ice, and great brown bears, and that is only the beginning. And I have no intention of telling you how it feels.

Marvin didn't want me to go. He said your place is here with me. He said that a lot but it didn't cut much ice where I live after how he did me, that time he threw his second heart attack and they flew him down to Seattle to the hospital. Sure, I'd

451

forgiven him, or whatever you want to call it, for his trespasses with that CCU nurse who'd saved him from dying when dying was his due, I'd taken him back because after all I was past my time and no children and somehow it just didn't mean that much to me. A woman thinks about it always, an older woman especially, what you would do if your husband puts you down, how you would feel when he wakes up one morning, convalescing, taking life easy, smoking again, happy to be alive, flexing his tattoos, and tells you over his second cup of coffee there was this nurse down in Seattle, and her and me, and she had soft pink skin and golden hair. I mean you think about it. But when it was over, and he told me, and he told me it was over, the thing that bothered me most was how little I cared, one way or the other, and I think he noticed. I think he filed that item away in his memory-box and pulled it out when I told him about the Noatak assignment, and he said no. He said no, but I said yes. I didn't even remind him of that nurse he'd seen in Seattle on his two visits back to the doctor after his surgery. It had never been like I'd wanted something from him in return. It wouldn't have been worth it. I couldn't exactly hold his hand to the fire where there was only the glint of sundown on a frozen ditch, and that's all there was. But from the moment I'd tried to care and couldn't, I'd wanted something—not so much from him as from myself. So I just told Marvin how he could reach me in Noatak. He never did.

This was for the Fairbanks Daily News-Miner, with whom I'd been employed for eight and a half years at that time. I'd never been to college but you didn't need that in those days and at that latitude, I was quick and I was Alaska and I guess I had a way of putting things. I'd always kept the bills and written my husband's advertisements, and I guess I put some life into them, and then they asked me to handle the union newsletter, and I put some life into that, and when I got to wanting a little money of my own I went to the newspaper and they took me on no questions asked. They set me to covering the Woman's Club and I got some Births and Deaths, and I guess I even put some life into the deaths because they set me to covering visiting dignitaries and local color and human interest, which was mostly all the paper at that time. I had a style. At the start they tried to tell me not to say "I" when I meant myself, for example I'd write in an obit "I used to know so-and-so to drink deeply but never to excess," and they'd

452

circle that word and scribble in the margin "1st person," as if I didn't know. I told them who the hell did they think wrote the story? Whose name was under the headline? First person *singular*, I said, I wasn't ignorant. They smiled at me, but when the mail came in they found the readers loved it, and of course they did. I was talking to *them*, I was. So the editor let me go but it was a big joke around the office, and when they finally gave me my own column they called it "First Person Singular." Everybody knew it was just plain Maggie Leithorn.

This Noatak thing was my own idea. In case you never heard of it, and most people down here haven't except for a few fat kabluna fishermen, one of whom sports a gill where his nostril should be, courtesy of yours truly, but that's another story—in case you never heard of it, Noatak is an Eskimo village on the Noatak River, which flows west out of the western Brooks Range through the palm of God's right hand into Kotzebue Sound. I'd done some pieces on some of the natives in Fairbanks, some of the tradesmen and some of the craftspeople and some of their festivals, and I couldn't help but notice the way they looked at you. Always polite and humble, always cooperative, eager to please, but amused inside like they knew something you'd never know, and it was secret, and it was shattering, and they didn't have to worry about how impolite it would be to refuse to tell you about it, because you were white, and would never in a hundred years of interviews even come close to the question. That's when I started to think maybe I was different. Maybe I was only part white, maybe my mother lay down in her Portland pantry with a Negro milkman to celebrate the first day of the new century. She was wild like me, but anyway that misses the point. It wouldn't have made any difference to the Inupiat if she had, because they know it goes deeper than color and call Negroes black white people. It goes down to something I was attuned to in the way even these young town Eskimos I was interviewing conducted their daily lives and imagined themselves vis-à-vis the whole shebang, something singular, yes, about me. Something in the way I saved my dry Communion bread at the Methodist Church till they'd passed around the little cup of grape juice, and dipped the one into the other and sucked the sour juice out of the bread-cube like a sponge, and this the 1950s, for God's sake, and me right up there in the choir, front and center. Something about how I

453

ribboned my ceilings with flypaper and scattered citronella candles three and four to a room through the buggy season, but never bothered having Marvin screen the windows, because it seemed like too much trouble, and Marvin didn't seem to feel like it, and the flypapers and citronella seemed to be working okay. Something in the way I drank, which was not normal for a white woman even in Alaska, which burns my hide even now to write about it. I mean it was all right for the entire Woman's Club to repair to a lounge and slosh four mixers every evening so they could stand to have their husbands or somebody else's lie on top of them, but me, I didn't take a drop for months at a time, and then for some reason, because of a smell in the air, or a look from Marvin, or maybe no reason at all, I'd get the taste, and I wouldn't quit for seven days straight, until I couldn't hoist a bottle or climb up off the floor to reach the bathroom. Marvin locked me in at times like that but he was smarter than to try and stop me, and naturally they all knew about it. They said Maggie drinks like a stinking Eskimo, and there was supposed to be something wrong with that, and they snickered and said poor Marvin married him a squaw, except this squaw never minded cussing people to their faces who were cussing me behind my back, which is not exactly what you'd call the Eskimo way, which is what I'm talking about. They hold their peace. Maggie Leithorn did not. Still and all, I saw things through their eyes, I had that power.

An Eskimo, see, might pitch his family's tent on the very edge of a river in the springtime when the ice is broken, to be close to the running pike. This is in the old days. When the water rises to the door of the tent, they all tear it down and move it, lock, stock, and barrel—two feet higher up the bank. Because it's a big tent and is full of their worldly belongings, this takes them most of the day, and two days later, because the water keeps rising, they do it again, and again, and again. But it never occurs to them simply to put the tent once and for all on the bluff a hundred yards from the river. A white person says it's because they're stupid. But ever since I heard that story from Jean-Baptiste Kelley I knew the reason, and it made perfect sense to me. For one thing, they *want* to be two feet from the river. The roar of the black water with the big pike dancing in it makes them a lot happier than the empty whine of the wind at the top

454

of the bank, and they only wish they were walruses, and could pitch their tent right smack in the middle of the waves. Maybe they make up a song to that effect. But there's something more, and it goes even deeper, and is the real and true reason they keep moving the tent: They enjoy moving it. And to that, there is no reason. If you don't understand, you'll never make an Eskimo, and I understood.

J.-B. Kelley was a half-Eskimo carpenter in Fairbanks, an employee of Marvin's, illegitimate son of an old Canuck trader in Kotzebue and one of the first I interviewed and wrote up for the paper. He was kind of a success story in those days, only 32 and had actually bought a house and was bringing all his family to live in it. Somebody shot him in a drunken argument not long after, but the thing I'll always remember about him was this pendant round his neck, which I asked if I could look at. He got embarrassed, but was not about to refuse a direct request from the boss's wife. He lifted it out from the V of his Pendleton shirt and held it there in his own fingers, away from mine. The light in the room was not that good and it just looked like an old stone, sort of a river pebble, brown and oval. I had to lean closer to see it, and J.-B. sort of tensed away as I did, so that the stone was still in shadows as I peered at it. What I saw, though, was a tiny human face carved on the stone, and I nearly fell down where I stood.

It was a face like you'd see in a nightmare, like you'd see in the deepest ward of a mental hospital sticking out from a strait-jacket that had its arms tightly buckled around the back—a face that looked like it had been screaming ever since it was born, like whatever it was screaming about had long since been forgotten and now it was just screaming and could never stop, which was why it had started screaming in the first place. I saw that scream split open in front of me and fell right through it and kept on falling, until J.-B. got worried and tucked it back in his shirt. He led me to a chair and said pretty scary, huh? But none of this went into my article, which was way behind deadline anyway because I didn't stop drinking for a week and a half, by which time I had almost succeeded in erasing the face from my memory. I didn't entirely, though, because before I had left him I'd managed to ask J.-B. where he'd gotten it, and he'd looked sheepish and said from some old folks. I asked what it meant, what it signified, what for the love of God the thing was *for*, and he got that old amused and secret look on his face and said it didn't mean nothing, that it came down from the old times when the people were confused and hadn't clearly heard the voice of Jesus. I asked him why he wore it, and he wouldn't answer, but passed me another cup of tea. I asked him where those old folks lived, and he said, Noatak.

Mary was there when the doctor came in that morning and told me what they'd found. He said that the tumor in my lung had spread to my brain and there wasn't any use in operating. He said chemotherapy might give me a few more months, with toxic effects. I didn't have much to say—who would?—but that poor kid looked like she wanted to bust out crying. There was something about her that got to me even then, though she seemed like a decent sort. The doctor told me he was sorry, and frowned at me as he left. Then right away Mary wanted to talk.

She told me *she* was sorry. I told her all was forgiven, which went right over her pretty blonde head, and she asked me what my reaction was. I said to what? She said, well, to dying. I said I'm not dead yet, honey. She put her hand on my arm and I guess she felt me go stiff because she took it away again. She said it's too soon to talk about it. Then she brightened and looked around, meaning to change the subject, and said, what are these?

I said, they're three pieces of jasper. She said, what is jasper? I said sort of a reddish-brown rock. She smiled and said I can see that, but what are they for? Are they a keepsake, or a good- luck charm, or are you some kind of fossil collector? She was laughing as if it were all a big joke, so I said all of the above. She said fossils? I said look a little closer. She put her head down to them where they sat on the bedside table, then she went very pale and quickly sat up again. She said, they have faces, and she wasn't smiling any more. I said, indeed they do. She said why do you have these things? I told her somebody gave them to me. She said who gave them to you, the cheeky pup. And I don't know why, it would have saved me a whole lot of breath if I hadn't, but I told her, Raigili.

A friend, an Eskimo, she said. You're from Fairbanks, of course. Are you—Eskimo yourself? Not that I know of, I told her. Then she asked me again, what are they for? and something in

456

the way she said it made me think she was a person like myself, and I felt sad to think how long it had been since I'd felt like that, and for that reason alone I told her everything.

I told her I didn't know much about necessity but if you're talking about today it is necessary that some will live and some will die and if you're talking about tomorrow and tomorrow and tomorrow, well, she knew what was necessary as well as I did. It was necessary that Aargun leave his ailing mother in a stand of cottonwoods where Tunarak Creek flows into the Noatak at the third bend upstream from the red-banded bluff, or else they all would have died. It was necessary each year for Aargun to go east from Noatak to revisit that spot, and that one year he should die there at the claws of a bear whom he passed on its left, as old lore says you mustn't. It was necessary that Raigili shoot that bear there and then to come into its power, wrap her husband in its skin, and bring him back to life. Apparently it was also necessary that there be three pieces of jasper—not bile rock, but hard, red jasper—in the gall-bag of that bear, that those stones should issue from the bear imprinted with the screams of three demented faces suggesting what archaeologists call the Dorset period, and finally that they should come, over time, into the possession of an old white woman from Fairbanks, who will not know what to do with them. As the good book says, she will ponder these things in her heart.

Mary was amazed and had a thousand questions, not all immediately, because you know how nurses are, they come and they go, always busy. But she wanted to hear everything, and over the next few days it came out between us, how I was introduced to Raigili and Aargun, her husband, on that very first trip to Noatak for the Fairbanks Daily News-Miner. When I got off the small plane from Kotzebue I went up to the cluster of nut-brown faces standing in the mud and made it clear in my straightforward fashion that I wanted something colorful, wanted to talk with someone in touch with the old times, and they nodded politely and took me to Raigili. She lived at that time in a rough plank house near the back of the village, which was a streetless collection of similar huts set at random angles to each other on a terrace above the river, with a Friends church, a trading post, a school, and a National Guard armory. The inside of her house looked the same as all the others that I saw, dark unless the door was open or the

457

seal-oil lamp was burning, furnished with a wooden table and bed around an iron wood-burning stove from which seemed to emanate the smell of old grease and sweat and urine. Over time, as I returned to Noatak yearly, flying in like the geese or by water like the salmon, I learned to see what was different about Raigili's house. One thing that didn't hit me for a long time was that the house wasn't square, but roughly six-sided, for no reason that I ever discovered, and standing against the walls among rusted coffee cans and empty tubs of margarine and ripsaws and blackened pots and big steel traps was a drum made of sealskin and bearclaws. On the bed was the skin of a silvery-brown bear, smelling musty and strong. Under the bed, covered with dust, was a portable record player, and dangling from the middle of the roof, right over the bed, was an insulated cable ending in an ungrounded socket. Finally, hardest to see, nailed to the wall over the doorway, next to a small postcard Jesus, was a sack of some kind, weighted and dangling like a scrotum, which, I found out much later, was exactly what it was.

But all this was for the future. For now, all I could see was a small wrinkled woman standing in that doorway, framed by two clumps of poison iris and surrounded by a pack of leaping sleddogs, with her grey hair loosely pulled back over horn-rimmed glasses. She took a piece of gum from her mouth and stuck it on her forehead for safekeeping. So softly I could hardly hear her over the yapping of the dogs, she said, you have come.

I didn't know what to make of that, except that indeed I had come, and for the first time in my life I felt like I had come to the right place for the right reasons. She called me by name— Maggi was how she pronounced it, with a round Inupiat "a"—and invited me in. The fact that she knew my name was a little disturbing, since no one had introduced us, and I hadn't done anything as organized as writing ahead. But I learned that her husband had been in Kotzebue doing construction work with their grown children when I laid-over there on my flight in, and he might have heard of me, and had time to send word home with one of the boatloads of Noataqmiut shuttling back and forth after the spring breakup. Either that or she had picked up my name via Jean-Baptiste Kelley, but she denied both, and I observed over the years that Raigili had an attachment to what whites call "the truth" which is unusual in an Eskimo. Ordinarily they see this truth as a harmful fetish, somewhat bizarre, and hold talk of their own emotions, or worse, yours, to be highly distasteful. But Raigili (she insisted on being called by her birth name, and everyone did, though her real name was Martha) was the only Eskimo I ever met who seemed to go out of her way to offend you with her honesty, to startle you with what she considered the truth, in which she resembled what white people call a prophet or philosopher, two concepts that do not exist in the Inupiat tongue because they involve human beings using words to set them apart. The nearest thing was the work of the old-time shamans, whose power was precisely the power to hurt other people with words if he or she saw fit, though the "truth" of the words, as near as I can tell, had nothing at all to do with it. But here again Raigili was one of a kind, because while the average Eskimo went as mute as a fish when the subject of shamanism was even hinted at, or assured you he wouldn't know the first thing about it since the last of the shamans had died old and poor in his grandmother's prime and all Eskimos were good Eskimos now that the word of Jesus Christ had freed them from ignorance and darkness, and made you feel like a racist for so much as besmirching his tidy little Methodism or Quakerhood with the memory of pre-Christian traumas, Raigili said straight out, and it was the first thing she said after my name, which no one had told her—she said *I am angatquq. That's why you are here.*

Well, no it wasn't. Fact is, the more she talked, then and on all the lengthening days of that first visit, about what she called her turning backward, her digging into the half-remembered mysteries of her people, her growing conviction that here lay her calling and the greatness of the Inupiat, the clearer it became to me that thanks anyway, but none of this was copy for the Fairbanks Daily News-Miner, bless its timid heart, not even under the colorful rubric of First Person Singular. What could I make of a middle-aged Eskimo woman who'd returned from her second stint in the state mental institution to the house where she lived with her husband and her old mother-in-law in the village of her birth, to find a younger woman wearing green galoshes in her bed, and commenced all over again to see great bestial shapes in the rolling fog who called her by name, not her Christian name but the melodious one her parents had called her in secret? Who shrieked at her husband until he tore her clothes and threatened

459

to send her back to the kabluna nuthouse? Who stabbed herself with knives in public places, Noatak village being nothing but public places, till her husband grew ashamed, and let her stay, provided she would stay inside? My audience of plumbers and plumbers' wives was not quite ready for this. Margaret Leithorn was not quite ready for this, but there I was, I had nowhere else to go. The villagers who had deposited me with this gum-chewing little Cassandra showed no inclination to rescue me and pretended to forget that I existed, while Raigili took it for granted that I was her guest with a capital C as in captive and brooded dangerously whenever I talked about leaving. My tea isn't good enough for you, she'd say, or you're horny, you wish that my husband was here. This made my mouth drop open because actually Aargun, as she called him, though the rest of the world knew him as Ralph, was due home any day from his construction job in Kotzebue for the annual hunting trip up-river, and I dreaded this prospect for all the reasons you might expect a lone white woman to dread it, although wanton rape, especially of kabluna females past their prime, was hardly in the Eskimo character, as even at that time I was well aware. But old notions die hard, and I would find that Aargun was as different in his way from the myths of "Eskimo character" as his wife was.

While Raigili had succeeded in persuading her husband not to send her away again, he hadn't exactly agreed to evict Sally Morgan, the well-heeled teenager from Kivalina he'd brought home with him during his wife's second sabbatical. His magnanimity extended only to keeping the both of them under one roof, which was not yet then so unheard-of a situation, especially for a good provider like he was, a talented janitor and hunter of seal and caribou, and handy as a wage-earner with hammer and saw to boot. It didn't sit pretty with the educational authorities, however, when several of the parents of the local scholars complained that the school's custodian was living in adultery like an old-fashioned umealik. But the school's white principal was fond of Ralph, as much for his jokes as the way he kept the school's generator running, so he shielded Ralph until he himself was recalled over the matter, which was probably his strategy. Even then, in leaving, he left his old Sears phonograph to the unregenerate sinner along with a collection of opera recordings and permission for Ralph to run a wire exclusively from the school,

460

which was the only building with electricity at that time, to his cabin, to empower the apocalyptic voices that rose off of them, so much like his wife's in their madness and vision. The similarity made a great impression on him and you might say effected his conversion to her way of thinking. While she got used to the idea of Sally Morgan, he started listening as hard to her as he did to his wonderful records, in the long winter hours of his unemployment, as the seal oil burned off the moss in the low stone bowl and it was just the three of them, plus mother, plus the voices he called his weeping music.

The rest of the village, hearing the weird mixture of sounds human and mechanical that issued from Ralph and Martha's and not being prepared to make any sense of them whatsoever, wrote the pair of them off as possessed (by properly Christian devils, of course) and the following summer, in the month when the geese can't fly, when Ralph left his mother to die at a bend of the river many days' journey upstream in the lap of the mountains where the water does not run fast, they knew he had finally left the pale along with his lunatic wife and taken that young girl with him. He defended himself to the native pastor when he returned, saying the old woman had expressed a wish to die in that very spot, which featured a stand of spruce along the watercourse and off to one side some cottonwoods, fragrant and light, sheltering a swale of arctic poppies whose yellow blooms had not yet fallen owing to the dryness of the season. He emphasized her age and her infirmity, pointing out that sudden pains in her chest had made it impossible to travel since the river was low and his boat was heavy and they'd had to line it a good ways already and she couldn't walk farther. Also it was unusually cold as well as dry and the ice was already coming to the shallow water. He added for good measure that despite the cold or perhaps because of it the spot was pleasantly free from mosquitoes, but his pastor waved at him as if he were a mosquito himself and simply said he shouldn't have taken his mother upstream in the first place. Ralph shrugged and said that he always had. He said she had no protectors in the village any more and as far as he knew she had wanted to go, though naturally they'd exchanged no words on the subject, and then Ralph would say no more because he saw they were against him.

461

She may have been infirm, said the pastor. She may even have been dying, as you say, but she was alive when you left her. That is a sin. She died alone and her mortal remains were thrown to the mercy of the beasts. Can you even say that it wasn't a beast that killed her? Can you say that you aren't that beast? The pastor went on in this way until Ralph felt so bad that he got up a Christian burial in absentia, with rocks to weight the coffin, but they hadn't enough of them, and in the spring, the frost had heaved the empty box up so it stood with its head half out of the soil, accusing them. From that time on, Ralph and Martha and Sally Morgan, or Aargun and Raigili and Kiva, as they began to call each other, were isolated in the village. They moved their hut to the outskirts near the airstrip. In the fledging time, as soon after break-up as possible, they headed up-river again, just the two of them now, because Kiva had come down with an ailment that wasted her flesh and afflicted her mind with darkness. I suspect also that the truce with Raigili, who remained subject to sudden fits and hallucinations, was getting on her nerves, though Raigili had mostly kept her own counsel through the dark months, chewing gum and meditating and listening to opera, visiting if at all only with the oldest crones of the village, who were unaware of how things stood with her soul and invited her in for tea because they themselves were lonely or they took pity on her. She asked many questions about the old times and they in their innocence did their best to answer, searching their memories, chewing the gum she gave them. She chewed gum in silence, too, when Aargun finally gunned the little motor that sliced their boat out into the chop of a chilly June breeze, and for days they hardly spoke, which is the Eskimo way.

They fished their way upstream, shooting waterfowl in the mornings, and after many days they came to the mouth of Tunarak Creek. The place was unchanged. The cottonwoods were in leaf and according to his mother's last instructions Aargun filled a small bowl with cottonwood greens and ate them and dried some of the sticky buds over a fire and ground them and smoked them in his pipe. The oils snapped and bubbled with perfume until Aargun began to see her spirit again, though no trace of her body remained. It had disappeared, no doubt, even as the pastor said, into the belly of some bear, perhaps the same one who walked into camp that evening, attracted by the smell of

462

spitted grayling, and charged straight at Aargun, who dodged too late and caught the bear's left paw on his right neck and shoulder, flying thirty feet through the air. Raigili, who had foreseen this, was waiting with the gun. One shot laid the bear down dead.

She asked the bear for strength and for understanding and the bear gave her his skin, wet and bloody, which she dragged to where Aargun lay crumpled on the riverbank. She told me his heart was still, and his blood had turned the Noatak bright red. She rolled him up in the bearskin and sang songs over him all that night, those she herself had made in her own tongue as well as others that had been given to her, including "Perche tarda la luna" from *Turandot*, whose meaning she felt she understood, as she put it, through the veil of language. By morning he was able to sit up and eat, which was the moment she knew that the bear's *angatquq* had become her own, the ancient power to heal or to refrain from healing, to steal another's soul, or to lock it in bone when it wanted to fly away. These were her words. She nursed her husband for several days, feeding him bear meat that she herself had chewed, and before they left Aargun had her cut out its gallbladder, which as an aphrodisiac and general elixir vitae would fetch a hundred dollars at the Chinese restaurant in Kotzebue. The bag came out heavy and hard in her gore-soaked hands and spilled the stones like dice when she sliced it open. She was not surprised by the faces she found on the stones. She washed them in the river, which rose and lifted their boat, drifting them west toward Noatak. She thanked the bear as the cottonwoods passed round the bend.

I didn't know what to make of it, then or now. As I told all this to Mary here in my hospital room in Seattle I felt again as I'd felt years before when Raigili told it to me in her hut in an Eskimo village that still seems more real in my mind than any of this plastic and formica or towers of steel seen through plate-glass windows streaming with winter rain. I'd felt like crying, like running, like pouring mocking laughter in her face, anything but sitting still and listening, waiting for her husband to come home, and stifling the question that grew bigger inside me every day. But Mary didn't laugh or cry or run, but asked straight out: Did you believe her? I felt again a kind of fury well up inside me at her terrible simplicity and wanted to strike at her, but instead I ignored what she had asked and went on to tell of the death of the ailing Kiva, who was buried in her green rubber footwear not long after Raigili and Aargun got home, and despite Kiva's death I spoke of Raigili, as everyone in Noatak came to speak of her, as a healer. Again Mary asked, without a thought: Did she ever heal anyone? I said that her power, if you wanted to call it that, tapped deep into the history of her people, that that was its source and its current, and if you're talking about healing maybe there was more biology between the ears than men in white coats have ever dreamt upon, and maybe it was not strictly necessary to cut and burn and poison in order to heal, if you could only get inside the sickness and move with it, kind of loosen things up. These were Raigili's phrases, not my own, which made me feel like I was pretending, but I don't think Mary noticed, because she nodded her head solemnly when I told her the stories of people Raigili had healed using the stones, people in Noatak or Sisualik or Kiana, people with fevers and wounds and ailments of various sorts, some from as far away as Kobuk who would come to see her in Kotzebue, and two people I myself had met who'd been in and out of asylums just like Raigili and who worshipped the ground she walked on because she had touched them and sung over them and rolled the stones in their hands, and made them whole again.

Mary was deeply impressed with this, I could tell, which for some reason made me as angry as her questioning. I tried to ignore the fact that I was starting to hate her. And because I could see what she was thinking I tried to ignore that these same three stones sat between us now on my bedside table, carved with faces from the asylum of the everlasting. But she with her hateful questions wouldn't allow it. She touched my arm and asked, are you a healer too?

I straightened my back which is usually bent nowadays from sitting on the edge of a hard bed without a cigarette, and told her I don't know much about healing. Five years these stones have been in my possession, I said, and I've never healed anyone, never attempted to heal anyone, and would dream least of all of attempting to heal myself.

She said heal yourself? Who mentioned healing yourself? She was smiling like she had me in a corner. I said you did, damn you, don't twist my words around. She put her arm around my shoulders. You did, Margaret, you, yourself, she said, and if

464

that's what you want, maybe you ought to try it. She looked at the stones. I pushed her arm off me and said maybe *you'd* like to try it. Try what that doc can't do, keep Maggie alive. But since you like questions so much, here's a question for you: Why? She blushed, and said I'm sorry, and my anger burst. You want them? I said. I felt the water rising inside me and knew the time had come to move my tent. I knew I would enjoy it. She backed away but I picked up the stones and threw them at her, hard. They hit and fell to the floor. You want them? I said again. They're yours.

She got down on her knees and fetched them from under the bed, where they had rolled. She kneeled in front of me and held them like they were precious.

I said, and it's Mrs. Leithorn, to you.

Guilt is a beaten thing, but sorrow is fierce. The feeling of sorrow is something the earth yields lavishly, but we've turned our backs on it. Nowadays we're only sorry, sorry for this, sorry for that, sorry it snowed last night and I missed your plane, sorry your husband lost his job, sorry, lady, but you just bought the farm. Me, I don't even feel sorry for my own death, much less for Mary's. I've never felt sorry for a single act in my life, not for what I did with Aargun, not even when I got home late to Fairbanks from that first summer in Noatak, summer having stretched out into fall, four months since I'd left, and found Marvin lying on the living room floor, his face smashed into the carpet, which was none too cushy. The breeze that blew through the unscreened windows had cleared the smell of citronella from the house, though the candles were freshly guttered. This told me it had not been all that long, just long enough for the mosquitoes to give up on him. I imagine the prospect of my homecoming made him nervous, not to say thrilled with anticipation, and that was enough right there to flood his carburetor. The coroner asked me if I had any questions. No questions, I said, all my questions have been answered.

I didn't feel much like drinking. My first inclination was to run back to Noatak. The way I pictured it, we'd sit smoking in the smoky hut as the ice skinned the river, and Aargun would pace around chanting "Avant de quitter ces lieux" from Gounod's *Faust*, and Raigili and I would laugh through our gum at my efforts to make a burnable wick of moss. We would eat whitefish

465

and caribou, and salmonberries with sugar and seal oil, and now and then I would treat for a can of peas or carrots from the store, and in a month or two Raigili and I would jig for trout through the ice while Aargun was gone hunting. This time I wouldn't dread his return, as I had that summer. We would know he was coming before we ever heard him and we'd go out into the snowy twilight and help him unharness the dogs. A goose, he'd announce sadly, that's all I could catch, a poor crippled goose who because of his heavy hooves and spreading antlers could not fly. Then he'd clap his mittens together with a grin and say Brrr! Cold! and we'd bring him tea, and chop the frozen moose-quarters up into chunks, and hand them around. Soon his frosty clothing would steam up the hut like a sauna. Pinkerton! he would laugh, spreading his arms theatrically, the returning hero, and Raigili and I would sing "Un bel di vedremo" a la Maria Callas, and I would read to them again from the stories on the backs of the record jackets, Butterfly, Parsifal, Rosenkavalier, as they listened like children.

That's what I wanted, with Marvin in the ground, or rather not in the ground but encrypted till the ground unfroze enough to bury him. But I still had my job, which I now needed more than ever, and besides, I knew in my heart that Maggie was not another Kiva, and was never meant to be. Winter would never find me in Noatak, although that grey village became heart's home to me. It was a summer home only, and winter became my exile. That first winter alone I did my work and paid my bills and read every book I could find about the North Alaskan Eskimo, Nansen and Stefansson and Rasmussen, Boas and Spencer. I practiced my Inupiat and read about sealing and hunting the whale, wife exchange and magic songs, how umiaks were built, what the Messenger Feast meant and why there were shamans and so-called arctic hysteria. Speaking of which, that was also the winter that Jean-Baptiste Kelley was shot dead, by a former co-worker who felt like J.-B. had taken over more than his fair share of Marvin's business. It was a white man who did it, as I had reason to know, and told the Fairbanks Police when they came for my deposition, but that man (whom I will not name) was never indicted. At J.-B.'s funeral at the Chapel of Chimes I sat on his family's side, behind his wife and mother, who were off in another world. I was surprised when they'd asked me to be one of the pallbearers—

I'm not that big, and hadn't known the family all that well. The coffin was huge and gleaming and mounded with hothouse flowers and I leaned over in the pew and whispered to the strapping Eskimo lad from Kotzebue who sat beside me, Looks heavy. He raised his eyebrows because I'd said it in Inupiat, but without taking his eyes off the coffin he whispered back, in English, You'd be surprised, they make most of them out of fiberglass these days. There was an old Methodist minister, my old minister, who went on in an angry voice for a long time about heaven and how our hearts may fail us but God is our strength forever. He said it so many times that he got it twisted around and started to shout, Our farts may hail us, but he saved himself just in time. I made a mental note to tell that one to Aargun, who would appreciate it, as they played a wobbly recording of some guy singing "Rock of Ages." Then we carried the coffin out to the hearse for the short drive to the encrypting vault, where Marvin also waited for the spring, when things would come alive enough, so to speak, for him to get dead and buried. And that kid was wrong, the coffin was as heavy as if it were full of cement.

I waited for spring, too, along with the dead. Somehow I could no longer bring myself to sing in the Methodist choir after they convicted an Eskimo acquaintance of murdering J.-B. and put him away. I let old friendships drop, except the people I saw at the Daily News-Miner. I lived for the lengthening days, and with them the break-up, which saw me off again on the Piper T-1040 to Noatak—that next year still as a Fairbanks feature reporter, and after my book came out (*Noatak Twilight*, The Mountaineers Press, now out of print) as ethnographer-general to the natives of the Kotzebue Basin, and finally just as a far-flung member of the family. Every summer I shipped upriver in the straining boat along with Aargun and Raigili for the return to Tunarak Creek, and beyond. We hunted and fished and skinned, and I began to push them farther up the tributaries, taking notes. In case you didn't know it, there are more than a few nooks and crannies in the Brooks and Schwatka Ranges that Margaret Leithorn was the first white person to visit without a lust for yellow metal, maybe the first ever. People in Fairbanks naturally talked about a 52-year-old white woman suddenly going off the deep end like I did, but I didn't see it as sudden—J.-B. was sudden—and they were

467

wrong to think my end of the gangplank was any deeper than their own, which they proceeded to drop from one by one like stones. I preferred my private version of oblivion.

All those summers of my new life as an Eskimo, I was haunted by the ghost of Sally Morgan. Aargun and Raigili talked about her often, recalling her well-spaced eyes and plump, round features. They laughed and said Maggie skins a porcupine just like Kiva, or Don't worry, Maggie, Kiva also hated pickled trout bellies. But they never mentioned the one thing Kiva did that Maggie didn't. What had happened between Aargun and me that first summer under the pressure of circumstances never happened again, and Raigili never spoke of it. I guess it was the only thing she never spoke of, because if over the years she became less oracular, more businesslike about her unusual abilities, she never lost her joy in the shocking insight. Aargun never alluded to it either, not even in fun, though he was renowned for his crude jokes and his gutter talk. He would describe to me how long his turds were, who had the thickest penis he'd ever seen, which of his neighbors let their wives be on top, all of this in a tone of innocent wonder, but I and Kiva knew he was not so innocent. Yet he always affected with me this paternal benevolence that ended by getting under my skin. You bet I was attracted to him. He had a charisma, a magnetism, a certainty that his position vis-à-vis the great questions of existence was unquestionably correct, which is the one barbaric stupidity. It is also a force and a source of power. But I've thought it over a lot in the twenty-some years since I first stumbled onto him, or he first stumbled over me, and I've come to believe that the power was his alone while the stupidity was held in common with so-called intelligent people the world over, witness my smooth-faced frowning doctor here. I believe also that it was his power and not his stupidity that took him out into a February storm ten years ago, a man in his seventies, to check traps on his brand-new snow machine. Something—call it that certitude of his—had set the trap for *him*, and he stepped grandly into it. Like that pastor had said so many years before, he could never be sure he was not one of his own animals. None of us can, but it must have been tough for Raigili to lose a snow-machine. I was at home in my study when it happened, and suddenly that old deep-winter feeling came over me like tiredness and despair, and I knew I was heading for a binge. It had been a long time. With no one in the house to mind me, I missed Raig-ili's phone call, I missed Aargun's funeral, and I missed the week of celebrating that followed. After that, something changed be-tween Raigili and me, and things were different, until that final call from Kotzebue.

She had moved there after she was widowed to be nearer her family and the people who constantly sought her out for her pow-ers. Come summer, I visited her in the first frame house she'd ever lived in, at the north end of town, across from the tank farm, on Turf Street. There was dust in the windless air. Her glazed windows and her tilted aluminum roof were dull with it. The red of the freshly-painted walls was brown with it. Even the waterfront smelled more like dust than salt, and the strips of salmon hung like wash by the street were dust-dry. It was the driest summer since Aargun's mother had died, stranded up-stream by a sinking river. Many Inupiat suffered from coughs and rashes and strange feelings of malaise. They paid Raigili in meat or money or firewood, whichever they were flush with, and her business was good. In the week that I spent there I watched them come in, through the door over which the sack of stones still hung, past the bed on which the bearskin, balding with age, still lay in state despite the record heat, and into a small back room. And I watched them go, looking the same as they had when they had entered, with the same cough or the same limp or the same inflamed skin, but also with that dumb self-consciousness of church-goers after communion. I had heard all the stories and followed the rise of her career, so to speak, but she'd never allowed me to watch what she did with the sick. It bothered me because my scientific interest was keen, and she knew that, but other than this one thing we were sisters, and got along just like people who'd grown up together and didn't always need a lot to say, even though I was fifty-something when we first met and she ten years older.

That first Kotzebue summer, though, I could feel the changes. We didn't talk about Aargun, but he was right there between us under the hot metal roof. I longed for the cool of the mountains but she had sold his boat for a bicycle and was feeling too old for the nomadic life. No Tunarak Creek for me, she said, refer-ring, I suppose, to what happened with Aargun's mother, and be-sides, she had found a new kind of belonging in Kotzebue that invigorated her more than the Brooks Range ever had, which I found depressing. The stores in town were full of things like Twinkies and Lo-Cal Hot Chocolate Mix and cheap white bread, and she'd mounted a campaign to teach some nutritional awareness, as she called it, to the people who more and more were her regular clientele—old Eskimos, like herself, moved in from the sticks, or younger Eskimos who'd never had a culture. Her talk was full of phrases like "junk food" and "empty calories" that she heard on the little TV set she'd bought with her Social Security money, and she frowned at me now if I didn't trim the fat from a piece of beef or a piece of caribou. To me, caribou isn't much with the fat trimmed off, but her number-one favorite evil of that summer had to be white bread. The Eskimos had never had a native grain or bread, and she was working hard within what she now called her "community" to promote a return to traditional foraged foods like sourdock and masru, the Eskimo potato. The use of those fluffy sweet slices to make something called "sandwiches" with something called "baloney" struck her as a cultural decline. I don't know about that, but all her preaching made me hot and thirsty. I thought maybe not all of the baloney was in those sandwiches. I felt cooped up and had just about decided to fly up to Noatak by myself when she leaned towards me over a bowl of fermented wild rhubarb and said, so tell me, Maggie, are you screwing anyone?

I guess she took my stunned silence for a negative because she plowed right on. Maggie, she said, just because we're old doesn't mean we can't screw any more. You think I don't do it? I told her I don't think, period, let's leave it that way. She said a woman like me can't live without a hot-blooded man. I said that's fascinating, Raigili, it really is, did you hear this on Donahue? Sarcasm was never a major factor among the Inupiat and to this she said sure, on Donahue, Dr. Ruth, you name it, the vibration is everywhere. Not where I live, I said. She said that's because you live alone. I said, Raigili, just stuff it, okay? which was the first time I'd ever really lost my temper with her. She looked at me then, also for the first time ever, like a grown-up looking at an unruly child or a sane person looking at a crazy one—in other words, and this cut me to the quick, like an Eskimo looking at a celibate white female, with a smile that covered the irritation she felt at being placed in a position of disadvantage by somebody else's weaknesses. I knew that smile well. Don't look at me like that, Raigili, I said. Like what, she smiled, and I slapped her face. You had Aargun once, she said, but I have him forever. Congratulations, I said, now you're just like me.

Well, it was ridiculous, a couple of old ladies, but the next summer I accepted an assignment in Barrow to write about the natives and the pipeline, and the summer after that I had to do research in Juneau and Anchorage. I sent my excuses to Raigili, who had asked me to come, but I was aware that a pattern established over fifteen years had been broken, and I tried not to think about what it was doing to me. The next year she didn't invite, and I sent no excuses. I retired that year from the Daily News-Miner and told myself all that life-is-a-river bullshit, how I had simply floated on downstream towards the delta, leaving Noatak and all that part of my life behind me. It was phony but I had to tell myself something to explain why I was spending my winters now and my summers too reacquainting myself with old friends of Marvin's at the cocktail lounges. They had finally accepted me, if for no better reason than that we had all grown more or less old, and I was some kind of writer, and had returned to the fold with lots of interesting Eskimo stories to tell. I even drank once or twice with a gang that included the man who shot J.-B. Kelley, though I used the occasion to throw some Scotch in his face. He had let himself get drunk enough to reach for my bony shoulder, which is pretty drunk. I wetted him down and called him a sad litle fucker. Everyone laughed and said Hoo, Maggie always was a hot one.

They didn't know the half of it, but somehow I didn't either any more, and that's how come I was there on Christmas Eve, boring some boring old-timers at a watering-hole on Cushman Street called The Persian Kingdom, where the temperature was a permanent 85° and conservationists be damned, allowing the waitresses to wear gauze pantaloons and see-through vests over their bikinis, when I was called to the phone. It was Raigili, in Kotzebue. I was tanked, and the only thing I could think of to say to this person I hadn't even talked to in three and a half years was not hello but How the hell did you find me in The Persian Kingdom? She said is that what they call it nowadays? I laughed and said Raigili, you havven shanged. She said from the sound of it, neither have you, and I started to cry, and she said, Maggie, I

471

need you. I said what do you need from a drunken old white lady? She said I need you to come. I said come where? She said to Kotzebue, now, right away. Something in her voice drained the whiskey out of my brain and I said what's wrong, Raigili? She said nothing, just come. I said I'll come, and she said Merry Christmas.

I didn't bother saying goodbye to my crowd at The Persian Kingdom. I never bothered saying goodbye to my crowd, they were used to my moods. They hollered party-pooper and threw popcorn at me through clouds of smoke as I made for the door, but the moment I stepped outside their words turned to ice-fog under the streetlights and tinkled to the pavement. That's how I was seeing things just then, like I was still in whiskey river, which I was, but with absolute wide-awake clarity. The cold seemed to empty my eyeballs and give me night-vision. As soon as I got home I got on the horn to Joe Melchior, my contact at Frontier Flying, and asked about my chances of hopping a bird to Kotzebue. Might as well try hopping a camel, he said, we're booked solid with natives, home for the holidays and all that song and dance. Bump someone, I said. He says Maggie, there's moss on the igloo since you last headed west, so what's the g-d hurry all of a sudden? I said mind your own business, Melchior. He said be here at nine tomorrow, and bring me a bottle.

The bottle was Johnnie Walker but the bag was brown paper, and I had another with contents of less exalted stamp for the nine Eskimos who gave me the evil eye when I took the tenth seat. Their smiles unfroze after I passed around the libation and asked after the uncles and aunts and distant in-laws of the two or three whose names I could still remember. After that I stared out the Piper's window, over the left-hand turboprop as it streamed an ice-blue haze back into the darkness, to the rising of the fat yellow star on the southern horizon. And I'd better tell you that I don't mean the sun, but the queen of night, Venus, the morning and the evening star, morning and evening being one short twilight in Kotzebue, on Christmas, where it would spark like a sun squeezed down to a point of light. On this moonless day it was far and away the biggest light out there, restless, jumpy, dancing as the Inupiat say, or used to say, which is a sign of deteriorating weather, and which I was probably the only person on that plane loaded with Eskimos who could still tell you, such is progress. As

472

we flew west by northwest at 10,000 feet over the empty black taiga, across the frozen Yukon and the frozen Koyukuk and down the frozen Kobuk River, the lovely word Aageluuleraavik was much on my mind, and not much else.

Kotzebue looked small between the snow-covered tundra and the snow-covered Sound as we came in low over Hotham Inlet, and the star sat smack-dab over the center of it like a beacon. On the beat-up yellow school-bus which was the airport shuttle I swallowed some more of the rot-gut and stuck two pieces of gum in my mouth to disguise the smell. I met Raigili at the new Dairy Queen, as she'd suggested. She smiled when she saw me and said you look thin, Maggie. I gave her my presents, which I'd picked up at the Fairbanks airport, some earrings, some cheap perfume, then she made some more small talk. I found myself listening with only half an ear and scanning the personals pinned to the bulletin board above her head, the tundra telegraph of births and deaths, break-ups and marriages, accidents, tragedies, lonely hearts. I nodded my head as her lips moved but I was staring at one small hand-lettered notice among the rest, which read: "You wore green galoshes last Saturday night. I'm dying to see you again. Call 443-0712, Kivalina." Suddenly the DQ was full of ghosts, swarming and singing, and the smell of frozen hamburger patties frying was the stench of bodies even mosquitoes wouldn't touch, and all the glassy-eyed kids were staring as I started to sob. Raigili stopped talking about whatever it was she was talking about and I blurted out, you heard about Jean-Baptiste? She said slowly, that was fifteen years ago, Maggie. I said don't look back, but they're gaining on us. She said they? I just kept crying and she said would you like a little black coffee? It came in an enormous sytrofoam container and tasted like silverware. I took the wad of gum from my mouth and thought about sticking it under the table. She said let me have it, Maggie. I handed it over and she put it in the middle of her forehead. Then she laughed and hugged me close.

The coffee helped but I still felt spooked as we walked up Shore Avenue toward Turf Street over a squeaking foot of snow. A few storefronts were trimmed with Christmas lights, half burned-out. On the utility poles, torn streamers of red and green tinsel flapped in the wind off the groaning Sound, where a man had been killed, ice-fishing alone, a week before. The surface had

473

shifted suddenly and sheared over his wind-break, rubbing him out. His family had come to Raigili. I shuddered and said, for what? His soul was still floating around, she said, we laid it to rest. I said was this before or after the Quaker funeral? If she noticed the sneer in my voice she didn't show it. After, she said, and she said that they talked about grief, how it would be okay for them to feel guilty, and to get in touch with the conflicts this person had left them. I said don't worry, they all come back, Raigili, all the dead. She looked at me and said of course they do, and some of the living, too. I said are you sure you've got me in the proper category? She said what makes you think I was talking about you? You were talking about me, I said. She said, I'm hearing fear and disillusion. I said you talk like one of these pop psychologists. She said maybe they talk like me. I laughed. And maybe you'll be on television one of these days. She said it's not impossible. I said don't hold your breath. She stopped me on the slippery street and unzipped my parka and put her two hands inside. If Christ came to Canaan, she said, then CBS can come to Kotzebue. Her hands made my belly shiver. I said, I've come, isn't that good enough?

Raigili's house was as full as it could be of her children and her children's children and their children too, only a few of whom I could actually say that I knew. There was lots of food and laughter and music from a tape deck. Andy Williams and Stevie Wonder and *Lohengrin*, opera and Christmas carols. There was a big bowl of Raigili's favorite, cooked char livers mashed to a paste with raspberries. That afternoon a storm blew in and the ground-blizzard swallowed the roadways but people came and went all night laughing and eating, and Raigili seemed to forget about me. The company was friendly but nobody drank in that household and I could see right away there was nothing here to have brought me from Fairbanks in somebody else's seat. As I sobered up I began to feel let down, but I held my peace. It was Christmas, after all. The less I said, though, the madder I got. After a couple of days the crowd began to thin and Raigili started to look at me like maybe she figured I ought to be doing the same. But the weather had pinned all the planes to the ground and I was stuck, stuck and angry, same as I'd been the first time I'd ever met her. At 2 a.m. on the morning of the 28th, I was sitting alone at her kitchen table smoking my umpteenth cigarette and staring

out her plastic-sheathed window into the snow that whipped hor-
izontally through the lights of Pacific-Alaska Fuel Services across
the street, thinking their sea-green holding tanks looked like so
many inside-out swimming pools, when Raigili came in and said
ugh, Maggi, how could you do that to your lungs? Because
they're my lungs, not yours, I said, which anyway are probably
black as night from eighty years of wood fires and seal-oil lamps,
so don't be so goddamned superior with your tape deck and your
television and your oil furnace that keeps me awake all night. Ah,
Maggi, she said, always the long, sharp tongue. Right, I said, and
it was Aargun, remember, who carried the long, sharp blade to
back me up. She said I do remember, though those days are
gone, and that's exactly what I wanted to talk to you about. Talk
away, Mrs. Dinah Shore, I said, there never was anything else to
keep me here. She said, Maggi, did I ever tell you I was sorry to
hear of your husband's death? Marvin was his name? I said who
gives a shit. Almost twenty years we've been like sisters, she
said, and I was never sure of his name. Tell me about Marvin.
   I shouldn't have looked at her because my anger made me feel
safe and I knew if I looked it would fade and I'd tell her what she
asked. I said Marvin was a carpenter, he built houses, mostly.
She just kept looking, so I said he was a simple man, proud of his
work, proud of his biceps, proud of the eagle tattoos that were on
them, fond of bowling. He never put screens on our windows. I
never asked him to. He didn't want children. He was younger
than me. She reached over and took the cigarette from my fingers and stubbed it out. She handed me some gum. I folded my
hands and said, he didn't want me to go. How did you feel about
leaving? she asked, and handed me a Kleenex. How did you feel
about Kiva, I asked right back. I killed her, she said, same as
you. I coughed and said do yourself a favor, don't mention that
when you go on television. It's only the truth, she said. That's not
what you told me before, I said, you told me she got sick and
died. What's the difference? she said again. I looked at her like
she was crazy, which, it is worthwhile to remember, not that long
before I met her she had been. For starters, I said, and I realize
this may not mean much to you, but I happen to have loved my
husband. She shrugged. And I loved Kiva, she said. The whole
wide world loved Kiva, she was young, she wore green galoshes,
and her parents owned two boats up in Kivalina. Kiva was a good

vibration, Maggi. Yes well, just for the record, I said, Marvin was not. But you loved him anyway, she said. I said that's what I'm telling you. She shrugged again. You're right, she said, that doesn't mean much to me. I said which word did you not understand? She said, the last one. I could play these games and I said the last one what? She said the last word: anyway. You loved him anyway. I don't understand that. I said it's called forgiveness. She said ah yes, the other face. I said the other cheek. She said face, cheek, whatever, the life of Jesus. How did he betray you? I said who said he betrayed me? She said, forgiveness. Sometimes you had to wonder about Raigili. I said, there was a girl down in Seattle. A nurse, she said. I just stared at her. He was sick, she went on, but he must have been handsome, a man with tattoos is attractive, he's sending out signals, and from both biceps yet. Sorry I could never arrange an introduction, I said. She blinked and said I'm sorry too, Maggi, that's how I started this conversation. I said I heard you. She said tell me about that nurse. I said bullshit. She said what was her name, where did she live, who was her daddy, come on, Maggi, tell. I said you really expect me to know all that, you loon. I said I couldn't care less than this about any nurse. I snapped my fingers. She said how about yourself?

I didn't say anything. She chewed on her gum and I lit another cigarette. I wanted to get off of it and I said you have teeth again, Raigili, I just now noticed. She smiled wide and tapped them. Christmas present from the kids, she said, thank heaven for plastic, I can eat meat again. But you shouldn't chew gum, I said, I mean won't they come loose? She shrugged. You know Maggi, she said, the Old People followed the meat. Ever hear that expression? I said sure I've heard it, it means they were nomadic, like Aargun, only more so, they went where the game was thickest. They followed the meat, she repeated. But we have meat down the street here at Hanson's and Alaska Commercial, and you know what? It don't go nowhere, and that is where we follow it. Guilt is our hunger nowadays, and we'll follow that hunger all the way to Seattle if we have to. Know what I mean? I never liked Raigili when she was in this vein, so I bit my tongue. You're welcome to your memories, Maggi, she said, but memory is a bear, he will eat you unless you eat him. Lay him down, Maggi, the meat is nourishing, and the skin mades a nice warm bed.

I was steaming and I couldn't hide it. Is that all you dragged me five hundred miles on false pretenses to tell me? I said. She said no, actually, it wasn't. I wanted to give you these. She got up from the table, slowly, so I could see how old she was. She went over to the door, which was slightly crooked now from the house sinking, and reached up with a meat-fork. She lifted down the wrinkled bag that held her healing stones. She brought it over, giggling. Did I ever tell you what this was? she said. It's the bag from the crotch of a musk-ox bull in rut. She held the handle of the meat-fork down at an angle over the sack, and swayed the apparatus back and forth. Aargun bought it for me when he sold that bear's gallbladder. She giggled again. You can get all kinds of nifty things in Kotzebue. I want you to have this. I said the bag? She said, the stones. You can keep them in a zip-lock freezer bag for all I care, the stones are the important thing. I said I don't understand. She said most of the time understanding is not necessary. I said, Raigili, I couldn't. She said you couldn't wield a buck-knife, but you did. I said I'm not taking them, they're your life. She said that's why you must take them. I said Raigili, but she sighed and covered her eyes with her hand. God damn it to hell, Maggi, she whispered, would you just shut up. Then she reached for one of my cigarettes and said, give me a light.

The next day was calm and very cold. Venus hung over the Sound in a shimmer of ice haze. She saw me to the airport and clutched my hands when I left. She told me to watch my salt and cholesterol, and especially my saccharin. That stuff gives cancer to rats, she said. A week later, when her oldest son called me at home in Fairbanks, her Quaker funeral had already taken place.

*　*　*　*

I hear it all. From my new room across from the nurses' station, I hear them coming and going, rattling their keys and fetching their pills and their needles, crying and chattering mournfully like pigeons, having their reactions, trying to make themselves feel like death changes something. They express their attitudes, then they express them again. They do all this outside my door, and all it does is make me feel like laughing. It's funny how people refuse to believe you can hear them. They stand right outside your door and talk about things too bad to talk about in front of you, as if the door wasn't open and cancerous old alcoholics didn't have ears or brains. In my room they call

477

this a safety vest, but out there they call it a restraint and say tie her down good, she's got the DT's, and don't turn your back or she'll try to throw something at you. You want me to tell you I'm sorry, don't you, I say. And they talk about Mary.

That's how I know that the Old Man nailed her yesterday, her day off, in the early afternoon, in the crosswalk in front of the hospital. The nurses get red on their clean white teeth from biting their painted lips and rub their mascara into each other's clean white uniforms. They call it a tragedy, they whisper of fluke and accident. Whales have flukes and Shakespeare wrote tragedies but I know something they don't know, there aren't any accidents. He hit her on the right side and threw her far down the street. The marks of his claws were found on her neck and shoulder. The car kept going. The stones are with her now, wherever she is, or in some detective's drawer or the garbage can of her mother and father's house. Either way, they have run their course. I think of her now with only a little regret and with fading bitterness. It's the same feeling I had flying home from Kotzebue for the last time, with the stones in my suitcase. In transferring them to me, Raigili must have known what a mockery she was making of her entire life. She must have known that the power was hers, but not hers to pass along. I never really knew what to do with those pieces of jasper. I put them on a shelf, where they gathered dust, and carried them with me when I travelled. But I wondered what they had to do with *me,* and in the end I passed them on, as she did. In the end. She said it was not always necessary to understand, but the point is I did. I understood, but I did not believe.

Mary believed, and that's the one thing I couldn't forgive her for. Apropos of which, there is something else I know that these nurses don't. They wonder why Mary was coming to the hospital on her day off, dressed in her street clothes. They say that if only she hadn't, she'd still be alive. The fact is, she was here on a little business of mine, what you might call a quasi-legal appointment. She'd been called to explain to certain interested parties, including my serious young doctor, why I woke up from a nap a few days ago to find my door closed, my curtain drawn, Mary sitting beside me with her eyes shut, and three red stones arranged on the covers over my belly in a sort of triangle. I felt their chill, and that's why I woke up. I said what the hell are you doing? She said lay him down, Maggi, lay him down. I said who do you think you are? She said how about yourself? and that was enough for me. I denounced her immediately to the hospital authorities for practicing shamanism without a license. They were calling her in, I suppose, for her version of the story.

She never made it, and so this story is mine. If you want the truth, I think it's a story of delusion. I think Raigili was deluded, pure and simple. But the not so simple thing, and not so pure, no, not so pure, is that when she dies and wills her delusions to you, well, you wonder who's the looney.

I set the point of my knife in the shit-hole and worked it up the belly with a sawing motion. I severed the gullet behind the mouth and ran my thumb bump-bump down the inside of the spine. The guts fell into my hand and I tore them away, heaving them as far out into the current as I could. I set the lightened grayling on the strand beside his brother, and reached for the next one, his rainbow sheen already dried to dull silver.

Suddenly the knife stood still as the howling hit me. I didn't breathe, and it happened again, high, looping, braided, and this time unmistakably human. The third wave told me what direction—from upriver beyond the little limestone canyon, where Aargun had gone with his wooden pole and his jig-line. I quickly cut a willow stem and threaded my fish through the gills, laying them in the shallows. I rinsed and folded the blade of my buck-knife and dropped it into my pocket without drying it.

A circle of wet spread over my thigh from the knife as I trotted up the bank. The walls of the tiny gorge were stepped and shelved, easy to climb though crusted with dry, black lichen, and lichen-slimy up near the waterfall. From the rocks, Tunarak Creek was blue as the sky, with soft white clouds drifting along it. The grey rock felt warm under my hand, but my heart pounded cold in the gorge's shadows. Then I was up and out on the sun-swept tundra.

Just above the falls, the Tunarak widened into a lake that rippled the floor of a hidden valley. By its near shore, a float-plane glistened white, rocking on the breeze. Two big orange tents stood close to it, and in front of them was a circle of men, maybe five of them, laughing at a woman in the center. Their laughter rolled on the down-valley wind like the baying of wolves. Two of

479

the men were taking pictures of the woman while another kept running up and putting more clothes on her. Although she appeared to be fully dressed already, he kept adding to her costume, shoving a pink beret on her head, or tying an apron around her thick waist. One after another they had their pictures taken with their arms around her. I couldn't see till I got down closer that the woman was Aargun.

He had a smile on his face that looked like it had been chopped there with an ax. He stood stock-still as the men clowned around him, smooching him on the cheek for the cameras and spitting disgustedly. Empty bottles of whiskey lay piled beside a catch of grayling. They didn't notice me until I was nearly on top of them, and when they did they rubbed their yellow beards and stared at me as if I had two heads. Then one of them said what filled me with rage: She's white.

Afternoon, missus, said another, he with you? meaning Aargun, but by then I had my buck-knife up his nostril and he wasn't talking. Aargun, I said, get those clothes off. He didn't move nor even stop smiling, though I fancy he looked at me with something like abomination. For a long few seconds we all stood wired in a powerful tension, until I screamed, Damn you, Aargun, I said take them off! but Aargun still didn't move. See, ma'am, somebody said, the boy don't mind, he knows we're just—Shut up, I said, or I'll fillet this fish's face. There was silence again, and then one of them slowly raised his hand. Hold on, now, lady, he said, don't do nothing rash. He cut his eyes at Aargun and said, tell her, boy. Aargun grinned and said, go on, put the knife down, Maggi. My hand started to shake and I looked at him through tears of frustration, and as I did I must have nicked the bastard's nose because he hollered and grabbed at my wrist and wrenched it down and the others all rushed in and reached for me and I felt myself falling, then suddenly they all fell back like scattered chickens.

The flensing-knife flew out from under the apron and whistled back and forth through the air like a great, long saber, flashing and dancing. The men rolled away as from an explosion and Aargun froze in a crouch between me and them, his blade held rigid at the end of his outstretched arm. He backed up and pushed me toward the falls, following me slowly. When we reached the lip of the little canyon, he was still pointing the knife at the five men, who were resting on the ground, shaking their heads. A woman had wandered out of the left-hand tent—a real woman, naked and brown—and begun without curiosity to gather up the odds and ends of her clothing. Then Aargun said to me, Go, and after a minute he quickly followed me down.

Not until we'd reached the Noatak did he stop and get out of the pink beret and the apron and wraparound skirt and the nylon bra stretched tightly over his chest. He grinned and spread his arms like a vaudevillian, saying, Cosi fan tutte. Soon we heard a low humming, and looted up to see the white float-plane climbing southeast across the river and away. When we got back to our camp by the cottonwoods, Raigili was gone with the blueberry pot. I built up the fire as Aargun paced back and forth. It was September, early evening, and the sun was getting low. The next morning we would drift on homeward. Yellow light bowled up the wide road of river and lit up the crowns of the cottonwoods like they were burning.

Suddenly Aargun stopped in front of me and lifted me to my feet. He wrapped his big fist around my belt-buckle, tugging it downwards. He led me to a bed of poppies in the cottonwood grove and said, damn you, take them off, but he was laughing. As he loosened his own belt he added, knife up the nose, crazy Maggi, that's a sharp kind of screwing. Then he laughed again, softly, to himself. The wind came up as he lay on me, stilling the mosquitoes. When he was done he climbed off and went back to Raigili, but I lay there for a long time before I got dressed. I watched the last of the sun burn up to the tops of the cottonwoods and I smelled their sweet incense, and when the wind shook, the dry leaves drifted down and piled between my legs, like pieces of gold.

Nominated by H. E. Francis and Alaska Quarterly Review

THE PYROXENES

by JAMES MERRILL

from THE FORMALIST

Well, life has touched me, too.
No longer infant jade,
What is the soul not made
To drink in, to go through

As it becomes itself!
Look at this forest scene,
Dendritic, evergreen,
On Leto's back-lit shelf—

A "forest" that predates
The kingdom of the trees.
Move on a step to these
Translucent spinach plates

Morbidly thin, which flake
On flake corundum-red
As weeping eyes embed.
You'd think poorhouse and wake,

Fury, bereavement, grief
Dwelt at Creation's core,
Maternal protoplast,
Millions of years before

Coming to high relief
Among us city folk.

Out of her woods at last,
On the Third Day we woke

From cradles deep in mire
At white heat: elements-
To-be of hard, scarred sense,
Strangers to fire.

Nominated by The Formalist

WHITE BOOT

by MICHAEL McCLURE

from NEW YORK QUARTERLY

In Golden Gate Park After the Storm

for Sterling Bunnell

STERLING BELIEVES THAT CHAOS ARISES FROM DEEP
INTRINSIC
ORDER
and is merely a quality of energy
in the scene that surrounds.
ORDER, he asserts, is earlier
than this universe,
preceding what a finger
or tongue touches on now;
order enhances and shapes
the buttercup and the moss
stirring on the storm-soaked ground
as well as the shark-colored jay that flies
to take popcorn from my hand.
Even the junco
there by my white boot
on the dripping flagstones
knows it.
The hail intermingling in silvery stripes
with the downrush of rain,
is the same structure as thought.
The flesh of the resonating psyche is free

and cannot be bought.
—BUT
ALL
SOME
KNOW
of such things
is the nuggetlike gold of hunger,
the rippling muscle of ongoing love,
and light that flashes
from a wild eye.

Nominated by Tony Quagliano

485

RAVENS AT DEER CREEK

by ROBERT WRIGLEY

from THE GETTYSBURG REVIEW

Something's dead in that stand of fir
one ridge over. Ravens circle and swoop
above the trees, while others
swirl up from below, like paper scraps
blackened in a fire. In the mountains
in winter, it's true: death is a joyful flame,
those caws and cartwheels pure celebration.
It is a long snowy mile I've come
to see this, thanks to luck, or grace.
I meant only a hard ski through powder,
my pulse in my ears, and sweat, the pace
like a mainspring, my breath louder and louder
until I stopped, body an engine
ticking to be cool. And now the birds.
I watch them and think, maybe I have seen
these very ones, speaking without words,
clear-eyed and clerical, ironic, peering in at me
from the berm of snow outside my window,
where I sprinkled a few crumbs of bread. We
are neighbors in the neighborhood of silence.
They've accepted my crumbs, and when the fire was hot
and smokeless huddled in ranks against
the cold at the top of the chimney. And they're not
without gratitude. Though I'm clearly visible
to them now, they swirl on and sing,
and if, in the early dusk, I should fall

on my way back home and—injured, crying—damn the stars
and the frigid night
and crawl awhile on my hopeless way
then stop, numb, easing into the darkening white
like a candle, I know they'll stay
with me, keeping watch, moving limb to limb,
angels down Jacob's ladder, wise
to the moon, and waiting for me, simple as sin,
that they may know the delicacy of my eyes.

Nominated by Greg Pape, Arthur Smith

487

SUN SPOTS

by CHRISTOPHER BUCKLEY

from THE IOWA REVIEW

Every eleven years they appear
like dark pores beneath the floating
photosphere, the atomic skin that makes
up the surface. The *auroras* erupt then too,
the irrepressible fiery hair of the sun torn loose and
thrown into space at us, a welter of flaming astral birds
lifting off the *limb*, that visible edge and hard limit of the star.
The magnetic whorls, paired anywhere from two to fifty, are then
several times larger than earth, and strain and pull at fission's invisible frame,
setting out against the rotation of burning equatorial seas, hovering above the blue-
hot center like a sickness in gravity. Yet, when the ocellated torrents and latitudinal drifts
are graphed, the *penumbras* echo the winged patterns of butterflies rather than some matrix of sinking
anti-matter. And after all our spinning about this source, this seething theme and variation, we have nothing new
to say about the spots outside of the old tales that still flare up and forebode havoc in the distant atmosphere of our lives.
So last winter when auroras blazed and the black fields swelled, it was no wonder that broadcasts were interrupted
with blank bursts. "Live from the Met," waffled out and in with a certain nothing on the air—
a soundless hiss and drop-out from the blue. And just weeks before, the opera at the Met
went, a first time ever, unfinished—and the stage turned dark after one un-
balanced soul threw himself mid-aria from a balcony to a break-
neck death. And so, the dread forecasts must have held
sway over at least one man as his will sparked
out and reason fumed in on itself.

It was reported he'd recently
been observed storming around
the mezzanine, stalking some absent
space—and with the house lights down he slipped
into the empty box and pitched himself head-long over
into the dark. He did not stand out in tuxedo and black tie
they said—there was no sound, no note. Only the lovely and loveless
Turandot, waiting high and star-white on the stage, with her riddle for the hero
who was confident as any tenor despite the heads of other suitors who'd been unable to answer
staggered about her on poles like disjunct planets, like moons bruised beyond all aspects of the light . . .
Is it coincidence then, that this year they discover the hole in our ozone to be much larger than first supposed,
that melanoma is on the rise, that the clear-cut Amazon is leaving us with thin air, a simmering rain?
Where on the scale finally are we—Galactic to Sub-Atomic? Our cells cluster and spiral

like galaxies, to or from what effect? Yet we're most open to what lies beyond us—
astronomers have now abandoned our own solar system in favor of great radio
telescopes fixed on the obfuscated heart of space—steely petals of the dishes
unfolding, like camera lenses, like slow and awkward flowers
craning toward sound instead of light. And anchored
firmly in those white sands and eroding shoals
of time, they focus toward some innuendo
sung down in dim, binomial bleeps—
too far away ever to be of use
to the future hanging fire.

Nominated by Lynne McMahon, Sherod Santos

ONE WAY

fiction by JESS MOWRY

from RATS IN THE TREES (John Daniel & Co.) and ZYZZYVA

R OBBY PUSHED OPEN the station door, carrying his board by the front truck, downside in. At least it was cool inside. He smelled burgers from the restaurant and his stomach growled, but five and change wouldn't go far. Maybe he could live off his fat awhile like those bears on TV? He saw a whole cigarette under a chair and snagged it fast. Matches were always a prob, but Jeffers had given him his Bic and it was still half full.

He walked across to a black plastic TV-chair, just like the one in Fresno. He slid behind the little screen and pulled out his lighter, wondering if they had the Thunder Cats or Ninja Turtles here. It wasn't worth risking a quarter to find out. The cigarette was one of those pussy kind, so he broke off the filter before firing. The smoke eased his hunger a little, but that cleaning shit they used on the floor was giving him a headache.

A rattler in a baggy uniform came over. He was white and bored. He glanced at the cigarette, but seemed to figure out there were better things to hassle about, "You got a ticket, kid?"

Robby dug it out. The rattler gave it a look, then flipped it back, jerking a thumb at the big clock over the doors. "Next one leaves at five-twenty, kid. Be on it." He smiled with his mouth. "And put a fucking quarter in or get outta the chair."

"Dipshit," came to Robby's mind. He took a big cool hit off the cigarette and blew smoke, watching the rattler's eyes narrow. Then he slid out of the chair and walked *the* walk toward the bathroom, feeling the rattler watching. "Lame-o," he whispered.

490

A tall skinny black boy stood by the door. They'd call him dribble-lips in Fresno. He looked about sixteen and also like he knew everything about Robby. "Crackers," he murmured. "A dollar."

Robby knew crackers, though they were called nukes in Fresno, and a dollar was way too much. He almost smiled. Like the TV said, "Just say no," asshole. He ignored the dude: scoring the right local word was worth the shove he got. He did smile then, hearing the rattler's squeaky cop-shoes cross the floor and the one word, *"Out!"*

"Yeah, right," the skinny dude yawned. Robby knew he'd be back.

The bathroom was all shiny tile under flickering fluorescents. It smelled like piss and Pine-Sol. There was a white dude, old, twenty-something, leaning on the line of sinks. He smiled at Robby.

Homo, Robby thought. Perv. Anybody who hung out where it smelled like piss had to be weird. Things weren't so different here. He saw the long trough and the dude watching him. He hated those things—out in the open, always too fucking high. How could anybody piss trying to stand on their toes? Everything else was a goddamn pay toilet except one and there was somebody in it. A fucking dime to piss! At least he could shut the door. He paid the box a dime and went in, sighing, yanking his zipper, and making as much water-noise as he could. He should've used the one right there on the bus; had to start figuring stuff like that.

He jerked up his zipper, flipped the cigarette in the toilet, and flushed. Then he laid the skateboard across the seat and sat, swinging his legs. Should he go for San Francisco? Trouble was, he didn't know how long that would take. It would probably be dark when he got there, too late for the ocean, and they'd run him off without a ticket. He'd slept on the street before, a few times when his folks were fighting, a couple more with Jeffers and Tad when they'd scored some beer and gotten too wasted to skate or even walk. It'd be a lot easier to find some place behind a dumpster. . . .

Somebody tapped on the door. Robby saw the perv's Adidas underneath. "Hey, kid, want to play a game?"

Robby grinned. Games were shit old people thought up for kids. He'd never let a perv touch him before but Jamie had, in

491

Rotting Park, and got $20. He'd said it was weird, but not bad. Jeffers said you could score a sixer that way, sometimes, but to get it first. Robby sat and kicked his legs. The door was locked, even if the perv put in another dime. What was he going to do, crawl under?

"How much?" Robby asked. That's what Jeffers would say.

The perv sounded like he had hurt feelings or something. "Hey, little guy, I just want to be your friend."

"Yeah right, duuude!" Suddenly Robby laughed and almost couldn't stop. It was *too* funny. A dime bought you a piss and a perv in Oakland. "Fuck-off, AIDSball," he said.

The perv said nothing, but the Adidas didn't move.

"I'll scream," Robby added. "Loud."

The Adidas went away.

Sunlight slanted yellow in hot evening air as Robby pushed open the station door. He'd figured he might as well check the place out. There must be an ocean around somewhere. A black kid went by on a board, a thrasher old VariFlex. They ignored each other but checked boards; Robby's was better and they both knew it. The kid wore ragged jeans and had his shirt tied around his waist, hanging down in back. Robby pulled his off and did the same. The cracker dude was standing by a streetlamp, looking like he wanted to kick the shit out of somebody. Robby decked and rolled. It didn't matter which way, but he thought of the ocean again. Jeffers said you could sleep on the beach.

Wheels clicked cracks and the blocks passed. Robby stayed on a straight line to somewhere. These sidewalks were crowded, and he was too busy dodging people to pay much attention to anything else. The concrete was old and rough. The curbs were different too, but there was a lot of scraped skateboard paint on them.

The sun lowered and grew orange in distant fog. The air cooled and he stopped sweating. He passed another boy on a board, a little black dude on a Punk-Size. The kid didn't seem to figure there was anything special about Robby and that felt good and bad at the same time.

The food smells from the restaurants bothered him: there were so many. He tailed in front of a Doggie Diner and thought about a hot dog, but there was another cigarette under a bus bench and he snagged that instead, firing as he rolled. It didn't seem to help his hunger much and it buzzed his head a little. He pinched it halfway, dropping it in the bag for later.

The streets were quiet now, and he heard a car come around the far corner. He tensed a moment, glancing up the street—van, Dodge, dark blue, maybe black, it was getting hard to see as the daylight faded. He looked around but there was no place to hide. Was there any reason to? Heavy-metal music echoed between the buildings. Robby flipped up his board and pretended to be checking the trucks while watching the van from the corner of his eye as it neared. It didn't have its lights on but the driver must have seen him because it eased toward the curb. Robby almost decked, but the music faded low and a kid-voice called, "Yo, shredder!"

The van pulled over and stopped. The voice was friendly, breaking in the middle the way Jeffers' did sometimes. "Want some beer, brother?"

Robby came slowly to the open passenger window, ready to book fast. The kid inside was white, thin, with super-long bleached metaler hair. He wore black Levis, black Iron Maiden T-shirt, big studded collar, and a heavy spiked wrist-cuff. He also had on those expensive studded riot-gloves. Total showtime, Robby thought, no good for skating. But his blue eyes were friendly.

Robby leaned on the door, looking in. If the kid was old enough for a license, it was just. The dude grinned at Robby. Both his front teeth were those stainless-steel kind they sometimes put in kids until they were old enough for real fake ones.

Total metaler or what, flashed through Robby's mind. But at the same time he felt a little sorry for the dude—other kids probably called him tin-grin, or something. The dude held out an open can of Bud. Robby took it, sipped, then chugged a decent hit. It was kid-beer, kind of flat and warm, but he was thirsty and warm beer kept you from being hungry.

"What's up, bro?" the dude asked.

Robby considered. "Um, just skatin' home, man."

Robby handed back the can and the dude nodded, chugging, not even wiping the top first. Robby stood on tiptoes, pressing closer to the door. The metal was still sun-warm and felt good.

"Yeah?" said the dude. "Figured you must live around here 'cause you've got a board. Um, what kind?"

493

Robby held it up. "Just a thrasher old Steadham. Nuthin' rad. You ride, man?"

The dude grinned again and passed back the Bud. "Not since I got my wheels!" He patted the dash. "Used to have a Roskopp."

"Yeah?" said Robby. "They're totally bad!"

"Where do you live? I could give you a ride if you want."

Robby eyes flicked to the back of the van. Carpeted, paneled, but totally empty, nowhere anybody else could be hiding. "Um, by the beach."

Robby left a couple swallows in the can and passed it back. It wasn't cool to kill it. The dude gave Robby another metal grin and finished it. *"Beach?* Oh yeah. I guess it would be for you. Well, guess that means you're almost home anyway, don't it?" He studied Robby a minute. "Um, how old are you, man?"

"Thirteen."

"Naw. Hey, open the door a second, let me see ya."

Robby did, stepping back. The dude checked him and grinned. "No way, man! You're way too big for thirteen."

Robby smiled a little. At least he hadn't said fat.

"Hey!" said the dude. "I got one more Bud left. You wanna slide in an' we'll just sit here an' split it? You like Slayer?"

Robby considered. It was getting darker by the minute and the street was empty and dead. The van smelled good inside—like leather and kids, beer and smoke. The dome light had come on when the door opened. It was painted red and made the interior look warm. Maybe with a half-Bud in his stomach he wouldn't be hungry tonight. Robby climbed in.

The dude pulled another Bud from between the seats and popped it, checking Robby again. "Hey, bro, no shit, you are big an' bad. I guess all you dudes are like that, huh?" He gave Robby firsts.

Robby frowned a little. "Um, what do you mean?"

"Aw, nothing." The kid smiled again. "Hey, I know how lame this's gonna sound, but my best friend is a black dude. I known him since third-grade. All you dudes are just naturally cool."

Robby sipped beer and smiled. "Or what."

The kid gave Robby another long look. For just a second, Robby wanted to cross his arms over his chest. "My little brother's thirteen too, only he's a total marshmallow compared to you.

494

I guess all you bros have to be super bad to live here, huh? I mean, you know how to fight, an' carry guns an' everything?"

Robby thought a second. "Yeah."

"Full-autos, huh?"

"Sometimes." Robby passed back the Bud. The dude studied him a few moments. "Um, could I touch you, bro? I mean, I ain't no homo or nothing! I just can't believe you're only thirteen."

Robby tensed and slid close to the door. "Um, no, man. I know you're not a homo. I just don't wanna be touched, okay? I, um, gotta get home anyways. Thanks for the beer, bro." Robby slid out, watching the dude watching him. The kid started to reach for something between the seats, then gave Robby another grin.

"Hey. It's cool, bro! I don't blame you. We had those pervert movies in school too."

Robby stood on the sidewalk for a moment then closed the van's door. "It's okay, bro. I just gotta get home, that's all. My dad'll get pissed. Um, thanks again for the Bud . . . an' I think your van is totally bad."

He rolled a couple blocks more, then stopped and looked around. The buildings were old and dirty brick, faded like rust in the evening light. No more stores, only a little corner market. The rest were garages and body shops, all closed. The sidewalk was totally thrashed, broken and littered with bottles and trash. There was a wino in a doorway. It was so ugly and familiar and stupid that it made him homesick. But the salt smell was strong and he rolled on.

Parked trucks and abandoned cars lined the curbs. Windows at street level were barred or covered with plywood. He looked at the spray-painted words and pictures, some familiar—the Anarchy sign, Hip-Hop, good old FUCK YOU. But there weren't any squared-off Chicano letters and there was lots of heavy-metal and punker stuff and rap.

Robby jumped the gutter, cut the street, and slapped the opposite curb. A spray-paint design in red and black, like a Tiger-Dog snarling from a letter A, faced him from a corner wall—a gang-mark for sure. It was old, but nobody'd painted "sucks" or something underneath or an "anti" sign over it. Whatever the Tiger-Dog stood for, it got respect. It wasn't very high on the wall, he noticed, just about where he'd have painted it. For sure,

495

there were kid-gangs in Fresno, but the big dudes always painted out their marks fast.

He rounded another corner and there it was. He tailed and stared and fought back tears. It sucked!

There was no surf. The water stretched away, silent and sullen. There was no beach. The water lapped at rotten pilings, broken rock, and rusty junk. No sand, only stinking black mud. Further up the shore, dim in a fog as gray and ugly as a tule fog in Fresno, was a short wharf alongside a crumbling warehouse.

Snagging his board, Robby walked over to a rusted chain-link gate. The wire on one corner was peeled back and he squeezed through. The wharf planking was rotten and gone in places. He walked to the end and sat, dangling his legs, looking down at dirty black water where garbage floated. He pulled out the half-cigarette and fired. Tears burned his eyes again, and this time he let them fall.

He should've figured it would be like this. The ocean was just as worn-out and thrashed as everything else in the whole fucking world! Things were no different anywhere; and, if there really were white sandy beaches and surf-kids, it would be a kind of mall-place with rattlers to keep him out. This was all the ocean he was ever going to get.

The last light faded and Robby sat alone in foggy darkness. He smoked until the cigarette burned his fingers. The fog was wet and cold and he put his shirt back on. He wished he had enough beer so he could drink until he couldn't see or feel anything anymore. Then he pulled his knees, put his head between his legs, and cried.

Something creaked behind him, but he didn't look. He didn't care. Let the Tiger-Dogs come and beat the shit out of him; maybe they'd kill him. Maybe that was better.

There was breathing, the deep kind, like you make when you're drunk. Then, a kid-voice: "Whitey?"

That was funny. Even now. Robby turned, looking up at the fattest kid he'd ever seen.

For sure, a lot of Mexican kids were fat, but this dude was black. He looked about Robby's age, though it was hard to tell in the dark. He wore jeans that sagged under his belly, thrasher Nikes that used to be white, and a ragged black T-shirt with what

496

looked like RATT on the front and couldn't cover his middle. The fat kid stopped a few feet away and checked Robby. "You ain't Whitey."

Robby shrugged. He couldn't see anybody else around and sure wasn't scared of this fat tub. "Duh."

That didn't seem to bother the fat kid. He smiled a little, funny, like he knew a secret or something and Robby wondered if he was a retard.

"Yeah? You ain't from here," the dude said.

"No shit."

"Yeah? So, where?"

"So nuthin'! I'm Panthro from Third-Earth, duuude!"

The fat kid only smiled wider and that bothered Robby.

"Yeah? I'm into the Thundercats too, man. You look more like one of Mum-ra's dipshits. Wanna get your ass wiped?"

"By *you*? I doubt!"

The fat kid grinned, teeth big and white. "Yeah? You in Animal-Land now, dude. Lion-o ain't gonna save your ass here."

Robby considered that and the fat kid moved a lot faster than it looked like he could, snagging Robby's board with a grunt. Robby jumped up, but the dude was checking his board like an expert, though he couldn't have ridden one for his life. Robby wanted to snatch it back and punch that huge belly, hard, but the dude handled the board with respect.

"Steadham," the fat kid said. He grinned even wider. "That's what Whitey rides too. Um, synchronicity, man!" He checked the downside, and pointed to a sticker. "Skully Brothers. I heard of them. They gots an ad in *Thrasher*. They in, um . . . "

"Fresno."

"Yeah." The fat kid handed the board back, and Robby couldn't help it, he asked, "You, um, *ride*, man?"

The dude smiled, shy. "Naw. But the other Animals all shred to the max, 'specially Randers an' Kevin." He studied Robby a minute. "Whitey's pretty intense too. You sure look a lot like him."

Robby was used to white kids saying stupid stuff like that, but a black dude should know better. Anyway, "How the fuck could I look like a whitey, man?"

"Whitey's black, an' kinda fat too."

"I ain't fat! Not like you!"

The fat kid giggled. "Yeah? Now you even *sound* like Whitey!"

497

"Fuckin' A!"

"Nobody says *that* anymore."

"Then, why's he called Whitey?"

"'Cause."

Robby thought a minute. There was an open doorway on the side of the warehouse and the other . . . Animals . . . were probably in there laughing. For sure, he was going to get beat up. He shrugged again. "What the fuck, man. I'm Robby. You got a smoke or you just gonna kick my ass? Go ahead. I don't give a shit."

The fat kid gave him that funny smile again, then dug a squashed Marlboro hardpack from a pocket and straightened two cigarettes. They fired off Robby's Bic.

"I'm Donny," the fat kid said. "Randers might kick it." He considered. "Or maybe just do you best-moves-for-keeps an' score himself another board."

Robby didn't say anything. He'd lost his last board that way. He took a big hit off the Marlboro and it buzzed his head. He didn't care about that either. The other dudes would probably show in a minute anyway.

Donny sank down and dangled his legs. Robby checked the doorway again, then slowly sat alongside. They smoked and spat in the water. Donny smelled a little like burger grease and Robby's belly rumbled.

"So, where's Fresno?" Donny asked.

"A long ways."

"Yeah? How'd you get here? You don't got to say."

"On a lame-o bus."

"Yeah? How come? You don't got to say."

"I ran away, man."

Donny blew smoke. "Yeah? Kevin don't hardly go home no more either. He didn't run as far as you. Just used to get wasted all the time an' sleep in dumpsters."

"I done that."

"Yeah? Only now he stays at the Center a lot with Nathaniel."

"Who's Nathaniel? Some kinda social-worker lady?"

Donny spat. "Nathaniel is a *boy,* man! Kinda."

Robby told himself to be cool. He could blow it easy with stupid questions and these dudes would figure him a squid and kick his ass. "That, um, Tiger-Dog your mark? It's pretty hot."

498

"Yeah. I do 'em." Donny looked back at the water. "I figure that's why they let me be a Animal."

Mascot, Robby thought. That figured. But some gang mascots were pretty important. He knew better than to ask how many Animals there were . . . or *where* they were. "Must be some bad dudes?"

"Or what! Even the dealers leave us alone. Most of the time." Donny sat a little straighter. "We kicked the shit outta some old perv what beat up Kevin a few weeks ago! Sent him bawlin' back to Silicone-land, man!" He looked at Robby. "So, where you sleepin'? You don't got to say."

Robby shrugged and looked back at the doorway. He really didn't feel like getting beat up.

Donny smiled. "Like King Kong?"

"Huh?"

"Any fuckin' place he wants to?"

Robby looked down at the water and nodded.

Donny glanced over his shoulder at the doorway, then back at Robby. "I'm alone, man." He flipped his cigarette away and stretched. "You hungry?"

Robby nodded again.

"Yeah? Me too. C'mon. My mom don't get home till around ten an' we got lots of stuff. You stay out here, for sure you get your ass wiped. Randers is cool, but he got no time for strange dudes, an' Kevin, shit, man, you wouldn't want to meet Kevin in the dark!" Donny struggled to his feet. "Um, why was you cryin', man? You don't got to say."

Robby thought a minute, then shrugged and pointed. "Your ocean sucks."

Donny looked out over the Bay. The fog was too thick to see San Francisco or even the Bridge going across. He gave Robby another funny smile. "Yeah."

Donny led through the doorway into blackness. They came out the front, walked a couple of blocks back up from the water, and turned into a door, then up a narrow box-stairs that smelled like old piss. The steps ended at a hall. A dim bulb burned halfway down and more light filtered through a window from a street-lamp. It looked to Robby like the floor tilted. The boards squeaked and popped and there was a lot of stuff spray-painted on the walls. Donny went to the far end, dug two keys from a

499

pocket, and undid the locks on a door that looked like some-body'd tried to kick down a couple of times. The hinges were loose as Donny shoved it open. He flipped a switch and Robby got that homesick feeling again. Not much was different anywhere.

There was one room, half of it kitchen. The other half had some thrashed furniture and pictures of Martin Luther King and JFK on top of an old TV. There was a messy bed under the win-dow, Donny's for sure. A half-open door showed a bathroom, and another door, closed, was probably his mom's room.

Donny pushed the hall door closed and snapped the locks. "Okay, huh?"

Robby nodded.

Donny pulled off his shirt and kicked out of his Nikes. "You like burgers, man?"

"Or what! Um, can I use your bathroom?"

"For sure. Um, pick up the seat or my mom has a cow." Donny snapped on the TV, then went to the fridge and started knocking stuff around inside. He held up a can of Budweiser as Robby came back. "Wanna beer, man?"

"For sure! Um, your mom *let* you drink beer?"

"Naw . . . leastways not at home. She seen me drunk on my ass a couple of times an' had a cow. I got this sixer from Weasel today an' gotta do somethin' with it before she gets back. We can drink it if you wanna."

"Um, don't Weasel get pissed?"

"Naw. The Animals always got beer."

Robby took the can and popped it, taking a small hit. He knew better than to chug on an empty stomach. "Um, you dudes do anything but beer, man?"

Donny squashed some globs of hamburger on the counter and plopped them in a big black pan. "Beer mostly. For sure every-body's checked out all the other shit, but it's hard to ride on most of that stuff. Kevin still does some rock once in a while an' Rix an' Randers both did some dust a couple weeks ago." He dropped the pan on the stove. "They both blew it an' Nathaniel had to chill 'em out. Nathaniel don't like that kinda shit. He's cool an' don't say nuthin', but you can tell. What you do in Fresno, man?"

"Me an' my friend Jeffers did some nuke a couple of weeks ago."

"What?"

500

"Um, cracker?"

"Yeah? Intense, huh?"

"Aw, only for a little while. You got to keep doin' more. Shit's cheap but it still runs into bucks. I don't like to mega-think anyways. Scary sometimes." He looked at the Bud can. "Figure most of the shredders only do this stuff . . . maybe some doob once in a while."

"Yeah. That's about like it is here. What's Fresno like, man? You got mountains an' stuff?"

"Naw, Fresno got total zip, man! It sucks!"

Donny turned. "Yeah? Didn't you see nuthin' nice comin' on the bus?"

"It was at night, mostly. Then today I was sleepin'. Ain't nuthin' nice nowhere, man."

"Yeah."

Robby looked at the TV. It was an old Silver Spoons rerun. Ricky was all bummed-out and crying because his dad wouldn't get him a new video game. Robby sipped beer. Behind him, Donny said, "*That* dude's got some nice shit."

"Yeah. But he's still got probs, man. He's got all that stuff an' still gots probs. I never seen him just hangin' with his friends, y'know? Just hangin' out somewhere an' doin' nuthin'? Like he don't really got no friends. Sometimes I feel sorry for him, man. Me an' Jeffers fuckin' get off more in a hour just curb-grindin' than I ever seen him do."

Donny nodded.

Robby walked to the bed and checked the posters—Iron Maiden, Mega-Deth. There were some drawings too, good ones, with the Tiger-Dog in color. "You do some hot shit, man. The Tiger-Dog should be a sticker!"

Donny pushed the burgers around with a fork, dodging grease spatters. "Um, thanks, dude." He looked up. "Um, you could probably stay here tonight if you wanna . . . The bed ain't very big, but I ain't no homo or nuthin'."

Robby sat on the rumpled bed. It smelled like sweaty-kid and burger grease. "Your mom get pissed?"

Donny flipped the meat. "Naw. But she ask you all kinds of stupid stuff, like where you live an' that sorta shit." He shrugged. "She's really pretty cool, but it might make you feel weird. You could make somethin' up."

501

Back against the wall by the bed was a good old Santa Cruz Slasher, ridden hard, but dusty now. "Um, that your board, man?"

Donny glanced up. "Naw. That was Duncan's. You can check it if you want."

Robby leaned down to snag it, then stopped. There was dried stuff all over, like old crumbly mud. Robby studied it a long time, but didn't touch it. "Um . . . Duncan get a new one or somethin'?"

Donny didn't look up. Robby hardly heard him above the burger sizzle. "Duncan's dead, man."

Donny mashed the meat hard with the fork. "He jumped off that warehouse by the wharf, man, a few months ago. I found his board in the mud between the rocks next day after the cops leave . . . like he tried to take it with him or somethin'! His mom was a bitch an' I wasn't gonna give it to her! None of the dudes wanted it either. Nobody's rode it again . . . figure the bearings all rusted now anyways. My mom don't like it. She won't even touch it, man!" He opened a cupboard and pulled out a pack of buns. "Duncan was my friend, kinda."

Robby took a big hit of beer. "Sorry, man. I just figured it was yours . . . before you got fat or somethin'."

Donny shrugged. "I always been fat."

Robby drank some more beer and turned to the pictures. Donny could draw to the max! There was one, five dudes on boards, sort of half-cartoon and half-serious. All were black except two, and none looked much over fourteen. One white kid was small and skinny but looked badder than hell. The other was like a total maller, blond and friendly. The black dude in the middle had muscles and it was easy to see he knew what is, is, and what ain't, wasn't worth nothing. That had to be Randers. Another was chubby and did look a little like Robby: Whitey. The last was like the cracker dude at the station, only younger.

Donny came over with two plates and four steaming burgers maxed with stuff and a beer under one arm. He sat beside Robby. "Scarf time."

"Or what!" Robby grabbed a burger and took a huge bite. He turned a little and pointed to the mean-looking white kid. "Weasel, right?"

Donny shook his head. "Naw. That's Kevin. Weasel's the other whitey."

"Don't look like no weasel."

Donny sucked beer and burped. "He put a rat in his mom's microwave once."

"Huh? Oh . . . yeah, right. I think I figured Randers—in the middle and, for sure, he could kick-ass. Who's the skinny dude with the teeth?"

"Rix."

"Ricks?"

"Naw. R-I-X, man. Wait. . . . " Donny slid to the floor and pulled a cardboard box from under the bed. It was full of magazines and had the Tiger-Dog on it. He dug out a Thundercats comic, flipped it open, and pointed to a Moleman. "Rix is the leader of the Molemen. Like, at first they hate the Thundercats an' keep tryin' to kill 'em, but then they get to be friends. There was this big monster-thing tryin' to kill the Molemen an' steal all their stuff an' it kept on blamin' the Thundercats, so Rix starts this big war. Then they finally figure out that they shouldn't be fightin' each other when it's this big monster-thing that's their real enemy."

Robby looked at the picture. The Molemen had huge front teeth. "Shit, they sure don't look friendly!"

"Yeah. Maybe that's why the Thundercats was ascared of 'em at first. Really, they was pretty good dudes behind them teeth."

Robby nodded. "You read a lot, man?"

Donny shrugged and stuck the book back. "Nuthin' else to do 'cept watch TV. The Animals all come up here a lot . . . probably 'cause my mom's not home. She don't mind, really, 'cept I figure she thinks they might not be good dudes, man."

"How come you ain't in the picture?"

"Aw, I drew it. Didn't seem right, y'know? 'Sides, I know what I look like."

"Shit, man. Killer dudes like you Animals could be makin' megabucks runnin' rock! There's one board-pack doin' that in Fresno. Even the little kids score a hundred a day just bein' watchers! Fuck. You dudes could have all new boards an' stuff!"

Donny shrugged. "Yeah. There's this bigger kid, fifteen or somethin', keeps comin' 'round tellin' Randers all that shit. He ain't even old enough for a license an' he drivin' a new Corvette, man! Randers think about it a lot, you can tell. Nathaniel don't like that dealer dude, kicked the shit outta him once. Dude say he gonna kill Nathaniel, only Nathaniel just laughs at him. 'Course, right then, the Animals would've killed the dude anyways, no prob."

Donny went to the fridge and snagged two more Buds. He brought them back, along with a box of Ding-Dongs, and sat. He looked at the old board and then out the window. "Duncan was a Animal then. This dealer dude finally talked him into bein' a runner. No prob an' he was makin' mega-money . . . scored everybody new wheels an' Swiss bearin's an' found some store'd sell him cases of Heinie at three times the price . . . 'cause he was only fourteen still." Donny shrugged. "He got sorta like that Ricky on Silver Spoons—all kinds of shit but nobody liked him much. Then he started into doin' rock himself. Max. Stayed wasted all the time an' didn't even ride no more. Spent all his money an' didn't have no friends. . . . Then he goes an' fuckin' jumps off the buildin' one night, man! Shit! I still wanted to be his friend only he wouldn't let me!"

Robby chugged the rest of his Bud, picked up a second. "Jeez, you gonna cry?"

"Naw!"

Robby ate a Ding-Dong and washed it down with beer. "They got this place in Fresno, man. The dudes call it the Rock House. It's for kids. You go there an' they kinda lock you inside, sellin' you rock an' give you food from Burger King." He shrugged. "One dude from school even sold his board so's he could keep goin' there a little more. I don't know, man. Maybe Randers is right? Sometimes I figure I don't know enough about shit, but ain't nobody tells you nuthin'! All that dogshit on TV looks like it's for squid-kids, man!"

"Yeah."

"So, how come this Nathaniel ain't in the picture?"

"Nathaniel ain't a Animal. He could be if he wanted, but maybe the other kids at the Center'd be ascared of him then?" Donny pointed to another drawing. "That's Nathaniel."

Robby looked. The dude was white, with really light blond hair like a surfer, down over his shoulders like a metaler. He was thin but not skinny and his face was hard but not mean. Robby studied the picture a long time. It was only a drawing but the dude was old. He looked about nineteen or something. "I thought you said Nathaniel was a boy?"

Donny ate a Ding-Dong and drank some more beer. "Naw. I said, *kinda*." He thought a while, "Ain't nobody knows what Nathaniel is. Sometimes he's a boy, but he can be a man when he gots to."

"Kinda like one of them homos that dresses like a kid?"

"Nathaniel ain't no homo, dude!"

"Aw, that ain't what I meant anyways."

Donny nodded and looked back at the picture. Then he whispered, "I figure he's some kinda werewolf."

"Naw! There ain't no such thing!" Robby turned back to the drawing. "Maybe in Germany or somethin'?"

Donny shrugged. "Yeah? Well, it's like he never gets no older . . . like he's gonna be what he is forever. He rides this ancient Hosoi Street board an' shreds to the max!" He chugged the last swallow and got up. "Anyways, if he is a werewolf or somethin', he's the coolest one you'll ever see! He *likes* kids, man! An' not the way all them pervs always tellin' you! He fuckin' *cried* about Duncan, man! Like it was his fault or somethin'! He talks real talk too . . . not like old people with all that dogshit stuff don't mean nuthin'. He ain't no pussy neither! Dude gots a prob, he can tell it to Nathaniel an' he *help!*"

Robby nodded and drank some more. "Wish we had a dude like that in Fresno."

Donny smiled. "I don't figure there's anybody else like Nathaniel anywheres! All the Animals would die for him, man! He don't tell us what to do neither. One time, Randers called slavers on him an' he didn't even hassle about it."

Robby finished the second Bud. He was a little buzzed and his belly was tight and full. It felt good. "Um, can I score another smoke off you, man? I'll pay you back."

"For sure." Donny held out the pack and they both fired from the Bic again.

"So, what's slavers?"

Donny got up and went to the fridge for the last two Buds. "You don't got that in Fresno?"

"I don't know. Maybe we call it somethin' else?"

505

"Yeah. Um, say you fuck-up on one of your friends? He gets to call slavers on you an' you got to do anything he wants till he calls it off again. Shit. Randers would call it on you right now just for bein' here!"

"Naw. We got nuthin' like that. If you fuck-over one of your friends or do something hurts all the dudes, you just get beat up."

Donny smiled and handed him a Bud. "Yeah? Slavers is better. The other dudes get to make you do stuff, *any* stuff, or they can just save it back till there's somethin' really gross or scary to get done." He shrugged. "You get your ass wiped an' it's over. Maybe it hurts awhile but no prob. Slavers makes you think about the shit you done longer an' you don't do it again."

"What if you don't wanna do it?"

"*Then* you get your ass wiped! You wouldn't be a Animal no more either!"

"Sounds like some little-kid shit. You ever get it called?"

"Yeah. Once."

"What'd you have to do, lick dog-piss or somethin'?"

"Naw. *That* would be little-kid shit!" Donny slid to the floor again and pulled out the box. He dug under all the skate magazines and comics and held up a black .45 automatic, then tossed it to Robby. "I had to roust it outta this dealer's car! Right in the street in the daytime!" He giggled. "Weasel helped a little. He threw a big handful of dogshit at the dealer-dude's bodyguard who's 'sposed to be watchin' the car. Right in the fuckin' *face,* man! Weasel booked on his board an' I score the gun while the guard was chasin' him! Dude had a Uzi, I think, but was ascared to use it on the street 'cause it was daytime."

Robby checked the big gun. "This's hot, man! It's like an army one! Jeffers gots this old thrasher .38 but I only seen this kind in movies. Eddie Murphy gots one." Robby held it in both hands and aimed at Donny's chest. He made a gun-sound and Donny grinned and fell back on the floor. Robby checked the gun again—heavy, black, and important as hell. "Ain't nobody gonna kick your ass when you got somethin' like this, man! Um, it loaded?"

Donny sat up and held out his hand. Robby gave him the gun and Donny pulled the clip and held it up. "Only seven. 'Sposed to have eight an' then you can keep one in the chamber too, but

I shot it once at the old Navy yard to see what it'd feel like." He grinned. "Slams your wrist, man, max!" He shoved the clip back in and threw it to Robby again.

"Awesome! How do you cock it?"

Donny sat on the bed. "Like this." He worked the slide. "Take off the safety. . . . " He did. "An' you ready to waste somebody."

Robby held it in both hands, arms out, finger on the trigger, and looked down the sight. "Wanted to waste this dude at school one time. Kept on beatin' me up . . . for *nuthin'*, man! Every fuckin' day!"

Donny nodded. "Yeah. I figure everybody gots somebody they wanna kill."

Robby lowered the gun and looked at it a while longer. Then he handed it back. Donny pulled the clip, worked the slide, and the bullet popped out. He pushed it back in the clip. "Randers said I could keep it. He already gots this huge .44 mag. Duncan give it to him when he was makin' all the money an' still tryin' to stay friends. Randers shot it a couple times. He say it kicks like hell."

"I like yours, man," Robby said. "Maybe I can score one too?"

Donny shrugged and put the gun back in the box, covering it with comics. "No prob if you gots the bucks. Kevin wants a Uzi like the dealers got, but he had to use some of his money to buy a new deck." He glanced at the dusty old board again. "Figure pretty soon he gonna try rock-runnin' too."

There was a clock on a box beside the bed and Donny glanced at it. "Nine-thirty, man. My mom'll be home in a little while." He handed Robby the last Ding-Dong. "She works at this bakery thrift-store; that's how come we always got lots of this stuff." He thought a minute. "Maybe I gots somethin' figured tonight. Chug the beer so's we can dump the empties."

Robby grinned and did. He stood up and fell against Donny, who laughed and caught him. "Hey, dude, three wimpy Buds an' you wasted?"

"Jeez, I ain't had nuthin' to eat in two days, man! What'd you expect?"

Donny held his shoulders. "Yeah? You ain't gonna puke or nuthin'?"

"Naw."

Donny kept hold of Robby's shoulders. "Um, I was gonna ask if you wanted to take the cans down to the garbage—climbin' them stairs sucks—but you out-of-it!"

"No I ain't! Shit, I could handle another sixer!"

"Yeah, right, dude. Get in bed against the wall. I'm so big mom'll never figure there's two kids in there. She might come over an' kiss me or somethin' but you just keep your head covered. Okay?"

"Or what." Robby pulled off his shirt and Donny had to catch him again.

"You totally ripped, man."

Robby laughed and fell back on the bed. He kicked off his Pumas. "Yeah? I wish I was like this all the time! No probs *forever!*"

Donny grinned. "Yeah. Be right back."

"I'm cool."

The window was open a little and that strange/familiar sea-smell drifted in on the breeze and played over Robby's body. He slid off his jeans and it felt good. Once in a while things didn't seem so bad, but it helped to be a little wasted. He was almost asleep when Donny came back and nudged him.

"Get under the blanket, dude."

"Huh? Oh, yeah, right."

Donny turned off the TV and the light, slid off his jeans, and climbed in the bed. Robby snuggled his head on the pillow. Donny's big body gave off heat like a radiator and the kid-smell was good. Except for the burger grease. Donny smelled a lot like Jeffers.

"Um, Robby?"

"Yeah?"

"Um, *you* ain't no homo, are you?"

"No way, man!"

"Sorry."

"It's cool. Um, Donny?"

"Yeah?"

"Why was you down there by the ocean tonight?"

"I don't know. I go there sometimes when there's nuthin' else to do. I think about Duncan, I guess. Nobody liked him anymore, but he used to be a pretty cool dude."

"Ain't your fault he's dead."

"Yeah. But I still think about him a lot. Nobody gives a shit, man."

"Or what. Um, I'm sorry I called you fat."

"That's cool. Night, man."

"Night."

Nominated by John Daniel & Co.

SPECIAL MENTION

(The editors also wish to mention the following important works published by small presses last year. Listing is in no particular order.)

FICTION

Tale Tales From the Mekong Delta—Kate Braverman (Story)
The Legend of Pig-Eye—Rick Bass (Paris Review)
A Perfectly Happy Woman—Patricia Matthews (Georgia Review)
A Perfect Day at Riis Park—Kerry Dolan (Quarterly West)
La Barca de la Illusion—Lucia Berlin (*Homesick,* Black Sparrow)
Quiet—Rick Rofihe (Grand Street)
Good Samaritans—R. D. Skillings (TriQuarterly)
Father's Mechanical Universe—Steve Heller (American Literary
    Review)
A&P Revisited—Greg Johnson (Southern Humanities Review)
The Cheater's Club—Maria Flook (Ploughshares)
Thieves—Elizabeth Evans (Crazyhorse)
The Earth's Crown—Robert Boswell (Ploughshares)
My Father Swims His Horse At Last—Robert Day (TriQuarterly)
Open Arms—Robert Olen Butler (Missouri Review)
Sen-Sen—Ewing Campbell (New England Review)
Nighthawks—Stuart Dybek (Paris Review)
The Whole World at Once—Sharon Oard Warner (The Gamut)
Riverman Five—H. Wessells (Temporary Culture)
Sweetness and Light—Clark Blaise (New Myths/MSS)
Whole Other Bodies—Walter Kirn (The Quarterly)
A Temporary Life—Amanda Jermyn (Peregrine)
Someday House—Barbara Croft (*Primary Colors,* New Rivers
    Press)
Quicksilver Carousel—Laura Ho Fineman (West/Word)

Closer To You—Scott Bradfield (Tampa Review)
Boat People—Joyce Thompson (Pulphouse)
Jump—Bill Roorbach (Sonora Review)
Seize The Day—Bonita Friedman (River Styx)
Brown Town—Linda Heller (Alaska Quarterly Review)
Candy—Reginald Gibbon (Colorado Review)
Spontaneous Combustion—Bradford Barkley (Other Voices)
Waiting for Elvis—Debra Lintz (Chariton Review)
The Shadow Child—Susan Kenney (*The Eloquent Edge*, Acadia
    Co.)
One Nothing—Stewart O'Nan (The New Renaissance)
Grace—Vickie Sears (*Simple Songs*, Firebrand Books)
Sons of Adam—Tony Ardizzone (Agni)
Fugitive—Jack Driscoll (West Branch)
Song and Dance—Darrell Spencer (High Plains Literary Review)
Solidarity Forever!—Gordon Weaver (Weber Studies)
The Loan—Peter Corodimas (Antioch Review)
A Man The Size of A Postage Stamp—Arnost Lustig (Kenyon
    Review)
Jordan Valley, 1977—Barry Lopez (ZYZZYVA)
In The Lurch—Jim Krusoe (Harbinger)
Down in Frenchburg—Lance Olsen (Alaska Quarterly Review)
The Disappeared—Charles Baxter (Michigan Quarterly Review)
The Kiss-Me-Quick—Rochelle Distelheim (North American
    Review)
Outings—Andrei Codrescu (New Directions)
Liza Wieland—Tommy Wadell (The Journal)
Barrier Methods—Sandy Huss (Crazyhorse)
Punishment—Melanie Rae Thon (Southern Review)
Collision—David Huddle (Shenandoah)
Robbery—Mark Spencer (Short Story)
Scrambled—Michael Stephens (Writ)
The Rabbit In The Moon—Gladys Swan (Colorado Review)
Mourning Dove—Annie Dawid (Folio)
The Skating Pond—Deborah Joy Corey (Carolina Quarterly)
Water Witch—Judith Slater (Sonora Review)
The One With Flowers—Eve Shelnutt (Mānoa)
Road of Thorns—June Wagner (Crazyhorse)
To The Western Wall, Luke Havergall—Thomas Kennedy
    (Margin)

Freedom, A Theory of—Lee K. Abbott (Gettysburg Review)
Jenny In Blue—Mark Spencer (Chariton Review)
The Parlor Game—Villy Sorensen (*Another Metamorphosis,* Fjord Press)
Overburden—Sharon Sheehe Stark (Prairie Schooner)
Mr. Irony—Padgett Powell (Paris Review)
Taco Mask—Steve Fisher (TriQuarterly)
Levidow—Gerald Shapiro (Kenyon Review)
I Was Aroused: To Dennis Cooper from Mina Karker—Dodie Bellamy (ZYZZYVA)
The Sound—Elizabeth Inness-Brown (Sycamore Review)
Speak Low—Melissa Lentricchia (New England Review)
The Reverse—Philip Graham (Florida Review)
Resurrection Bay—Caroline Patterson (Epoch)
Lily—Cynthia Wyatt (Chelsea)
One Hundred Foreskins—Louis Berney (Ploughshares)
The Commissar of Splendor—Lane von Herzen (Indiana Review)
The Welder's Cup—Gerald Haslam (American Literary Review)
Me Dying Trial—Patricia Powell (Caribbean Writer)
Patria—K. C. Frederick (Fiction International)
The Rabbit In The Moon—Gladys Swan (Colorado Review)
Solace—Patricia Lear (The Quarterly)
Whatever Happened to Jack Ruby's Dog—Geoff Schmidt (Chariton Review)
The Beautiful Baby—Monica Wood (Mānoa)
Stars—Jean Thompson (Indiana Review)
The Government Man—Ken Smith (TriQuarterly)
Streets—Paul K. Haeder (Turnstile)
Her Perfect Life—Sharon Solwitz (Other Voices)
Lord Royston's Tour—Lydia Davis (Conjunctions)
Raising the Dead in Cliffside, North Carolina—Ron Rash (Carolina Literary Companion)
Thief—Paul Griner (Caesura)
The World and Other Places—Jeanette Winterson (Grand Street)
What We Are Up Against—Dale Ray Phillips (Story)
The Girl on the Mountain—David Michael Kaplan (Beloit Fiction Journal)
Jocko—Joe David Bellamy (Boulevard)
Lives of the Fathers—Steven Schwartz (Ploughshares)
Hard Sell—Arnold E. Sabatelli (Ploughshares)

Overland—Sharon Sheehe Stark (Boulevard)

The Virgin Suicides—Jeffrey Eugenides (Paris Review)

Look At The Animals—Nicholas McDowell (Ontario Review)

Between the Flags—B. H. Friedman (Witness)

Mr. Tangible—Jerry Bumpus (Witness)

Throne of Blood—Abby Frucht (Ontario Review)

What Have You Been Doing? What Are You Doing Now?—
Christine Schutt (Quarterly)

Sunday Mornings—Andre Dubus (Boston Review)

Dragon's Seed—Madison Smartt Bell (Boulevard)

Kabuki Everything—Maxine Chernoff (Another Chicago
Magazine)

In Which Francesco Melzi Discovers Fiction—R. M. Berry
(Apalachee Quarterly)

Variations on the Robe—Steve Fisher (Epoch)

Retreat—Arthur Morey (TriQuarterly)

Courting Laura Providencia, And The Cost of Living—Jack Pu-
laski (Ohio Review)

Like A Normal Human Being—E. J. Graff (Iowa Review)

Mama—Ann Henry (City Lights Review)

South of Kittatinny—Hilding Johnson (Story)

"29"—Jill Peacock (Alaska Quarterly Review)

from The Jade Cabinet—Rikki Ducornet (Ontario Review)

How We Die—Gordon Lish (Antioch Review)

Propriety—Bret Lott (Story)

Little Miracles, Kept Promises—Sandra Cisneros (Grand Street)

The Epoxy-Resin Mao—Thomas Bradley (Berkeley Fiction
Review)

Safe Forever—Rich DeMarinis (Story)

Ophelia—Julie Blackwomon (*Voyages Out 2*, Seal Press)

The Robe—Wayne Karlin (Antietam Review)

The Run—Robert Canzoneri (Story)

In A Word, Trowbridge—Richard Stern (Antioch Review)

Common Sense—Rai Berzins (Malahat Review)

The Great Vomito—Crad Kilodney (*Junior Brain Tumors In Action*, Charnel House)

Timothydammit—Kent Meyers (Black Warrior Review)

The Trucker—Michael Henson (StoryQuarterly)

India—Peter Najarian (Five Fingers)

Constructing Alex Wetzelberg—Doris Vidaver (Chelsea)

Fishbone—Donna Trussell (Triquarterly)
The Isle of Love—Vicki Lindner (Ploughshares)
When Dolphins Dance—Richard Neumann (Laurel Review)
Speaking To The Fish—Lisa Sandlin (Shenandoah)
The Last Man To Die In The Nebraska Electric Chair—Margaret
    Fiske (Laurel Review)
Playing for Keeps—Joe Ashby Porter (New American Writing)
Bologoye—Mikhail Iossel (Boulevard)
The Eye of God—Josip Novakovich (Boulevard)
Hogs From Hell—Mark Spencer (Laurel Review)
Dakota Crossing—David Cates (Ontario Review)
Ballad—Dagoberto Gilb (Threepenny Review)
Fireflies—David Michael Kaplan (TriQuarterly)
Little Nightmares, Little Dreams—Rachel Simon (Story)
Xmas—Russell Banks (Antaeus)
Cousin Aubrey—Peter Taylor (Kenyon Review)

ESSAYS

Shortages—William Matthews (New England Review)
The Degradation of Money—Sam Hamill (ZYZZYVA)
Philip Larkin—Katha Pollitt (Grand Street)
Christopher Isherwood: Getting Things Right—Thom Gunn
    (Threepenny Review)
Death and the Image—Jay Cantor (TriQuarterly)
Taken by Haros: Death in a Cycladic Village—Alison Cadbury
    (Georgia Review)
Biograms—Paul West (City Lights Review)
A Border Tale—C. A. Fiedler (Yale Review)
Life with Daughters: Watching The Miss America Pageant—
    Gerald Early (Kenyon Review)
Six, Alas!—Ronald Johnson (Chicago Review)
A Long Game of Scrabble: A Memoir of Graham Greene—
    Michael Meyer (Paris Review)
from Hole In The Sky—William Kittredge (Ploughshares)
Deceptive Cadences—Norma Marder (Georgia Review)
Summer Storms—Larry Woiwode (Paris Review)
Swiss Army Knife—Bill Holm (Milkweed)
Not The Oprah Show—Jerry Herron (Ploughshares)

My Introduction to Katherine Anne Porter—Eudora Welty (Georgia Review)
A Trip With V. S. Naipaul—James Applewhite (Raritan Review)
Lament for A Maker—Donald Hall (AWP Chronicle)
Notes Toward A History of Scaffolding—Susan Mitchell (Provincetown Arts)
Taming Rio Bravo—Gerald Haslam (Pacific Discovery)
Living With Indians—Lewis P. Simpson (Southern Review)
James Wright At Kenyon—E. L. Doctorow (Gettysburg Review)
Mother Tongue—Amy Tan (Threepenny Review)
Delft: An Essay Poem—Albert Goldbarth (Kenyon Review)

POETRY

Carolina Steel Co. Canticle—Donald Platt (Poetry Northwest)
Flower of Five Blossoms—Galway Kinnell (American Poetry Review)
Sestina at 3 AM—Linda Pastan (Poetry)
Crossing the Desert—Steve Kowit (Spirit That Moves Us)
Bullhead Lily—Eric Ormsby (Blueline)
Thinking About My Father—David Huddle (Kenyon Review)
The Fast—Philip Levine (Beloit Poetry Journal)
Extinctions—David Wojahn (New England Review)
Male Image—Ted Solotaroff (American Poetry Review)
Triage—Chris Gompert (Poet & Critic)
Poem For My Brother, Manager of a Go-Go Bar in Roselle Park, NJ—Andrea Hollander Budy (Zone 3)
Crèche—Maura Stanton (Crazyhorse)
Le Courier de Jeanne D'Arc—Linda McCarriston (Georgia Review)
Patriotics—David Baker (Shenandoah)
G-9—Tim Dlugos (Paris Review)
Sometimes The First Boys Don't Count—Denise Duhamel (North Dakota Quarterly)
Tiananmen Square—Patrick Daly (Americas Review)
The Rape—Ray Lopez (Occident)
Somnium—Dennis Saleh (The Windhorse Review)
"Too Much," Albert Goldbarth (Georgia Review)
Chimera—Carol Frost (*Chimera*, Gibbs Smith)

The Light of the World—Louie Skipper (Alabama Poets)
Rapture—Christopher Davis (Hayden's Ferry Review)
What I Remember of What They Told Me—John Engman (Crazy-
    horse)
An Observer of Incidentality—Russell Edson (Parnassus)
One-Legged Wooden Red-Wing—Stanley Plumly (Field)
Small Talk—Coleman Barks (Kenyon Review)
Suite—Mark Jarman (Crazyhorse)
Benediction—Richard Jackson (Prairie Schooner)
Party—Joe Bolton (Galileo Press)
Graveyard Shift—Henry Carlile (Shenandoah)
Forgetfulness—Billy Collins (Poetry)
Texas—Jan Conn (*South of the Tudo Bem Cafe*, Vehicule Press)
Ghazal 84—Jim Daniels (The MacGuffin)
Plantation Road—Barbara Fritchie (New Delta Review)
After The Last Practice—Edward Hirsch (Kenyon Review)
Butcher Scraps—Faye Kicknosway (Mānoa)
The Accident—Lisa Lewis (Western Humanities Review)
The Inn—Barbara Moore (*Farewell to the Body*, Word Works)
The Troubadour—Rosalie Moore (Blue Unicorn)

PRESSES FEATURED IN THE PUSHCART PRIZE EDITIONS (1976–1991)

Acts
Agni Review
Ahsahta Press
Ailanthus Press
Alaska Quarterly Review
Alcheringa/Ethnopoetics
Alice James Books
Ambergris
Amelia
American Literature
American PEN
American Poetry Review
American Scholar
The American Voice
Amicus Journal
Amnesty International
Anaesthesia Review
Another Chicago Magazine
Antaeus
Antietam Review
Antioch Review
Apalachee Quarterly
Aphra
The Ark
Ascensius Press
Ascent
Aspen Leaves

Aspen Poetry Anthology
Assembling
Bamboo Ridge
Barlenmir House
Barnwood Press
The Bellingham Review
Bellowing Ark
Beloit Poetry Journal
Bennington Review
Bilingual Review
Black American Literature Forum
Black Rooster
Black Scholar
Black Sparrow
Black Warrior Review
Blackwells Press
Bloomsbury Review
Blue Cloud Quarterly
Blue Unicorn
Blue Wind Press
Bluefish
BOA Editions
Bookslinger Editions
Boulevard
Boxspring
Brown Journal of the Arts
Burning Deck Press

Caliban
California Quarterly
Callaloo
Calliope
Calliopea Press
Canto
Capra Press
Carolina Quarterly
Cedar Rock
Center
Chariton Review
Charnel House
Chelsea
Chicago Review
Chouteau Review
Chowder Review
Cimarron Review
Cincinnati Poetry Review
City Lights Books
Clown War
CoEvolution Quarterly
Cold Mountain Press
Colorado Review
Columbia: A Magazine of Poetry
    and Prose
Confluence Press
Confrontation
Conjunctions
Copper Canyon Press
Cosmic Information Agency
Crawl Out Your Window
Crazyhorse
Crescent Review
Cross Cultural Communications
Cross Currents
Cumberland Poetry Review
Curbstone Press
Cutbank
Dacotah Territory
Daedalus
Decatur House
December
Denver Quarterly

Domestic Crude
Dragon Gate Inc.
Dreamworks
Dryad Press
Duck Down Press
Durak
East River Anthology
Ellis Press
Empty Bowl
Epoch
Exquisite Corpse
Fiction
Fiction Collective
Fiction International
Field
Firebrand Books
Firelands Art Review
The Formalist
Five Fingers Review
Five Trees Press
Frontiers: A Journal of Women
    Studies
Gallimaufry
Genre
The Georgia Review
Gettysburg Review
Ghost Dance
Goddard Journal
David Godine, Publisher
Graham House Press
Grand Street
Granta
Graywolf Press
Green Mountains Review
Greenfield Review
Greensboro Review
Guardian Press
Hard Pressed
Hermitage Press
Hills
Holmgangers Press
Holy Cow!
Home Planet News

Hudson Review
Icarus
Iguana Press
Indiana Review
Indiana Writes
Intermedia
Intro
Invisible City
Inwood Press
Iowa Review
Ironwood
Jam To-day
The Kanchenjuga Press
Kansas Quarterly
Kayak
Kelsey Street Press
Kenyon Review
Latitudes Press
Laughing Waters Press
Laurel Review
L'Epervier Press
Liberation
Linquis
The Little Magazine
Living Hand Press
Living Poets Press
Logbridge-Rhodes
Lowlands Review
Lucille
Lynx House Press
Magic Circle Press
Malahat Review
Mānoa
Manroot
Massachusetts Review
Mho & Mho Works
Micah PUblications
Michigan Quarterly
Milkweed Editions
Milkweed Quarterly
The Minnesota Review
Mississippi Review
Mississippi Valley Review

Missouri Review
Montana Gothic
Montana Review
Montemora
Moon Pony Press
Mr. Cogito Press
MSS
Mulch Press
Nada Press
New America
New American Review
The New Criterion
New Delta Review
New Directions
New England Review and Bread
    Loaf Quarterly
New Letters
New Virginia Review
New York Quarterly
Nimrod
North American Review
North Atlantic Books
North Dakota Quarterly
North Point Press
Northern Lights
Northwest Review
O. ARS
Obsidian
Oconee Review
October
Ohio Review
Ontario Review
Open Places
Orca Press
Oxford Press
Oyez Press
Painted Bride Quarterly
Paris Review
Parnassus: Poetry in Review
Partisan Review
Penca Books
Pentagram
Penumbra Press

Pequod
Persea: An International Review
Pipedream Press
Pitcairn Press
Ploughshares
Poet and Critic
Poetry
Poetry East
Poetry Northwest
Poetry Now
Prairie Schooner
Prescott Street Press
Promise of Learnings
Puerto Del Sol
Quarry West
The Quarterly
Quarterly West
Raccoon
Rainbow Press
Raritan A Quarterly Review
Red Cedar Review
Red Clay Books
Red Dust Press
Red Earth Press
Release Press
Revista Chicano-Riquena
River Styx
Rowan Tree Press
Russian *Samizdat*
Salmagundi
San Marcos Press
Sea Pen Press and Paper Mill
Seal Press
Seamark Press
Seattle Review
Second Coming Press
The Seventies Press
Sewanee Review
Shankpainter
Shantih
Sheep Meadow Press
Shenandoah
A Shout In The Street

Sibyl-Child Press
Small Moon
The Smith
Some
The Sonora Review
Southern Poetry Review
Southern Review
Southwest Review
Spectrum
The Spirit That Moves Us
St. Andrews Press
Story
Story Quarterly
Streetfare Journal
Stuart Wright, Publisher
Sulfur
The Sun
Sun & Moon Press
Sun Press
Sunstone
Tar River Poetry
Teal Press
Telephone Books
Telescope
Temblor
Tendril
Texas Slough
13th Moon
THIS
Thorp Springs Press
Three Rivers Press
Threepenny Review
Thunder City Press
Thunder's Mouth Press
Tombouctou Books
Toothpaste Press
Transatlantic Review
TriQuarterly
Truck Press
Tuumba Press
Undine
Unicorn Press
University of Pittsburgh Press

Unmuzzled Ox
Unspeakable Visions of the
    Individual
Vagabond
Virginia Quarterly
Wampeter Press
Washington Writers Workshop
Water Table
Western Humanities Review
Westigan Review
Wickwire Press

Wilmore City
Word Beat Press
Word-Smith
Wormwood Review
Writers Forum
Xanadu
Yale Review
Yardbird Reader
Yarrow
Y'Bird
ZYZZYVA

CONTRIBUTING SMALL PRESSES

(These presses made or received nominations for this edition of *The Pushcart Prize*. See the *International Directory of Little Magazines and Small Presses,* Dustbooks, Box 1056, Paradise, CA 95969, for subscription rates, manuscript requirements and a complete international listing of small presses.)

A

Aardvaark Enterprises, 204 Millbank Dr., S.W., Calgary, Alberta *CANADA* T2Y 2H9

Abattoir Editions, Annex 22, Univ. of Nebraska, Omaha, NE 68182

Abraxas Press, Inc., 2518 Gregory St., Madison, WI 53711

Acadia Publishing Co., P.O. Box 170, Bar Harbor, ME 04609

Adastra Press, 101 Strong St., Easthampton, MA 01027

ADD, see A Different Drummer

Agni, 236 Bay State Rd., Boston Univ., Boston, MA 02215

Agog Magazine, c/o Scott Gray, 372 5th Ave., Brooklyn, NY 11215

AHA Books, see Mirrors

Ahsahta Press, Boise State Univ., 1910 University Dr., Boise, ID 83725

Aim Magazine, P.O. Box 20554, Chicago, IL 60620

Alabama Literary Review, 253 Smith Hall, Tory State Univ., Troy, AL 36082

Alaska Quarterly Review, English Dept., Univ. of Alaska, Anchorage, AK 99508

The Alchemist, P.O. Box 123, LaSalle, Que, *CANADA*

Alice James Books, 33 Richdale Ave., Cambridge, MA 02140

Alpha Beat Soup, 68 Winter Ave., Scarborough, Ont, *CANADA* M1K 4M3

Amador Publishers, P.O. Box 12335, Albuquerque, NM 87195

Ambergris, P.O. Box 29919, Cincinnati, OH 45229

Amelia, 329 "E" St., Bakersfield, CA 93304

American Poetry Review, 1721 Walnut St., Philadelphia, PA 19103

The American Voice, 332 W. Broadway, Ste. 1215, Louisville, KY 40202

The Animals' Agenda, 456 Monroe Turnpike, Monroe, CT 06468

Anna's House, P.O. Box 438070, Chicago, IL 60643

Another Chicago Magazine (& Press), 3709 N. Kenmore, Chicago, IL 60613

Ant Farm, P.O. Box 15513, Santa Fe, NM 87506

Antaeus, 26 W. 17th, New York, NY 10011

Antietam Review, 82 W. Washington St., Hagerstown, MD 21740

The Antioch Review, P.O. Box 148, Yellow Springs, OH 45387

Anvil Press, P.O. Box 1575, Sta. A, Vanvouver, B.C., *CANADA* V6C 2P7

Apalachee Quarterly, P.O. Box 20106, Tallahassee, FL 32316

Applezaba Press, P.O. Box 4134, Long Beach, CA 90804

Arbiter Press, P.O. Box 592540, Orlando, FL 32859

ARCHAE, 10 Troilus, Old Bridge, NJ 08857

Ariadne Press, 4817 Tallahassee Ave., Rockville, MD 20853

Artful Dodge, English Dept., College of Wooster, Wooster, OH 44691

Ashley Books, Inc., 4600 W. Commercial Blvd., Ft. Lauderdale, FL 33319

Ashod Press, P.O. Box 1147, New York, NY 10159

Atlantic Advocate, P.O. Box 3370, Fredericton, N.B. *CANADA* E3B 5A2

AVEC, P.O. Box 1059, Penngrove, CA 94951

AWP Chronicle, Associated Writing Programs, Old Dominion Univ., Norfolk, VA 23529

B

Bad Haircut, 3115 S.W. Roxbury St., Seattle, WA 98126

Bakunin, 100 Atrium Way, #124, Davis, CA 95616

Bamberger Books, P.O. Box 1126, Flint, MI 48501

Bamboo Ridge, P.O. Box 61781, Honolulu, HI 96822

Bay Windows, 1523 Washington St., Boston, MA 02118

Bear House Publishing, 2711 Watson, Houston, TX 77009

The Bellingham Review, 1007 Queen St., Bellingham, WA 98226

Bellowing Ark, P.O. Box 45637, Seattle WA 98145

Beloit Poetry Journal, Box 154, RFD 2, Ellsworth, ME 04605

The Bench Press, 1355 Raintree Dr., Columbia, SC 29212

Bennett & Kitchel, P.O. Box 4422, East Lansing, MI 48826

Berkeley Fiction Review, 700 Eshelman Hall, Univ. of Calif., Berkeley, CA 94720

Berkeley Poets Workshop & Press, P.O. Box 459, Berkeley, CA 94701

Bilingual Review/Press, Hispanic Research Center, Arizona State Univ., Tempe, AZ 85287

Black Moss Press, 1939 Alsace, Windsor, Ont. *CANADA* N8W 1M5

Black River Review, 855 Mildred Ave., Lorain, OH 44052

Black Warrior Review, P.O. Box 2936, Tuscaloosa, Al 35487

Blue Unicorn, 22 Avon Rd., Kensington, CA 94707

Blueline, English Dept., Potsdam College, Potsdam, NY 13676

BLUR, Boston Literary Review, Box 357, W. Somerville, MA 02144

Bone & Flesh, P.O. Box 349, Concord, NH 03302

Border/Lines, 183 Bathurst St., #301, Toronto, Ont. *CANADA* M5T 2R7

The Boston Review, 33 Harrison Ave., Boston, MA 02111

Bottom Dog Press, c/o Firelands College, Huron, OH 44839

Bottomfish, DeAnza College, 21250 Stevens Creek Blvd., Cupertino, CA 95024

Boulevard, 2400 Chestnut St., #2208, Philadelphia, PA 19103

Branden Publishing Co., Inc., 17 Station St., Box 843, Brookline Village, Boston, MA 02147

Breakthrough!, see Aardvaark Enterprises

Breitenbush Books, P.O. Box 82157, Portland, OR 97282

Brick Books, Box 38, Sta. B, London, Ont., *CANADA* N6A 4V3

Burning Books, 690 Market, Ste. 1501, San Francisco, CA 94104

Burning Deck, 71 Elmgrove Ave., Providence, RI 02906

Butler, Geoff, P.O. Box 29, Granville Ferry, Nova Scotia, CANADA B0S 1K0

Byline Magazine, P.O. Box 130596, Edmond, OK 73013

C

Cacanadadada Press, Ltd., 3350 W. 21st Ave, Vancouver, B.C. *CANADA* V6S 1G7

Cafe Gaga, 2630 Robert Walker Place, Arlington, VA 22207

Calapooya Collage, P.O. Box 309, Monmouth, OR 97361

Caliban, P.O. Box 4321, Ann Arbor, MI 98106

Calliope, Creative Writing Program, Roger Williams College, Bristol, RI 02809

Calypso, 175 E. Washington, #C, El Cajon, CA 92020

Calyx, P.O. Box B, Corvallis, OR 97339

The Camel Press, Big Cove Tannery, PA 17212

Caravan Press, 343 S. Broadway, Los Angeles, CA 90013

The Caribbean Writer, Univ. of The Virgin Islands, RR02, Box 10,000, St. Croix, U.S. Virgin Islands, 00850

Carpenter Press, P.O. Box 14387, Columbus, OH 43214

Catalyst, 511 E. Mariposa, #116, Phoenix, AZ 85012

Cemetery Dance (Magazine), P.O. Box 858, Edgewood, MD 21040

Charnel House, P.O. Box 281, Sta. S, Toronto, Ont. *CANADA* M5M 4L7

The Chattahoochee Review, DeKalb College, 2101 Womack Rd., Dunwoody, GA 30338

Chelsea, Box 5880, Grand Central Sta., New York, NY 10163

Chicago Review, 5801 S. Kenwood Ave, Chicago, IL 60637

Chips off the Writer's Block, P.O. Box 83371, Los Angeles, CA 90083

Chiron Review, 1514 Stone, Great Bend, KS 67530

Cimarron Review, English Dept., Oklahoma State Univ., Stillwater, OK 74078

Cincinnati Poetry Review, English Dept., Univ. of Cincinnati, Cincinnati, OH 45221

Cinco Puntos Press, 2709 Louisville, El Paso, TX 79930

City Lights, 261 Columbus Ave, San Francisco, CA 94133

Cleveland State Univ. Poetry Center, English Dept., Rhodes Tower, Cleveland, OH 44115

The Climbing Art, P.O. Box 816, Alamosa, CO 81101

Clockwatch Review, English Dept., Illinois Wesleyan Univ., Bloomington, IL 61702

Confluence Press, Lewis-Clark State College, Lewiston, ID 83501

Confrontation, English Dept., C. W. Post of Long Island Univ., Greenvale, NY 11548

Context South, P.O. Box 291, State University, AR 72467

Council Oak Books, 1428 S. St. Louis, Tulsa, OK 74120

Creeping Bent, 1023 Main St., Bethlehem, PA 18018

The Crescent Review, P.O. Box 15065, Winston-Salem, NC 27113

The Critic, c/o The Thomas More Assoc., 205 W. Monroe St., 6th fl., Chicago, IL 60606

Crooked Roads, see Wheel of Fire Press

CutBank, English Dept., Univ. of Montana, Missoula, MT 59812

D

Dalkey Archive Press, 5700 College Rd., Lisle, IL 60532

Damascus Works, 1101 N. Calvert St., #1605, Baltimore, MD 21202

John Daniel & Co., Publishers, P.O. Box 21922, Santa Barbara, CA 93121

Dawn-Rose Press, 12470 Fiori Lane, Sebastopol, CA 95472

Dawnwood Press, 387 Park Avenue S, New York, NY 10016

Delirium, c/o Muggwart Press, Rte. 1, Box 7X, Harrison, ID 83833

Denver Quarterly, Univ. of Denver, University Park, Denver, CO 80208

Devil Mountain Books, P.O. Box 4115, Walnut Creek, CA 94596

A Different Drummer, 84 Bay 28th St., Brooklyn, NY 11214

Dreams & Visions, c/o Skysong Press, RR1 Washago, Ont., CANADA L0K 2B0

Druid Press, 2724 Shades Crest Rd., Birmingham, AL 35216

Dryad Press, 15 Sherman Ave., Takoma Park, MD 20912

Dufour Editions, Inc., P.O. Box 449, Chester Springs, PA 19425

E

Earthwise Review, P.O. Box 680536, Miami, FL 33168

Edgewood Press, P.O. Box 264, Cambridge, MA 02238

Wm. B. Eerdmans Publishing Co, 255 Jefferson Ave. SE, Grand Rapids, MI 49503

the eleventh MUSE, P.O. Box 2413, Colorado Springs, CO 80901

Embers, Box 104, Guilford, CT 06437

Empyreal Press, P.O. Box 1746, Place du Parc, Montreal, Que CAN H2W 2R7

EOTU, 1810 W. State #115, Boise, ID 83702

EPOCH, 251 Goldwin Smith Hall, Cornell Univ., Ithaca, NY 14853

Event, Douglas College, P.O. Box 2503, New Westminster, B.C. CANADA V3L 5B2

Exit 13 Magazine, c/o Tom Plante, P.O. Box 423, Fanwood, NJ 07023

Experiment in Words, P.O. Box 470186, Fort Worth, TX 76147

F

Farragut Publishing Co., 2033 M St., NW, Ste. 640, Washington, DC 20036

Fiction International, English Dept., San Diego State Univ., San Diego, CA 92182

Field, Creative Writing Program, Rice Hall 17, Oberlin College, Oberlin, OH 44074

The Figures, 5 Castle Hill, Great Barrington, MA 01230

Fine Madness, P.O. Box 31138, Seattle, WA 98103

Firebrand Books, 141 The Commons, Ithaca, NY 14850

1st Amendment Publishers, 1505 Llano St., Ste. H-3, Santa Fe, NM 87501

Five Fingers Review, 949 Fell St., #4, San Francisco, CA 94117

Fjord Press, P.O. Box 16501, Seattle, WA 98116

The Florida Review, English Dept., Univ. of Central Florida, Orlando, FL 32816

Folio, Dept. of Literature, The American Univ., 4400 Mass Ave., Washington, DC 20016

For Poets Only, P.O. Box 4855, Schenectady, NY 12304

The Formalist, 525 S. Rotherwood, Evansville, IN 47714

Forum, English Dept., Ball State Univ., Muncie, IN 47306

Forum, Kansas City Artists Coalition, 201 Wyandotte, Kansas City, MO 64105

Free Focus, see Ostentatious Mind
Free Lunch, P.O. Box 7647, Laguna Niguel, CA 92607
French Broad Press, The Asheville School, Asheville, NC 28806
Frogpond, 970 Acequia Madre, Santa Fe, NM 87501

G

Galileo Press, 7215 York Rd., Ste. 210, Baltimore, MD 21212
Gamut, 1218 Fenn Tower, Cleveland State Univ., Cleveland, OH 44115
Gauntlet, 309 Powell Rd., Springfield, PA 19064
Georgia Review, Univ. of Georgia, Athens, GA 30602
Gettysburg Review, Gettysburg College, Gettysburg, PA 17325
Giants Play Well in the Drizzle, 326A Fourth St., Brooklyn, NY 11215
The Gopherwood Review, Box 58784, Houston, TX 77256
Grand Street, 135 Central Park West, New York, NY 10023
Green Mountain Review, Johnson State College, Johnson, VT 05686
Green Stone Publications, P.O. Box 15623, Seattle, WA 98115
The Greenfield Review, 2 Middle Grove Rd., P.O. Box 308, Greenfield Center, NY 12833
Green's Magazine, P.O. Box 3236, Regina, Saskatchewan, CANADA S4P 3H1
The Greensboro Review, English Dept., Univ. of North Carolina, Greensboro, NC 27412
Gypsy, 10708 Gay Brewer, El Paso, TX 79935

H

Hamilton Haiku Press, 4 E. 23rd St., Hamilton, Ont., CANADA L8V 2W6
Hammers, c/o Doublestar Press, 1718 Sherman Ave, Ste. 205, Evanston, IL 60201
Hanging Loose, 231 Wyckoff St., Brooklyn, NY 11217
Harp-Strings, 310 S. Adams St., Beverly Hills, FL 32665
Haypenny Press, 211 New Street, West Paterson, NJ 07424
Helikon Press, 120 W. 71st St., New York, Ny 10023

Hen's Teeth, P.O. Box 689, Brookings, SD 57006

High Plains Literary Review, 180 Adams St., Ste. 250, Denver, CO 80206

High Plains Press, P.O. Box 123, Glendo, WY 82213

Hob-Nob, 994 Nissley Rd., Lancaster, PA 17601

Home Planet News, P.O. Box 415, Stuyvesant Sta., New York, NY 10009

Hot Springs Gazette, Box 480740, Los Angeles, CA 90048

the howling mantra, P.O. Box 1821, La Crosse, WI 54602

Hubbub, English Dept., Reed College, Portland, OR 97202

The Hudson Review, 684 Park Avenue, New York, NY 10021

Hutton Publications, P.O. Box 1870, Hayden, ID 83835

I

In One Ear Press, 3527 Voltaire St., San Diego, CA 92106

Indiana Review, 316 N. Jordan Ave, Bloomington, IN 47405

Infinity Limited, P.O. Box 2713, Castro Valley, CA 94546

Innisfree, P.O. Box 277, Manhattan Beach, CA 90266

Invisible City, see Red Hill Press

The Iowa Review, 308 EPB, Univ. of Iowa, Iowa City, IA 52242

Iowa Woman, P.O. Box 2938, Waterloo, IA 50704

ipsissima verba/ the very words, see Haypenny Press

J

The Journal, English Dept., Ohio State Univ., Columbus, OH 43210

Journal of New Jersey Poets, County College of Morris, Randolph, NJ 07869

Journal of Regional Criticism, 1025 Garner St, #18, Colorado Springs, CO 80905

K

K, 351 Dalhousie St., Brantford, Ont. CANADA N3S 3V9

Kalliope, Florida Community College, 3939 Roosevelt Blvd., Jacksonville, FL 32205

Karamu, English Dept., Eastern Illinois Univ., Charleston, IL 61920
Kelsey Review, Mercer Co. Community College, P.O. Box B, Trenton, NJ 08690
Kelsey St. Press, P.O. Box 9235, Berkeley, CA 94709
The Kenyon Review, Kenyon College, Gambier, OH 43022
Key West Review, P.O. Box 2082, Key West, FL 33045
Kingfisher, P.O. Box 9783, North Berkeley, CA 94709
Knights Press, 190 Henry St., Stamford, CT 06902

L

Lambda Book Report, 1625 Connecticut Ave, NW, Washington, DC 20009
Laughing Bear Press, P.O. Box 36159, Denver, CO 80236
The Laurel Review, English Dept., Northwest Missouri State Univ., Maryville, MO 64468
The Literary Review, Fairleigh Dickinson Univ., 285 Madison Ave., Madison, NJ 07940
Literary Sketches, P.O. Box 810571, Dallas, TX 75381
Little Free Press, Rt. 1, Box 102, Cushing, MN 56443
The Little Magazine, English Dept., SUNY, Albany, NY 12222
litspeak, Universität Regensburg, Institut fur Anglistik, PT 3.2.86 W-8400 Regensburg, GERMANY
The Long Story, 11 Kingston St., North Andover, MA 01845
Loonfeather, 426 Bemidji Ave, Bemidji, MN 56601
Los Arboles Publications, P.O. Box 7000–54, Redondo Beach, CA 90277
Lost Creek Letters, Box 373A, Rushville, MO 64484
Lost Generation Journal, Rt. 5, Box 134, Salem, MO 65401
Lost Roads Publishers, P.O. Box 5848, Providence, RI 02903
Lowlands Press, 6109 Magazine, New Orleans, LA 70118
Lullwater Review, Box 22036, Emory Univ., Atlanta, GA 30322
Lynx, P.O. Box 169, Toutle, WA 98649
The Lyric, 307 Dunton Dr., SW, Blacksburg, VA 24060

M

MacDonald & Reinecke, The Press of, P.O. Box 840, Arroyo Grande, CA 93420

The MacGuffin, Schoolcraft College, 18600 Haggerty Rd., Livonia, MI 48152

The Madison Review, English Dept., Univ. of Wisconsin, Madison, WI 53703

Magnificat Press, P.O. Box 365, Avon, NJ 07717

The Malahat Review, Univ. of Victoria, P.O. Box 3045, Victoria, B.C. CANADA V8W 3P4

The Manhattan Review, 440 Riverside Dr., New York, NY 10027

manic d press, P.O. Box 410804, San Francisco, CA 94141

Mankato Poetry Review, English Dept., Box 53, Mankato State Univ., Mankato, MN 56001

Mānoa, English Dept., Univ. of Hawaii, 1733 Donaghho Rd., Honolulu, HI 96822

The Massachusetts Review, Memorial Hall, Univ. of Massachusetts, Amherst, MA 01003

McFarland & Co., Publishers, Box 611, Jefferson, NC 28640

Metrosphere, Metropolitan State College of Denver, P.O. Box 173362, Campus Box 57, Denver, CO 80217

Micah Publications, 255 Humphrey St., Marblehead, MA 01945

Michigan Quarterly Review, Univ. of Michigan, 3032 Rackham Bldg., Ann Arbor, MI 48109

Mid-List Press, 2300 Bryant Ave S, Minneapolis, MN 55405

The Midland Review, 205 Morrill Hall, OSU, Stillwater, OK 74078

Midstream, 515 Park Avenue, New York, NY 10022

Midwest Farmer's Market, P.O. Box 1272, Galesburg, IL 61402

Milkweed Editions, P.O. Box 3226, Minneapolis, MN 55403

Mind in Motion, P.O. Box 1118, Apple Valley, CA 92307

M.I.P. Company, P.O. Box 27484, Minneapolis, MN 55427

Mirrors, P.O. Box 1250, Gualala, CA 95445

Mississippi Valley Review, English Dept., Western Illinois Univ., Macomb, IL 61455

The Missouri Review, 1507 Hillcrest Hall, Univ. of Missouri, Columbia, MO 65211

Moonstone Blue, see Night Roses

Mosaic, c/o Y. David Shulman, 324 Ave F, Brooklyn, NY 11218

Mr. Cogito, Box 627, Pacific Univ., Forest Grove, OR 97116

Mudfish, c/o Box Turtle Press, Inc, 184 Franklin St., New York, NY 10013

The Nebraska Review, Creative Writing Prog., Univ. of Nebraska, Omaha, NE 68182

NER/BLQ, see New England Review

New American Writing, 2920 W. Pratt, Chicago, IL 60645

New Delta Review, English Dept., Louisiana State Univ., Baton Rouge, LA 70803

New England Review, Middlebury College, Middlebury, VT 05753

New Hope Press, 304 S. Denton St., Dothan, AL 36301

New Letters, UMKC, 5100 Rockhill Rd., Kansas City, MO 64110

New Mexico Humanities Review, Humanities Dept., New Mexico Tech., Socorro, NM 87801

New Renaissance, 9 Heath Rd., Arlington, MA 02174

New Rivers Press, 420 N. 5th St., Ste. 910, Minneapolis, MN 55401

New Victoria Publishers, Inc., Box 27, Norwich, VT 05055

New World Library, 58 Paul Drive, San Rafael, CA 94903

New York Quarterly, P.O. Box 693, Old Chelsea Station, New York, NY 10019

Night Roses, P.O. Box 393, Prospect Heights, IL 60070

Nimrod, Arts & Humanities Council of Tulsa, Harwelden, 2210 S. Main, Tulsa, OK 74114

North American Review, Univ. Northern Iowa, Cedar Falls, IA 50614

North Country Press, P.O. Box 440, Belfast, ME 04915

North Dakota Quarterly, P.O. Box 8237, Univ. of North Dakota, Grand Forks, ND 58202

Northern Lights, P.O. Box 8084, Missoula, MT 59807

The Northern Review, Univ. of Wisconsin, Stevens Point, WI 54481

Northwest Review, 369 PLC, Univ. of Oregon, Eugene, OR 97403

Norton Coker Press, P.O. Box 640543, San Francisco, CA 94164

Nostalgia, P.O. Box 2224, Orangeburg, SC 29118

Now & Then, c/o CASS, Box 19180A, East Tenn. State Univ., Johnson City, TN 37614

now it's up to you publications, 157 S. Logan, Denver, CO 80209

NRG Magazine, 6735 S.E. 78th St., Portland, OR 97206

Nuts to Us!, see New Hope Press

O

Occident Press, 70 Eshleman Hall, Univ. of Calif., Berkeley, CA 94720

The Ohio Review, Ellis Hall, Ohio Univ., Athens, OH 45701

Oktoberfest, see Druid Press

Ontario Review, 9 Honey Brook Dr., Princeton, NJ 08540

Open Street Review, P.O. Box 746, Louisville, KY 40201

Orchises, P.O. Box 20602, Alexandria, VA 22320

Osiris, Box 297, Deerfield, MA 01842

Ostentatious Mind, 224 - 82nd St., Brooklyn, NY 11209

The Other Side, 1225 Dandridge St., Fredericksburg, VA 22401

Other Voices, 820 Ridge Rd., Highland Park, IL 60035

Ox Head Press, Rte. 3, Box 136, Browerville, MN 56438

Oxford Magazine, 356 Bachelor Hall, Miami Univ., Oxford, OH 45056

P

Pacific Review, English Dept., California State Univ., San Bernardino, CA 92407

Pandit Press, 24843 Del Prado, Ste. 405, Dana Point, CA 92629

Paper Bag, P.O. Box 268805, Chicago, IL 60626

Paris Review, 541 E. 72nd St., New York, NY 10021

Parnassus Literary Journal, P.O. Box 1384, Forest Park, GA 30051

Passage House, 42 Cleveland Lane, Princeton, NJ 08540

Pegasus, 525 Avenue B, Boulder City, NV 89005

Peninhand, P.O. Box 82699, Portland, OR 97282

Perceptions, 1945 S. 4th W, Missoula, MT 59801

Peregrine, P.O. Box 1076, Amherst, MA 01004

Persephone Press, 22-B Pine Lake Dr., Whispering Pines, NC 28327

Piedmont Literary Review, 1017 Spanish Moss Lane, Breaux Bridge, LA 70517

Pig Iron, P.O. Box 237, Youngstown, OH 44501

PIVOT, 250 Riverside Dr., #23, New York, NY 10025

Plain View Press, P.O. Box 33311, Austin, TX 78764

Ploughshares, Emerson College, 100 Beacon St., Boston, MA 02116

Poet & Critic, Iowa State Univ., 203 Ross Hall, Ames, IA 50011

Poetpourri, Box 3737 Taft Rd., Syracuse, NY 13220

Poetry East, English Dept., DePaul Univ., 802 W. Belden Ave, Chicago, IL 60614

Poetry Magic Publications, 1630 Lake Dr., Haslett, MI 48840

Poetry on Wings/Silver Wings, P.O. Box 1000, Pearblossom, CA 93553

The Poetry Peddler, P.O. Box 250, W. Monroe, NY 13167

Poets & Writers, 72 Spring St., New York, NY 10012

Poets At Work, RD #1, Portersville, PA 16051

Poets. Painters. Composers., 10254 35th Ave. SW, Seattle, WA 98146

The Porcupine's Quill, 68 Main St., Erin, Ont, CANADA N0B 1T0

Portmanteau Editions, P.O. Box 159, Littleton, NH 03561

Potato Eyes Magazine, P.O. Box 76, Troy, ME 04987

Potpourri, P.O. Box 8278, Prairie Village, KS 66208

Prairie Schooner, 201 Andrews Hall, Univ. of Nebraska, Lincoln, NE 68588

Press Gang Publishers, 603 Powell St., Vancouver, B.C., CANADA V6A 1H2

Primal Publishing, 107 Brighton Ave., Allston, MA 02134

Prophetic Voices, 94 Santa Maria Dr., Novato, CA 94947

Provincetown Arts, P.O. Box 35, Provincetown, MA 02657

Puerto del Sol, Box 3E, New Mexico State Univ., Las Cruces, NM 88003

Pulphouse, P.O. Box 1227, Eugene, OR 97440

Q

Queen's Quarterly, Queen's Univ., Kingston, Ont., CANADA K7L 3N6

The Quarterly, 201 E. 50th, New York, NY 10022

R

Rainy Day Press, P.O. Box 3035, Eugene, OR 97403

Ramalo Publications, 2107 N. Spokane St., Post Falls, ID 83854

Raritan, Rutgers Univ., 165 College Ave, New Brunswick, NJ 08903

Raw Dog Press, 128 Harvey Ave, Doylestown, PA 18901

The Raystown Review, RD #1, Box 205, Schellsburg, PA 15559

The Real Comet Press, 3131 Western Ave, #410, Seattle, WA 98121

Red Hill Press, P.O. Box 2853, San Francisco, CA 94126

Redneck Review, P.O. Box 730, Twin Falls, ID 83303

Resurgens, P.O. Box 725006, Atlanta, GA 30339

Review of Contemporary Fiction, see Dalkey Archive Press

The Richmond Quarterly, 2405 Vollmer Rd., Richmond, VA 23229

Rio Arts Projects, 582 East Second St., Brooklyn, NY 11218

River City, English Dept., Memphis State Univ., Memphis, TN 38152

Riverside Quarterly, 807 Walters, #107, Lake Charles, LA 70605

The Runaway Spoon Press, Box 3621, Port Charlotte, Fl 33949

Russian River Writers' Guild, P.O. Box 1123, Sebastopol, CA 95473

S

Samisdat, 456 Monroe Turnpike, Monroe, CT 06468

San Diego Poets Press, P.O. Box 8638, LaJolla, CA 92038

Santa Monica Review, 1900 Pico Blvd., Santa Monica, CA 90405

Saroff, Raymond, Publisher, Acorn Hill Rd, Box 269, Olive Bridge, NY 12461

SCORE, 491 Mandana Blvd., #3, Oakland, CA 94610

Seal Press, 3131 Western Ave., #410, Seattle, WA 98121

Seems, Lakeland College, P.O. Box 359, Sheboygan, WI 53081

Seneca Review, English Dept., Hobart & Wm. Smith Colleges, Geneva, NY 14456

Sensations Magazine, 2 Radio Ave., Ste. A5, Secaucus, NJ 07094

Shenandoah, Box 722, Lexington, VA 24450

Silver Forest Publishing, P.O. Box 3520, Evergreen, CO 80439

Sing Heavenly Muse!, P.O. Box 13320, Minneapolis, MN 55414

Singular Speech Press, 10 Hilltop Drive, Canton, CT 06019

Sisyphus, 8 Asticou Rd., Boston, MA 02130

Snake Nation Review, 2920 North Oak, Valdosta, GA 31602

Sonora Review, English Dept., Purdue Univ., West Lafayette, IN 47907

Sound Board Books, 1016 E. El Camino, Ste. 124, Sunnyvale, CA 94087

South Coast Poetry Journal, English Dept., Calif. State Univ., Fullerton, CA 92634

Southern California Anthology, c/o Professional Writing Prog., Univ. of So. Calif., Los Angeles, CA 90089

Southern Poetry Review, English Dept., Univ. of North Carolina, Charlotte, NC 28223

Southwest Review, 6410 Airline Rd., So. Methodist Univ., Dallas, TX 75275

Sou'wester, Box 1438, So. Illinois Univ., Edwardsville, IL 62026

The Sow's Ear, 245 McDowell St., Bristol, TN 37620

Spirit, Seton Hall Univ., South Orange, NJ 07079

Spirit that Moves Us Press, P.O. Box 820, Jackson Heights, NY 11372

Spitball, 6224 Collegeville Pl., Cincinnati, OH 45224

St. Andrews Review & Press, St. Andrews College, Laurinburg, NC 28352

Star Route Journal, P.O. Box 1451, Redway, CA 95560

Starlight Press, Box 3107, Long Island City, NY 11103

Story, 1507 Dana Ave., Cincinnati, OH 45207

Story Quarterly, P.O. Box 1416, Northbrook, IL 60065

Strange Plasma, see Edgewood Press

sub-TERRAIN, see Anvil Press

The Sun, 107 N. Roberson, Chapel Hill, NC 27516

SUN DOG: The Southeast Review, 406 Williams, Florida State Univ., Tallahassee, FL 32306

Swamp Root, Rt. 2, Box 1098, Hiwassee One, Jacksboro, TN 37757

Swan Books, P.O. Box 2498, Fair Oaks, CA 95628

Sycamore Review, English Dept., Purdue Univ., West Lafayette, IN 47907

T

Tampa Review, Univ. of Tampa, P.O. Box 19F, Tampa, FL 33606

Tar River Poetry, English Dept., East Carolina Univ., Greenville, NC 27834

Tesseract Publications, 3001 W. 57th St., Sioux Falls, SD 57106

Thema, c/o Bothomos Enterprises, P.O. Box 74109, Metairie, LA 70033

III Publishing, P.O. Box 170363, San Francisco, CA 94117

The Threepenny Review, P.O. Box 9131, Berkeley, CA 94709

ThornTree Press, Inc., 547 Hawthorn Lane, Winnetka, IL 60093

Tikkkun, 5100 Lerna St., Oakland, CA 94619

Timberline, Rt. 1, Box 1434, Fulton, MO 65251

Tory Corner Editions, P.O. Box 8100, Glen Ridge, NJ 07028

TriQuarterly, Northwestern Univ., 2020 Ridge Ave., Evanston, IL 60208

Trivia, P.O. Box 606, N. Amherst, MA 01059

Trout Creek Press, 5976 Billings Rd., Parkdale, OR 97041

Tucumcari Literary Review, 3108 W. Bellevue Ave, Los Angeles, CA 90026

Turnstile, 175 Fifth Ave, Ste. 2348, New York, NY 10010

U

Underpass, #574–21, 10405 Jasper Ave, Edmonton, Alberta, CANADA T5J 3S2

Univ. of Windsor Review, English Dept., Univ. of Windsor, Windsor, Ont., CANADA N9B 3P4

V

Véhicule Press, P.O. Box 125, Sta. "La Cité", Montreal, CANADA H2X 3M0

Verve, P.O. Box, 3205, Simi Valley, CA 93093

Virgina Quarterly Review, One West Range, Charlottesville, VA 22903

W

Washington Review, Box 50132, Washington, DC 20004

We Press, P.O. Box 1503, Santa Cruz, CA 95061

Webster Review, Webster Univ., 470 E. Lockwood, Webster Groves, MO 63119

West Anglia Publications, P.O. Box 2683, LaJolla, CA 92038

West Branch, English Dept., Bucknell Univ., Lewisburg, PA 17837

West/Word, UCLA Extension, The Writers' Prog., 10995 Le Conte Ave. #313, Los Angeles, CA 90024

Wheat Forder's Press, P.O. Box 6317, Washington, DC 20015

Wheel of Fire Press, P.O. Box 32631, Kansas City, MO 64111

Whetstone, B.A.A.C., P.O. Box 1266, Barrington, IL 60011

White Clouds Revue, see Wind Vein Press

Whole Notes, P.O. Box 1374, Las Cruces, NM 88004

Willow Springs (Magazine), P.O. Box 1063, Eastern Washington Univ., Cheney, WA 99004

Jim Wilson Publications, Box 14B, Monterville, W.VA 26282

Wind Vein Press, P.O. Box 462, Ketchum, ID 83340

The Windhorse Review, R.R.3, Box 3140, Yarmouth, Nova Scotia, CANADA B5A 4A7

The Windless Orchard, English Dept., Indiana Univ., Fort Wayne, IN 46805

Wineberry Press, 3207 Macomb St., NW, Washington, DC 20008

WIRE Magazine, 2696 Summit Ave, Highland Park, IL 60035

The Wise Woman, 2441 Cordova St., Oakland, CA 94602

Without Halos, Ocean Co. Poets Collective, P.O. Box 1342, Point Pleasant Beach, NJ 08742

Witness, 31000 Northwestern Hwy, Ste. 200, Farmington Hills, MI 48018

Woodhenge Press, N2493 Kunz Rd., Fort Atkinson, WI 53538

Woods Colt Press, P.O. Box 22524, Kansas City, MO 64113

Word Works, Inc., P.O. Box 42164, Washington, DC 20015

The Wormwood Review, P.O. Box 4698, Stockton, CA 95204

WRIT Magazine, Two Sussex Ave, Toronto, Ont., CANADA M5S 1J5

The Writers' Bar-B-Q, 924 Bryn Mawr, Springfield, IL 62703

Writers' Forum, P.O. Box 7150, Univ. of Colorado, Colo. Springs, CO 80933

Writers' Lifeline, P.O. Box 1641, Cornwall, Ont. CANADA K6H 5V6

X

Xanthyros Foundation, P.O. Box 91980, West Vancouver, B.C. CANADA V7V 4S4

Y

The Yale Review, P.O. Box 1902A Yale Sta., New Haven CT 06520
Yardbird Books, P.O. Box 10214, State College, PA 16805
Yellow Silk, P.O. Box 6374, Albany, CA 94706

Z

Zephyr Press, see Empyreal Press
Zoland Books, Inc., 384 Huron Ave, Cambridge, MA 02138
Zymergy, see Empyreal Press
ZYZZYVA, 41 Sutter St., Ste. 1400, San Francisco, CA 94104

INDEX

The following is a listing in alphabetical order by author's last name of works reprinted in the first sixteen *Pushcart Prize* editions.

542

543

545

557

558

560

Contributors' Notes

FELIPE ALFAU was born in Barcelona in 1902. He emigrated to the United States during World War I and his first novel appeared here in 1936. This selection is from *Chromos*, written in 1946–48 but unpublished until Dalkey Archive Press issued it in 1990. He now lives on Long Island, New York.

CHARLES BAXTER is author of the novel, *First Light*, a book of poems, and three editions of stories. He lives in Ann Arbor.

MARVIN BELL previously appeared in these pages in PPV. His *New and Selected Poems* was published by Atheneum (1987) and his *Iris of Creation* is just out from Copper Canyon.

NELSON BENTLEY taught in the English Department at the University of Washington. His books include *Sea Lion Caves* and *The Collected Shorter Poems*. He died in December, 1990.

SUSAN BERGMAN lives and writes in Barrington, Illinois. This essay is from a work in progress.

GWENDOLYN BROOKS was born in 1917 in Topeka, Kansas and had her first book published in 1945. Her *Anne Allen* won a Pulitzer Prize in 1949. She teaches at several colleges in the Chicago area.

CHRISTOPER BUCKLEY's *Blue Autumn* is out from Copper Beech Press (1990). He lives in Coatesville, Pennsylvania.

F. L. CHANDONNET is a newspaper reporter living and working in Alaska.

ERIC CHOCK works in the Poets-In-The-Schools program in Hawaii. He has published many poems in little magazines around the country.

JANE COOPER's most recent book is *Scaffolding: New and Selected Poems* (Anvil, 1984). She lives in New York City.

TED COHEN is a professor of philosophy at the University of Chicago. This is his first essay to appear in a literary magazine. More recent work is just out in *Raritan.*

MELINDA DAVIS is the author of *Text*, forthcoming from Knopf. She lives in New York.

JEANNE DIXON was born in Two Medicine in a remote corner of north-central Montana, where her father was a hunter and trapper. She still lives in Montana next to Rattlesnake Creek with her dog Amy.

ALAN DUGAN is the author most recently of *Poems 6* (Ecco). Ecco also published his *New and Collected Poems: 1961–1983* (1983).

STEPHEN DUNN is the author of *Local Time* (Morrow, 1986) and *Between Angels* (Norton, 1989). He lives in Port Republic, New Jersey.

LINDA GREGG's third collection is *The Sacraments of Desire.* She lives in Northampton, Massachusetts.

BEN GROFF is a registered nurse living with his wife and children in Lynwood, Washington. This is his first published story.

MARK HALLIDAY's first book of poems, *Little Star,* was a National Poetry selection. His newest collection, *Tasker Street,* won the 1991 Juniper Prize.

GWEN HEAD lives in Berkeley, California and her most recent book is *The Ten Thousandth Night* (University of Pittsburgh).

BRENDA HILLMAN has two collections forthcoming from Wesleyan—*Death Tractates* and *Bright Existence.* She is poet in residence at St. Mary's College of California.

TONY HOAGLAND has published recent poems and essays in *American Poetry Review, Crazyhorse, Black Warrior Review, Passages North, Sonora Review* and *Georgia Review.* He lives in Albany, California.

JOSEPHINE JACOBSEN lives in Cockeysville, Maryland. She last appeared here in *Pushcart Prize VI.* She is the author of many stories and poems and this year is co-judge of the Lenore Marshall Award.

DAVID JAUSS is the author of the story collection, *Crimes of Passion* (Story Press, 1984). His fiction has appeared in the *O'Henry, Best American Short Stories* and Pushcart Prize (XIV) collections.

GEORGE KEITHLEY lives in Chico, California. His *The Donner Party* was published by Braziller in 1989.

WILLIAM KENNEDY's most recent novel is *Quinn's Book* (1988). *Very Old Bones* is forthcoming. He won the Pulitzer Prize for fiction in 1985.

URSULA K. LE GUIN's story is part of a collection, *Searoad: Chronicles of Klatsand* out soon from HarperCollins. She is the author of fifteen novels, about sixty stories and many poems and essays. She lives in Berkeley.

LI-YOUNG LEE is the author of two poetry collections: *Rose* and *The City In Which I Love You* (BOA Editions). He lives in Chicago.

MICHAEL McCLURE lives in Oakland, California. *Selected Poems* (1986) and *Fragments of Perseus* (1983) were published by New Directions.

RENÉE MANFREDI's stories have appreared in *Mississippi Review, Black Warrior Review,* and *Cimarron,* among others. She lives in Bloomington, Indiana.

YANN MARTEL is a Canadian writer living in Paris. Earlier work appeared in *Malahat* #84.

JACK MARSHALL's most recent poetry collection is *Arabian Nights* (Coffee House, 1987). *Chaos Comics,* a new long poem, is just out as a Pennywhistle Press chapbook.

WILLIAM MATTHEWS' most recent books are *Blues If You Want* (poems, Houghton Mifflin) and *Curiosities* (essays, University of Michigan).

JAMES MERRILL won the Bollingen Poetry Prize in 1973 and the Pulitzer Prize in 1977. His most recent poetry collections are *From The First Nine: Poems 1947–1976* and *Late Settings*, both from Atheneum.

JESS MOWRY was born in 1960, grew up in Oakland and was educated through the eighth grade. He skateboards eight to ten miles a day and works at a drop-in center for inner city young people. His novel, *Children of The Night*, is just out from Holloway House, and his third book is due from Farrar, Straus and Giroux.

HOWARD NEMEROV was a recent Poet Laureate of the Library of Congress. His many prizes include an award from the National Institue of Arts and Letters, a Guggenheim Fellowship and a Pulitzer Prize for his collected poems (1978).

HELEN NORRIS lives in Alabama and has published four novels, most recently *Walk With The Sickle Moon*. She has also published two volumes of short fiction and has been honored with O'Henry selections and Andrew Lytle awards.

NAOMI SHIHAB NYE is the author of three poetry collections from Breitenbush Books of Oregon. She received the I. B. Lavan Younger Poets Award from the Academy of American Poets in 1988.

JOYCE CAROL OATES is the author of two recent novellas, *I Lock My Door Upon Myself* (Ecco) and *The Rise of Life on Earth* (New Directions). She teaches at Princeton University where she helps edit *The Ontario Review* with Raymond Smith.

SHARON OLDS is director of the creative writing department at New York University. Her collection, *The Father*, will soon be out from Knopf.

MARY OLIVER won the Pulitzer Prize in 1984. Her most recent poetry collection is *House of Light* (Beacon).

JANET PEERY has work due soon in *American Short Fiction*, *Kansas Quarterly* and *First*. She lives in Kansas, where she is working on a first novel.

ELLEN POLLACK teaches at Tufts University. Her first fiction collection is *The Rabbi In The Attic*, just out from Delphinium.

KATHA POLLITT lives in New York City and has published poems recently in *The New Yorker* and *The New Republic.*

LEN ROBERTS' latest book was *Black Wings,* a National Poetry Series selection. He is currently a Guggenheim Fellow in Poetry.

CAROL ROH-SPAULDING is a graduate student in English at the University of Iowa. Her work has appeared in *Beloit Fiction Journal* and elsewhere.

DAVID ROMTVEDT is author of *Moon; Free and Compulsory for All;* and *How Many Horses.* He lives with his wife and daughter in Buffalo, Wyoming.

SUSAN STRAIGHT's stories have appeared in *Passages North, Ploughshares, TriQuarterly* and *Contact.* She teaches at the University of California, Riverside.

WILLIAM J. SCHEICK teaches at the University of Texas, where he also edits *Texas Studies.* He has published books on Edward Taylor, Jonathan Edwards, Ralph Waldo Emerson and H. G. Wells.

WILLIAM STAFFORD has won The National Book Award, the Award in Literature of the American Academy and Institute of Arts and Letters and the Shelley Memorial Award. He is a past co-poetry editor of *The Pushcart Prize* and he lives in Lake Oswego, Oregon.

JEAN VALENTINE's most recent collection is *Home, Deep, Blue: New and Selected Poems* (Alice James, 1989). She lives in New York City,

ELLEN BRYANT VOIGT is the author most recently of *Two Trees,* forthcoming from Norton in 1992. Her collection, *The Lotus Flowers* (1987), is also available from Norton.

PAUL WEST is the author of many novels and has won the Aga Khan Fiction Prize and an award in Literature from the American Academy and Institute of Arts and Letters.

DIANE WILLIAMS' first collection of stories, *This Is About the Body, the Mind, the Soul, The World, Time, and Fate* is just out in paperback from Grove Weidenfeld. Her next collection is due in late 1992 from the same publisher. She is co-editor of *StoryQuarterly.*

ROBERT WRIGLEY'S third poetry collection, *What My Father Believed*, is just published by The University of Illinois Press. He lives in Lewiston, Idaho.

ADAM ZAGAJEWSKI was born in Poland in 1945. His books in English include *Tremor* (1985) and *Solidarity, Solitude* (essays, 1990).